THE IMPLEMENTATION GUIDE TO
STUDENT LEARNING SUPPORTS
IN THE CLASSROOM AND SCHOOLWIDE

D1305191

Two young ones playing restaurant:

"How do you want your steak?"

"Medium."

"I'm sorry, we only have large."

To those whose answers make us think.

HOWARD S. ADELMAN ▪ LINDA TAYLOR

THE IMPLEMENTATION GUIDE TO STUDENT LEARNING SUPPORTS

IN THE CLASSROOM AND SCHOOLWIDE

New Directions for Addressing Barriers to Learning

CORWIN PRESS
A SAGE Publications Company
Thousand Oaks, California

For information:

Corwin Press
A Sage Publications Company
2455 Teller Road
Thousand Oaks, California 91320
www.corwinpress.com

Sage Publications Ltd.
1 Oliver's Yard
55 City Road
London EC1Y 1SP
United Kingdom

Sage Publications India Pvt. Ltd.
B-42, Panchsheel Enclave
Post Box 4109
New Delhi 110 017 India

Printed in the United States of America

Library of Congress Cataloging-in-Publication Data

Adelman, Howard S.
The implementation guide to student learning supports in the classroom and schoolwide: New directions for addressing barriers to learning / Howard S. Adelman & Linda Taylor.
    p. cm.
Includes bibliographical references and index.
ISBN 1-4129-1452-3 (cloth)—ISBN 1-4129-1453-1 (pbk.)
    1. School failure—United States—Prevention. 2. Learning disabled children—Education—United States. I. Taylor, Linda (Linda L.) II. Title.
LB3063.A33 2006
371.9—dc22

                                        2005002358

This book is printed on acid-free paper.

05 06 07 08 09 10 9 8 7 6 5 4 3 2 1

Acquisitions Editor:	Faye Zucker
Editorial Assistant:	Gem Rabanera
Production Editor:	Melanie Birdsall
Copy Editor:	Barbara Coster
Typesetter:	C&M Digitals (P) Ltd.
Proofreader:	Cheryl Rivard
Indexer:	Kathy Paparchontis
Cover Designer:	Tracy E. Miller

Contents

Exhibits and Guides: Tools for Analyses and Capacity Building

Preface

"*What more can I do to help the children in my class who are not making it?*" the teacher asked with a note of despair.

Before either of us could respond, someone shouted, "*Why don't we talk about improving schools to keep kids from having problems?*" It was more a statement than a question, and the feelings accompanying it were strong. Some in the audience nodded their agreement. Others, concerned about their children with special needs, said that they wanted more specialized programs and staff. They didn't feel general classroom and school improvements would do the job, and it was too late to prevent their kids' problems. And so it goes whenever student problems and learning supports are discussed.

Every day a wide range of learning, behavioral, emotional, and physical problems interfere with students participating effectively and fully benefiting from the instruction teachers provide. Even the best schools find that *too many* youngsters are growing up in situations where significant barriers regularly interfere with their reaching full potential. This book is concerned with a broad range of learning and related behavior problems and the types of learning supports needed to address barriers to learning and teaching.

The notion of *barriers to learning* encompasses both external and internal factors. Some students bring with them to school a wide range of problems stemming from restricted opportunities associated with poverty, difficult and diverse family conditions, high rates of mobility, lack of English language skills, violent neighborhoods, problems related to substance abuse, inadequate health care, and lack of enrichment opportunities. Some youngsters also bring with them intrinsic conditions that make learning and performing difficult.

As a result, at every grade level there are students who come to school each day not quite ready to perform and learn in the most effective manner. Students' learning and behavior problems are exacerbated as they internalize the frustrations of confronting barriers to learning and the debilitating effects of performing poorly at school. All this and the conditions under which they must teach interfere with teachers' effectiveness.

The world around us is changing at an exponential rate—so must the way we approach learning and related behavior problems. As we all are called upon to play a role in doing something about the many individuals who have trouble learning academic skills, it is essential that we all have a broad understanding of what causes such problems and what society in general and schools in particular need to do. It is time to move forward in the discussion of what it means to ensure that all youngsters have an equal opportunity to succeed at school.

To these ends, this volume is designed as a guide for ensuring that every school has a comprehensive and adaptable system of learning supports in the classroom and schoolwide. The frameworks and practices presented are based on our many years of work in classrooms and schoolwide and from efforts to enhance school-community collaboration.

Some of what we have learned comes from our direct efforts to introduce, sustain, and scale up innovations. Other insights come from theory and the large body of relevant research. And equally instructive is what we have derived from lessons learned and shared by many school leaders and on-the-line staff who strive every day to do their best for children.

Although we emphasize the need to address barriers, we hasten to stress that this is not at odds with a focus on strengths, resilience, assets, and protective factors. Efforts to enhance positive development and improve instruction clearly can improve readiness to learn. However, it is the case that preventing problems often requires direct action to remove or at least minimize the impact of barriers.

Previous initiatives for enhancing student supports provide evidence about what must be changed and what new directions hold promise. Educators recognize, and research supports, that barriers to learning and teaching demand high-level, consistent, systemwide attention. The need for new directions in no way is meant to demean anyone's current efforts. We know that the demands placed on those working in the field go well beyond what common sense says anyone should be asked to endure. And we know that school staff often feel as if they are swimming against the tide and making too little progress.

Our objectives in writing this guide are to highlight some of the systemic reasons it feels that way, to improve the situation, and to enhance school outcomes. Some of what we propose is difficult to accomplish. We hope that the fact that there are schools, districts, and state agencies already trailblazing the way will engender a sense of hope and encouragement to those committed to improving how schools address barriers to learning.

Throughout the book, we include a variety of tools. They offer details about teacher and learning support staff practices that can make new directions a reality every day. They provide guides for capacity building as teachers and support staff team together for planning and implementation. And because leadership is essential in developing a comprehensive system of learning supports, a companion to this volume is available: *The School Leader's Guide to Student Learning Supports: New Directions for Addressing Barriers to Learning.*

Acknowledgments

It will be obvious that our work owes much to many.

We are especially grateful to those who are pioneering major systemic changes across the country—so many in the field have generously offered their insights and wisdom. And, of course, we are indebted to hundreds of scholars whose research and writing is a shared treasure, to Perry Nelson and the host of graduate and undergraduate students at UCLA who contribute so much to our work each day, and to the many young people and their families who continue to teach us all.

PUBLISHER'S ACKNOWLEDGMENTS

Corwin Press acknowledges with gratitude the important contributions of the following manuscript reviewers:

Jane Belmore, Assistant Superintendent
Madison Metropolitan School District
Madison, WI

Linda Miller, Consultant
Strategic Systems Development
Iowa Department of Education
Des Moines, IA

Sandra Screen, Director
Office of Psychological Services
Detroit Public Schools
Detroit, MI

Susan Wooley, Executive Director
American School Health Association
Kent, OH

About the Authors

Howard S. Adelman is professor of psychology and codirector (along with Linda Taylor) of the School Mental Health Project and its federally supported national Center for Mental Health in Schools at UCLA. He began his professional career as a remedial classroom teacher in 1960 and received his PhD in psychology from UCLA in 1966. He directed the Fernald School and Laboratory at UCLA from 1973–1986 and has codirected the School Mental Health Project since 1986. His research and teaching focus on addressing barriers to students' learning (including educational, psychosocial, and mental health problems). In particular, he is interested in system variables (e.g., environmental determinants and interventions, models and mechanisms for system change) and intrinsic motivational factors (e.g., self-perceptions of control, competence, relatedness) relevant to the causes and correction of emotional, behavioral, and learning problems. In recent years, he has been involved in large-scale systemic reform initiatives to enhance school and community efforts to address barriers to learning and promote healthy development.

Linda Taylor is codirector of the School Mental Health Project and its federally supported national Center for Mental Health in Schools at UCLA. Throughout her career, she has been concerned with a wide range of psychosocial and educational problems experienced by children and adolescents. Her early experiences included community agency work. From 1973 to 1986, she was assistant director at the Fernald Laboratory School and Clinic at UCLA. In 1986, she became codirector of the School Mental Health Project. From 1986 to 2000, she also held a clinical psychologist position in the Los Angeles Unified School District and directed several large-scale projects for the school district. These projects led to her involvement in systemic reform initiatives designed to enhance school and community efforts to address barriers to learning and enhance healthy development.

Introduction

The single most characteristic thing about human beings is that they learn.

—Jerome Bruner

Our schools have a long history of assisting teachers in dealing with problems that interfere with school learning. Prominent examples are seen in the continuous focus on inservice professional development for teachers; the range of counseling, psychological, and social service programs at schools; and in initiatives for enhancing students' assets and resiliency.

A great deal is done, but efforts are fragmented and marginalized. As a result, they are less effective than they could be. For the situation to improve, we must all broaden our understanding of what causes learning and behavior problems and what society in general and schools in particular need to do. Human development, learning, and behavior are shaped by the continuous interplay between the individual and the overlapping, multilayered contexts in which learning and behavior occur. The well-being of a significant proportion of the nation's youth depends on schools and communities appreciating the full implications of this.

Our emphasis in this volume is on frameworks and strategies for dealing with the entire range of learning and behavior problems. Throughout, we stress the importance of incorporating the invaluable understanding of *intrinsic* motivation developed over the past 50 years.

It is evident to any teacher that the range of problems that must be addressed are complex, and therefore the solutions must be comprehensive and multifaceted. For schools, this means addressing barriers to learning and teaching, as well as promoting healthy development. It also means that schools, families, and community resources must learn to collaborate *effectively* to enhance policy and practice and pursue essential systemic changes.

All this leads to the conclusion that school improvement planning and practices must include a comprehensive and fully integrated system of learning supports in the classroom and schoolwide. A comprehensive system of learning supports provided in a timely and effective manner can ensure that fewer students require intensive and expensive services. And by fully integrating the system with instructional improvements, the learning, achievement, and performance of all children and youth will improve in ways that enable them to become self-sufficient and successful members of society.

Given the large numbers of students who are not doing well in school, it is essential to begin with an appreciation of who we are talking about and why so many students are experiencing learning and behavior problems. In Part I, we offer perspectives for understanding the nature and scope of students' problems and what is involved in dealing with such problems in a comprehensive way. We stress the need to change learning environments as well as provide specialized assistance when necessary. From this perspective, we highlight the importance of a comprehensive, multifaceted, and cohesive *Enabling* or *Learning Supports Component.*

We end Part I by exploring how important motivational factors are in understanding and correcting learning and behavior problems, particularly for students who have become disengaged from classroom learning. In this context, we raise cautions about the trend toward overreliance on techniques that overemphasize social control at the expense of engaging and reengaging youngsters in classroom learning.

Part II explores what needs to change in classrooms. We probe the question: *What supports good teaching?* and outline frameworks for improving current classroom practices. We offer specific ideas and procedures for personalizing instruction and providing special assistance, emphasizing the importance of matching motivation and development, providing a comprehensive curriculum, and using a personalized approach to teaching. We spell out why personalizing instruction is the first step in preventing and correcting problems. Then we detail the process of providing special assistance in those instances when personalized instruction is insufficient.

The focus in Part III is on what must be done schoolwide and in collaboration with families and the community at large. Using the concept of an Enabling or Learning Supports Component, we outline the "curriculum" for such an approach. We also discuss the infrastructure that must be established so that such a component is not marginalized in school policy and practice and that enables teachers and learning support staff to team for planning and implementation. We then explore the potential of school-family-community collaboration for strengthening students, families, schools, and neighborhoods. We end Part III with comments on the changes ahead of us, and in Part IV we offer specific additional resources that we hope will be of use.

Throughout this book, we reflect the thinking of a growing group of stakeholders who understand that enabling all students to benefit more fully from their schooling depends on intervention strategies that go well beyond current *instructional* reforms. Closing the achievement gap and leaving no child behind must be more than maxims; they must represent a policy and practice agenda that effectively addresses barriers to learning and teaching.

Do you understand
the questions?

Sure. The questions
are easy.

It's the answers
that are hard!

PART I

So You Want All Kids to Succeed at School. Then It's Time to Rethink What We Are Doing!

Someone is in trouble . . . at school each day the words go by, too quickly to make sense. So attention turns from reading to avoidance, pain, pretense.

We approach the integrally related topics of learning, behavior, and emotional problems within the context of changing schools and a changing world. And we do so with a sense of urgency because too many youngsters are having trouble in and out of school.

The good news is that there are many schools where the majority of students are doing just fine, and in any school, one can find youngsters who are succeeding. The bad news is that in any school, one can find youngsters who are failing, and there are too many schools, particularly those serving lower income families, where large numbers of students and their teachers are in trouble. And, too often, schools are ill-prepared to address the needs of those in trouble.

Schools must move forward in proactive and positive ways if they are to effectively address learning and behavior problems and enable all students to have an equal opportunity to succeed at school. And they must do so with a fundamental appreciation of what motivates learning and appropriate behavior.

Part I begins by answering the question: *Why do students have problems?* By the end of Chapter 2, it will be evident that learning and behavior problems are multifaceted and that the solutions must be too. In Chapter 3, we stress that the solution requires a comprehensive approach that can engage and reengage students in learning. At schools, a shared perspective of these matters is the basis for moving in new directions for addressing barriers to learning to enable an equal opportunity for succeeding at school.

Why Students Have Problems

1

Many well-known adolescent difficulties are not intrinsic to the teenage years but are related to the mismatch between adolescents' developmental needs and the kinds of experiences most junior high and high schools provide.

—Linda Darling-Hammond (1997)

Consider the American penchant for ignoring the structural causes of problems. We prefer the simplicity and satisfaction of holding individuals responsible for whatever happens: crime, poverty, school failure, what have you. Thus, even when one high school crisis is followed by another, we concentrate on the particular people involved—their values, their character, their personal failings—rather than asking whether something about the system in which these students find themselves might also need to be addressed.

—Alfie Kohn (1999)

I failed every subject but algebra.

That's not too surprising since you didn't take algebra.

ORIENTING QUESTIONS

? Why must we be careful about compelling correlates?
? How can common learning and behavior problems be differentiated from learning disabilities and ADHD?
? How are barriers to learning grouped?

In the last analysis, we see only what we are ready to see. We eliminate and ignore everything that is not part of our prejudices.

—Charcot (1857)

What causes most learning and behavior problems? In this chapter, we look first at the difficulty of determining cause and effect and at general models that shape thinking about the causes of human behavior. Then, using a broad framework, we explore the causes for a full continuum of learning and behavior problems.

THE PROBLEM OF COMPELLING CLUES

At one time, there was a tribe of South Pacific natives who believed that lice were responsible for keeping a person healthy (Chase, 1956). They had noticed that almost all the healthy people in the tribe had lice, while those who were sick had no lice. Thus, it seemed reasonable to them that lice caused good health.

A teacher-in-training working with children with learning and/or behavior problems notices that most of them are easily distracted and more fidgety than students without such problems. They are also less likely to listen or to do assignments well, and they often flit from one thing to another. The new teacher concludes that there is something physically wrong with these youngsters.

Every day we puzzle over our experiences and, in trying to make sense of them, arrive at conclusions about what caused them to happen. It is a very basic and useful part of human nature for people to try to understand cause and effect. Unfortunately, sometimes we are wrong. The South Pacific Islanders didn't know that sick people usually have a high fever, and since lice do not like the higher temperature, they jump off!

The teacher-in-training is right in thinking that some children with learning problems may have a biological condition that makes it hard for them to pay attention. However, with further training and experience, teachers learn that there are a significant number of students whose attention problems stem from a lack of interest or from the belief that they really can't do the work or from any number of other psychological factors.

Errors in Logic

Whenever I read the obituary column, I can never understand how people always seem to die in alphabetical order.

Because it is so compelling to look for causes, and because people so often make errors in doing so, logicians and scientists have spent a lot of time discussing the problem. For example, logicians have pointed out the fallacy of assuming (as the Islanders did) that one event (lice) caused another (good health) just because the first event preceded the second. We make this type of error every time we *presume* that a person's learning or behavior problems are due to a difficult birth, a divorce, poor nutrition, a dysfunctioning brain, or other factors that preceded the problem.

Another kind of logical error occurs when one event may affect another, but only in a minor way, as part of a much more complicated set of events. There is a tendency to think that people who behave nicely have been brought up well by their parents. We all know, however, of cases in which the parents' actions seem to have very little to do with the child's behavior. This can be especially true of teenagers, who are strongly influenced by their friends.

A third logical error can arise when two events repeatedly occur together. After a while, it can become impossible to tell whether one causes the other or whether both are caused by something else. For instance, frequently children with learning problems also have behavior problems. Did the learning problem cause the behavior problem? Did the behavior problem cause the learning problem? Did poor parenting or poor teaching or poor peer models cause both the learning and behavior problems? The longer these problems exist, the harder it is to know.

Causes and Correlates

In trying to understand learning and behavior problems, researchers and practitioners look for all sorts of clues, or *correlates*. When faced with compelling clues, it is important to understand the difference between causes and correlates. *Correlates* are simply events that have some relation to each other: lice and good health, no lice and sickness. A *cause* and its effect show a special type of correlation, one in which the nature of the relationship is known. Some events that occur together fit so well with "common sense" that we are quick to believe they are cause and effect. However, we may overlook other factors important in understanding the actual connection.

Some correlates are particularly compelling because they fit with current theories, attitudes, or policies. The more intuitively logical the connection, the harder it is to understand that they may not be causally related. They are compelling clues but may be misleading.

CAUSAL MODELS

Many factors shape thinking about human behavior and learning and the problems individuals experience. It helps to begin with a broad transactional view, such as currently prevails in scientific explanations of human behavior.

A Transactional Model

Before the 1920s, dominant thinking saw human behavior as determined primarily by factors within a person, especially inborn characteristics. As behaviorism gained influence, a strong competitive view arose. Behavior was seen as primarily shaped by environmental influences, with a particular emphasis on the reinforcers one encounters.

Times have changed. Now the prevailing model for understanding human functioning is a transactional view that emphasizes the interplay of person and environment. This view is sometimes referred to as reciprocal determinism (Bandura, 1978).

Let's apply a transactional model to a learning situation. In teaching a lesson, the teacher will find that some students learn easily and some do not. And even a good student may appear distracted on a given day.

Why the Differences?

A commonsense answer suggests that each student brings something different to the situation and therefore experiences it differently. And that's a pretty good answer—as far as it goes. What gets lost in this simple explanation is the reciprocal impact student and situation have on each other—resulting in continuous change in both.

To clarify the point: any student can be viewed as bringing to each situation *capacities, attitudes, and behaviors accumulated over time*, as well as *current states of being and behaving.* These "person" variables transact with each other and also with the environment.

At the same time, the situation in which students are expected to function consists not only of *instructional processes and content* but also the *physical and social context* in which instruction takes place. Each part of the environment also transacts with the others.

Obviously, the transactions can vary considerably and can lead to a variety of positive and/or negative outcomes. In general, the types of outcomes can be described as

- *Enhancement of learning and positive behavior.* Capacities, attitudes, and behavior change and expand in desirable ways.
- *Delayed and arrested learning.* There is little change in capacities.
- *Disrupted functioning.* There is interference with learning and performance, an increase in dysfunctional behaving, and possibly a decrease in capacities.
- *Deviant functioning.* Capacities, attitudes, and behaviors change and expand but not in desirable ways.

The Transactional Model as a Comprehensive Framework

Professionals tend to use models that view the cause of an individual's problems as either within the person or coming from the environment. Actually, two "person-oriented" models are discussed widely: (1) the disordered or "ill" person model and (2) the slow maturation model. Those using an environment model emphasize inadequate and pathological environments.

In contrast, a transactional view encompasses the position that problems may be caused by person, environment, or both. This broad paradigm encourages a comprehensive perspective of cause and correction. A transactional view acknowledges that there are cases in which an individual's disabilities or disorders predispose him or her to problems even in highly accommodating settings. At the same time, such a view also accounts for instances in which the environment is so inadequate or hostile that individuals have problems despite having no disability. Finally, it recognizes problems caused by a combination of person and environment factors.

It might seem reasonable to continue to use person models and environment models and add the transactional model. However, a transactional view actually provides an umbrella encompassing the others and provides the kind of comprehensive perspective needed to differentiate among learning and behavior problems.

The value of a broad transactional perspective, then, is that it asks whether the *primary* instigating causes are to be found in

- *The individual* (e.g., a neurological dysfunction, cognitive skill and/or strategy deficits, developmental and/or motivational differences)

- *The environment* (e.g., the primary environment, such as poor instructional programs, parental neglect; the secondary environment, such as racially isolated schools and neighborhoods; or the tertiary environment, such as broad social, economic, political, and cultural influences)
- The *reciprocal interplay* of individual and environment

The need for a comprehensive perspective in labeling problems is illustrated by efforts to diagnose youngsters' learning, behavior, and emotional problems. Systems used in special education and by those who diagnose "mental disorders" tend to overemphasize symptoms (i.e., correlates) and focus on whether the symptoms reach criteria to qualify for one (or more) personal disorder categories. The result has been a bias that emphasizes person pathology and minimizes the role played by environmental factors.

The following conceptual example illustrates how a broad framework can offer a useful *starting* place for understanding behavioral, emotional, and learning problems. No simple typology can do justice to

Guide 1.1   Applying a Transactional View of the Primary Cause of Problems

Problems primarily caused by factors in the environment (E)	Problems caused equally by environment and person	Problems primarily caused by factors in the person (P)
E (E ↔ p)	(E ↔ P)	(e ↔ P) P
|—————————————————————|	—————|—————	——————————————————————|
Type I Problems	Type II Problems	Type III Problems (e.g., LD, ADHD, other disorders)
• Caused primarily by environments and systems that are deficient and/or hostile	• Caused primarily by a significant *mismatch* between individual differences and vulnerabilities and the nature of that person's environment	• Caused primarily by personal disabilities/ disorders
• Problems may be mild to moderately severe and narrow to moderately pervasive	• Problems may be mild to moderately severe and pervasive	• Problems may be moderate to profoundly severe and moderate to broadly pervasive

the complexities involved in classifying students' problems. However, even a simple framework based on a transactional view can be helpful in differentiating among problems (Adelman, 1995; Adelman & Taylor, 1994).

As indicated in Guide 1.1, problems can be differentiated along a continuum that separates those caused by internal factors, environmental variables, or a combination of both. Problems caused by the environment are placed at one end of the continuum and referred to as Type I problems. Many people grow up in impoverished and hostile environmental circumstances. Such conditions should be considered first in hypothesizing what *initially* caused an individual's behavioral, emotional, and learning problems. At the other end are problems caused primarily by personal disabilities and disorders; these are designated as Type III problems. The Type II group consists of persons who do not function well in situations where their individual differences and minor vulnerabilities are poorly accommodated or are responded to hostilely. The problems for individuals in this group are a relatively equal product of person characteristics and failure of the environment to accommodate that individual.

There are, of course, variations along the continuum that do not precisely fit a category. That is, at each point between the extreme ends, environment-person transactions are the cause, but the degree to which each contributes to the problem varies.

What's in a Name?

There is a tendency among the general public to refer to anyone with a learning problem as LD, and anyone with problems at school who manifests a high activity level often is seen as having ADHD. Diagnostic labels need to be used cautiously. Strong images are associated with such labels, and people act upon these notions. Sometimes the images are useful generalizations; sometimes they are harmful stereotypes. Sometimes they guide practitioners toward good ways to help; sometimes they contribute to "blaming the victim," by making young people the focus of intervention rather than pursuing system deficiencies that are causing the problem. In all cases, such labels can profoundly shape a person's future. Clearly, schools want to account for individual differences when they are important in preventing and correcting learning, behavior, and emotional problems. It's just not as easy to do as we would like.

"What's the use of *their* having names," the Gnat said, "if they won't answer to them?"

"No use to *them*," said Alice; "but it's useful to the people who name them, I suppose."

—Lewis Carroll,
Through the Looking-Glass

The above way of thinking about learning, behavior, and emotional problems illustrates the value of starting with a broad model of cause. It can counter tendencies to jump prematurely to the conclusion that a problem is caused by deficiencies or pathology within the individual. It can help combat practices that "blame the victim" (Ryan, 1971). It highlights the notion that improving the way the environment accommodates individual differences often can be a sufficient intervention strategy.

Response to Intervention as a Diagnostic Strategy

Available data suggest that minimally 95% of all children can be taught to read. Yet about 50% of those students designated as in need of special education were labeled as having LD. With specific respect to LD, direct instruction or "scientifically based reading instruction" is being advocated as the key to reducing the numbers labeled. The claim is that findings from early intervention and prevention studies suggest that "reading failure rates as high as 38–40 percent can be reduced to six percent or less" (Lyon, 1998). Thus, before a student is diagnosed, advocates want students provided with "well-designed and well-implemented early intervention." This approach to the problem of diagnosis is dubbed *response to intervention* (RTI).

One controversy related to RTI stems from the emphasis on using the type of direct instruction described by the National Reading Panel sponsored by the National Institute of Child Health & Human Development (NICHD, 2000). Direct instruction is heavily oriented to development of specific skills, with the skills explicitly laid out in lesson plans for teachers in published reading programs and with frequent testing to identify what has and hasn't been learned.

On the other side of the controversy are critics who argue that the evidence base for direct instruction is so limited that no one can be confident that the approach will produce the type of reading interest and abilities that college-bound students must develop. These professionals are especially critical of the work of the National Reading Panel, which they argue was overloaded with proponents of direct instruction and inappropriately relied on correlational data to infer causation.

In sum, the continuum, generated by using a transactional model, encompasses a full range of learning and behavior problems—including learning disabilities (LD) and attention-deficit/hyperactivity disorder (ADHD). From this perspective, a transactional view provides a comprehensive framework for appreciating the full range of learning and behavior problems. A sample of specific instigating factors that can cause learning and behavior problems based on a transactional view is offered in Guide 1.2.

WHY WORRY ABOUT CAUSE?

Not all professionals are concerned about what originally instigated a learning or behavior problem. Many express the view that initial causes usually cannot be assessed; and even if they could, little can be done about the cause once the problem exists. Such practitioners tend to see appropriate corrective procedures as focused on (a) helping the individual acquire skills and strategies that should have been learned previously and (b) eliminating factors that *currently* are contributing to problems. Thus, they see little point in looking for initial causes.

All interveners are concerned about *current* factors that interfere with effective learning and performance. For example, poor study habits or the absence of particular social skills may be identified as causing poor attention to a task or failure to remember what apparently was learned earlier. In attempting to correct ongoing problems, the assumption sometimes is made that the inappropriate habits can be overcome and the missing skills can be learned.

Any of the factors indicated in Guide 1.2 may negatively affect current functioning. For example, a student may be a rather passive learner at school (e.g., not

Guide 1.2 Factors Instigating Learning, Behavior, and Emotional Problems

Environment (E) (Type I problems)

1. *Insufficient stimuli* (e.g., prolonged periods in impoverished environments; deprivation of learning opportunities at home or school such as lack of play and practice situations and poor instruction; inadequate diet)

2. *Excessive stimuli* (e.g., overly demanding home, school, or work experiences, such as overwhelming pressure to achieve and contradictory expectations; overcrowding)

3. *Intrusive and hostile stimuli* (e.g., medical practices, especially at birth, leading to physiological impairment; contaminated environments; conflict in home, school, workplace; faulty child-rearing practices, such as long-standing abuse and rejection; dysfunctional family; migratory family; language used is a second language; social prejudices related to race, sex, age, physical characteristics, and behavior)

Person (P) (Type III problems)

1. *Physiological insult* (e.g., cerebral trauma, such as accident or stroke, endocrine dysfunctions and chemical imbalances; illness affecting brain or sensory functioning)

2. *Genetic anomaly* (e.g., genes that limit, slow down, or lead to any atypical development)

3. *Cognitive activity and affective states experienced by self as deviant* (e.g., lack of knowledge or skills such as basic cognitive strategies; lack of ability to cope effectively with emotions, such as low self-esteem)

4. *Physical characteristics shaping contact with environment and/or experienced by self as deviant* (e.g., visual, auditory, or motoric deficits; excessive or reduced sensitivity to stimuli; easily fatigued; factors such as race, sex, age, or unusual appearance that produce stereotypical responses)

5. *Deviant actions of the individual* (e.g., performance problems, such as excessive performance errors; high or low levels of activity)

Interactions and Transactions Between E and P (Type II problems)

1. *Severe to moderate personal vulnerabilities and environmental defects and differences* (e.g., person with extremely slow development in a highly demanding environment—all of which simultaneously and equally instigate the problem)

2. *Minor personal vulnerabilities not accommodated by the situation* (e.g., person with minimal disorders in auditory perceptual ability trying to do auditory-loaded tasks; very active person forced into situations at home, school, or work that do not tolerate this level of activity)

3. *Minor environmental defects and differences not accommodated by the individual* (e.g., person is in the minority racially or culturally and is not participating in many social activities because he or she thinks others may be unreceptive)

paying adequate attention) because of physical and emotional stress caused by inappropriate child-rearing practices, illness, poor nutrition, and so forth. Obviously, few will disagree that such factors should be assessed and corrected whenever feasible.

From an intervention viewpoint, the answer to *Why worry about cause?* is simple. Understanding cause can be the key to prevention and, in some cases, is the best guide to appropriate corrective strategies.

LEARNING AND BEHAVIOR
PROBLEMS: COMMON PHENOMENA

Data from the National Center for Education Statistics (NCES, 2000) indicate that 37% of fourth graders cannot read at a basic level. Best estimates suggest that at least 20% of elementary students in the United States have significant reading problems. Among those from poor families and those with limited English language skills, the percentage shoots up to 60–70%. At the same time, best estimates suggest that minimally 95% of all children can be taught to read.

By the late 1990s, about 50% of those students designated as in need of special education were labeled LD. This translates into 2.8 million children. (The proportion of school-age children so labeled rose from 1.8% in 1976–1977 to 5.2% in 2001.) Reading and behavior problems were probably the largest source of the referrals that led to these students being so designated (Lyon, 2002). In testimony to Congress, federal officials have stressed that "of the children who will eventually drop out of school, over seventy-five percent will report difficulties in learning to read" (Pasternack, 2002). The disproportionate number of students diagnosed as LD have led to questions about whether many of these youngsters actually represent commonplace reading and related behavior problems.

Given that learning is a function of the transactions between the learner and the environment, it is understandable that certain groups would have higher rates of problems. One such group consists of those individuals living in poverty. However, keep in mind that poverty is a correlate, not the cause.

It is important to understand the factors that lead many who grow up in poverty to manifest learning and behavior problems. It is equally important, as we highlight later in the chapter, to understand what enables those who overcome the negative impact of such conditions.

For some time, official data have indicated that youngsters under age 18 were the age group with the greatest percentage (16.2%) living in poverty in the United States (U.S. Census Bureau, 2000). It is acknowledged widely that poverty is highly correlated with school failure, high school dropout, delinquency, teenage pregnancy, and other problems.

In comparison to students coming from middle or higher income families, many young children residing in poverty have less opportunity to develop the initial capabilities and positive attitudes to learning that most elementary school programs require for success. Most poverty families simply do not have the resources to provide the same preparatory experiences for their children as those who are better off financially. Moreover, many reside in the type of hostile environment that can generate so much stress as to make school adjustment and learning excessively difficult.

It is no surprise, then, that so many youngsters from poor families enter kindergarten and over the years come to school each day less than ready to meet the demands made of them. The mismatch may be particularly bad for individuals who have recently migrated from a different culture, do not speak English, or both.

There is a poignant irony in all this. Children of poverty often have developed a range of other cultural, subcultural, and language abilities that middle-class-oriented schools are unprepared to accommodate, never mind capitalize upon. As a result, many of these youngsters struggle to survive without access to their strengths. It should surprise no one that a high percentage of these youngsters soon are seen as having learning and behavior problems and may end up diagnosed as having LD, ADHD, and/or other disorders.

Of course, a youngster does not have to live in poverty to be deprived of the opportunity to develop the initial capabilities and attitudes to succeed in elementary school programs. There are youngsters who in the preschool years develop a bit slower than their peers. Their learning potential in the long run need not be affected by this fact. However, if early school demands do not accommodate a wide range of differences, the youngsters are vulnerable. When a task demands a level of development they have not achieved, they cannot do it. For example, youngsters who have not yet developed to a level where they can visually discriminate between the letters *b* and *d* or make auditory discriminations between words such as *fan* and *man* are in trouble if the reading curriculum demands they do so. And months later, when their development catches up to that curriculum demand, the reading program relentlessly has moved on, leaving them farther behind. Given what we know about the normal range of developmental variations, it is no surprise that many of these youngsters end up having problems.

When students have trouble learning at school, they frequently manifest behavior problems. This is a common reaction to learning problems. And, of course, behavior problems can get in the way of learning. Furthermore, both sets of problems may appear simultaneously and stem from the same or separate causes. It is important to remember that an individual can have more than one problem. Given all this, it is not surprising that there is considerable confusion about the relationship between learning and behavior problems.

The strong relationship between learning and behavior problems makes it essential that practitioners, researchers, and policymakers strive

to understand this association. A transactional view of cause provides a framework for doing so.

BARRIERS TO LEARNING

Another way to discuss why children have problems at school is to think in terms of barriers to learning and what the role of schools should be in addressing such factors. Such a perspective blends well with a transactional view of the causes of human behavior because it emphasizes that for a great many students, *external* not *internal* factors often are the ones that should be the primary focus of attention.

Implicit in democratic ideals is the intent of ensuring that *all* students succeed at school and that "no child is left behind." If all students came ready and able to profit from "high standards" curricula, then there would be little problem. But *all* encompasses those who are experiencing external and/or internal barriers that interfere with benefiting from what the teacher is offering. Providing all students an equal opportunity to succeed requires more than higher standards and greater accountability for instruction, better teaching, increased discipline, reduced school violence, and an end to social promotion. It also requires addressing barriers to development, learning, and teaching.

Based on a review of over 30 years of research, Hawkins and Catalano (1992) identify common risk factors that reliably predict such problems as youth delinquency, violence, substance abuse, teen pregnancy, and school dropout. These factors also are associated with such mental health concerns as school adjustment problems, relationship difficulties, physical and sexual abuse, neglect, and severe emotional disturbance. The majority of factors identified by Hawkins and Catalano are external barriers to healthy development and learning. Such factors are not excuses for anyone not doing his or her best; they are, however, rather obvious impediments, and ones to which no good parent would willingly submit his or her child. Following is our effort to synthesize various analyses of external and internal barriers:

External Factors*	Internal Factors (Biological and Psychological)
Community Availability of drugs Availability of firearms Community laws and norms favorable toward drug use, firearms, and crime Media portrayals of violence Transitions and mobility Low neighborhood attachment and community disorganization Extreme economic deprivation	*Differences* (e.g., being further along toward one end or the other of a normal developmental curve; not fitting local "norms" in terms of looks and behavior)
Family Family history of the problem behavior Family management problems Family conflict Favorable parental attitudes and involvement in the problem behavior	*Vulnerabilities* (e.g., minor health/vision/hearing problems and other deficiencies/deficits that result in school absences and other needs for special accommodations; being the focus of racial, ethnic, or gender bias; economical disadvantage; youngster and/or parent lacks interest in youngster's schooling, is alienated, or rebellious; early manifestation of severe and pervasive problem/antisocial behavior)
School Academic failure beginning in late elementary school	*Disabilities* (e.g., true learning, behavior, and emotional disorders)
Peer Friends who engage in the problem behavior Favorable attitudes toward the problem behavior	

*Other examples of external factors include exposure to crisis events in the community, home, and school; lack of availability and access to good school readiness programs; lack of home involvement in schooling; lack of peer support, positive role models, and mentoring; lack of access and availability of good recreational opportunities; lack of access and availability to good community housing, health and social services, transportation, law enforcement, sanitation; lack of access and availability to good school support programs; sparsity of high-quality schools.

The terrible fact is that too many youngsters are growing up and going to school in situations that not only fail to promote healthy development but are antithetical to the process. Some also bring with them personal factors that make learning and performing difficult. At one time or another, most students bring problems with them to school that affect their learning and perhaps interfere with the teacher's efforts to teach. As a result, some youngsters at every grade level come to school unready to meet the setting's demands effectively. As long as school reforms fail to address such barriers in comprehensive and multifaceted ways, especially in schools where large proportions of students are not doing well, it is unlikely that achievement test score averages can be meaningfully raised.

ADDRESSING BARRIERS/RISKS, ESTABLISHING PROTECTIVE BUFFERS, AND PROMOTING FULL DEVELOPMENT

Schools tend to address barriers to learning as a last resort. This is not surprising, since their assigned mission is to educate, and school staff are under increasing pressure both to leave no child behind and avoid discussing matters that may sound like excuses for not doing so. The irony, of course, is that most school staff are painfully aware of barriers that must be addressed. Moreover, the widespread emphasis on high stakes testing not only underscores how many students are not performing well but also the degree to which such testing is adding another barrier that keeps some students from having an equal opportunity to succeed at school.

All this leads to concerns about what the role of schools is and should be in handling such problems. Critics point out that the tendency is for schools to be reactive—waiting until problems become severe and pervasive. At the same time, because schools have been accused of having a *deficit orientation* toward many youngsters, they have increasingly tried to avoid terms denoting risks and barriers or an overemphasis on remediation.

It is good that schools realize that a focus solely on fixing problems is too limited and may be counterproductive. Overemphasis on remediation can diminish efforts to promote healthy development, limit opportunity, and be motivationally debilitating to all involved. And undermining motivation works against resiliency in responding to adversity. One important outcome of the reaction to overemphasizing risks and problems is that increasing attention is being given to strengths, assets, resilience, and protective factors. Among the benefits of this focus is greater understanding of how some youngsters born into poverty overcome this potential barrier to success.

However, as Scales and Leffert (1999) indicate in their work on developmental assets, focusing just on enhancing assets is an insufficient approach.

> Young people also need adequate food, shelter, clothing, caregivers who at the minimum are not abusive or neglectful, families with adequate incomes, schools where both children and teachers feel safe, and economically and culturally vibrant neighborhoods—not ones beset with drugs, violent crime, and infrastructural decay. For example, young people who are disadvantaged by living in poor neighborhoods are consistently more likely to engage in risky behavior at higher rates than their affluent peers, and they show consistently lower rates of positive outcomes (Brooks-Gunn & Duncan, 1997). Moreover, young people who live in abusive homes or in neighborhoods with high levels of violence are more likely to become both victims and perpetrators of violence. (Garbarino, 1995, p. 10)

As advocates have argued the merits of their respective positions about risks versus assets, and as terms such as *resilience* and *protective factors* are popularized, confusion and controversy have arisen. The following distinctions are offered in support of the position that the need is to address barriers, establish protective buffers, and promote full development.

Risk Factors

One way to think about risks is in terms of potential external and internal barriers to development and learning. Research indicates that the primary causes for most youngsters' learning, behavior, and emotional problems are external factors (related to neighborhood, family, school, and/or peers). For a few, problems stem from individual disorders and differences. An appreciation of the research on the role played by external and internal factors makes a focus on such matters a major part of any comprehensive, multifaceted approach for addressing barriers to learning, development, and teaching.

Protective Factors

Protective factors are conditions that *buffer* against the impact of barriers (risk factors). Such conditions may prevent or counter risk-producing conditions by promoting the development of neighborhood, family, school, peer, and individual strengths, assets, and coping mechanisms through special assistance and accommodations. The term *resilience* usually refers to an individual's ability to cope in ways that buffer. Research on protective buffers also guides efforts to address barriers.

Promoting Full Development

As often is stressed, being problem-free is not the same as being well developed. Efforts to reduce risks and enhance protection can help minimize problems but are insufficient for promoting full development, well-being, and a value-based life. Those concerned with establishing systems for promoting healthy development recognize the need for direct efforts to promote development and empowerment, including the mobilization of individuals for self-direction. In many cases, interventions to create buffers and promote full development are identical, and the payoff is the cultivation of developmental strengths and assets. However, promoting healthy development is not limited to countering risks and engendering protective factors. Efforts to promote full development represent ends that are valued in and of themselves and to which most of us aspire.

Considerable bodies of research and theory have identified major correlates that are useful guideposts in designing relevant interventions (see Guide 1.3). And as the examples illustrate, there is a significant overlap in conceptualizing the various factors. Some risk factors (barriers) and protective buffers are mirror images; others are distinct. Many protective

Guide 1.3   Examples of Barriers to Learning/Development, Protective Buffers, and Promoting Full Development*

Environmental Conditions**			Person-based Factors**
1. Barriers to Development and Learning *(risk-producing conditions)*			
Neighborhood	*Family*	*School and Peers*	*Individual*
• Extreme economic deprivation • Community disorganization, including high levels of mobility • Violence, drugs, etc. • Minority and/or immigrant status	• Chronic poverty • Conflict/disruptions/violence • Substance abuse • Models problem behavior • Abusive caretaking • Inadequate provision for quality child care	• Poor quality school • Negative encounters with teachers • Negative encounters with peers and/or inappropriate peer models	• Medical problems • Low birth weight/neurodevelopmental delay • Psychophysiological problems • Difficult temperament and adjustment problems
2. Protective Buffers *(conditions that prevent or counter risk-producing conditions, strengths, assets, corrective interventions, coping mechanisms, special assistance and accommodations)*			
Neighborhood	*Family*	*School and Peers*	*Individual*
• Strong economic conditions/emerging economic opportunities • Safe and stable communities • Available and accessible services • Strong bond with positive other(s) • Appropriate expectations and standards • Opportunities to successfully participate, contribute, and be recognized	• Adequate financial resources • Nurturing supportive family members who are positive models • Safe and stable (organized and predictable) home environment • Family literacy • Provision of high-quality child care • Secure attachments, early and ongoing	• Success at school • Positive relationships with one or more teachers • Positive relationships with peers and appropriate peer models • Strong bond with positive other(s)	• Higher cognitive functioning • Psychophysiological health • Easy temperament, outgoing personality, and positive behavior • Strong abilities for involvement and problem solving • Sense of purpose and future • Gender (girls less apt to develop certain problems)
3. Promoting Full Development *(conditions, over and beyond those that create protective buffers, that enhance healthy development, well-being, and a value-based life)*			
Neighborhood	*Family*	*School and Peers*	*Individual*
• Nurturing and supportive conditions • Policy and practice promote healthy development and sense of community	• Conditions that foster positive physical and mental health among all family members	• Nurturing and supportive climate schoolwide and in classrooms • Conditions that foster feelings of competence, self-determination, and connectedness	• Pursues opportunities for personal development and empowerment • Intrinsically motivated to pursue full development, well-being, and a value-based life

*For more on these matters, see Adelman & Taylor (1994), Deci & Ryan (1985), Hawkins & Catalano (1992), Huffman, Mehlinger, & Kerivan (2000), and Strader, Collins, & Noe (2000).

**A transactional view of behavior recognizes the interplay of environment and person variables.

buffers are natural by-products of efforts to engender full development. From this perspective, addressing barriers to learning and development and promoting healthy development are two sides of the same coin. And the best way to engender resilient behavior, individual assets, and healthy behavior in children and adolescents probably is to focus intervention on both sides of the coin.

CONCLUDING COMMENTS

In this chapter, we have stressed that it is a mistake to jump too quickly from research that identifies compelling correlates to making assumptions about cause and effect. We underscored that this trend masks how many problems are caused by the environment and person-environment trans-actions. We also have explored the problem of mislabeling commonplace learning and behavior problems. And we stressed the value of under-standing that behavior is reciprocally determined (i.e., is a function of person and environment transactions).

A comprehensive understanding of the barriers to student learning is essential to the integrity of efforts related to prevention, early intervention, and treatment, as well as training and research. The same is true with respect to protective buffers and positive development.

The implications of a transactional view for intervention are profound. As we discuss in Chapter 2, any school where large numbers of students manifest learning, behavior, and emotional problems needs to implement a comprehensive, multifaceted, and cohesive continuum of interventions. This continuum must address barriers (reducing risks, enhancing buffers) and promote full development. Policymakers and researchers must move beyond the narrow set of empirically supported programs to a research and development agenda that braids together systematic, comprehensive, multifaceted approaches. It is by moving in this direction that schools can increase their effectiveness in reengaging the many students who have become disengaged from classroom learning.

REFLECTION AND STIMULUS FOR DISCUSSION

Key Insights About "Why Students Have Problems"

Based on what you learned so far,

Identify (and discuss)

1. The key factors that result in students experiencing learning and related behavior problems

2. How schools are affected by barriers to learning

If there is an opportunity for group discussion, you may find the following group process guidelines helpful:

- Start by identifying someone who will facilitate the group interchange.
- Take a few minutes to make a few individual notes on a worksheet.
- Be sure all major points are compiled for sharing with other groups.
- Ask someone else to watch the time so that the group doesn't bog down.

Here is what a student wrote in class one day.

> I am 13 years old and learning disabled. I have had problems along time. People say I am smart but I lak eny ability and I am tired of trying. My parrents tryed to help me, but I dont deserve there support or concern, I am just not worth if I do not get allong with people eneywhere and never have been able to. I am affraid of every one and hate being told to wake up or come out of my dreemworld. I dont know how to deel with eney thing eneywhere.

Make some notes about what you think should be done and then discuss your ideas with others.

If there is an opportunity for group discussion, you may find the following group process guidelines helpful:

- Start by identifying someone who will facilitate the group interchange.
- Take a few minutes to make a few individual notes on a worksheet.
- Be sure all major points are compiled for sharing with other groups.
- Ask someone else to watch the time so that the group doesn't bog down.

ACTIVITY

Observe a classroom. Identify students who appear to be having difficulty. After observing for a while, write down your views about

1. Why the students are having difficulty

2. What was tried in an effort to help

3. What seemed to help and why

4. What didn't work and why

5. What new strategies you would add

It's funny and poignant.

In describing anatomy, one seventh grader wrote:

Anatomy is the human body made up of three parts, the head, the chest, and stummick. The head holds the skull and the brains if there is any. The chest holds the liver, and the stummick holds the vowels which are *a, e, i, o, u,* and sometimes *w* and *y.*

REFERENCES

Adelman, H. S. (1995). Clinical psychology: Beyond psychopathology and clinical interventions. *Clinical Psychology: Science and Practice, 2,* 28–44.

Adelman, H. S., & Taylor, L. (1994). *On understanding intervention in psychology and education.* Westport, CT: Prager.

Bandura, A. (1978). The self system in reciprocal determinism. *American Psychologist, 33,* 344–358.

Brooks-Gunn, J., & Duncan, G. J. (1997). The effects of poverty on children. *The Future of Children, 7,* 55–71. Los Altos, CA: Packard Foundation.

Charcot, J. M. (1857). *De l'expectoration en médecine.* Charcot-Leyden crystals. Retrieved from http://www.whonamedit.com.

Chase, S. (1956). *Guides to straight thinking.* New York: Harper & Brothers.

Darling-Hammond, L. (1997). *The right to learn: A blueprint for creating schools that work.* San Francisco: Jossey-Bass.

Deci, E., & Ryan, R. (1985). *Intrinsic motivation and self-determination in human behavior.* New York: Plenum.

Garbarino, J. (1995). *Raising children in a socially toxic environment.* San Francisco: Jossey-Bass.

Hawkins, J. D., & Catalano, R. F. (1992). *Communities that care.* San Francisco: Jossey-Bass.

Huffman, L., Mehlinger, S., & Kerivan, A. (2000). *Research on the risk factors for early school problems and selected federal policies affecting children's social and emotional development and their readiness for school.* The Child and Mental Health Foundation and Agencies Network. Retrieved from http://www.nimh.nih.gov/childp/goodstart.cfm.

Kohn, A. (1999). Constant frustration and occasional violence: The legacy of American high schools. *American School Board Journal.* Retrieved from http://www.asbj.com/security/contents/0999kohn.html.

Lyon, G. R. (1998). Reading: A research-based approach. In California State Board of Education (Eds.), *Read all about it: Readings to inform the profession.* Sacramento, CA: County Office of Education.

Lyon, G. R. (2002). Testimony before the Subcommittee on Educational Reform, U.S. Senate.

National Center for Educational Statistics. (2000). *The nation's report card: Fourth-grade reading 2000.* Washington, DC: Author. Retrieved from http://nces.ed.gov/nationsreportcard.

National Institute of Child Health & Human Development (NICHD). (2000). *Report of the national reading panel: Teaching children to read.* Retrieved from http://www.nichd.nih.gov/publications/nrp/smallbook.htm.

Pasternack, R. (2002). Testimony before the Subcommittee on Educational Reform, U.S. Senate.

Ryan, W. (1971). *Blaming the victim.* New York: Random House.

Scales, P. C., & Leffert, N. (1999). *Developmental assets.* Minneapolis, MN: Search Institute.

Strader, T. N., Collins, D. A., & Noe, T. D. (2000). *Building healthy individuals, families, and communities: Creating lasting connections.* New York: Kluwer Academic/Plenum.

U.S. Census Bureau. (2000). *Households and families: Census 2000 brief* (issued September 2001). Washington, DC: U.S. Department of Commerce. (http://www.census.gov/prod/2001pubs/c2kbr01-8.pdf).

U.S. Office of Education. (1977). Education of handicapped children. *Federal Register, 42,* 65082–65085.

*Chapter 14 contains a list of special resources related
to the above matters available at no cost from the national
Center for Mental Health in Schools, which is at UCLA and is
directed by the authors of this book. Go to http://smhp.psych.ucla.edu.*

Problems Are Multifaceted; Solutions Must Be Too!

2

It is either naive or irresponsible to ignore the connection between children's performance in school and their experiences with malnutrition, homelessness, lack of medical care, inadequate housing, racial and cultural discrimination, and other burdens.

—Harold Howe II

What's easy to get into but hard to get out of?   Trouble!

25

ORIENTING QUESTIONS

? What's wrong with the way schools currently use resources for learning supports?
? Why is a full continuum of learning supports needed?
? What are the six arenas covered by an Enabling or Learning Supports Component?

School systems are not responsible for meeting every need of their students. But when the need directly affects learning, the school must meet the challenge.

—Carnegie Task Force on
Education of Young Adolescents (1989)

It was February. Ms. Harris was feeling overwhelmed. As a math teacher with five years of experience in middle schools, she had seen it all. But that didn't make it easier to handle. There were just too many students who didn't like math class. Some were frequently truant, and when they did show up, they hadn't done the homework and were disruptive.

James was a typical example. He preferred talking to classmates to doing his work. When reprimanded, he argued back. Any form of discipline seemed just fine with him. He didn't like teachers or much else about school.

In desperation, Ms. Harris reached out to the school's student support staff. They added James's name to the long list waiting for review. The length of the list made it unlikely that they would get to James before the end of the year.

Given the range of learning, behavior, and emotional problems that teachers and student support staff encounter, meeting the challenge is difficult. The sparsity of resources available to do the work almost always is cited as a limiting factor. Related concerns are the way interventions are conceived, organized, and implemented.

Current policy and practices in schools and districts tend to be reactive—responding mostly to squeaky wheels and crises. A considerable proportion of the sparse resources for "student supports" are directed at addressing discrete problems and doing so in piecemeal ways. Reactive and fragmented practices arise from the large number of referrals from teachers who want some help and from the need to categorize students to justify receiving and using special funding.

All this leads to designing interventions first and foremost to focus on specific students exhibiting flagrant problems. In most schools, however, the number of students referred by teachers overwhelms available supports. At the same time, the situation is confounded by categorical funding. The paradox of such funding is that it brings in extra resources but limits use to specific types of problems. As a result, it is not uncommon for one student identified as having multiple problems to be involved in programs with several professionals working independently of each other. All this limits the number of students who can be helped and usually fragments intervention in undesirable ways.

So, in this age of data-driven decision making, the data are clear. The majority of teacher and student support resources address a relatively small proportion of students and do so in a fragmented manner. This means that relatively little is done about the majority of those students who are overwhelming teachers such as Ms. Harris.

Teachers and support staff tend to be unhappy with the current state of affairs. Teachers need much more help, not just for individual students, but to effectively redress the range of complex yet commonplace problems that affect the learning and achievement of a larger proportion of students (e.g., the achievement gap, students who have disengaged from classroom learning, truancy, dropouts, and bullying).

Given that teachers need more from student support staff and that support staff would like to be more helpful, we need to look closely at what needs to change, and then teachers and support staff have to work together to make things better. In doing so, the guiding questions are: *How do schools address barriers to learning and teaching? What can be done to more effectively enable students to learn and teachers to teach?*

WHAT SCHOOLS ARE DOING

Currently, there are about 91,000 public schools in about 15,000 districts. Over the years, most (but obviously not all) schools have instituted programs designed with a range of learning, behavior, and emotional problems in mind. There is a large body of research supporting the promise of much of this activity.

School-based and school-linked programs have been developed for purposes of early intervention, crisis intervention and prevention, treatment, and promotion of positive social and emotional development. Some programs are provided throughout a district, others are carried out at or linked to targeted schools. The interventions may be offered to all students in a school, to those in specified grades, or to those identified as at risk. The activities may be implemented in regular or special education classrooms or as "pull out" programs and may be designed for an entire class, groups, or individuals. There also may be a focus on primary prevention and enhancement of healthy development through use of health education, health services, guidance, and so forth—though relatively few resources usually are allocated for such activity.

Staffing for Learning Support

School districts use a variety of *personnel* to address student problems. These may include resource teachers, special education staff, "pupil services" or "support services" specialists, such as school psychologists, counselors, social workers, and nurses, as well as a variety of related therapists (e.g., art, dance, music, occupational, physical, speech, language-hearing, and recreation therapists). Their *functions* can be grouped as (a) direct services and instruction, (b) coordination, development, and leadership related to programs, services, resources, and systems, and (c) enhancement of connections with community resources. Federal and state mandates play a significant role in determining how many personnel are employed to address problems.

In addition to responding to crises, prevailing direct intervention approaches encompass identification of the needs of targeted individuals, prescription of one or more interventions, brief consultation, and gatekeeping procedures (such as referral for assessment, corrective services, triage, and diagnosis). In some situations, however, resources are so limited that specialists can do little more than assess for special education eligibility, offer brief consultations, and make referrals to special education and/or community resources.

More Effective Use of Resources

Inadequate data are available on how much schools spend to address learning, behavior, and emotional problems. Figures most often gathered and reported focus on pupil service personnel. These data suggest that about 7% of a school district's budget goes to paying the salaries of such personnel. As to numbers employed, the *School Health Policies and Program Study 2000* conducted by the National Center for Chronic Disease Prevention and Health Promotion (see http://www.cdc.gov) sampled 51 state departments of education, 560 school districts, and 950 schools. Findings indicate that 77% of schools have a part- or full-time guidance counselor, 66% have a part- or full-time school psychologist, and 44% have a part- or full-time social worker.

While ratios change with economic conditions, professional-to-student ratio for school psychologists or school social workers has averaged 1:2,500 students; for school counselors, the ratio has been about 1:1,000 (Carlson, Paavola, & Talley, 1995). At the same time, estimates indicate that more than half the students in many schools are encountering major barriers that interfere with their functioning. Given existing ratios, it is obvious that more than narrow-band (individual and small-group-oriented) approaches must be used in such schools if the majority are to receive the help they need. Yet the prevailing orientation remains that of focusing on discrete problems and overrelying on specialized services provided to small numbers of students.

Because the need is so great, a variety of individuals often are called upon to play a role in addressing problems of youth and their families. These include other health professionals (such as school nurses and physicians), instructional professionals (health educators, other classroom teachers, special education staff, resource staff), administrative staff (principals, assistant principals), students (including trained peer counselors), family members, and almost everyone else involved with a school (aides, clerical and cafeteria staff, custodians, bus drivers, paraprofessionals, recreation personnel, volunteers, and professionals-in-training). In addition, some schools are using specialists employed by other public and private agencies, such as health departments, hospitals, social service agencies, and community-based organizations, to provide services to students, their families, and school staff.

In calculating how much schools spend on addressing learning, behavior, and emotional problems, to focus only on pupil service personnel salaries probably is misleading and a major underestimation. This is particularly so for schools receiving special funding. Studies are needed to clarify the entire gamut of resources that school sites devote to student problems. Budgets must be broken apart in ways that allow tallying all resources allocated from general funds, support provided for compensatory and special education, and underwriting

---

> ### What Is Spent in Schools?
>
> • Federal government figures indicate $5.2 million are spent on special education (U.S. Department of Education, 2001). Overall costs are about $43 billion (and rising), with the federal government funding only about $5.3 billion. Estimates in many school districts indicate that about 20% of the budget can be consumed by special education. How much is used directly for efforts to address learning, behavior, and emotional problems is unknown, but remember that more than 50% of those in special education are diagnosed as learning disabled and more than 8% are labeled as emotionally/behaviorally disturbed.
>
> • Looking at total education budgets, one group of investigators report that nationally, 6.7% of school spending (about $16 billion) is used for student support services, such as counseling, psychological services, speech therapy, health services, and diagnostic and related special services for students with disabilities (Monk, Pijanowski, & Hussain, 1997). Again, the amount specifically devoted to learning, behavior, and emotional problems is unclear. The figures do not include costs related to time spent on such matters by other school staff such as teachers and administrators. Also not included are expenditures related to initiatives such as safe and drug-free schools programs and arrangements such as alternative and continuation schools and funding for school-based health, family, and parent centers.

related to programs for dropout prevention and recovery, safe and drug-free schools, pregnancy prevention, teen parents, family literacy, homeless students, and more. In some schools, it has been suggested that as much as 25–30% of the budget is expended on problem prevention and correction.

Whatever the expenditures, it is common knowledge that few schools come close to having enough resources to deal with a large number of students with learning, behavior, and emotional problems. Moreover, the contexts for intervention often are limited and makeshift because of how current resources are allocated and used. A relatively small proportion of space at schools is earmarked specifically for programs that address student problems. Many special programs and related efforts to promote health and positive behavior are assigned space on an ad hoc basis. Support service personnel often must rotate among schools as "itinerant" staff. These conditions contribute to the tendency for such personnel to operate in relative isolation of each other and other stakeholders. To make matters worse, little systematic inservice development is provided for new support staff when they arrive from their preservice programs. Clearly, all this is not conducive to effective practice and is wasteful of sparse resources.

In sum, analyses show that support interventions are developed and function in relative isolation of each other and they rarely are envisioned comprehensively. Organizationally, the tendency is for policymakers to mandate and planners and developers to focus on specific services and programs, with too little thought or time given to mechanisms for program development and collaboration. Functionally, most practitioners spend their time using specialized interventions with targeted problems, usually individual or small groups of students. Consequently, programs to address learning, behavior, emotional, and physical problems rarely are coordinated with each other or with educational programs. Intervention planning and implementation are widely characterized as being fragmented and piecemeal, which is an ineffective way for schools to deal with the complex sets of problems confronting teachers such as Ms. Harris.

Now that you've been in school for a while, how do you like it?

Closed!

NEEDED: A FULL CONTINUUM OF LEARNING SUPPORTS

As we have noted, when students are not doing well, a prevailing trend is for teachers to refer them to support staff. In some schools and classrooms, the number of referrals is dramatic. Where special teams exist to review students for whom teachers request help, the list grows as the year proceeds. The longer the list, the longer the lag time for review—often to the point that by the end of the school year, the team has reviewed just a small percentage of those referred. *And no matter how many are reviewed, there are always more referrals than can be served.*

One solution might be to convince policymakers to fund more special programs and services at schools. However, even if the policy climate favored more special programs, such interventions alone are not a comprehensive approach for addressing barriers to learning. More services to treat problems certainly are needed. But so are programs for prevention and early-after-problem onset that can reduce the number of students teachers send to student review teams. Multifaceted problems that affect large numbers of students usually require comprehensive, integrated solutions applied concurrently and over time. This means developing the full continuum of interventions illustrated in Guide 2.1.

Development of a full continuum involves the efforts of school and community. Such a continuum must be *comprehensive, multifaceted,* and *integrated* and woven into three overlapping *systems:* systems for positive development and prevention of problems, systems of early intervention to address problems as soon after their onset as feasible, and systems of care for those with chronic and severe problems. Accomplishing all this requires that society's policymakers work toward fundamental systemic reforms that will enable redeployment of how current resources are used.

The three systems highlighted in Guide 2.1 must encompass an array of effective programmatic activities along the continuum. For example, moving through the continuum, the emphasis is on (a) public health protection, promotion, and maintenance to foster opportunities, positive development, and wellness, (b) preschool-age support and assistance to enhance health and psychosocial development, (c) early-schooling targeted interventions, (d) improvement and augmentation of ongoing regular support, (e) other interventions prior to referral for intensive, ongoing targeted treatments, and (f) intensive treatments. Examples of each are listed in Guide 2.2.

The continuum of interventions framed in Guides 2.1 and 2.2 encompasses a holistic and developmental emphasis. The focus is on individuals, families, and the contexts in which they live, learn, work, and play. A basic underlying assumption is that, initially, the emphasis should be on the least restrictive and nonintrusive forms of intervention required to address problems and accommodate diversity. Another assumption is that problems are not discrete, and therefore, interventions that address root causes should be used. Although schools cannot do everything outlined, they must play a much greater role in developing the programs and systems essential for all students to benefit from higher standards and improved instruction. Central to this is expanding efforts to prevent and correct learning, behavior, and emotional problems (Adelman, 1995; Adelman & Taylor,

Guide 2.1   A Comprehensive, Multifaceted, and Integrated Approach to Addressing Barriers to Learning and Promoting Healthy Development

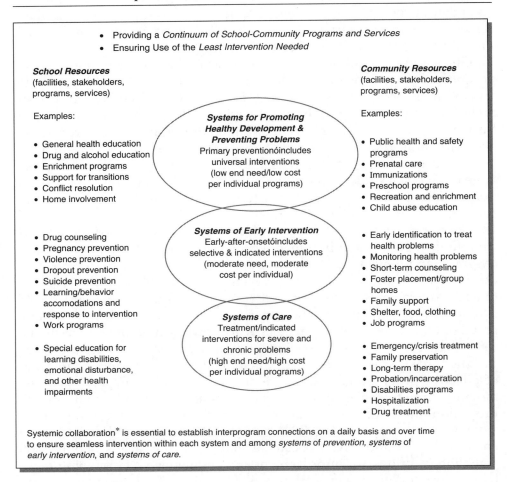

Providing a *Continuum of School-Community Programs and Services*

Ensuring Use of the *Least Intervention Needed*

School Resources
(facilities, stakeholders, programs, services)

Examples:

- General health education
- Drug and alcohol education
- Enrichment programs
- Support for transitions
- Conflict resolution
- Home involvement

- Drug counseling
- Pregnancy prevention
- Violence prevention
- Dropout prevention
- Suicide prevention
- Learning/behavior accomodations and response to intervention
- Work programs

- Special education for learning disabilities, emotional disturbance, and other health impairments

Community Resources
(facilities, stakeholders, programs, services)

Examples:

- Public health and safety programs
- Prenatal care
- Immunizations
- Preschool programs
- Recreation and enrichment
- Child abuse education

- Early identification to treat health problems
- Monitoring health problems
- Short-term counseling
- Foster placement/group homes
- Family support
- Shelter, food, clothing
- Job programs

- Emergency/crisis treatment
- Family preservation
- Long-term therapy
- Probation/incarceration
- Disabilities programs
- Hospitalization
- Drug treatment

Systems for Promoting Healthy Development & Preventing Problems
Primary prevention—includes universal interventions
(low end need/low cost per individual programs)

Systems of Early Intervention
Early-after-onset—includes selective & indicated interventions
(moderate need, moderate cost per individual)

Systems of Care
Treatment/indicated interventions for severe and chronic problems
(high end need/high cost per individual programs)

Systemic collaboration* is essential to establish interprogram connections on a daily basis and over time to ensure seamless intervention within each system and among *systems* of *prevention, systems* of *early intervention*, and *systems of care*.

*Such collaboration involves horizontal and vertical restructuring of programs and services (a) within jurisdictions, school districts, and community agencies (e.g., among departments, divisions, units, schools, clusters of schools) or (b) between jurisdictions, school and community agencies, public and private sectors; among schools; among community agencies

1997). This includes working closely with teachers in classrooms to provide students with academic and social supports and increasing recreational and enrichment opportunities. For families, teachers and support staff can work with adult educators to bring classes to school and neighborhood sites and facilitate enrollment of family members who want to improve their literacy, learn English, and develop job skills. To accomplish all this, schools must outreach to connect with community resources.

Guide 2.2   From Primary Prevention to Treatment of Serious Problems:
A Continuum of Community School Programs to Address
Barriers to Learning and Enhance Healthy Development

Intervention Continuum	Examples of Focus and Types of Intervention (Programs and services aimed at system changes and individual needs)
Systems for health promotion and primary prevention	1. *Public health protection, promotion, and maintenance to foster opportunities, positive development, and wellness* • Economic enhancement of those living in poverty (e.g., work/welfare programs) • Safety (e.g., instruction, regulations, lead abatement programs) • Physical and mental health (including healthy start initiatives, immunizations, dental care, substance abuse prevention, violence prevention, health/mental health education, sex education and family planning, recreation, social services to access basic living resources, and so forth)
	2. *Preschool-age support and assistance to enhance health and psychosocial development* • Systems' enhancement through multidisciplinary team work, consultation, and staff development • Education and social support for parents of preschoolers • Equality day care • Quality early education • Appropriate screening and amelioration of physical and mental health and psychosocial problems
Systems for early-after-problem onset intervention	3. *Early-schooling targeted interventions* • Orientations, welcoming and transition support into school and community life for students and their families (especially immigrants) • Support and guidance to ameliorate school adjustment problems • Personalized instruction in the primary grades • Additional support to address specific learning problems • Parent involvement in problem solving • Comprehensive and accessible psychosocial and physical and mental health programs (including a focus on community and home violence and other problems identified through community needs assessment)
	4. *Improvement and augmentation of ongoing regular support* • Enhance systems through multidisciplinary team work, consultation, and staff development • Preparation and support for school and life transitions • Teaching "basics" of support and remediation to regular teachers (including use of available resource personnel, peer and volunteer support) • Parent involvement in problem solving • Resource support for parents-in-need (including assistance in finding work, legal aid, ESL and citizenship classes, and so forth) • Comprehensive and accessible psychosocial and physical and mental health interventions (including health and physical education, recreation, violence reduction programs, and so forth) • Academic guidance and assistance • Emergency and crisis prevention and response mechanisms
	5. *Other interventions prior to referral for intensive, ongoing targeted treatments* • Enhance systems through multidisciplinary team work, consultation, and staff development • Short-term specialized interventions (including resource teacher instruction and family mobilization; programs for suicide prevention, pregnant minors, substance abusers, gang members, and other potential dropouts)
Systems for treatment for severe/chronic problems	6. *Intensive treatments* • Referral, triage, placement guidance and assistance, case management, and resource coordination • Family preservation programs and services • Special education and rehabilitation • Dropout recovery and follow-up support • Services for severe-chronic psychosocial/mental/physical health problems

When the framework outlined in Guides 2.1 and 2.2 is used to analyze a school's programs and those in the surrounding community, it usually becomes evident that both the school and its surrounding community have some related but separate initiatives. Such an analysis highlights the degree of fragmentation (and marginalization) that characterizes efforts to address barriers to learning and teaching. More important, it suggests the need for systemic collaboration to braid resources and establish interprogram connections on a daily basis and over time. This involves horizontal and vertical restructuring of programs and services within and between jurisdictions (e.g., among departments, divisions, units, schools, clusters of schools, districts, community agencies, and public and private sectors). Such connections are essential to counter tendencies to develop separate programs in different venues for every observed problem.

In support of specific types of programs exemplified in Guides 2.1 and 2.2, a little bit of data can be gleaned from various facets of the research literature, most often project evaluations and dissertations. For obvious reasons, no study has ever looked at the impact of implementing the full continuum in any one geographic catchment area. However, we can make inferences from naturalistic "experiments" taking place in every wealthy and most upper-middle-income communities. Across the country, concerned parents who have financial resources, or who can avail themselves of such resources when necessary, will purchase any of the interventions listed in order to ensure their children's well-being. This represents a body of empirical support for the value of such interventions that cannot be ignored. (As one wag put it: *The range of interventions is supported by a new form of validation—market validity!*)

RETHINKING SCHOOL REFORM TO INCLUDE LEARNING SUPPORTS

Keeping the full continuum in mind, let's look at school reform. It is clear that prevailing reforms give short shrift to how schools and communities can meet the challenge by addressing persistent barriers to learning and teaching.

Our analyses of dominant policies for improving schools indicate that the primary focus is on two major components: (1) enhancing instruction and curriculum and (2) restructuring school governance/management. The implementation of such efforts is shaped by demands for every teacher and school to adopt high standards and expectations and be accountable for results, as measured by standardized achievement tests. Toward these ends, the calls have been to enhance direct academic support and move away from a "deficit" model by adopting a strengths or resilience-oriented paradigm. All this is reflected in federal education legislation. Even when legislation provides for "supplemental services," the emphasis primarily is on tutoring, thereby paying little attention to the multifaceted nature of the barriers that interfere with students' learning and performing well at school.

Given that the primary focus of school improvement efforts is on instruction, concern arises about what the agenda is for helping teachers such as Ms. Harris be more effective with those students who are overwhelming her. Our analyses find the agenda inadequate.

One or more of three types of approaches might be mentioned in a school improvement plan, but even when they are included, they are marginalized in policy and daily practice in classrooms and schoolwide. One approach stresses targeted problems. Such "categorical" initiatives generate auxiliary programs, some supported by school district general funds and some underwritten by federal and private-sector money. Examples of activities include those related to special and compensatory education; ending social promotion; violence reduction; prevention of substance abuse, youth pregnancy, suicide, and dropouts; early identification; school-based health centers; and family and youth resource centers.

A second set of approaches stems from overlapping policies intended to link community resources to schools. Terms used for these initiatives include *school-linked services, full-service schools, school-community partnerships,* and *community schools.* In a few states where such initiatives are under way, discussion is turning to how to enhance linkage between school improvement and efforts to integrate community services and strengthen neighborhoods. Paralleling these efforts is a natural interest in promoting healthy development and productive citizens and workers.

A third and narrower set of initiatives flows down from federal and state policies designed to promote coordination and collaboration among *governmental* departments and their service agencies. The intent is to foster integrated services, with an emphasis on greater local control, increased involvement of parents, and locating services at schools when feasible. To facilitate coordinated planning and organizational change, local, state, and federal intra- and interagency councils have been established. Relatedly, legislative bodies are rethinking their committee structures, and some states have gone so far as to create new executive branch structures (e.g., combining education and all agencies and services for children and families under one cabinet-level department). Locally, the most ambitious collaborations are pursuing comprehensive community initiatives with an emphasis on community building.

The various initiatives do help *some* teachers and *some* students who are not succeeding at school. However, they come nowhere near addressing the scope of need. Indeed, their limited potency further suggests the degree to which efforts to address barriers to learning and development are *marginalized* in policy and practice.

The limited impact of current policy points to the need to rethink school reform. Our analyses indicate that the two component models upon which current reforms are based is inadequate for improving schools in ways that will be effective in preventing and correcting learning and behavior problems. Movement to a three-component model is necessary for enabling teachers to teach and all young people to have an equal opportunity to succeed at school (see Guide 2.3).

Stated simply, the prevailing approaches to school reform do not address barriers to learning, development, and teaching in comprehensive and multifaceted ways, especially in schools where large proportions of students are not doing well. Rather, the emphasis is mostly on intensifying and narrowing the attention paid to curriculum/instruction and class-room management. This ignores the need to fundamentally restructure school and community support programs and services and continues to marginalize efforts to design the types of environments that are essential to the success of school reforms.

A three-component model calls for elevating efforts to address barriers to development, learning, and teaching to the level of one of three fundamental facets of education reform. We call the third component an *Enabling Component*; others use terms such as a *Learning Supports Component*. All three components are seen as essential, complementary, and overlapping.

THE CONCEPT OF AN ENABLING COMPONENT

Enabling is defined as "providing with the means or opportunity; making possible, practical, or easy; giving power, capacity, or sanction to." The concept of an Enabling Component is formulated on the proposition that a comprehensive, multifaceted, integrated continuum of enabling activity *is essential* for addressing the needs of youngsters who encounter barriers that interfere with their benefiting satisfactorily from instruction. From this perspective, schools committed to the success of all children should be redesigned to *enable learning* by addressing barriers to learning and teaching. That is, schools must not only focus on improving instruction and how they make decisions and manage resources, but they must also improve how they enable students to learn and teachers to teach.

The concept of an Enabling Component is meant to provide a unifying framework for reforms that fully integrate a comprehensive focus on addressing barriers to student learning as school improvement moves forward. It underscores the need to weave together school and community resources to address a wide range of factors interfering with young people's learning, performance, and well-being. It embraces efforts to promote healthy development and foster positive functioning as the best way to prevent many learning, behavior, emotional, and health problems and as a necessary adjunct to correcting problems experienced by teachers, students, and families.

Guide 2.3 Moving From a Two- to a Three-component Model for Reform and Restructuring

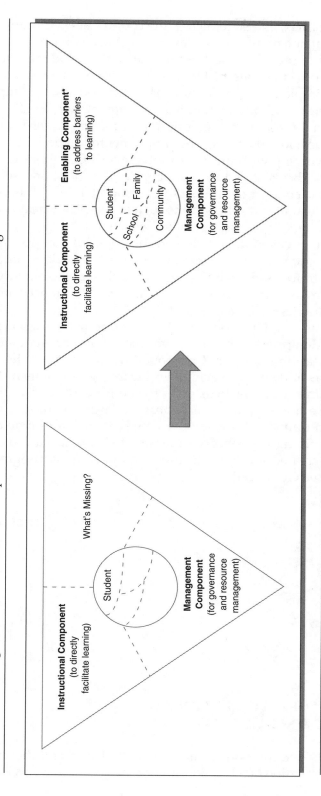

*The third component (an Enabling Component) is established in policy and practice as primary and essential and is developed into a comprehensive approach by weaving together school and community resources.

Schools, districts, and states across the country are beginning to explore the value of enhancing efforts to develop a comprehensive, multifaceted, and integrated approach to addressing barriers to student learning. One example is seen in the state of Hawaii. The entire state has adopted and has begun to implement the framework. They call their component for addressing barriers a *Comprehensive Student Support System* (CSSS). Another statewide example is seen in the design for a *Learning Supports Component* that has been developed and is being implemented by Iowa's Department of Education working with the state's Interagency Collaborative for Youth Development. Other state education agencies, districts, and schools have taken note of the concept of an Enabling Component for addressing barriers to learning, usually adopting terms such as *Learning Supports Component* or a *Component for a Supportive Learning Environment.*

Whatever it is called, a key element of the third component involves building the capacity of classrooms to enhance instructional effectiveness. Such "classroom-focused enabling" involves personalized instruction that accounts for motivational and developmental differences and special assistance in the classroom as needed.

However, an emphasis on only the classroom risks ignoring necessary schoolwide approaches. Thus, we operationalize the concept of an Enabling or Learning Support Component to cover five other arenas to address barriers and enable teaching and learning. These include an array of schoolwide interventions to respond to and prevent crises, support transitions, increase home involvement, provide targeted student and family assistance, and outreach to develop greater community involvement and support. By defining the concept in terms of six arenas, a broad unifying framework is created around which education support programs can be restructured (see Guide 2.4).

Do you have a solution for the problem?   No, but I'm sure good at admiring it.

NEW DIRECTIONS FOR LEARNING SUPPORT AT A SCHOOL SITE

Adoption of a three-component model is intended to end the marginalization and fragmentation of education support programs and services at school

Guide 2.4   A School Site Component to Address Barriers to Learning and Enhance Healthy Development

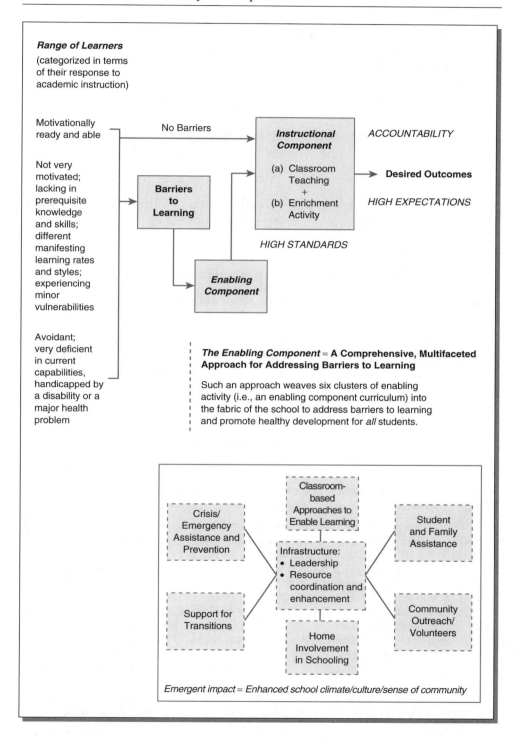

Range of Learners
(categorized in terms of their response to academic instruction)

Motivationally ready and able

Not very motivated; lacking in prerequisite knowledge and skills; different manifesting learning rates and styles; experiencing minor vulnerabilities

Avoidant; very deficient in current capabilities, handicapped by a disability or a major health problem

No Barriers

Barriers to Learning

Instructional Component

(a) Classroom Teaching
+
(b) Enrichment Activity

Enabling Component

ACCOUNTABILITY

Desired Outcomes

HIGH EXPECTATIONS

HIGH STANDARDS

The Enabling Component = **A Comprehensive, Multifaceted Approach for Addressing Barriers to Learning**

Such an approach weaves six clusters of enabling activity (i.e., an enabling component curriculum) into the fabric of the school to address barriers to learning and promote healthy development for *all* students.

Crisis/ Emergency Assistance and Prevention

Classroom-based Approaches to Enable Learning

Infrastructure:
• Leadership
• Resource coordination and enhancement

Student and Family Assistance

Support for Transitions

Home Involvement in Schooling

Community Outreach/ Volunteers

Emergent impact = Enhanced school climate/culture/sense of community sites. Moreover, the notion of a third component can be operationalized in ways that unify a school's efforts in developing a comprehensive, multi-faceted, and cohesive approach.

For example, the framework outlined in Guide 2.4 reflects an extensive analysis of the activity schools use to address barriers to learning. The six arenas are used to guide development of an Enabling or Learning Supports Component.

As can be seen in Guide 2.4, the framework covers

1. Enhancing the classroom teacher's capacity to address problems and foster social, emotional, intellectual, and behavioral development

2. Responding to, minimizing impact of, and preventing crises

3. Enhancing the capacity of schools to handle the many transition concerns confronting students and their families

4. Enhancing home involvement

5. Outreaching to the surrounding community to build linkages

6. Providing special assistance for students and families

Combined, these constitute the content or "curriculum" of an Enabling or Learning Support Component. Each of the six arenas is briefly highlighted in Guide 2.5 and discussed in greater detail in Chapter 7.

Guide 2.5   "Curriculum" Areas for an Enabling Component

---

1. Enhancing teacher capacity for addressing problems and for fostering social, emotional, intellectual, and behavioral development

This arena provides a fundamental example not only of how an Enabling or Learning Supports Component overlaps regular instructional efforts but also how it adds value to prevailing efforts to improve instruction. Classroom-based efforts to enable learning can (a) prevent problems, (b) facilitate intervening as soon as problems are noted, (c) enhance intrinsic motivation for learning, and (d) reengage students who have become disengaged from classroom learning. This is accomplished by increasing teachers' effectiveness so they can account for a wider range of individual differences, foster a caring context for learning, and prevent and handle a wider range of problems when they arise. Effectiveness is enhanced through personalized staff development and opening the classroom door to others who can help.

One objective is to provide teachers with the knowledge and skills to develop a classroom infrastructure that transforms a big class into a set of smaller ones. Such a focus is essential for increasing the effectiveness of regular classroom instruction, supporting inclusionary policies, and reducing the need for specialized services.

Work in this arena requires programmatic approaches and systems designed to personalize professional development of teachers and support staff, develop the capabilities of paraeducators and other paid assistants and volunteers, provide temporary out-of-class assistance for students, and enhance resources. For example: personalized help is provided to increase a teacher's array of strategies for accommodating, as well as teaching students to compensate for, differences, vulnerabilities, and disabilities. Teachers learn to use paid assistants, peer tutors, and volunteers in targeted ways to enhance social and academic support.

As appropriate, support *in the classroom* also is provided by resource and itinerant teachers and counselors. This involves restructuring and redesigning the roles, functions, and staff development of resource and itinerant teachers, counselors, and other pupil service personnel so they are able to work closely with teachers and students in the classroom and on regular activities.

2. Responding to minimizing impact, and preventing crises

Schools must respond to minimize the impact of and prevent school and personal crises. This requires schoolwide and classroom-based systems and programmatic approaches. Such activity focuses on (a) emergency/crisis response at a site, throughout a school complex, and communitywide (including a focus on ensuring follow-up care), (b) minimizing the impact of crises, and (c) prevention at school and in the community to address school safety and violence reduction, suicide prevention, child abuse prevention, and so forth.

Desired outcomes of crisis assistance include ensuring immediate emergency and follow-up care so students are able to resume learning without too much delay. Prevention outcome indices reflect a safe and productive environment where students and their families display the type of attitudes and capacities needed to deal with violence and other threats to safety.

A key mechanism in this arena often is development of a crisis team. Such a team is trained in emergency response procedures, physical and psychological first aid, aftermath interventions, and so forth. The team also can take the lead in planning ways to prevent some crises by facilitating development of programs to mediate and resolve conflicts, enhance human relations, and promote a caring school culture.

3. Enhancing school capacity to handle the variety of transition concerns confronting students and their families

Students and their families are regularly confronted with a variety of transitions—changing schools, changing grades, encountering other daily hassles and major life demands. Many of these interfere with productive school involvement. A comprehensive focus on transitions requires schoolwide and classroom-based systems and programs to (a) enhance successful transitions, (b) prevent transition problems, and (c) use transition periods to reduce alienation and increase positive attitudes toward school and learning. Examples of programs include schoolwide and classroom-specific activities for welcoming new arrivals (students, their families, staff) and rendering ongoing social support; counseling and articulation strategies to support grade-to-grade and school-to-school transitions and moves to and from special education, college, and postschool living and work; and before- and afterschool and intersession activities to enrich learning and provide recreation in a safe environment.

(Continued)

(Continued)

Anticipated overall outcomes are reduced alienation and enhanced motivation and increased involvement in school and learning activities. Examples of early outcomes include reduced tardies resulting from participation in beforeschool programs and reduced vandalism, violence, and crime at school and in the neighborhood resulting from involvement in afterschool activities. Over time, articulation programs can reduce school avoidance and dropouts, as well as enhance the number who make successful transitions to higher education and postschool living and work. It is also likely that a caring school climate can play a significant role in reducing student transiency.

4. Enhancing home involvement

This arena expands concern for parent involvement to encompass anyone in the home influencing the student's life. In some cases, grandparents, aunts, or older siblings have assumed the parenting role. Older brothers and sisters often are the most significant influences on a youngster's life choices. Thus, schools and communities must go beyond focusing on parents in their efforts to enhance home involvement.

This arena includes schoolwide and classroom-based efforts designed to strengthen the home situation, enhance family problem-solving capabilities, and increase support for student well-being. Accomplishing all this requires a range of schoolwide and classroom-based systems and programs to (a) address the specific learning and support needs of adults in the home, such as offering ESL, literacy, vocational, and citizenship classes, enrichment and recreational opportunities, and mutual support groups, (b) help those in the home improve how basic student obligations are met, such as providing guidance related to parenting and how to help with schoolwork, (c) improve forms of basic communication that promote the well-being of student, family, and school, (d) enhance the home-school connection and sense of community, (e) foster participation in making decisions essential to a student's well-being, (f) facilitate home support of student learning and development, (g) mobilize those at home to problem solve related to student needs, and (h) elicit help (support, collaborations, and partnerships) from those at home with respect to meeting classroom, school, and community needs. The context for some of this activity may be a *parent or family center* if one has been established at the site. Outcomes include indices of family member learning, student progress, and community enhancement specifically related to home involvement.

5. Outreaching to the community to build linkages and collaborations

Schools can do their job better when they are an integral and positive part of the community. For example, it is a truism that learning is neither limited to what is formally taught nor to time spent in classrooms. It occurs whenever and wherever the learner interacts with the surrounding environment. All facets of the community (not just the school) provide learning opportunities. *Anyone in the community who wants to facilitate learning might be a contributing teacher.* This includes aides, volunteers, parents, siblings, peers, mentors in the community, librarians, recreation staff, college students, and so forth. They all constitute what can be called *the teaching community.* When a school successfully joins with its surrounding community, everyone has the opportunity to learn and to teach.

Another key facet of community involvement is opening up school sites as places where families and other community residents can engage in learning, recreation, and enrichment, and find services they need. This encompasses outreach to the community to collaborate to enhance the engagement of young people to directly strengthen youngsters, families, and neighborhoods. In this respect, increasing attention is paid to interventions to promote healthy development, resiliency, and assets.

For schools to be seen as an integral part of the community, steps must be taken to create and maintain linkage and collaboration. The intent is to maximize mutual benefits, including better student progress, an enhanced sense of community, community development, and more. In the long run, the aims are to strengthen students, schools, families, and neighborhoods. Outreach focuses on public and private agencies, organizations, universities, colleges, and facilities; businesses and professional organizations and groups; and volunteer service programs, organizations, and clubs. Greater volunteerism on the part of families, peers, and others from the community can break down barriers and increase home and community involvement in schools and schooling. Over time, this arena can include systems and programs designed to (a) recruit a wide range of community involvement and support, (b) train, screen, and maintain volunteers, (c) reach out to families and students who don't come to school regularly, including truants and dropouts, (d) connect school and community efforts to promote child and youth development, and (e) enhance community-school connections and sense of community.

6. Providing special assistance for students and families

Specialized assistance for students and their families is designed for the relatively few problems that cannot be handled without adding special interventions. The emphasis is on providing special services in a personalized way to assist with a broad range of needs. To begin with, social, physical, and mental health assistance available in the school and community is used. As community outreach brings in other resources, these are linked to existing activity in an integrated manner. Additional attention is paid to enhancing systems for triage, case and resource management, direct services for immediate needs, and referral for special services and special education as appropriate. Ongoing efforts are made to expand and enhance resources. While any office or room can be used, a valuable context for providing such services is a center facility, such as a family, community, health, or parent resource center.

A programmatic approach in this arena requires systems designed to provide special assistance in ways that increase the likelihood that a student will be more successful at school while also reducing the need for teachers to seek special programs and services. The work encompasses providing all stakeholders with information clarifying available assistance and how to access help, facilitating requests for assistance, handling referrals, providing direct service, implementing case and resource management, and interfacing with community outreach to assimilate additional resources into current service delivery. It also involves ongoing analyses of requests for services as a basis for working with school colleagues to design strategies that can reduce inappropriate reliance on special assistance. Thus, major outcomes are enhanced access to special assistance as needed, indices of effectiveness, *and* the reduction of inappropriate referrals for such assistance.

Unfortunately, most school reformers seem unaware that for all students to benefit from improved instruction, schools must play a major role in developing such an enabling curriculum. Without it, the resolution of learning and behavior problems is left to current strategies for improving instruction and controlling behavior. It is time to expand thinking to include a comprehensive component for addressing barriers to learning and pursue this third component with the same priority devoted to the other efforts for improving schools. Teachers, support staff, and administrators need to team together to ensure that this happens.

CONCLUDING COMMENTS

In Chapter 1, we stressed the importance of appreciating the full range of learning and behavior problems and differentiating them in terms of internal and external causes. The main emphasis in this chapter has been on enhancing what teachers and support staff do to address such a complex set of problems. By this point, the following state of affairs is evident. Early in the 21st century,

- Too many kids are not doing well in schools.
- To change this, schools must play a major role in addressing barriers to learning.
- However, support programs and services as they currently operate are *marginalized* in policy and practice and can't do enough to help teachers meet the needs of the majority of students experiencing learning, behavior, and emotional problems.
- Rather than address the problems surrounding school-owned support programs and services, policymakers and schools seem to have become enamored with the concept of school-linked services, as if adding a few community health and social services to a few schools is a sufficient solution.

Teachers and those who want to support teachers and students need to appreciate the full implications of all this. For example, with respect to achievement test averages for schools and districts trying to close the achievement gap, it means a *plateau effect* is likely to occur. Reports from across the country are verifying the earlier predictions that the overemphasis on direct strategies to increase test averages results in modest immediate test score increases followed by a longer-term plateau. Researchers note that after a steady few years' climb in student achievement during the 1990s, states experienced faltering achievement levels (e.g., California, Florida, Michigan, Texas). In some cases, test scores showed a decline in student proficiency.

In general, limited efficacy seems inevitable as long as the full continuum of necessary programs is unavailable and staff development remains deficient. Limited cost-effectiveness seems inevitable as long as related interventions are carried out in isolation of each other. Limited systemic change is likely as long as the entire enterprise is marginalized in policy and practice. Given all this, it is not surprising that many in the field doubt that major breakthroughs can occur without a comprehensive, multifaceted, and integrated continuum of interventions. Such views add impetus to major initiatives that are under way designed to restructure the way schools operate in providing learning supports.

A major shift in thinking is long overdue. We all must rethink how schools, families, and communities can meet the challenge of addressing persistent barriers to student learning and at the same time enhance how all stakeholders work together to promote healthy development.

Fortunately, pioneering initiatives around the country are demonstrating ways to broaden policy and practice. These initiatives recognize that to enable students to learn and teachers to teach, there must not only be effective instruction and well-managed schools, but also barriers to learning must be handled in a comprehensive way. Those leading the way are introducing new frameworks for comprehensive, multifaceted, and cohesive approaches. In doing so, their work underscores that (a) current reforms are based on an inadequate two-component model for restructuring schools, (b) movement to a three-component model is necessary if schools are to benefit all young people appropriately, (c) the third component encompasses a comprehensive continuum of enabling activity to address barriers to learning and teaching, and (d) all three components are essential, complementary, and overlapping and must be integrated fully in school improvement initiatives. Whatever it is called (e.g., an Enabling Component, a Learning Supports Component, a Comprehensive Student Support System), the emphasis is on ensuring that efforts to address barriers to development, learning, and teaching are not marginalized in policy and practice.

The next decade must mark a turning point in how schools and communities address the problems of children and youth. In particular, the focus must be on initiatives to reform and restructure how schools work to prevent and ameliorate the many learning, behavior, and emotional problems experienced by students so that all have an equal opportunity to succeed at school. This means reshaping the functions of all school personnel who have a role to play in addressing barriers to learning and promoting healthy development. It also means rethinking how schools respond to misbehavior. As we stress in the next chapter, there must be a shift in emphasis from social control as an end in itself to strategies that address behavior problems in ways that maximize the reengagement of students in classroom learning. There is much work to be done as public schools across the country are called upon to leave no child behind.

REFLECTION AND STIMULUS FOR DISCUSSION

Key Insights About "Problems Are
Multifaceted; Solutions Must Be Too!"

Based on what you learned so far,

> *Identify (and discuss) key insights about what*
> *is needed to ensure that schools play an effective role in*
> *addressing barriers to student development and learning.*

If there is an opportunity for group discussion, you may find the following group process guidelines helpful:

- Start by identifying someone who will facilitate the group interchange.
- Take a few minutes to make a few individual notes on a worksheet.
- Be sure all major points are compiled for sharing with other groups.
- Ask someone else to watch the time so that the group doesn't bog down.

ACTIVITY

Observe what is going on at a school to address barriers to learning and teaching. After observing for a while, write down

1. Your views about how the school handles student and teacher concerns

2. What seemed to help and why

3. What didn't work and why

"The Board meeting is called to order; the problem for today is whether to hire three security guards or two teachers."

REFERENCES

Adelman, H. S. (1995). Education reform: Broadening the focus. *Psychological Science, 6*, 61–62.

Adelman, H. S., & Taylor, L. (1997). Addressing barriers to learning: Beyond school-linked services and full service schools. *American Journal of Orthopsychiatry, 67*, 408–421.

Carlson, C., Paavola, J., & Talley, R. (1995). Historical, current, and future models of schools as health care delivery settings. *School Psychology Quarterly, 10*, 184–202.

Carnegie Council on Adolescent Development's Task Force on Education of Young Adolescents. (1989). *Turning points: Preparing American youth for the 21st century.* Washington, DC: Author.

Monk, D. H., Pijanowski, J. C., & Hussain, S. (1997). How and where the education dollar is spent. *The Future of Children, 7*, 51–62.

U.S. Department of Education. (2001). To assure the free appropriate public education of all children with disabilities. *Twenty-third annual report to Congress on the implementation of the Individuals with Disabilities Education Act.* Jessup, MD: Education Publications Center.

*Chapter 14 contains a list of special resources related
to the above matters available at no cost from the national
Center for Mental Health in Schools, which is at UCLA and is
directed by the authors of this book. Go to http://smhp.psych.ucla.edu.*

It's Not About Controlling Behavior; It's About Engaging and Reengaging Students in Learning

3

Many students say that . . . they feel their classes are irrelevant and boring, that they are just passing time . . . [and] are not able to connect what they are being taught with what they feel they need for success in their later life. This disengagement from the learning process is manifested in many ways, one of which is the lack of student responsibility for learning. In many ways the traditional educational structure, one in which teachers "pour knowledge into the vessel" (the student), has placed all responsibility for learning on the teacher, none on the student. Schools present lessons neatly packaged, without acknowledging or accepting the "messiness" of learning-by-doing and through experience and activity. Schools often do not provide students a chance to accept responsibility for learning, as that might actually empower students. Students in many schools have become accustomed to being spoon-fed the material to master tests, and they have lost their enthusiasm for exploration, dialogue, and reflection—all critical steps in the learning process.

—American Youth Policy Forum (2000)

I suspect that many children would learn arithmetic, and learn it better, if it were illegal.

—John Holt (1989)

ORIENTING QUESTIONS

? What are optimal ways to address behavior problems at school?

? Why is an understanding of how to reengage students in classroom learning essential in developing learning supports?

? What is intrinsic motivation, and what are the implications for addressing barriers to student learning?

External reinforcement may indeed get a particular act going and may lead to its repetition, but it does not nourish, reliably, the long course of learning by which [one] slowly builds in [one's] own way a serviceable model of what the world is and what it can be.

—Jerome Bruner (1966)

As we have stressed, curriculum content is learned as a result of transactions between the learner and the environment. The essence of the teaching process is to create an environment that first can mobilize the learner to pursue the curriculum and then can maintain that mobilization while effectively facilitating learning. Behavior problems clearly get in the way of all this.

Misbehavior disrupts. In some forms, such as bullying and intimidating others, it is hurtful. And observing such behavior may disinhibit others.

When a student misbehaves, a natural reaction is to want that youngster to experience and other students to see the consequences of misbehaving. One hope is that public awareness of consequences will deter subsequent problems. As a result, a considerable amount of time at schools is devoted to discipline; a common concern for teachers is "classroom management."

In their efforts to deal with deviant and devious behavior and to create safe environments, unfortunately, schools increasingly overrely on negative consequences and other control techniques. Such practices model behavior that can foster rather than counter development of negative values and often produce other forms of undesired behavior. Moreover, the tactics often make schools look and feel more like prisons than community treasures.

To move schools beyond overreliance on punishment and control strategies, there is ongoing advocacy for social skills training, positive behavior support, and new agendas for emotional "intelligence" training, asset development, and character education. Relatedly, there are calls for greater home involvement, with emphasis on enhanced parent responsibility for their children's behavior and learning. More comprehensively, some reformers want to transform schools in ways that create an atmosphere of "caring," "cooperative learning," and a "sense of community." Such advocates usually argue for schools that are holistically oriented and family centered. They want curricula to enhance values and character, including responsibility (social and moral), integrity, self-regulation (self-discipline), and a work ethic, and also want schools to foster self-esteem, diverse talents, and emotional well-being. These trends are important. When paired with a contemporary understanding of human motivation, they recognize that the major intent in dealing with behavior problems at school must be the engagement and reengagement of students in classroom learning (Adelman & Taylor, 1993; Center for Mental Health in Schools, 2001).

DISENGAGED STUDENTS AND SOCIAL CONTROL

After an extensive review of the literature, Fredricks, Blumenfeld, and Paris (2004) conclude: Engagement is associated with positive academic outcomes, including achievement and persistence in school; and it is higher in classrooms with supportive teachers and peers, challenging and authentic tasks, opportunities for choice, and sufficient structure. Conversely, for many students, disengagement is associated with behavior problems, and behavior and learning problems lead to eventual dropout. The degree of concern about student engagement varies depending on school population.

In general, teaching involves being able to apply strategies focused on content to be taught and knowledge and skills to be acquired—with some degree of attention given to the process of engaging students. All this works fine in schools where most students come each day ready and able to deal with what the teacher is ready and able to teach. Indeed, teachers are fortunate when they have a classroom where the majority of students show up and are receptive to the planned lessons. In schools that are the

The review by Fredricks et al. (2004) notes that

Engagement is defined in three ways in the research literature:

1. *Behavioral engagement* draws on the idea of participation; it includes involvement in academic and social or extracurricular activities and is considered crucial for achieving positive academic outcomes and preventing dropping out.

2. *Emotional engagement* encompasses positive and negative reactions to teachers, classmates, academics, and school and is presumed to create ties to an institution and influence willingness to do the work.

3. *Cognitive engagement* draws on the idea of investment; it incorporates thoughtfulness and willingness to exert the effort necessary to comprehend complex ideas and master difficult skills.

Antecedents of engagement can be organized into

- *School-level factors*. Voluntary choice, clear and consistent goals, small size, student participation in school policy and management, opportunities for staff and students to be involved in cooperative endeavors, and academic work that allows for the development of products
- *Classroom context*. Teacher support, peers, classroom structure, autonomy support, task characteristics
- *Individual needs*. Need for relatedness, need for autonomy, need for competence

Engagement can be measured as follows:

- *Behavioral engagement*. Conduct, work involvement, participation, persistence (e.g., completing homework, complying with school rules, absent/tardy, off-task)
- *Emotional engagement*. Self-report related to feelings of frustration, boredom, interest, anger, satisfaction; student-teacher relations; work orientation
- *Cognitive engagement*. Investment in learning, flexible problem solving, independent work styles, coping with perceived failure, preference for challenge and independent mastery, commitment to understanding the work

greatest focus of public criticism, this certainly is not the case. What most of us realize, at least at some level, is that teachers in such settings are confronted with an entirely different teaching situation. Among the various supports they absolutely must have are ways to reengage students who have become disengaged and often resistant to broadband (non-personalized) teaching approaches (see Guide 3.1). To the dismay of most teachers, however, strategies for reengaging students in *learning* rarely are a prominent part of pre- or inservice preparation and seldom are the focus of interventions pursued by professionals whose role is to support teachers and students (National Research Council and the Institute of Medicine, 2004).

It is commonplace to find that when a student is not engaged in the lessons at hand, he or she tends to pursue other activity. As teachers and other staff try to cope with those who are disruptive, the main concern usually is "classroom management." At one time, a heavy dose of punishment was the dominant approach. Currently, the stress is on more positive practices designed to provide "behavior support" in and out of the classroom. For the most part, however, the strategies are applied as a form of *social control* aimed directly at stopping disruptive behavior.

An often-stated assumption is that stopping the behavior will make the student amenable to teaching. In a few cases, this may be so. However, the assumption ignores all the work that has led to

Guide 3.1   Broadband (Nonpersonalized) Teaching

Once upon a time, the animals decided that their lives and their society would be improved by setting up a school. The basics identified as necessary for survival in the animal world were swimming, running, climbing, jumping, and flying. Instructors were hired to teach these activities, and it was agreed that all the animals would take all the courses. This worked out well for the administrators, but it caused some problems for the students.

The squirrel, for example, was an A student in running, jumping, and climbing but had trouble in flying class, not because of an inability to fly, for she could sail from the top of one tree to another with ease, but because the flying curriculum called for taking off from the ground. The squirrel was drilled in ground-to-air takeoffs until she was exhausted and developed charley horses from overexertion. This caused her to perform poorly in her other classes, and her grades dropped to D's.

The duck was outstanding in swimming class—even better than the teacher. But she did so poorly in running that she was transferred to a remedial class. There she practiced running until her webbed feet were so badly damaged that she was only an average swimmer. But since average was acceptable, nobody saw this as a problem—except the duck.

In contrast, the rabbit was excellent in running, but, being terrified of water, he was an extremely poor swimmer. Despite a lot of makeup work in swimming class, he never could stay afloat. He soon became frustrated and uncooperative and was eventually expelled because of behavior problems.

The eagle naturally enough was a brilliant student in flying class and even did well in running and jumping. He had to be severely disciplined in climbing class, however, because he insisted that his way of getting to the top of the tree was faster and easier.

It should be noted that the parents of the groundhog pulled him out of school because the administration would not add classes in digging and burrowing. The groundhogs, along with the gophers and badgers, got a prairie dog to start a private school. They all have become strong opponents of school taxes and proponents of voucher systems.

By graduation time, the student with the best grades in the animal school was a compulsive ostrich who could run superbly and also could swim, fly, and climb a little. She, of course, was made class valedictorian and received scholarship offers from all the best universities.

SOURCE: George H. Reeves is credited with giving this parable to American educators.

understanding *psychological reactance* and the need to restore one's sense of self-determination (Deci & Flaste, 1995). Moreover, it belies two painful realities: the number of students who continue to manifest poor academic achievement and the staggering dropout rate in too many schools.

The wrong socialization practices have been used or have been implemented incorrectly. In particular, schools have been criticized for overemphasizing punishment. To move schools beyond overreliance on punishment, there is ongoing advocacy for social skills training, asset development, character education, and positive behavior support initiatives. The move from punishment to positive approaches is a welcome one. However, most of the new initiatives have not focused enough on a basic system failure that must be addressed if improved behavior is to be maintained. That is, strategies that focus on positive behavior have paid too little attention to helping teachers deal with student engagement in classroom learning.

Student engagement encompasses not only engaging and maintaining engagement but also *reengaging* those who have disengaged. Of particular concern is what teachers do when they encounter a student who has disengaged and is misbehaving. In most cases, the emphasis shouldn't be first and foremost on implementing social control techniques. (See Chapter 11 for more on the topic of addressing behavior problems.)

What teachers need even more are ways to reengage students who have become disengaged and resistant to standard instruction. Despite this need, strategies that have the greatest likelihood of reengaging students in *learning* rarely are a prominent part of pre- or inservice preparation. And such strategies seldom are the focus of interventions applied by professionals whose role is to support teachers and students. To correct these deficiencies, the developmental trend in intervention thinking must be toward practices that embrace an expanded view of engagement and human motivation (see Guide 3.2).

MOTIVATION AND LEARNING

Maria doesn't want to work on improving her reading. Not only is her *motivational readiness* for learning in this area low, but she also has a fairly high level of *avoidance motivation* for reading. Most of the time during reading instruction, she is disengaged and acting out.

In contrast, David is motivationally ready to improve reading skills, but he has very little motivation to do so in the ways his teacher proposes. He has high motivation for the *outcome* but low motivation for the *processes* prescribed for getting there.

Matt often is highly motivated to do whatever is prescribed to help him learn to read better, but his motivation starts to disappear after a few weeks of hard work. He has trouble maintaining a sufficient amount of ongoing or *continuing motivation,* and his attention and behavior wander.

Helena appeared motivated to learn and did learn many new vocabulary words and improved her reading comprehension on several occasions over the years she was in special school programs. Her motivation to read after school, however, has never increased. It was assumed that as her skills improved, her attitude toward reading would too. But it never has.

No one expected James to become a good reader because of low scores on tests related to phonics ability and reading comprehension in second

Guide 3.2   Developmental Trend in Intervention Thinking: Behavioral
Initiatives and Beyond

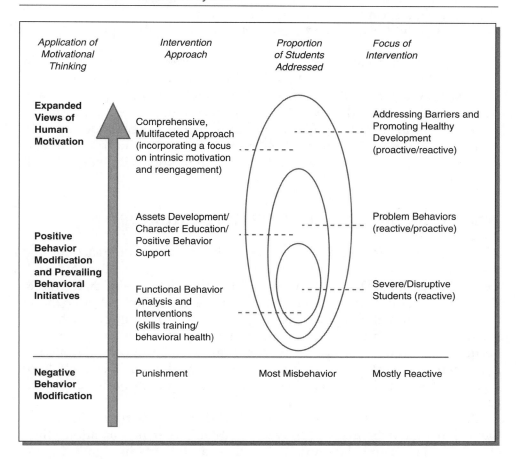

grade. However, his teacher found some beginning-level books on his
favorite sport (baseball) and found that he really wanted to read them. He
asked her and other students to help him with words and took the books
home to read (where he also asked an older sister for some help). His skills
started to improve rapidly, and he was soon reading on a par with his peers.

What the preceding examples illustrate is that

- Motivation is a learning prerequisite, and its absence may be a cause
  of learning and behavior problems, a factor maintaining such problems, or both.
- Individuals may be motivated toward the idea of obtaining a certain
  learning outcome but may not be motivated to pursue certain learning processes.
- Individuals may be motivated to start to work on overcoming
  their learning and behavior problems but may not maintain their
  motivation.

- Individuals may be motivated to learn basic skills but maintain negative attitudes about the area of functioning and thus never use the skills except when they must.
- Motivated learners can do more than others might expect.

Obviously, intrinsic motivation is a fundamental consideration in designing learning supports. An increased understanding of motivation clarifies how essential it is to avoid processes that limit options, make students feel controlled and coerced, and focus mostly on "remedying" problems. From a motivational perspective, such processes are seen as likely to produce avoidance reactions in the classroom and to school and thus reduce opportunities for positive learning and for development of positive attitudes.

DON'T LOSE SIGHT OF INTRINSIC MOTIVATION

Engaging and reengaging students in learning is the facet of teaching that draws on what is known about human motivation (e.g., see Brophy, 2004; Deci & Flaste, 1995; Deci & Ryan, 1985, 2002; Fredricks et al., 2004; Ryan & Deci, 2000; Stipek, 1998). What many of us have been taught about dealing with student misbehavior and learning problems runs counter to what we intuitively understand about human motivation. Teachers and parents, in particular, often learn to overdepend on reinforcement theory, despite the appreciation they have about the importance of intrinsic motivation. Those who argue we must focus on "basics" are right. But the basics that need attention have to do with motivation.

As we have stressed, the essence of teaching is creating an environment that mobilizes the student and maintains that mobilization while effectively facilitating learning. And when a student disengages, reengagement in learning depends on the use of interventions that minimize conditions that negatively affect motivation and maximize conditions that have a positive motivational effect.

Of course, teachers, parents, and support staff cannot control all factors affecting motivation. Indeed, when any of us address learning and behavior concerns, we have direct control over a relatively small segment of the physical and social environment. We try to maximize the likelihood that opportunities to learn are a good fit with the current capabilities of a given youngster. And with learning engagement in mind, we try to match individual differences in motivation.

Matching individual differences in *motivation* means attending to matters such as

- *Motivation as a readiness concern.* Optimal performance and learning require motivational readiness. The absence of such readiness can cause and/or maintain problems. If a learner does not have enough motivational readiness, strategies must be implemented to develop it (including ways to reduce avoidance motivation). Readiness should not be viewed in the old sense of waiting until an individual is interested. Rather, it should be understood in the contemporary sense of establishing environments that are perceived by students as caring, supportive places and as offering stimulating activities that are valued and challenging, and doable.

- *Motivation as a key ongoing process concern.* Many learners are caught up in the novelty of a new subject, but after a few lessons, interest often wanes. Some students are motivated by the idea of obtaining a given outcome but may not be motivated to pursue certain processes and thus may not pay attention or may try to avoid them. For example, some are motivated to start work on overcoming their problems but may not maintain that motivation. Strategies must be designed to elicit, enhance, and maintain motivation so that a youngster stays mobilized.

- *Minimizing negative motivation and avoidance reactions as process and outcome concerns.* Teachers and others at school and at home not only must try to increase motivation—especially intrinsic motivation—but also take care to avoid or at least minimize conditions that decrease motivation or produce negative motivation. For example, care must be taken not to overrely on extrinsics to entice and reward because to do so may decrease intrinsic motivation. At times, school is seen as unchallenging, uninteresting, overdemanding, overwhelming, overcontrolling, nonsupportive, or even hostile. When this happens, a student may develop negative attitudes and avoidance related to a given situation and, over time, related to school and all it represents.

- *Enhancing intrinsic motivation as a basic outcome concern.* It is essential to enhance motivation as an outcome so the desire to pursue a given area (e.g., reading, good behavior) increasingly is a positive intrinsic attitude that mobilizes learning and behaving outside the teaching situation. Achieving such an outcome involves use of strategies that do not overrely on extrinsic rewards and that do enable youngsters to play a meaningful role in making decisions related to valued options. In effect, enhancing intrinsic motivation is a fundamental *protective factor* and is the key to developing *resiliency*.

Students who are intrinsically motivated to learn at school seek out opportunities and challenges and go beyond requirements. In doing so, they learn more and learn more deeply than do classmates who are extrinsically motivated. Facilitating the learning of such students is a fairly straightforward matter and fits well with school improvements that primarily emphasize enhancing instructional practices. The focus is on helping establish ways for students who are motivationally ready and able to achieve and, of course, to maintain and enhance motivation. The process involves knowing when, how, and what to teach and also knowing when and how to structure the situation so they can learn on their own.

In contrast, students who manifest learning, behavior, and/or emotional problems may have developed extremely negative perceptions of teachers and programs. In such cases, they are not likely to be open to people and activities that look like "the same old thing." Major changes in approach are required if youngsters are even to perceive that something has changed in the situation. Minimally, exceptional efforts must be made to have them (a) view the teacher and other interveners as supportive (rather than controlling and indifferent) and (b) perceive content, outcomes, and activity options as personally valuable and obtainable. Thus, any effort to reengage disengaged students must begin by addressing negative perceptions. School support staff and teachers must work together to reverse conditions that led to such perceptions.

> Increasing intrinsic motivation involves affecting a student's thoughts, feelings, and decisions. In general, the intent is to use procedures that can potentially reduce negative and increase positive feelings, thoughts, and coping strategies with respect to learning. For learning and behavior problems, in particular, this means identifying and minimizing experiences that maintain or may increase avoidance motivation.

TWO KEY COMPONENTS OF MOTIVATION: VALUING AND EXPECTATIONS

Two common reasons people give for not bothering to learn something are "It's not worth it" and "I know I won't be able to do it." In general, the amount of time and energy spent on an activity seems dependent on how much the activity is valued by the person and on the person's expectation that what is valued will be attained without too great a cost.

About Valuing

What makes something worth doing? Prizes? Money? Merit awards? Praise? Certainly! We all do a great many things, some of which we don't even like to do, because the activity leads to a desired reward. Similarly, we often do things to escape punishment or other negative consequences that we prefer to avoid.

Rewards and punishments may be material or social. For those with learning, behavior, and emotional problems, there has been widespread use of such "incentives" (e.g., systematically giving points or tokens that can be exchanged for candy, prizes, praise, free time, or social interactions). Punishments have included loss of free time and other privileges, added work, fines, isolation, censure, and suspension. Grades have been used both as rewards and punishments. Because people will do things to obtain rewards or avoid punishment, rewards and punishment often are called *reinforcers.* Because they generally come from sources outside the person, they often are called *extrinsics.*

Extrinsic reinforcers are easy to use and can immediately affect behavior. Therefore, they have been widely adopted in the fields of special education and psychology. Unfortunately, the immediate effects are usually limited to very specific behaviors and often are short-term. Moreover, extensive use of extrinsics can have some undesired effects. And sometimes the available extrinsics simply aren't powerful enough to get the desired results.

It is important to remember that what makes some extrinsic factor rewarding is the fact that it is experienced by the recipient as a reward. What makes it a highly valued reward is that the recipient highly values it. If someone doesn't like candy, there is not much point in offering it as a reward. Furthermore, because the use of extrinsics has limits, it's fortunate that people often do things even without apparent extrinsic reason. In fact, a lot of what people learn and spend time doing is done for intrinsic reasons. *Curiosity* is a good example. Curiosity seems to be an innate quality that leads us to seek stimulation, avoid boredom, and learn a great deal.

People also pursue some things because of what has been described as an innate *striving for competence.* Most of us value feeling competent. We try to conquer some challenges, and if none are around, we usually seek one out. Of course, if the challenges confronting us seem unconquerable or make us too uncomfortable (e.g., too anxious or exhausted), we try to put them aside and move on to something more promising.

Another important intrinsic motivator appears to be an internal push toward *self-determination.* People seem to value feeling and thinking that they have some degree of choice and freedom in deciding what to do. And human beings also seem intrinsically moved toward establishing and maintaining relationships. That is, we value the feeling of *interpersonal connection.*

About Expectations

We may value something a great deal, but if we believe we can't do it or can't obtain it without paying too great a personal price, we are likely to look for other valued activities and outcomes to pursue. Expectations about these matters are influenced by past experiences.

Previously unsuccessful arenas usually are seen as unlikely paths to valued extrinsic rewards or intrinsic satisfactions. We may perceive past failure as the result of our lack of ability, or we may believe that more effort was required than we were willing to give. We may also feel that the help we needed to succeed was not available. If our perception is that very little has changed with regard to these factors, our expectation of succeeding now will be rather low. *In general, then, what we value interacts with our expectations, and motivation is one product of this interaction* (see Guide 3.3).

Guide 3.3   A Bit of Theory

Motivation theory has many facets. At the risk of oversimplifying things, the following discussion is designed to make a few big points.

$$E \times V$$

Can you decipher this? (Don't go on until you've tried.)

Hint: the "$\times$" is a multiplication sign.

In case the equation stumped you, don't be surprised. The main introduction to motivational thinking that many people have been given in the past involves some form of reinforcement theory (which essentially deals with extrinsic motivation). Thus, all this may be new to you, even though motivational theorists have been wrestling with it for a long time, and intuitively, you probably understand much of what they are talking about.

E represents an individual's *expectations* about outcome (in school this often means expectations of success or failure). *V* represents *valuing,* with valuing influenced by what is valued both intrinsically and extrinsically. Thus, in a general sense, motivation can be thought of in terms of expectancy times valuing. *Such theory recognizes that human beings are thinking and feeling organisms and that intrinsic factors can be powerful motivators. This understanding of human motivation has major implications for learning, teaching, parenting, and mental health interventions.*

Within some limits (which we need not discuss here), high expectations and high valuing produce high motivation, while low expectations (*E*) and high valuing (*V*) produce relatively weak motivation.

Youngsters may greatly value the idea of improving their reading. They usually are not happy with limited skills and know they would feel a lot better about themselves if they could read. But often they experience that everything the teacher asks them to do is a waste of time. They have done it all before, and they *still* have a reading problem. Sometimes they will do the exercises, but just to earn points to go on a field trip and to avoid the consequences of not cooperating. Often, however, they try to get out of doing the work by distracting the teacher. After all, why should they do things they are certain won't help them read any better?

(Expectancy $\times$ Valuing = Motivation)

$$0 \times 1.0 = 0$$

High expectations paired with low valuing also yields low approach motivation. Thus, the oft-cited remedial strategy of guaranteeing success by designing tasks to be very easy is not as simple a recipe as it sounds. Indeed, the approach is likely to fail if the outcome (e.g., improved reading, learning math fundamentals, applying social skills) is not valued or if the tasks are experienced as too boring or if doing them is seen as too embarrassing. In such cases, a strong negative value is attached to the activities, and this contributes to avoidance motivation.

(Expectancy $\times$ Valuing = Motivation)

$$1.0 \times 0 = 0$$

Appropriate appreciation of all this is necessary in designing a match for optimal learning and performance.

There are many intervention implications to derive from understanding intrinsic motivation. For example, mobilizing and maintaining a youngster's motivation depends on how a classroom program addresses concerns about valuing and expectations. Schools and classrooms that offer a broad range of opportunities (e.g., content, outcomes, procedural options) and involve students in decision making are best equipped to meet the challenge.

OVERRELIANCE ON EXTRINSICS: A BAD MATCH

Throughout this discussion of valuing and expectations, the emphasis has been on the fact that motivation is not something that can be determined solely by forces outside the individual. Others can plan activities and outcomes to influence motivation and learning; however, how the activities and outcomes are experienced determines whether they are pursued (or avoided) with a little or a lot of effort and ability. Understanding that an individual's perceptions can affect motivation has led researchers to important findings about some undesired effects resulting from overreliance on extrinsics (see Guide 3.4).

Because of the prominent role they play in school programs, grading, testing, and other performance evaluations are a special concern in any discussion of the overreliance on extrinsics as a way to reinforce positive learning. Although grades often are discussed as simply providing information about how well a student is doing, many, if not most, students perceive each grade as a reward or a punishment. Certainly, many teachers use grades to try to control behavior—to reward those who do assignments well and to punish those who don't (see Guide 3.5). Sometimes parents add to a student's perception of grades as extrinsic reinforcers by giving a reward for good report cards.

We all have our own horror stories about the negative impact of grades on ourselves and others. In general, grades have a way of reshaping what students do with their learning opportunities. In choosing what to study, students strongly consider what grades they are likely to receive. As deadlines for assignments and tests get closer, interest in the topic gives way to interest in maximizing one's grade. Discussion of interesting issues and problems related to the area of study gives way to questions about how long a paper should be and what will be on the test. None of this is surprising, given that poor grades can result in having to repeat a course or being denied certain immediate and long-range opportunities. It is simply a good example of how systems that overemphasize extrinsics may have a serious negative impact on intrinsic motivation for learning. *And if the impact of current practices is harmful to those who are able learners, imagine the impact on students with learning and behavior problems!*

The point is that extrinsic rewards can undermine intrinsic reasons for doing things. Although this is not always the case and may not always be

Guide 3.4   Is It Worth It?

In a small town, there were a few youngsters who were labeled as handicapped. Over the years, a local bully had taken it upon himself to persecute them. In one recent incident, he sent a gang of young ragamuffins to harass one of his classmates who had just been diagnosed as having learning disabilities. He told the youngsters that the boy was retarded and they could have some fun calling him a "retard."

Day after day in the schoolyard the gang sought the boy out. "Retard! Retard!" they hooted at him.

The situation became serious. The boy took the matter so much to heart that he began to brood and spent sleepless nights over it. Finally, out of desperation, he told his teacher about the problem, and together they evolved a plan.

The following day, when the little ones came to jeer at him, he confronted them, saying, "From today on I'll give any of you who calls me a retard a quarter."

Then he put his hand in his pocket and, indeed, gave each boy a quarter.

Well, delighted with their booty, the youngsters, of course, sought him out the following day and began to shrill, "Retard! Retard!"

The boy looked at them—smiling. He put his hand in his pocket and gave each of them a dime, saying, "A quarter is too much—I can only afford a dime today."

Well, the boys went away satisfied because, after all, a dime was money too.

However, when they came the next day to hoot, the boy gave them only a penny each.

"Why do we get only a penny today?" they yelled.

"That's all I can afford."

"But two days ago you gave us a quarter, and yesterday we got a dime. It's not fair!"

"Take it or leave it. That's all you're going to get."

"Do you think we're going to call you a retard for one lousy penny?"

"So don't."

And they didn't.

SOURCE: Adapted from a fable presented by Ausubel, 1948.

a bad thing, it is an important consideration in deciding to rely on extrinsic reinforcers in addressing learning, behavior, and emotional problems.

REENGAGEMENT IN SCHOOL LEARNING

Many individuals with learning problems also are described as hyperactive, distractible, impulsive, behavior disordered, and so forth. Their behavior patterns are seen as interfering with efforts to remedy their learning problems. Although motivation has always been a concern to those who work with learning and behavior problems, the emphasis in handling these interfering behaviors usually is on using extrinsics as part of efforts to directly control and/or in conjunction with direct skill instruction. For example, the interventions are designed to improve impulse control, perseverance, selective attention, frustration tolerance, sustained attention and

Guide 3.5   Rewards—To Control or Inform?

As Ed Deci (1975) has cogently stressed:

Rewards are generally used to control behavior. Children are sometimes rewarded with candy when they do what adults expect of them. Workers are rewarded with pay for doing what their supervisors want. People are rewarded with social approval or positive feedback for fitting into their social reference group. In all these situations, the aim of the reward is to control the person's behavior—to make [the person] continue to engage in acceptable behaviors. And rewards often do work quite effectively as controllers. Further, whether it works or not, each reward has a controlling aspect. Therefore, the first aspect to every reward (including feedback) is a controlling aspect. However, rewards also provide information to the person about his effectiveness in various situations. . . . When David did well at school, his mother told him she was proud of him, and when Amanda learned to ride a bike, she was given a brand new two-wheeler. David and Amanda knew from the praise and bicycle that they were competent and self-determining in relation to school and bicycling. The second aspect of every reward is the information it provides a person about his competence and self-determination.

When the controlling aspect of the reward is very salient, such as in the case of money or the avoidance of punishment, [a] change in perceived locus of causality . . . will occur. The person is "controlled" by the reward and s/he perceives that the locus of causality is external.

---

follow-through, and social awareness and skills. In all cases, the emphasis is on reducing or eliminating interfering behaviors, usually with the presumption that then the student will reengage in learning. However, there is little evidence that these strategies enhance a student's motivation toward classroom learning (National Research Council, 2004).

For motivated students, facilitating learning is a fairly straightforward matter and fits well with school improvements that primarily emphasize enhancing instructional practices (see Guide 3.6). The focus is on helping establish ways for students who are motivationally ready and able to achieve and, of course, to maintain and enhance their motivation. The process involves knowing when, how, and what to teach and also knowing when and how to structure the situation so they can learn on their own. However, students who manifest learning, behavior, and/or emotional problems often have developed extremely negative perceptions of teachers, programs, and school in general. Any effort to reengage these students must begin by recognizing such perceptions. Thus, the first step in addressing the problem is for the school leadership to acknowledge its nature and scope. Then school support staff and teachers must work together to pursue a major initiative focused on reengaging those who have become disengaged and reversing conditions that led to the problem.

Guide 3.6   Meaningful, Engaged Learning

In recent years, researchers have formed a strong consensus on the importance of engaged learning in schools and classrooms. This consensus, together with a recognition of the changing needs of the 21st century, has stimulated the development of specific indicators of engaged learning. Jones, Valdez, Nowakowski, and Rasmussen (1994) developed the indicators described below.

1. Vision of Engaged Learning

Successful, engaged learners are responsible for their own learning. These students are self-regulated and able to define their own learning goals and evaluate their own achievement. They are also energized by their learning, their joy of learning leads to a lifelong passion for solving problems, understanding, and taking the next step in their thinking.

2. Tasks for Engaged Learning

In order to have engaged learning, tasks need to be challenging, authentic, and multidisciplinary. Such tasks are typically complex and involve sustained amounts of time. They are authentic in that they correspond to the tasks in the home and workplaces of today and tomorrow. Collaboration around authentic tasks often takes place with peers and mentors within school as well as with family members and others in the real world outside of school. These tasks often require integrated instruction that incorporates problem-based learning and curriculum by project.

3. Assessment of Engaged Learning

Assessment of engaged learning involves presenting students with an authentic task, project, or investigation, and then observing, interviewing, and examining their presentations and artifacts to assess what they actually know and can do. This assessment, often called performance-based assessment, is generative in that it involves students in generating their own performance criteria and playing a key role in the overall design, evaluation, and reporting of their assessment. The best performance-based assessment has a seamless connection to curriculum and instruction so that it is ongoing. Assessment should represent all meaningful aspects of performance and should have equitable standards that apply to all students.

4. Instructional Models & Strategies for Engaged Learning

The most powerful models of instruction are interactive. Instruction actively engages the learner, and is generative. Instruction encourages the learner to construct and produce knowledge in meaningful ways. Students teach others interactively and interact generatively with their tacher and peers.

5. Learning Context of Engaged Learning

For engaged learning to happen, the classroom must be conceived of as a knowledge-building learning community. Such communities not only develop shared understandings collaboratively but also create empathetic learning environments that value diversity and multiple perspectives. These communities search for strategies to build on the strengths of all of its members.

6. Grouping for Engaged Learning

Collaborative work that is learning-centered often involves small groups or teams of two or more students within a classroom or across classroom boundaries. Heterogeneous groups (including different sexes, cultures, abilities, ages, and socio-economic backgrounds) offer a wealth of background knowledge and perspectives to different tasks. Flexible grouping, which allows teachers to reconfigure small groups according to the purposes of instruction and incorporates frequent heterogeneous groups, is one of the most equitable means of grouping and ensuring increased learning opportunities.

7. Teacher Roles for Engaged Learning

The role of the teacher in the classroom has shifted from the primary role of information giver to that of facilitator, guide, and learner. As a facilitator, the teacher provides the rich environments and learning experiences needed for collaborative study. The teacher also is required to act as a guide—a role that incorporates mediation, modeling, and coaching. Often the teacher also is a co-learner and co-investigator with the students.

8. Student Roles for Engaged Learning

One important student role is that of explorer. Interaction with the physical world and with other people allows students to discover concepts and apply skills. Students are then encouraged to reflect upon their discoveries, which is essential for the student as a cognitive apprentice. Apprenticeship takes place when students observe and apply the thinking processes used by practitioners. Students also become teachers themselves by integrating what they've learned.

Psychological scholarship over the past 50 years has brought renewed attention to motivation as a central concept in understanding learning and attention problems. This work is just beginning to find its way into applied fields and programs. One line of work has emphasized the relationship of learning and behavior problems to deficiencies in intrinsic motivation. This work clarifies the value of interventions designed to increase

- Feelings of self-determination
- Feelings of competence and expectations of success
- Feelings of interpersonal relatedness
- The range of interests and satisfactions related to learning

Activities to correct deficiencies in intrinsic motivation are directed at improving awareness of personal motives and true capabilities, learning to set valued and appropriate goals, learning to value and to make appropriate and satisfying choices, and learning to value and accept responsibility for choice.

> You have to get up and go to school!
>
> I don't want to. It's too hard and the kids don't like me.
>
> But you have to go. You're the teacher.

The point for emphasis here is that engaging and reengaging students in learning involves matching motivation. Matching motivation requires an appreciation of the importance of a student's perceptions in determining the right mix of intrinsic and extrinsic reasons. It also requires understanding the key role played by expectations related to outcome. Without a good match, social control strategies can suppress negative attitudes and behaviors, but reengagement in classroom learning is unlikely.

General Strategies

To clarify matters with respect to designing new directions for student support for disengaged students, below are four general strategies to think about in planning ways to work with such students:

1. Clarifying Student Perceptions of the Problem

It is desirable to create a situation where it is feasible to talk openly with students about why they have become disengaged. This provides an invaluable basis for formulating a personalized plan for helping to alter their negative perceptions and for planning ways to prevent others from developing such perceptions.

2. Reframing School Learning

As noted above, in the case of those who have disengaged, major reframing in teaching approaches is required so that these students (a) view the teacher as supportive (rather than controlling and indifferent) and (b) perceive content, outcomes, and activity options as personally valuable and obtainable. It is important, for example, to eliminate threatening evaluative measures; reframe content and processes to clarify purpose in terms of real-life needs and experiences and underscore how it all builds on previous learning; and clarify why the procedures are expected to be effective—especially those designed to help correct specific problems.

3. Renegotiating Involvement in School Learning

New and mutual agreements must be developed and evolved over time through conferences with the student and, where appropriate, including parents. The intent is to affect perceptions of choice, value, and probable outcome. The focus throughout is on clarifying awareness of valued options, enhancing expectations of positive outcomes, and engaging the student in meaningful, ongoing decision making. For the process to be most effective, students should be assisted in sampling new processes and content, options should include valued enrichment opportunities, and there must be provision for reevaluating and modifying decisions as perceptions shift.

4. Reestablishing and Maintaining an Appropriate Working Relationship

This requires the type of ongoing interactions that creates a sense of trust and open communication and provides personalized support and direction.

To maintain reengagement and prevent disengagement, the above strategies must be pursued using processes and content that

- Minimize threats to feelings of competence, self-determination, and relatedness to valued others.
- Maximize such feelings (included here is an emphasis on a school taking steps to enhance public perception that it is a welcoming, caring, safe, and just institution).
- Guide motivated practice (e.g., providing opportunities for meaningful applications and clarifying ways to organize practice).
- Provide continuous information on learning and performance in ways that highlight accomplishments.
- Provide opportunities for continued application and generalization (e.g., ways in which students can pursue additional, self-directed learning or can arrange for additional support and direction).

Obviously, it is no easy task to decrease well-assimilated negative attitudes and behaviors. And the task is likely to become even harder with the escalation toward high-stakes testing policies (no matter how well intentioned). It also seems obvious that *for many schools, enhanced achievement test scores will be feasible only when the large number of disengaged students are reengaged in learning at school.*

All this argues for (a) minimizing student disengagement and maximizing reengagement by moving school culture toward a greater focus on intrinsic motivation and (b) minimizing psychological reactance and enhancing perceptions that lead to reengagement in learning at school by rethinking social control practices. From a motivational perspective, key facets of accomplishing this involve enhancing learner options and decision making as highlighted below and discussed in greater detail in Chapter 6.

Options and Student Decision Making as Key Facets

A greater proportion of individuals with avoidance or low motivation for learning at school are found among those with learning, behavior, and/or emotional problems. For these individuals, few currently available options may be appealing. How much greater the range of options needs to be depends primarily on how strong avoidance tendencies are. In general, however, the initial strategies for working with such students involve

- Further expansion of the range of options for learning (if necessary, this includes avoiding established curriculum content and processes)
- Primarily emphasizing areas in which the student has made personal and active decisions
- Accommodation of a wider range of behavior than usually is tolerated (e.g., a widening of limits on the amount and types of "differences" tolerated)

From a motivational perspective, one of the most basic concerns is the way in which students are involved in making decisions about options. Critically, decision-making processes can lead to perceptions of coercion and control or to perceptions of real choice (e.g., being in control of one's destiny, being self-determining). Such differences in perception can affect whether a student is mobilized to pursue or avoid planned learning activities and outcomes.

People who have the opportunity to make decisions among valued and feasible options tend to be committed to following through. In contrast, people who are not involved in decisions often have little commitment to what is decided. And if individuals disagree with a decision that affects them, besides not following through, they may react with hostility.

Thus, essential to programs focusing on motivation are decision-making processes that affect perceptions of choice, value, and probable outcome. Three special points should be noted about decision making.

1. Decisions are based on current perceptions. As perceptions shift, it is necessary to reevaluate decisions and modify them in ways that maintain a mobilized learner.

2. Effective and efficient decision making is a basic skill and one that is as fundamental as the three R's. Thus, if an individual does not do it well initially, this is not a reason to move away from learner involvement in decision making. Rather, it is an assessment of a need and a reason to use the process not only for motivational purposes but also to improve this basic skill.

3. Among students manifesting learning, behavior, and/or emotional problems, it is well to remember that the most fundamental decision some of these individuals have to make is whether they want to participate or not. That is why it may be necessary in specific cases temporarily to put aside established options and standards. As we have stressed, before some students will decide to participate in a proactive way, they have to perceive the learning environment as positively

different—and quite a bit so—from the one in which they had so much failure.

Reviews of the literature on human motivation suggest that providing students with options and involving them in decision making are key facets of addressing the problem of engagement in the classroom and at school (Deci & Flaste, 1995; Deci & Ryan, 1985; Stipek, 1998). For example, numerous studies have shown that opportunities to express preferences and make choices lead to greater motivation, academic gains, increases in productivity and on-task behavior, and decreases in aggressive behavior. Similarly, researchers report that student participation in goal setting leads to more positive outcomes (e.g., higher commitment to a goal and increased performance). We have more to say about all this in our discussion of personalized instruction (Chapter 6).

CONCLUDING COMMENTS

Getting students involved in their education programs is more than having them participate; it is connecting students with their education, enabling them to influence and affect the program and, indeed, enabling them to become enwrapped and engrossed in their educational experiences.

—Wehrmeyer & Sands (1998)

Whatever the initial cause of someone's learning and behavior problems, the longer the individual has lived with such problems, the more likely he or she will have negative feelings and thoughts about instruction, teachers, and schools. The feelings include anxiety, fear, frustration, and anger. The thoughts may include strong expectations of failure and vulnerability and low valuing of many learning "opportunities." Such thoughts and feelings can result in avoidance motivation or low motivation for learning and performing in many areas of schooling.

Low motivation leads to halfhearted effort. Avoidance motivation leads to avoidance behaviors. Individuals with avoidance and low motivation often also are attracted to socially disapproved activity. Poor effort, avoidance behavior, and active pursuit of disapproved behavior on the part of students are surefire recipes for failure and worse.

It remains tempting to focus directly on student misbehavior. And it also is tempting to think that behavior problems at least can be exorcized by laying down the law. We have seen many administrators pursue this line of thinking. For every student who shapes up, ten others experience a Greek tragedy that inevitably ends in the student's being pushed out of school through a progression of suspensions, "opportunity" transfers, and expulsions. Official dropout figures don't tell the tale. What we see in most high schools in cities such as Los Angeles, Baltimore, D.C., Miami, and Detroit is that only about half of those who were enrolled in the ninth grade are still around to graduate from twelfth grade.

Most of these students entered kindergarten with a healthy curiosity and a desire to learn to read and write. By the end of second grade, we start seeing the first referrals by classroom teachers because of learning and behavior problems. From that point on, increasing numbers of students become disengaged from classroom learning, and most of these manifest some form of behavioral and emotional problems.

It is not surprising, then, that many are heartened to see the shift from punishment to positive behavior support in addressing unwanted behavior. However, as long as factors that lead to disengagement are left unaffected, we risk perpetuating the phenomenon that William Ryan identified as *blaming the victim.*

From an intervention perspective, the point for emphasis is that engaging and reengaging students in classroom learning involves matching motivation. Matching motivation requires factoring in students' perceptions in determining the right mix of intrinsic and extrinsic reasons. It also requires understanding the key role played by expectations related to outcome. Without a good match, social control strategies can temporarily suppress negative attitudes and behaviors, but reengagement in classroom learning is unlikely. And without reengagement in classroom learning, unwanted behavior is very likely to reappear.

The remainder of this book is concerned with new directions for learning support that can help reverse negative trends related to student attendance, participation, and achievement. We explore what needs to change in classrooms and what must be done schoolwide and in collaboration with families and the community at large.

REFLECTION AND STIMULUS FOR DISCUSSION

Key Insights About "It's Not About Controlling Behavior; It's About Engaging and Reengaging Students in Learning"

Based on what you learned so far:

> *Identify (and discuss) what is involved in engaging and reengaging students in classroom learning.*

As an aid, see the Tool for Reflection Activity below, which reflects the main categories of a self-study survey related to classroom-based efforts to enhance learning and performance (see Chapter 12).

Tool for Reflection Activity: From Adelman and Taylor's Self-study Survey on Classroom-focused Efforts to Enable Learning

I. **Opening the Classroom Door**
   A. Are others invited into the classroom to assist in enhancing classroom approaches?
      1. Aides (e.g., paraeducators, other paid assistants)?
      2. Older students?
      3. Other students in the class?
      4. Volunteers?
      5. Parents?
      6. Resource teacher?

   (Continued)

(Continued)

       7. Specialists?

       8. Other? (specify) _____

  B. Are there programs to train aides, volunteers, and other assistants who come into the classrooms to work with students who need help?

II. **Redesigning Classroom Approaches to Enhance Teacher Capability to Prevent and Handle Problems and Reduce Need for Out-of-Class Referrals**

  A. Is instruction personalized (i.e., designed to match each student's motivation and capabilities)?

  B. When needed, is in-classroom special assistance provided?

  C. Are there small-group and independent learning options?

  D. Are behavior problems handled in ways designed to minimize a negative impact on student attitudes toward classroom learning?

  E. Is there a range of curricular and instructional options and choices?

  F. Are prereferral interventions used?

  G. Are materials and activities upgraded to

       1. Ensure that there are enough basic supplies in the classroom?

       2. Increase the range of high-motivation activities (keyed to the interests of students in need of special attention)?

       3. Include advanced technology?

       4. Other? (specify) _____

  H. Are regular efforts to foster social and emotional development supplemented?

  I. Which of the following can teachers request as special interventions?

       1. Family problem-solving conferences?

       2. Exchange of students to improve student-teacher match and for a fresh start?

       3. Referral for specific services?

       4. Other? (specify) _____

  J. What programs are there for temporary out-of-class help?

       1. A family center providing student and family assistance?

       2. Designated problem remediation specialists?

       3. A time-out situation?

       4. Other? (specify) _____

K. What is done to assist a teacher who has difficulty with limited-English-speaking students?
1. Is the student reassigned?
2. Does the teacher receive professional development related to working with limited-English-speaking students?
3. Does a bilingual coordinator offer consultation?
4. Is a bilingual aide assigned to the class?
5. Are volunteers brought in to help (e.g., parents, peers)?
6. Other? (specify) _____

III. Enhancing and Personalizing Professional Development
A. Are teachers clustered for support and staff development?
B. Are demonstrations provided?
C. Are workshops and readings offered regularly?
D. Is consultation available from persons with special expertise such as
1. Learning supports staff (e.g., psychologist, counselor, social worker, nurse)?
2. Resource specialists and/or special education teachers?
3. Members of special committees?
4. Bilingual and/or other coordinators?
5. Other? (specify) _____
E. Is there a formal mentoring program?
F. Is team teaching or coteaching used for teachers to learn on the job?
G. Is the school creating a learning community?
H. Is there staff social support?
I. Is there formal conflict mediation/resolution for staff?
J. Is there a focus on learning how to integrate intrinsic motivation into teaching and classroom management?
K. Is there assistance in learning to use advanced technology?
L. Other (specify) _____

IV. Curricular Enrichment and Adjunct Programs
A. What types of technology are available to the classroom?
1. Are there computers in the classroom?
2. Is there a computer lab?
3. Is computer-assisted instruction offered?
4. Are there computer literacy programs?
5. Are computer programs used to address ESL needs?
6. Does the classroom have video recording capability?
7. Is instructional TV used in the classroom?

(Continued)

(Continued)

    8. Is there a multimedia lab?

    9. Other? (specify) _____

  B. What curricular enrichment and adjunct programs do teachers use?

    1. Are library activities used regularly?

    2. Is music/art used regularly?

    3. Is health education a regular part of the curriculum?

    4. Are student performances regular events?

    5. Are there several field trips a year?

    6. Are there student council and other leader opportunities?

    7. Are there school environment projects such as

      a. Mural painting?

      b. Horticulture/gardening?

      c. School cleanup and beautification?

      d. Other? (specify) _____

    8. Are there special schoolwide events such as

      a. Sports?

      b. Clubs and similar organized activities?

      c. Publication of a student newspaper?

      d. Sales events?

      e. Poster contests?

      f. Essay contests?

      g. A book fair?

      h. Pep rallies/contests?

      i. Attendance competitions?

      j. Attendance awards/assemblies?

      k. Other? (specify) _____

    9. Are guest contributors used (e.g., outside speakers/performers)?

   10. Other? (specify) _____

V. Classroom and Schoolwide Approaches Used to Create and Maintain a Caring and Supportive Climate

  A. Are there schoolwide approaches for

    1. Creating and maintaining a caring and supportive climate?

    2. Supporting high standards for positive behavior?

    3. Other? (specify) _____

  B. Are there classroom approaches for

    1. Creating and maintaining a caring and supportive climate?

    2. Supporting high standards for positive behavior?

    3. Other? (specify) _____

VI. Capacity Building for Classroom-based Approaches

A. Are there programs to enhance broad stakeholder involvement in classroom-based approaches?

B. Are there programs used to meet the educational needs of personnel related to classroom-based approaches?

   1. Is there ongoing training for learning support staff with respect to classroom-based approaches?

   2. Is there ongoing training for others involved in providing classroom-based approaches (e.g., teachers, peer buddies, office staff, administrators)?

   3. Other? (specify) _____

C. Which of the following topics are covered in educating stakeholders?

   1. How others can work effectively in the classroom

   2. Reengaging students who have disengaged from classroom learning

   3. Personalizing instruction

   4. Addressing learning, behavior, and emotional problems

   5. Enriching options and facilitating student and family involvement in decision making

D. Other things you think a school should do to assist a teacher's efforts to address barriers to students' learning.

ACTIVITY

Observe a group of students who are involved in the same classroom activity. Identify one who appears highly engaged in learning and one who seems very bored.

After observing for a while, write down your views about why each of the students is responding so differently to the same activity.

Think about the bored student whom you observed (or another one you know about).

Make some notes about what you think
should be done and then discuss your ideas with others.

1. Begin the group discussion with a brief exchange of what each member thinks causes students not to be engaged in a classroom learning activity.

2. Then discuss ideas for increasing the likelihood that such students will engage in learning.

If there is an opportunity for group discussion, you may find the following group process guidelines helpful:

- Start by identifying someone who will facilitate the group interchange.
- Take a few minutes to make a few individual notes on a worksheet.
- Be sure all major points are compiled for sharing with other groups.
- Ask someone else to watch the time so that the group doesn't bog down.

Teacher:	Yes, Chris, what is it?
Chris:	I don't want to scare you, but my dad says if I don't get better grades, someone is in for a spanking.

REFERENCES

Adelman, H. S., & Taylor, L. (1993). *Learning problems and learning disabilities: Moving forward.* Pacific Grove, CA: Brooks/Cole.

American Youth Policy Forum. (2000). *High schools of the millennium report.* Washington, DC: American Youth Policy Forum.

Ausubel, N. (Ed.). (1948). Applied psychology. In *A Treasury of Jewish Folklore.* New York: Crown.

Brophy, J. (2004). *Motivating students to learn* (2nd ed.). Mahwah, NJ: Lawrence Erlbaum.

Bruner, J. S. (1966). *Toward a theory of instruction.* Cambridge, MA: Belknap Press.

Center for Mental Health in Schools. (2001). *Enhancing classroom approaches for addressing barriers to learning: Classroom focused enabling.* Los Angeles: Center for Mental Health in Schools at UCLA.

Deci, E. L. (1975). *Intrinsic motivation.* New York: Plenum.

Deci, E. L., & Flaste, R. (1995). *Why we do what we do.* New York: Penguin Books.

Deci, E. L., & Ryan, R. M. (1985). *Intrinsic motivation and self-determination in human behavior.* New York: Plenum Press.

Deci, E. L., & Ryan, R. M. (2002). The paradox of achievement: The harder you push, the worse it gets. In J. Aronson (Ed.), *Improving academic achievement: Contributions of social psychology* (pp. 59–85). New York: Academic Press.

Fredricks, J. A., Blumenfeld, P. C., & Paris, A. H. (2004). School engagement: Potential of the concept, state of the evidence. *Review of Educational Research, 74,* 59–109.

Holt, J. (1989). *Learning all the time.* Reading, MA: Addison-Wesley.

Jones, B., Valdez, G., Nowakowski, J., & Rasmussen, C. (1994). *Designing learning and technology for educational reform.* Oak Brook, IL: North Central Regional Educational Laboratory. Excerpted from article on NCREL: North Central Regional Educational Laboratory.

National Research Council and the Institute of Medicine. (2004). *Engaging schools: Fostering high school students' motivation to learn.* Washington, DC: National Academies Press.

Ryan, R. M., & Deci, E. L. (2000). Intrinsic and extrinsic motivations: Classic definitions and new directions. *Contemporary Educational Psychology, 25,* 54–67.

Stipek, D. J. (1998). *Motivation to learn: From theory to practice* (3rd ed.). Boston: Allyn & Bacon.

Wehrmeyer, M. L., & Sands, D. J. (1998). *Making it happen: Student involvement in education planning, decision making, and instruction.* Baltimore: Paul Brookes.

*Chapter 14 contains a list of special resources related
to the above matters available at no cost from the national
Center for Mental Health in Schools, which is at UCLA and is
directed by the authors of this book. Go to http://smhp.psych.ucla.edu.*

PART II

Learning Supports
in the Classroom

Kids need us most when they're at their worst.

Schools are getting better and better at building systems for referring students for assistance when they manifest learning, behavior, and/or emotional problems. Not surprisingly, this leads to the "field of dreams" effect. (*Build it, and they will come.*) In some schools, the number of referrals is so large that the system is overwhelmed and unable to handle more than a small percentage of students. As stressed in Part I, schools committed to the success of all children must be redesigned so that teachers and support staff are better equipped to help such students. In this respect, we clarified the need for schools to develop a major component for addressing barriers to learning and promoting healthy development. Such a component is key to appropriately stemming the tide of referrals out of the classroom. And a major element of the component involves enhancing what goes on in the classroom to address learning and behavior problems in ways that *enable learning*. We have more to say about this in Part III.

Good schools want to do their best for *all* students. This, of course, reflects our society's commitment to equity, fairness, and justice. But if this commitment is to be meaningful, it cannot be approached simplistically. (It was said of the legendary coach Vince Lombardi that he was always fair because he treated all his players the same—like dogs!) For schools and teachers, equity, fairness, and justice start with designing instruction in ways that account for a wide range of individual differences and circumstances. But the work can't stop there if we are to assure all students an equal opportunity to succeed at school. Teachers and student support staff must be prepared to design classrooms to accommodate and assist the many learning, behavior, and emotional problems they encounter. Such preparation involves considerably more than most school staff will have learned before being hired.

Good teachers and support staff are continuing learners. They are keenly interested in what others have found works well. As a result, most end up being rather eclectic in their daily practice. Thoughtfully put together, an effective approach for helping students who manifest problems can be a healthy alternative to fads, fancies, and dogmatisms. But care must be taken to avoid grabbing hold of almost every new idea one learns about. (If it looks appealing, it is adopted—regardless of whether it is valid or consistent with other practices being used.) This is naive eclecticism and can result in more harm than good. No one should use a casual and undiscriminating approach in teaching and helping others. And no one should think there is a magic bullet that will solve the many dilemmas school staff encounter every day.

The way to avoid naive eclecticism is to build one's intervention approaches on a coherent and consistent set of

- Underlying concepts
- Practice guidelines that reflect these concepts
- Best practices that fit the guidelines
- Valid scientific data as they become available

Each of these considerations guides the following discussion, which focuses on developing that facet of an enabling or learning support component we call "classroom-focused enabling." This aspect of the component is the foundation around which a comprehensive approach should be built to enable all students to have an equal opportunity to succeed at school. Going beyond what teacher education programs usually stress, classroom-focused enabling encompasses a host of ways to enhance the effectiveness of classroom instruction by preventing problems and responding in motivationally sensitive ways when problems appear. Particular emphasis is placed on (a) personalizing instruction to account for motivational and developmental differences and (b) providing special assistance to address specific problems as soon as they arise.

Although Part II was written with teachers and others who work with teachers in mind, we believe all stakeholders in education should develop a basic understanding of the matters discussed. Student support staff, especially those who have not invested years as classroom teachers, need to enhance their appreciation of the type of classroom changes that can make a difference in preventing and correcting learning, behavior, and emotional problems. The following chapters obviously also have relevance for those who supervise and teach teachers. Finally, we recognize that parents are teachers. And while they aren't in classrooms, they can benefit from thinking about applying the concepts, principles, guidelines, and practices both to their parenting and to their role as advocates for school improvement.

Because kids need us most when they are at their worst, we must redesign classrooms and prepare school staff to meet the challenge.

Kids can walk around trouble if there is some place to walk to and someone to walk with.
— Tito (quoted by McLaughlin & Talbert, 1993)

Classrooms and Teaching Revisited

4

We believe the strength in education resides in the intelligent use of [a] powerful variety of approaches—matching them to different goals and adapting them to the student's styles and characteristics. Competence in teaching stems from the capacity to reach out to different children and to create a rich and multi-dimensional environment for them. . . . We believe the world of education should be a pluralistic one—that children and adults alike should have a "cafeteria of alternatives" to stimulate their growth and nurture both their unique potential and their capacity to make common cause in the rejuvenation of our troubled society.

—Bruce Joyce and Marsha Weil (1980)

Education is not the filling of a pail, but the lighting of a fire.

—William Butler Yeats

ORIENTING QUESTIONS

? What are the characteristics of good schools and teaching?
? Why should teachers "open the classroom door," and why should support staff do more of their work in classrooms?
? What's involved in creating a stimulating and manageable learning environment?

Any experience can be a learning activity . . . any learning activity can be an experience!

Every encounter at school results in something learned—for better or for worse. So every transaction with an adult in the school setting is teaching youngsters something.

Teachers, of course, play the primary role in formal instruction. Support staff, administrators, and others often are called on to play a primary "teaching" role when a student is not doing well. Generally, this happens after a problem has worsened over a period of time. The usual scenario is that (a) the teacher requests help, (b) the student is sent to someone who provides some form of intervention, which may involve the family and may result in referring the student for special services, and (c) if removal from the class is not recommended, the intervener reports back to the teacher what was done and offers some ideas for what the teacher should do when the student returns to class. Throughout the process, the student has been learning—but not always absorbing the intended messages.

From the perspective of addressing barriers to learning and preventing problems, we need to revisit teaching in the classroom (Adelman & Taylor, 1997). And we need to change the above scenario so that those who play a primary teaching role outside classrooms are invited inside to team with teachers in ways that prevent problems and respond when problems first arise.

New directions for student support call for changing the scenario. For such a change to become part of the culture of schools, teachers must open the classroom door, and all who enter must learn much more about classroom life and good teaching. These matters are the focus in this and the next two chapters.

We start with a brief exploration of what schooling is all about and the principles underlying good schools and good teaching. We stress the importance of creating a caring context for learning and the value of collaboration in the classroom as basic building blocks for good teaching in schools. In presenting these basic building blocks, we do so with the awareness that learning and teaching are dynamic, nonlinear processes and that some learners experience problems that require additional and sometimes specialized assistance (see Guide 4.1).[1]

Guide 4.1   Good Teaching—Promotion of Assets, Prevention of Problems, and Addressing the Problems in Keeping With the Principle of Least Intervention Needed

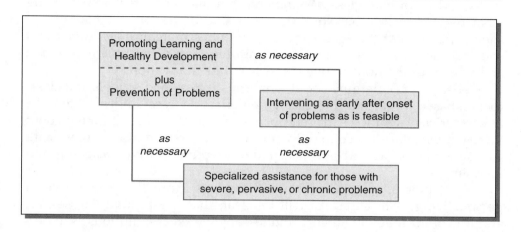

PRINCIPLES, GUIDELINES, AND CHARACTERISTICS OF GOOD SCHOOLS AND TEACHING

Most public school curriculum guides and manuals reflect efforts to prepare youngsters to cope with what may be called *developmental* or *life tasks*. Reading, math, biology, chemistry, social studies, history, government, physical and health education—all are seen as preparing an individual to assume an appropriate role in society as a worker, citizen, community member, and parent. Most educators and parents, however, also want to foster individual well-being, talents, and personal integrity. Thus, good teaching is not simply a matter of conveying content and mastering instructional techniques (Richardson, 2001).

Underlying any discussion of schooling and teaching is a *rationale* regarding what constitutes the right balance between societal and individual interests under a system of compulsory education. One rationale is that in the context of society's institutions for educating the young, good schooling and teaching require accomplishing society's intentions in ways that promote the well-being of youngsters. This is the perspective to which we subscribe.

Because the rationale adopted by teachers and other school staff is so important, we begin with a brief outline of principles, guidelines, and characteristics that have been synthesized over the years. Their complexity warrants more exploration, and we leave that for you to pursue.

The commonsense view of good teaching is captured by the old adage *Good teaching meets learners where they are.* Unfortunately, this adage often is interpreted only as a call for *matching* a student's current *capabilities* (e.g., knowledge and skills). The irony in this, of course, is that most school staff recognize that motivational factors often play a key role in accounting for poor instructional outcomes. One of the most common laments among teachers is "They could do it, if only they *wanted* to!" Teachers also know that good abilities are more likely to emerge when students are not only motivated to pursue class assignments but also are interested in using what they learn in other contexts. After the discussion in Chapter 3, it should be evident that good teaching requires matching *motivation* and encompasses practices that reflect an appreciation of *intrinsic* motivation and what must be done to overcome *avoidance* motivation.

Consensus is emerging about what constitutes good schools and classrooms, based in part on the research on effectiveness. Guides 4.2 and 4.3 offer a series of syntheses that encapsulate some of the best thinking about these matters. We all need to reflect on such matters and discuss them with colleagues as we revisit and articulate our philosophy of teaching and schooling.

In Chapter 5, we approach good teaching from the perspective of personalizing instruction. As will be clear, that perspective stresses the addition of the following theory and research-based assumptions as underlying efforts to meet learners where they are.

- Learning is a function of the ongoing transactions between the learner and the learning environment.
- Optimal learning is a function of an optimal match between the learner's accumulated capacities and attitudes and current state of being and the program's processes and content.
- Matching both a learner's motivation and capacities must be primary procedural objectives.
- The learner's perception is the critical criterion for evaluating whether a good match exists between the learner and the learning environment.
- Within reasonable limits, the wider the range of options that can be offered and the more the learner is made aware of the options and has a choice about which to pursue, the greater the likelihood that he or she will perceive the match as a good one.
- Besides improved learning, personalized programs enhance intrinsic valuing of learning and a sense of personal responsibility for learning. Furthermore, such programs increase acceptance and even appreciation of individual differences, as well as independent and cooperative functioning and problem solving.

A Note About Adopting Principles

Discussions of principles related to intervention have become so diffuse that almost every guideline is called a principle. With respect to school and classroom practice, especially with vulnerable and disenfranchised populations, a principled approach certainly is needed. The literature discussing the fundamental social philosophical concerns raised by schooling, teaching, and other intervention decisions suggests that what

Guide 4.2   A Synthesis of Principles and Guidelines Underlying Good
Schools and Teaching*

The following are widely advocated guidelines that provide a sense of the philosophy for school efforts to address barriers to development and learning and promote healthy development. This synthesis is organized around concerns for (a) stakeholders, (b) the teaching process, and (c) school and classroom climate.

1. With respect to stakeholders, good schools and good teaching

- Employ a critical mass of high-quality leadership and line staff who believe in what they are doing, value the search for understanding, see errors as valuable sources of learning, and pursue continuing education and self-renewal
- Involve all staff and a wide range of other competent, energetic, committed, and responsible stakeholders in planning, implementation, evaluation, and ongoing renewal
- Identify staff who are not performing well and provide personalized capacity-building opportunities, support, or other corrective remedies

2. With respect to the teaching process, good schools and good teaching use the strengths and vital resources of all stakeholders to

- Ensure the same high quality for all students
- Formulate and effectively communicate goals, standards, and quality indicators for cognitive, physical, emotional, and social development
- Facilitate continuous cognitive, physical, emotional, and social development and learning using procedures that promote active learning in and out of school
- Ensure use of comprehensive, multifaceted, and integrated approaches (e.g., approaches that are extensive and intensive enough to ensure that students have an equal opportunity to succeed at school and develop in healthy ways)
- Make learning accessible to all students (including those at greatest risk and hardest to reach) through development of a full continuum of learning supports (i.e., an enabling component)
- Tailor processes so they are a good fit in terms of both motivation and capability and are no more intrusive and disruptive than is necessary for meeting needs and accounting for distinctive needs, resources, and other forms of diversity
- Deal with students holistically and developmentally, as individuals and as part of a family, neighborhood, and community
- Tailor appropriate measures for improving practices and for purposes of accountability

3. With respect to school and classroom climate, good schools and good teaching

- Delineate the rights and obligations of all stakeholders
- Guide and foster a commitment to social justice (equity) and to creating a sense of community
- Ensure that staff, students, family members, and all other stakeholders have the time, training, skills, and institutional and collegial support necessary to create an accepting and safe environment and build relationships of mutual trust, respect, equality, and appropriate risk taking

And, in general, good schools and good teaching are experienced by all stakeholders as user-friendly, flexibly implemented, and responsive.

---

*Synthesized from many sources, including the vast research literature on good schools and good teaching. These sources overlap but are not as restricted in their focus as the literature on effective schools and classrooms (see Guide 4.3).

Guide 4.3   A Synthesis of Characteristics of Effective Schools and Classrooms That Account for *All* Learners*

Effective Schools

- Commitment to shared vision of equality
  - High expectations for student learning
  - Emphasis on academic work that is meaningful to the student
- Daily implementation of effective processes
  - Strong administrative leadership
  - Alignment of resources to reach goals
  - Professional development tied to goals
  - Discipline and school order
  - A sense of teamwork in the school
  - Teacher participation in decision making
  - Effective parental outreach and involvement
- Monitoring student progress through measured indicators of achievement
  - Setting local standards
  - Use of national standards
  - Use of data for continuous improvement of school climate and curricula
- Optimizing school size through limited enrollment, creation of small schools within big schools (e.g., academies, magnet programs), and other ways of grouping students and staff
- Strong involvement with the community and with surrounding family of schools
  - Students, families, and community are developed into a learning community
  - Programs address transitions between grades, school, school to career, and higher education

Effective Classrooms

- Positive classroom social climate that
  - Personalizes contacts and supports in ways that build trust over time and meets learners where they are
  - Offers accommodation so all students have an equal opportunity to learn
  - Adjusts class size and groupings to optimize learning
  - Engages students through dialogue and decision making and seizing "teachable moments"
  - Incorporates parents in multiple ways
  - Addresses social-emotional development
- Designing and implementing quality instructional experiences that
  - Involve students in decision making
  - Contextualize and make learning authentic, including use of real-life situations and mentors
  - Are appropriately cognitively complex and challenging
  - Enhance language/literacy
  - Foster joint student products
  - Extend the time students engage in learning through designing motivated practice
  - Ensure that students learn how to learn and are prepared for lifelong learning
  - Ensure the use of prereferral intervention strategies
  - Use a mix of methods and advanced technology to enhance learning
- Instruction is modified to meet students' needs based on ongoing assessments using
  - Measures of multiple dimensions of impact
  - Authentic assessment tools
  - Students' input based on their self-evaluations
- Teachers collaborate and are supported with
  - Personalized inservice, consultation, mentoring, grade-level teaming
  - Special resources who are available to come into the classroom to ensure that students with special needs are accommodated appropriately

---

*Synthesized from many sources, including the vast research literature on effective schools and classrooms.

must be addressed first and foremost are overlapping concerns about distributive justice (equity and fairness) and empowerment.

Equity is the legal facet of distributive justice. It ensures and protects individual rights and addresses inequities related to access to "goods" in life and meeting needs. Fairness is the more social philosophical application that deals with such ethical questions as: *Fair for whom? Fair according to whom? Fair using what criteria and what procedures for applying the criteria?* Obviously, what is fair for the society may not be fair for an individual; what is fair for one person or group may cause an inequity for another (see Beauchamp, Feinberg, & Smith, 1996). A good example of the dilemma is provided by high stakes testing, which is experienced by some students as fair and others as cutting them off from future opportunities. Another example is provided by the Individuals with Disabilities Education Act, which attempts to meet the special needs of a subgroup of individuals in ways that are fair to them and to the rest of society.

Equity and fairness do not guarantee empowerment. Empowerment is a multifaceted concept. In discussing power, theoreticians distinguish "power over" from "power to" and "power from." *Power over* involves explicit or implicit dominance over others and events; *power to* is seen as increased opportunities to act; *power from* implies ability to resist the power of others (see Hollander & Offermann, 1990; Riger, 1993).

From the perspective of school and classroom practice, the above overlapping principles raise complex concerns because there are three involved parties in any intervention: the society, the intervener(s), and those who are identified as participants (e.g., students, families). Each is a stakeholder; each brings vested and often conflicting interests to the enterprise; each party wants to be treated equitably, fairly, and in ways that promote empowerment (Adelman & Taylor, 1994; Strupp & Hadley, 1977). The profound implications of all this require greater attention by us all, especially with an eye to stakeholder motivation, setting standards, and cost-benefit analyses.

I told her the dog ate my homework. So she gave my dog an F and sent me to the doghouse!

ABOUT SCHOOL AND CLASSROOM CLIMATE

The concept of *climate* plays a major role in shaping the quality of school life, teaching, learning, and support. School and classroom climate are temporal, and somewhat fluid, perceived qualities of the immediate setting that emerge from the complex transaction of many factors. In turn, the climate reflects the influence of the underlying, institutionalized values and belief systems, norms, ideologies, rituals, and traditions that constitute the school *culture.* And, of course, the climate and culture at a school also are shaped by the surrounding political, social, cultural, and economic contexts (e.g., home, neighborhood, city, state, country).

School and classroom climate sometimes is referred to as the learning environment, as well as by terms such as *atmosphere, ambience, ecology,* and *milieu.* Depending on quality, the impact on students and staff can be beneficial for or a barrier to learning.

Key concepts for understanding school and classroom climate are social system organization; social attitudes; staff and student morale; power, control, guidance, support, and evaluation structures; curricular and instructional practices; communicated expectations; efficacy; accountability demands; cohesion; competition; fit between learner and classroom; system maintenance, growth, and change; orderliness; and safety. Moos (e.g., 1979) groups such concepts into three dimensions: (1) relationship (i.e., the nature and intensity of personal relationships within the environment; the extent to which people are involved in the environment and support and help each other), (2) personal development (i.e., basic directions along which personal growth and self-enhancement tend to occur), and (3) system maintenance and change (i.e., the extent to which the environment is orderly, clear in expectations, maintains control, and is responsive to change).

Research has indicated a range of strategies for enhancing a positive climate. All school staff have a significant role to play in ensuring that such strategies are well implemented and maintained.

Importance of Classroom Climate

Classroom climate is seen as a major determiner of classroom behavior and learning. Understanding the nature of classroom climate is a basic element in improving schools.

The concept of classroom climate implies the intent to establish and maintain a positive context that facilitates classroom learning, but in practice, classroom climates range from hostile or toxic to welcoming and supportive and can fluctuate daily and over the school year. Moreover, because the concept is a psychological construct, different observers may have different perceptions of the climate in a given classroom. Therefore, for purposes of his early research, Moos (1979) measured classroom environment in terms of the shared perceptions of those in the classroom.

Prevailing approaches to measuring classroom climate use (a) teacher and student perceptions, (b) external observers' ratings and systematic coding, and/or (c) naturalistic inquiry, ethnography, case study, and interpretative assessment techniques (Fraser, 1998; Freiberg, 1999).

Analyses of research suggest significant relationships between classroom climate and matters such as student engagement, behavior, self- efficacy, achievement, social and emotional development, principal leadership style, stages of educational reform, teacher burnout, and overall quality of school life. For example, studies report strong associations between achievement levels and classrooms that are perceived as having greater cohesion and goal direction and less disorganization and conflict. Research also suggests that the impact of classroom climate may be greater on students from low income homes and groups that often are discriminated against.

Given the correlational nature of classroom climate research, cause-and-effect interpretations remain speculative. The broader body of organizational research does indicate the profound role accountability pressures play in shaping organizational climate (Mahony & Hextall, 2000). Thus, it seems likely that the increasing demands for higher achievement test scores and control of student behavior contribute to a classroom climate that is reactive, overcontrolling, and overreliant on external reinforcement to motivate positive functioning.

Promoting a Positive School and Classroom Climate

Analyses of practice and research suggest that a proactive approach to developing a positive school and classroom climate requires careful attention to (a) enhancing the quality of life at school and especially in the classroom for students and staff, (b) pursuing a curriculum that promotes not only academic but also social and emotional learning, (c) enabling teachers and other staff to be effective with a wide range of students, and (d) fostering intrinsic motivation for learning and teaching. With respect to all this, the literature advocates

- A welcoming, caring, and hopeful atmosphere
- Social support mechanisms for students and staff
- An array of options for pursuing goals
- Meaningful participation by students and staff in decision making
- A transformed classroom infrastructure from a big classroom into a set of smaller units organized to maximize intrinsic motivation for learning and not based on ability or problem-oriented grouping
- Personalized instruction and response to problems
- Use of a variety of strategies for preventing and addressing problems as soon as they arise
- A healthy and attractive physical environment that is conducive to learning and teaching

CREATING A CARING CONTEXT FOR LEARNING

By this point, it should be evident that creating a caring context for learning requires considerable commitment on the part of all concerned. Teaching can be done in any context. Whenever a surrounding environment tries to promote learning, the process can be called teaching. Teaching occurs at school, at home, and in the community at large. It may be formalized or informally transmitted. Teaching in no way guarantees that learning will take place. Teaching in an uncaring way probably does guarantee that problems will arise.

From a psychological perspective, learning and teaching are experienced most positively when the learner cares about learning and the teacher cares about teaching. *Moreover, the whole process benefits greatly when all the participants care about each other.* Thus, good schools and good teachers work diligently to create an atmosphere that encourages mutual support, caring, and a sense of community. Such an atmosphere can play a key role in preventing learning, behavior, emotional, and health problems and promoting social and emotional learning and well-being.

Caring has moral, social, and personal facets. And when all facets of caring are present and balanced, they can nurture individuals and facilitate the process of learning. At the same time, caring in all its dimensions should be a major focus of what is taught and learned. This means a focus throughout on fostering positive social-emotional and physical development.

Caring begins when students (and their families) first arrive at a school. Classrooms and schools can do their job better if students feel they are truly welcome and have a range of social supports. A key facet of welcoming encompasses effectively connecting new students with peers and adults who can provide social support and advocacy.

On an ongoing basis, caring is best maintained through use of personalized instruction, regular student conferences, activity that fosters social and emotional development, and opportunities for students to attain positive status. Efforts to create a caring classroom climate benefit from programs for cooperative learning, peer tutoring, mentoring, advocacy, peer counseling and mediation, human relations, and conflict resolution. Clearly, a myriad of strategies can contribute to students' feeling positively connected to the classroom and school.

Given the importance of home involvement in schooling, attention also must be paid to creating a caring atmosphere for family members. Increased home involvement is more likely if families feel welcome and have access to social support at school. Thus, teachers and other school staff need to establish a program that effectively welcomes and connects families with school staff and other families to generate ongoing social support and greater participation in home involvement efforts.

Also, just as with students and their families, school staff need to feel truly welcome and socially supported. Rather than leaving this to chance, a caring school develops and institutionalizes a program to welcome and connect new staff with those with whom they will be working. And it does so in ways that effectively incorporate newcomers into the organization.

A COLLABORATIVE AND CARING CLASSROOM: OPENING THE CLASSROOM DOOR

Recently heard:

In some schools, it seems that teachers and students enter their classrooms ready to do battle. And at the end of the class, whoever is able to walk out "alive" is the winner.

This, of course, is a gross exaggeration . . . isn't it?

For a long time, teachers have gone into their classrooms and figuratively and often literally have shut their doors behind them. As a result, for better or worse, they have been on their own. On the positive side, the closed door limits outside meddling and inappropriate monitoring. The downside is that in too many instances, teachers are deprived of opportunities to learn from colleagues, and too often the isolation from others leads to feelings of alienation and burnout. Moreover, students are cut off from a variety of resources and experiences that appear essential to ensuring that all students have an equal opportunity to learn.

Because the negatives outweigh the potential gains, there are increasing calls for "opening the classroom door" to enhance collegial collaboration, consultation, mentoring, and greater involvement of expert assistance, volunteers, family members, and the community at large. Such fundamental changes in the culture of schools and classrooms are seen as routes to enhancing a caring climate, a sense of community, and teaching effectiveness. These changes are especially important for preventing commonplace learning, behavior, and emotional problems and for responding soon after the onset of a problem.

We have already discussed some of these matters. Guide 4.4 and the following discussion offer some additional details to consider.

Opening the Door to Enhance Teacher Support

New teachers need as much on-the-job training and in-classroom support as can be provided. All teachers need to learn more about how to enable learning in their classrooms. All school staff need to team in ways that enhance their effectiveness in supporting each other and enhancing student outcomes.

In opening the classroom door to enhance support, staff development, and outcomes, the crux of the matter is to ensure that effective teaming, mentoring, and other collegial practices are used. Learning effectively

Guide 4.4   Working Together

Teaching Benefits From Organizational Learning

Organizational learning requires an organizational structure "where people continually expand their capabilities to understand complexity, clarify vision and improve shared mental models" (Senge, 1990) by engaging in different tasks, acquiring different kinds of expertise, experiencing and expressing different forms of leadership, confronting uncomfortable organizational truths, and searching together for shared solutions (Hargreaves, 1994).

Collaboration and Collegiality

As Hargreaves and others have noted, these concepts are fundamental to improving morale and work satisfaction and to the whole enterprise of transforming schools to meet the needs of individuals and society. *Collaborative cultures* foster collaborative working relationships that are spontaneous, voluntary, development-oriented, pervasive across time and space, and unpredictable. When collegiality is *mandated,* it often produces what has been called *contrived collegiality,* which tends to breed inflexibility and inefficiency. Contrived collegiality is administratively regulated, compulsory, implementation-oriented, fixed in time and space, and predictable.

Welcoming for New Staff and Ongoing Social Support for All Staff

Just as with students and their families, there is a need for those working together at a school to feel that they are truly welcome and have a range of social supports. Thus, a major focus for stakeholder development activity is the establishment of a program that welcomes and connects new staff with others with whom they will be working and does so in ways that effectively incorporates them into the community.

Barriers to Working Together

Problems related to working relationships are a given. To minimize such problems, it is important for participants to understand barriers to working relationships and for sites to establish effective problem-solving mechanisms to eliminate or at least minimize such barriers.

Rescue Dynamics

A special problem that arises in caring communities are rescue dynamics. Such dynamics arise when caring and helping go astray, when those helping become frustrated and angry because those being helped don't respond in desired ways or seem not to be trying. It is important to minimize such dynamics by establishing procedures that build on motivational readiness and personalized interventions.

from each other is not just a talking game. It involves opportunities for modeling and guiding change (e.g., demonstrating and discussing new approaches, guiding initial practice and eventual implementation, and following up to improve and refine). Preferably, it takes place in every teacher's classroom and through visits to colleagues' classrooms.

Videotapes of and workshops on good practices can provide supplementary learning opportunities.

Team teaching with a mentor or a colleague provides a more intensive form of shared learning arrangement. Colleagues include specialist personnel, such as special education resource teachers and student support staff. Such staff can and need to do much more than "consult." That is, rather than just making recommendations to teachers about what to do about student learning, behavior, and emotional problems, specialists can be trained to go into classrooms to model, guide, and team with teachers as they practice and implement new approaches.

Opening the Door to Assistance and Partnerships

Opening the classroom door allows for the addition of a variety of forms of assistance and useful partnerships. As Hargreaves (1994) cogently notes:

> The way to relieve the uncertainty and open-endedness that characterizes classroom teaching is to create communities of colleagues who work collaboratively [in cultures of shared learning and positive risk taking] to set their own professional limits and standards, while still remaining committed to continuous improvement. Such communities can also bring together the professional and personal lives of teachers in a way that supports growth and allows problems to be discussed without fear of disapproval or punishment. (p. 156)

Increasingly, it is becoming evident that teachers need to work closely with other teachers and school personnel, as well as with parents, professionals-in-training, volunteers, and so forth. Collaboration and teaming are key facets of addressing barriers to learning. They allow schools to broaden the resources and strategies available in and out of the classroom to enhance learning and performance.

As noted, student learning is neither limited to what is formally taught nor to time spent in classrooms. Learning may occur whenever and wherever the learner interacts with the surrounding environment. All facets of the community (not just the school) provide learning opportunities. Anyone in the community who wants to facilitate learning might be a contributing teacher. When a classroom successfully joins with its surrounding community, everyone has the opportunity to learn and to teach. Indeed, many schools would do their job better if they were an integral and positive part of the community. The array of people who might be of assistance are aides and a variety of volunteers from the community and from institutions of higher education, other regular classroom teachers, family members, students, specialist teachers and support service personnel, school administrators, classified staff, and teachers-in-training and other professionals-in-training. Together they all constitute what can be called the teaching community. A few examples are highlighted in Guide 4.5.

Guide 4.5   Examples of Opening the Door to Assistance and Partnerships

Using Aides and Volunteers in Targeted Ways

Chronically, teachers find classroom instruction disrupted by some student who is less interested in the lesson than in interacting with a classmate. The first tendency usually is to use some simple form of social control to stop the disruptive behavior (e.g., using proximity and/or a mild verbal intervention). Because so many students today are not easily intimidated, teachers find that such strategies do not solve the problem. So the next steps escalate the event into a form of Greek tragedy. The teacher reprimands, warns, and finally sends the student to time-out or to the front office for discipline. In the process, the other students start to titter about what is happening, and the lesson usually is disrupted.

In contrast to this scenario, teachers can train their aides (if they have one) or a volunteer who has the ability to interact with students to work in ways that target such youngsters. The training of such individuals focuses on what the teacher wants them to do when a problem arises and what they should be doing to prevent such problems. In reaction to a problem, the aide or volunteer should expect the teacher to indicate that it is time to go and sit next to the designated youngster. The focus is on reengaging the student in the lesson. If this proves undoable, the next step involves taking the student for a walk outside the classroom. It is true that this means the student won't get the benefit of instruction during that period, but he or she wouldn't anyway.

Using this approach and not having to shift into a discipline mode has multiple benefits. For one, the teacher is able to carry out the day's lesson plan. For another, the other students do not have the experience of seeing the teacher having a control contest with a student. (Even if the teacher wins such contests, it may have a negative effect on how students perceive them. And if the teacher somehow loses it, that definitely conveys a wrong message. Either outcome can be counterproductive with respect to a caring climate and a sense of community.) Finally, the teacher has not had a negative encounter with the targeted student. Such encounters build up negative attitudes on both sides that can be counterproductive with respect to future teaching, learning, and behavior. Because there has been no negative encounter, the teacher can reach out to the student after the lesson is over and start to think about how to use an aide or volunteers to work with the student to prevent future problems.

Team Teaching

The obvious point here is that partnering with a compatible colleague enables the teachers to complement each other's areas of competence, provide each other with nurturance and personal support, and allow for relief in addressing problems.

Collaborating With Special Educators and Other Specialists

Almost every school has some personnel who have special training relevant to redesigning the classroom to work for a wider range of students. These specialists range from those who teach music or art to those who work with students designated as in need of special education. They can bring to the classroom not only their special expertise but also ideas for how the classroom design can incorporate practices that will engage students who have not been doing well and can accommodate those with special needs.

CREATING A STIMULATING AND MANAGEABLE LEARNING ENVIRONMENT

Everyone who works in schools knows that the way the classroom setting is arranged and instruction is organized can help or hinder learning and teaching. The ideal is to have an environment where students and teachers feel comfortable, positively stimulated, and well supported in pursuing the learning objectives of the day. To these ends and from the perspective of enhancing intrinsic motivation, a classroom benefits from (a) ensuring that available options encourage active learning (e.g., authentic, problem-based, and discovery learning; projects, learning centers, enrichment opportunities) and (b) grouping students in ways that turn big classes into smaller learning units and that enhance positive attitudes and support for learning.

Designing the Classroom for Active Learning

Teachers are often taught to group instructional practices under topics such as

- *Direct instruction* (structured overviews, explicit teaching, mastery lectures, drill and practice, compare and contrast, didactic questions, demonstrations, guides for reading, listening, and viewing)
- *Indirect instruction* (problem solving, case studies, inquiry, reading for meaning, reflective study, concept formation, concept mapping, concept attainment)
- *Interactive instruction* (debates, role playing, panels, brainstorming, peer practice, discussion, laboratory groups, cooperative learning groups, problem solving, circle of knowledge, tutorial groups, interviewing)
- *Independent study* (essays, computer-assisted instruction, learning activity packages, correspondence lessons, learning contracts, homework, research projects, assigned questions, learning centers)
- *Experiential learning* (field trips, conducting experiments, simulations, games, focused imaging, field observations, role playing, model building, surveys)

All these forms of instruction are relevant. However, *teaching* strategies must always have as their primary concern producing effective *learning.* Effective learning requires ensuring that the student is truly engaged in learning. Student engagement is especially important in preventing learning, behavior, and emotional problems and is essential at the first indications of such problems. And it is the key to using *response to intervention* as a diagnostic tool (Fletcher & Reschly, 2005). Thus, the focus here is on discussing the concept of *active learning* and instructional approaches designed to enhance motivation to learn.

One definition of active learning is "students actively constructing meaning grounded in their own experience rather than simply absorbing and reproducing knowledge transmitted from subject-matter fields" (Newmann, Marks, & Gamoran, 1996). Examples include small-group discussions; cooperative learning tasks; independent research projects; use of hands-on manipulatives; scientific equipment and arts and crafts materials; use of computer and video technology; and community-based projects such as surveys, oral histories, and volunteer service.

Simply stated, active learning is *learning by doing, listening, looking, and asking;* but it is not just being active that counts. It is the mobilization of the student to seek out and learn. Specific activities are designed to capitalize on student interests and curiosity, involve them in problem solving and guided inquiry, and elicit their thinking through reflective discussions and appropriate products. Moreover, the activities are designed to do all this in ways that not only minimize threats to feelings of competence, self-determination, and relatedness to others but enhance such feelings.

There are many examples of ways to promote active learning at all grade levels. It can take the form of class discussions, problem-based and discovery learning, a project approach, involvement in "learning centers" at school, experiences outside the classroom, and independent learning in or out of school. For example, students may become involved in classroom, schoolwide, or community service or action projects. Older students may be involved in "internships." Active methods can be introduced gradually so students learn how to benefit from them and can be provided appropriate support and guidance.

Active learning in the form of interactive instruction; authentic, problem-based discovery; and project-based learning does much more than motivate learning of subject matter and academic skills. Students also learn how to cooperate with others, share responsibility for planning and implementation, develop understanding and skills related to conflict resolution and mediation, and much more. Moreover, such formats provide a context for building collaborations with other teachers and school staff and with a variety of volunteers. Chapter 11 provides brief overviews of a variety of approaches that encompass strategies for actively engaging students in learning and practicing what has been learned.

Why do you say you're wasting your time by going to school?   Well, I can't read or write — and they won't let me talk!

Grouping Students and Turning Big Classes Into Smaller Units

In its report titled *High Schools of the Millennium,* the American Youth Policy Forum (2000) states:

> The structure and organization of a High School of the Millennium is very different than that of the conventional high school. First and foremost, [the school] is designed to provide small, personalized, and caring learning communities for students. . . . The smaller groups allow a number of adults . . . to work together with the students . . . as a way to develop more meaningful relationships and as a way for the teachers to better understand the learning needs of each student.
>
> Time is used differently. . . . Alternative schedules, such as a block schedule or modified block schedule, create longer class periods that allow students to become more actively engaged in their learning through more in-depth exploration. . . . The longer instructional times also allow for multiple learning activities that better meet the different learning styles of students. (pp. 26–27)

Grouping

When done appropriately, grouping has many benefits. At a fundamental level, grouping is an essential strategy in turning classrooms with large enrollments into a set of simultaneously operating small classes. Just as it is evident that we need to turn schools with large enrollments into sets of small schools, we must do the same in the classroom every day.

Aside from times when a learning objective is best accomplished with the whole class, the general trend should be to create small classes out of the whole. This involves grouping students in various ways, as well as providing opportunities for individual activity.

Clearly, students should never be grouped in ways that harm them. This applies to putting students in low ability tracks and segregating those with learning, behavior, or emotional problems. But grouping is essential for effective teaching. *Appropriate grouping* facilitates student engagement, learning, and performance. Besides enhancing academic learning, it can increase intrinsic motivation by promoting feelings of personal and interpersonal competence, self-determination, and positive connection with others. Moreover, it can foster autonomous learning skills, personal responsibility for learning, and healthy social-emotional attitudes and skills.

A well-designed classroom enables spending most of the time (a) working directly with a group while the rest of the students work in small groups and on independent activities or (b) rotating among small groups and individual learners. When staff team teach or collaborate in other ways, such grouping can be done across classrooms.

Effective grouping is facilitated by ensuring that teachers have adequate resources (including space, materials, and help). The key to effective grouping, however, is to take the time needed for youngsters to learn to work well with each other, with other resource personnel, and at times independently.

Done appropriately, students are grouped and regrouped flexibly and regularly, based on individual interests, needs, and for benefits to be derived from diversity. Small learning groups are established for cooperative inquiry and learning, concept and skill development, problem solving, motivated practice, peer- and cross-age tutoring, and other forms of activity that can be facilitated by peers, aides, and/or volunteers. In a small group (e.g., two to six members), students have more opportunities to participate. In heterogeneous, cooperative learning groups, each student has an interdependent role in pursuing a common learning goal and can contribute on a par with his or her capabilities.

Three types of groupings that are common are

1. *Needs-based grouping.* Short-term groupings are established for students with similar learning needs (e.g., to teach or reteach them particular skills and to do so in keeping with their current interests and capabilities).

2. *Interest-based grouping.* Students who already are motivated to pursue an activity usually can be taught to work together well on active learning tasks.

3. *Designed-diversity grouping.* For some objectives, it is desirable to combine sets of students who come from different backgrounds and have different abilities and interests (e.g., to discuss certain topics, foster certain social capabilities, engender mutual support for learning).

All three types provide opportunities to enhance interpersonal functioning and an understanding of working relationships and of factors affecting group functioning.

Tomlinson, in her 1999 book *The Differentiated Classroom: Responding to the Needs of All Learners,* delineates ways to minimize whole-class instruction through use of flexible small-group teaching and facilitating independent learning. She notes that nearly all educators agree with the need to differentiate instruction, but school staff may lack strategies to make it happen. To avoid lockstep instruction, she suggests strategies such as using *stations* (setting up different spots where students work on various tasks simultaneously) and *orbital studies* (with guidance and support, students are involved in short-term—three to six weeks—independent investigations related to a facet of the curriculum).

Differentiated instruction is not a form of tracking—just the opposite. It enables teachers to give every child access to the curriculum and ensures that each makes appropriate progress (see examples in Guide 4.6).

In all forms of grouping, approaches such as cooperative learning and computer-assisted instruction are relevant, and obviously, it helps to have multiple collaborators in the classroom. An aide and/or volunteers, for example, can assist with establishing and maintaining well-functioning groups, as well as providing special support and guidance for designated individuals. As teachers increasingly open their doors to others, assistance can be solicited from tutors, resource and special education teachers, pupil services personnel, and an ever-widening range of volunteers (e.g., tutors, peer buddies, parents, mentors, and any others who can bring special abilities into the classroom and offer additional options for learning). And of course, team teaching offers a potent way to expand the range of options for personalizing instruction.

Recognizing and Accommodating Diversity

Every classroom is diverse to some degree. Diversity arises from many factors: gender, ethnicity, race, socioeconomic status, religion, capability, disability, interests, and so forth. In grouping students, it is important to draw on the strengths of diversity. For example, a multiethnic classroom enables teachers to group students across ethnic lines to bring different perspectives to the learning activity. This allows students not only to learn about other perspectives, but it can enhance critical thinking and other higher order conceptual abilities. It also can foster the type of intergroup understanding and relationships essential to establishing a school climate of caring and mutual respect. And of course, the entire curriculum and all instructional activities must incorporate an appreciation of diversity, and teachers must plan ways to appropriately accommodate individual and group differences.

Collaborative or Team Teaching

Grouping can be facilitated through teacher collaboration. Not only can such teaming benefit students, but it can be a great boon to teachers. A good collaboration is one where colleagues mesh professionally and personally. It doesn't mean that there is agreement about everything, but there must be agreement about what constitutes good teaching and effective learning.

Collaborations can take various forms. Usually, when the focus is on classrooms, the tendency is to think in terms of two or more teachers teaming to share the instructional load in any way they feel works. New directions for student support will involve expanding the team to include support staff.

Guide 4.6   Differentiated Instruction and Making Smaller Units out of
Larger Classes

The Winter 2000 issue of *Curriculum,* the newsletter of the Association for Supervision and Curriculum Development (ASCD), offered the following example:

> First grade teachers Gail Canova and Lena Conltey . . . use supported reading activities to help young learners of various abilities strengthen reading skills. On Mondays, [they] read stories to the entire class but break the class into groups according to challenge levels for the next three days. On Fridays, the whole class reviews the story once more to measure improvements and reinforce learning. To help students of differing abilities improve writing skills, [they] have established peer tutoring groups. In the groups, children read their work aloud and help one another with spelling and editing as they create their own books.
>
> Penny Shockly . . . uses tiered assignments to engage her 5th graders at all levels of ability. When she begins the unit on perimeter, area, and volume, [she] first presents a short, hands-on lesson that defines the whole-class objective and lays the foundation for individual practice. Together, she and the students measure various sizes of cereal boxes so that everyone is clear about definitions and processes. Then, in groups of two, students receive activity packets. The more concrete learners receive packets with worksheets that direct them to measure their own desks and classroom furniture. In this highly structured activity, students practice calculating the perimeters, areas, and volumes of things they can actually see and touch. Shockley is on hand to offer help and to extend the activity, for those who are ready, by helping students find a way to arrange the desks so that they have the smallest possible perimeter. Other students with greater abstract reasoning skills receive packets that direct them to design their own bedrooms and to create scale drawings. They also calculate the cost and number of five-yard rolls of wallpaper borders needed to decorate their rooms. From catalogs, they select furniture and rugs that will fit into their model rooms. These details provide extensive practice, beginning with such tasks as determining how many square feet of floor space remain uncovered. This open-ended assignment offers higher-ability students an opportunity to extend their learning as far as they want to take it.
>
> Rob Frescoln, a seventh-grade science teacher, has students whose reading levels range from second through beyond seventh grade. "To help all his students succeed with research papers, [he] provides science texts at several reading levels and uses mixed-ability groupings. Each of five students in a mixed-ability group might research a different cell part by gathering information from books at her own reading level. Then groups split up so that all students with the same cell assignment compare notes and teach one another. Finally, students return to their original groups so that every member of each group can report to the others and learn about the other cell parts. 'It's the coolest thing in the world to see a lower ability kid teaching a higher-ability kid what he's learned,' says Frescoln."
>
> A high school social studies teacher, Leon Bushe uses mock trials to differentiate instruction according to interest, task, and readiness. "Dividing his class of 30 into three groups of 10, [he] gives each a court case involving a legal concept such as *beyond reasonable doubt.* Students choose whether to be lawyers, witnesses, or defendants—whichever they feel most comfortable with. Every student has at least two roles because each trial group also serves as the jury for another trial group. To prepare for their roles, students must complete individualized reading and writing assignments, but they all learn the basics of trial by jury. One factor . . . that heightens interest is that each jury deliberates in a fishbowl environment—that is, the rest of the class gets to observe the deliberations but may not speak or interfere."

Teaming may take the form of

- *Parallel teaching.* Team members combine their classes or other work and teach to their strengths. This may involve specific facets of the curriculum (e.g., one teacher covers math, another reading; they cover different aspects of science) or different students (e.g., for specific activities, they divide the students and work with those to whom each relates to best or can support in the best way).
- *Complementary teaching.* One team member takes the lead with the initial lessons and another facilitates the follow-up activity.
- *Special assistance.* While one team member provides basic instruction, another focuses on those students who need special assistance.

In all forms of teaming, others are involved in the collaborative effort. This includes aides, volunteers, and designated students to help in creating small groupings for teaching and learning. And with access to the Internet and distance learning, the nature and scope of collaboration have the potential to expand in dramatic fashion. Teachers and support staff can work together to recruit and train others to join in the collaborative effort.

Student Helpers

Besides the mutual benefits students get from cooperative learning groups and other informal ways they help each other, formal peer programs can be invaluable assets. Students can be taught to be peer tutors, group discussion leaders, role models, and mentors. Other useful roles include peer buddies (to welcome, orient, and provide social support as a new student transitions into the class and school), peer conflict mediators, and much more. Student helpers benefit their peers, themselves, and the school staff and enhance the school's efforts to create a caring climate and a sense of community.

Volunteers as an Invaluable Resource

Volunteers may help students on a one-to-one basis or in small groups. Group interactions are especially important in enhancing a student's cooperative interactions with peers. One-to-one work is often needed to develop a positive relationship with a particularly aggressive or withdrawn student, in reengaging a student who has disengaged from classroom learning, and in fostering successful task completion with a student easily distracted by peers. Volunteers can help enhance a student's motivation and skills and, at the very least, can help counter negative effects that arise when a student has difficulty adjusting to school. Working under the direction of the teacher and student support staff, they can be especially helpful establishing a supportive relationship with students who are having trouble adjusting to school.

Every teacher has had the experience of planning a wonderful lesson and having the class disrupted by one or two unengaged students. As noted above, properly trained volunteers are a great help in minimizing such disruptions and reengaging an errant student. When a volunteer is trained to focus on designated students, the volunteer knows to watch for and move quickly at the first indication that the student needs special guidance and support. The strategy involves going to sit next to the student and quietly trying to reengage the youngster. If necessary, the volunteer can take the student to a quiet area in the classroom and initiate another type of activity or even go out for a brief walk and talk if this is feasible. None of this is a matter of rewarding the student for bad behavior. Rather, it is a strategy for avoiding the tragedy of disrupting the whole class while the teacher reprimands the culprit and in the process increases that student's negative attitudes toward teaching and school. This use of a volunteer allows teaching to continue, and as soon as time permits, it makes it possible for staff to explore with the student ways to make the classroom a mutually satisfying place to be. Moreover, by handling the matter in this way, the teacher is likely to find the student more receptive to discussing things than if the usual "logical consequences" have been administered (e.g., loss of privileges, sending the student to time-out or to the assistant principal).

Volunteers can be a multifaceted resource in a classroom and throughout a school (see Guide 4.7). For this to be the case, however, the school staff must value volunteers and learn how to recruit, train, nurture, and use them effectively. When implemented properly, school volunteer programs can enable teachers to individualize instruction, free teachers and other school personnel to meet students' needs more effectively, broaden students' experiences through interaction with volunteers, strengthen school-community understanding and relations, enhance home involvement, and enrich the lives of volunteers. In the classroom, volunteers can provide just the type of extra support needed to enable staff to conference and work with students who require special assistance.

Volunteers can be recruited from a variety of sources: parents and other family members, others in the community such as senior citizens and workers in local businesses, college students, and peers and older students at the school. There also are organized programs that can provide volunteers, such as VISTA, America Reads, and local service clubs. And increasingly, institutions of higher education are requiring students to participate in learning through service. Schools committed to enhancing home and community involvement in schooling can pursue volunteer programs as a productive element in their efforts to do so.

Guide 4.7   The Many Roles for Volunteers in the Classroom and Throughout the School

---

I. Welcoming and Social Support
  A. In the front office
    1. Greeting and welcoming
    2. Providing information to those who come to the front desk
    3. Escorting guests, new students/families to destinations on the campus
    4. Orienting newcomers
  B. Staffing a welcoming club
    1. Connecting newly arrived parents with peer buddies
    2. Helping develop orientation and other information resources for newcomers
    3. Helping establish newcomer support groups

II. Working With Designated Students in the Classroom
  A. Helping to orient new students
  B. Engaging disinterested, distracted, and distracting students
  C. Providing personal guidance and support for specific students in class to help them stay focused and engaged

III. Providing Additional Opportunities and Support in Class and on the Campus as a Whole
  A. Recreational activity
  B. Enrichment activity
  C. Tutoring
  D. Mentoring

IV. Helping Enhance the Positive Climate Throughout the School, Including Assisting With "Chores"
  A. Assisting with supervision in class and throughout the campus
  B. Contributing to campus "beautification"
  C. Helping to get materials ready

Before leaving this topic, we want to amplify a bit on a few key ways volunteers are used.

Tutoring

One of the most direct and effective ways to provide extra instructional assistance is through individual and small-group tutoring. Volunteer tutors (including peer tutors and cross-age tutors) provide a way to make such assistance feasible on a large scale. Volunteers who are bilingual provide a special resource for students with limited English skills. They not only can help students with lessons but also can assist with the development of English language skills and can help the teacher communicate with family members. In the case of students tutoring other students, various benefits may accrue for the tutor in terms of enhanced knowledge, skills, attitudes, and behavior.

Planning and Implementing Instruction

As the teacher develops lesson plans and prepares instructional activities, volunteers can help gather resources and contribute any special knowledge and skills they have acquired. During class, they can help support and guide the work of small groups.

Social Support

Throughout any school day and at critical times throughout the school year, students require social as well as academic support. Who needs social support? New students and their families, students who are shy, those who are uncertain about how to make friends, those who feel alienated, those experiencing temporary emotional upsets, those who misbehave, students making the transition to a new grade and classroom, students transitioning back from special education, and many others. Here too peer volunteers can be used. For example, trained peer buddies may commit to a buddy for several weeks—eating lunch together, participating in various activities, and facilitating connections with other students.

Mentoring

It is well known that a good relationship with a caring adult is a fundamental ingredient in helping children succeed. In one form or another, all children need role models and advocates. Ideally, family members fulfill this role; teachers and others who work with young people can do so as well. To expand the range of role models and to ensure that all youngsters do have an advocate, volunteers can be recruited as mentors. Mentoring is another tool in efforts to provide social support and a sense of future options and hope, develop positive behavior and skills, increase engagement in school and life, and reduce school dropout.

Few teachers have the time to recruit and train a cadre of volunteers. Teachers can work with student support staff and the school administration to set up a volunteer program for the school. Initially, a small group of volunteers can be recruited and taught how to implement and maintain the volunteer program (e.g., how to recruit a large pool of volunteers, help train them, nurture them, work with them to recruit replacements when they leave).

The cost of volunteer programs is relatively small compared to the impact they can have on school climate and the quality of life for students and school staff.

CONCLUDING COMMENTS

With respect to improving schools, a major goal of legislation at state and federal levels is to have a qualified teacher in every classroom. New directions for student support can expand that notion to include teamwork that enhances the quality of teaching, learning, and caring in the classroom and schoolwide.

Classroom teaching is not easy. As Patricia Woodin-Weaver (2000) states:

> There's no bigger challenge than trying to insert kids in a one-size-fits-all [classroom] and then having to deal with the spillover of emotional and behavioral reactions. If kids are not in a place where they can learn, they let us know loud and clear. (p. 6)

Or as one colleague put it: "Kids would rather look bad than stupid!"

Good schools and good teaching are essential to preventing many learning and behavior problems at schools, minimizing the impact of those that arise, and providing the foundation upon which correction of problems must be built. Moreover, good teaching in a caring context contains the elements for countering staff burnout.

Finally, as important as the research on *effective* teaching is, we must not lose sight of the fact that *good* teaching encompasses much more. The literature on the elements of effective teaching stresses comparative data showing factors that have produced better outcomes than others. But we must always remember that the term *better* doesn't necessarily mean *good*, and the factors studied have yet to encompass many of the most valued principles that concerned parents and informed citizens want schooling to encapsulate in the best interests of children and society.

We now turn, in Chapter 5, to two specific facets of good teaching: personalizing instruction and providing special assistance as soon as and whenever a student needs it.

REFLECTION AND STIMULUS FOR DISCUSSION

Key Insights About "Classrooms and Teaching Revisited"

Based on what you learned so far,

> *Identify (and discuss) what principles and*
> *practices teachers should adopt to create a positive*
> *context for learning and to facilitate appropriate learning.*

If there is an opportunity for group discussion, you may find the following group process guidelines helpful:

- Start by identifying someone who will facilitate the group interchange.
- Take a few minutes to make a few individual notes on a worksheet.
- Be sure all major points are compiled for sharing with other groups.
- Ask someone else to watch the time so that the group doesn't bog down.

NOTE

1. It is worth noting that the 2004 reauthorization of the Individuals With Disabilities Education Act (IDEA) calls for a "Response to Intervention" (RTI) model that reflects facets of the type of sequential and least-intervention-needed approach diagrammed here and disussed in Chapters 5 and 6. However, the RTI approach focuses narrowly on instruction and particularly what has come to be known as "direct" instruction.

REFERENCES

Adelman, H. S., & Taylor, L. (1994). *On understanding intervention in psychology and education.* Westport, CT: Prager.

Adelman, H. S., & Taylor, L. (1997). System reform to address barriers to learning: Beyond school-linked services and full service schools. *American Journal of Orthopsychiatry, 67,* 408–421.

American Youth Policy Forum. (2000). *High schools of the millennium report.* Washington, DC: Author.

Beauchamp, T. L., Feinberg, J., & Smith, J. M. (1996). *Philosophy and the human condition.* Englewood Cliffs, NJ: Prentice Hall.

Fletcher, J. M., & Reschly, D. J. (2005). Changing procedures for identifying learning disabilities: The danger of perpetuating old ideas. *The School Psychologist, 59,* 10–15.

Fraser, B. J. (1998). Classroom environment instruments: Development, validity, and applications. *Learning Environments Research, 1,* 7–33.

Freiberg, H. J. (Ed.). (1999). *School climate: Measuring, improving, and sustaining healthy learning environments.* London: Falmer Press.

Hargreaves, A. (1994). *Changing teachers, changing times: Teachers' work and culture in the postmodern age.* New York: Teachers College Press.

Hollander, E. P., & Offermann, L. R. (1990). Power and leadership in organizations: Relationships in transition. *American Psychologist, 45,* 179–189.

Joyce, B., & Weil, M. (1980). *Models of teaching.* Boston: Allyn & Bacon.

Mahony, P., & Hextall, I. (2000). *Reconstructing teaching: Standards, performance and accountability.* New York: Routledge Falmer.

McLaughlin, M., & Talbert, I. (1993*). Contexts that matter for teaching and learning.* Stanford, CA: Stanford University.

Moos, R. H. (1979). *Evaluating educational environments.* San Francisco: Jossey-Bass.

Newmann, F., Marks, H., & Gamoran, A. (1996). Authentic pedagogy and student performance. *American Journal of Education, 104,* 280–312.

Richardson, V. (Ed.). (2001). *Handbook of research on teaching* (4th ed.). Washington, DC: American Educational Research Association.

Riger, S. (1993). What's wrong with empowerment. *American Journal of Community Psychology, 21,* 278–292.

Senge, P. (1990*). The fifth discipline: The art and practice of the learning organization.* New York: Currency Doubleday.

Strupp, H. H., & Hadley, S. M. (1977). A tripartite model for mental health and therapeutic outcomes with special reference to negative effects in psychotherapy. *American Psychologist, 32,* 187–196.

Tomlinson, C. A. (1999). *The differentiated classroom: Responding to the needs of all learners.* Alexandria, VA: Association for Supervision and Curriculum Development.

Woodin-Weaver, P. (2000). Cited in S. Willis & L. Mann, Differentiating instruction: Finding manageable ways to meet individual needs. *ASCD Curriculum Update.* Retrieved from www.ascd.org.

Chapter 14 contains a list of special resources related
to the above matters available at no cost from the national
Center for Mental Health in Schools, which is at UCLA and is
directed by the authors of this book. Go to http://smhp.psych.ucla.edu.

Personalizing Learning

5

Let the main object . . . be as follows: To seek and to find a method of instruction, by which teachers may teach less, but learners learn more; by which schools may be the scene of less noise, aversion, and useless labour, but of more leisure, enjoyment, and solid progress.

—Comenius (1632)

I'm thinking of suing the school for unfair practices.

Because you have a disability?

No, because the teacher gave him a D.

ORIENTING QUESTIONS

? How does personalized instruction differ from individualized instruction?
? What are the key features of a personalized classroom?
? Why should personalization precede special assistance?

It is the supreme art of the teacher to awaken joy to creative expression and knowledge.

—Albert Einstein

Teaching is a fascinating and somewhat mysterious process. It is one of the most basic forms of human interaction. We've all been taught; we've all experienced satisfaction when we succeed in helping others learn; and we've all experienced frustration when those we teach don't "get it."

Frustration is a common feeling when teaching doesn't go smoothly. The frustration often leads to a conclusion that something is wrong with the students—a lack of effort (*they would have learned it if they had really been trying*)—or a lack of ability (*they would have learned if they were smarter or didn't have LD or ADHD*).

Sometimes the frustration isn't just with a particular individual; it is with the poor performance at school of large numbers of children and adolescents. Such frustration leads to conclusions that something is wrong with the schools (*teachers need to get back to basics! Teachers need to be held accountable*) or with certain groups of people (*these youngsters do badly because their parents don't value education*).

The frustration is more than understandable. And with the frustration has come accusations and blaming. Blaming, of course, does not solve the problem. Neither does just demanding higher standards and accepting no excuses. If legislation is to produce good outcomes, it must support classrooms and schools in ways that help school staff effectively pursue the art, craft, and science of teaching. The intent in this and the next chapter is to outline a framework that encompasses regular instruction and special assistance. We begin with general strategies for personalizing instruction and mobilizing active learning.

THE CONCEPT OF PERSONALIZED INSTRUCTION

We have already introduced the concept of the match as applied to teaching (meeting learners where they are—in terms of both their motivation and capabilities). This also is referred to as the problem of "fit." For the most part, any of us can only approximate an *optimal* match. When we teach, we strive to design instruction that is a close enough fit for good learning. The best approximation probably is achieved through personalized instruction.

Even in the best classrooms, there can be a serious mismatch (a very poor fit), which results in students not learning what they are taught. As discussed in Part I, many factors can produce such a mismatch. Indeed, the possibilities are so extensive it is hardly surprising we all have occasions when learning is a problem.

When a teacher finds it difficult to create an appropriate match for any given student over many days, significant learning problems develop. With the learning problems comes emotional overlay and often behavior problems. It doesn't take long for a teacher to realize which students need special assistance.

Defining Personalization

For some time, efforts to improve the match for learning in the classroom have revolved around the concepts of individualized or personalized instruction. The two concepts overlap in their emphasis on developmental differences. Indeed, the major thrust in most *individualized* approaches is to account for individual differences in developmental capability. *Personalization,* however, is defined as the process of accounting for individual differences in both capability and motivation.

For motivated learners, either individualized or personalized instruction can be quite effective in helping learners attain their goals. Sometimes all that is needed is to provide the opportunity to learn. At other times, teaching facilitates learning by leading, guiding, stimulating, clarifying, and supporting. Both approaches require knowing when, how, and what to teach and when and how to structure the situation so students can learn on their own.

For students with learning, behavior, and emotional problems, motivation for classroom learning often has become a problem. In such cases, motivation is a primary consideration, and the concept of personalization provides the best guide to practice (and research).

Personalization needs to be understood as a psychological construct. From a motivational perspective, the *learner's perception* is a critical factor in defining whether the environment is a good fit. Given this, the key to a good match is ensuring that learning opportunities are *perceived by learners* as good ways to reach their goals. And therefore, a basic assessment concern is that of eliciting learners' perceptions of how well teaching and learning environments match both their interests and abilities.

Outlined in Guide 5.1 are the underlying assumptions and major program elements of personalized programs (Adelman & Taylor, 1993, 1994). Properly

Guide 5.1   Underlying Assumptions and Major Program Elements of a Personalized Program

1. Underlying Assumptions

The following are basic assumptions underlying personalized programs as we conceive them.

- Learning is a function of the ongoing transactions between the learner and the learning environment.
- Optimal learning is a function of an optimal match between the learner's accumulated capacities and attitudes and current state of being and the program's processes and context.
- Matching both learner motivation and capacities must be primary procedural objectives.
- The learner's perception is the critical criterion for evaluating whether a good match exists between the learner and the learning environment.
- The wider the range of options that can be offered and the more the learner is made aware of the options and has a choice about which to pursue, the greater the likelihood that he or she will perceive the match as a good one.
- Besides improved learning, personalized programs enhance intrinsic valuing of learning and a sense of personal responsibility for learning. Furthermore, such programs increase acceptance and even appreciation of individual differences, as well as independent and cooperative functioning and problem solving.

2. Program Elements

Major elements of personalized programs as we have identified them are

- Regular use of informal and formal conferences for discussing options, making decisions, exploring learners' perceptions, and mutually evaluating progress
- A broad range of options from which learners can make choices with regard to types of learning content, activities, and desired outcomes
- A broad range of options from which learners can make choices with regard to facilitation (support, guidance) of decision making and learning
- Active decision making by learners in making choices and in evaluating how well the chosen options match their motivation and capability
- Establishment of program plans and mutual agreements about the ongoing relationships between the learners and the program personnel
- Regular reevaluations of decisions, reformulation of plans, and renegotiation of agreements based on mutual evaluations of progress, problems, and learners' perceptions of the "match"

designed and carried out, such programs can reduce the need for special assistance. That is, matching motivation and developmental capability can be a sufficient condition for learning among youngsters whose difficulties are not due to interfering internal factors, such as a true disability.

Personalizing regular classroom programs also can improve the effectiveness of prevention, inclusion, mainstreaming, and prereferral interventions.

In such classrooms, personalization represents a regular classroom application of the principle of least intervention needed (which encompasses the concept of "least restrictive environment").

Enhancing Motivation Is a Core Concern

Matt and Jerry both are in Mr. Phillips's class. Jerry may not say so in so many words, but the class seems to fit him very well. He likes most of what he does in class each day, and he finds it just challenging enough (not too easy and not too hard). All indications suggest that he experiences the situation as a good match motivationally and developmentally. And this should continue as long as the situation changes in ways that reflect his ongoing learning and development.

Matt finds few things to like about the class. Although the teacher planned remedial activities that Matt is able to do rather easily, they don't interest him. He is bored and feels unhappy. From his perspective, the learning environment is not a good one.

By now it should be evident that at its core, personalized instruction is about attending as much to motivational differences as to differences in capabilities. Indeed, there are instances when the primary focus is on motivation. For this reason and because the practices used in too many schools still reflect a limited appreciation of human motivation, we need to reiterate and build on ideas we touched upon in Chapter 3.

No one has control over all the important elements involved in facilitating learning. Teachers and other school staff actually affect a small portion of the various environments in which learning occurs (e.g., classrooms, school, home, and neighborhood). Because this is so, it is essential that teachers and support staff begin with an appreciation of what is likely to affect a student's positive and negative motivation to learn. The following points warrant particular attention:

1. Optimal Performance and Learning Require Motivational Readiness

Readiness is understood in terms of offering stimulating environments where learning can be perceived as vivid, valued, and attainable.

Motivation is a key antecedent condition in any learning situation. It is a prerequisite to student attention, involvement, and performance. Poor motivational readiness may be a cause of poor learning and a factor in maintaining learning, behavior, and emotional problems. Thus, strategies are called for that can result in a high level of motivational readiness (including reduction of avoidance motivation) so students are mobilized to participate.

2. Motivation Represents Both a Process and an Outcome Concern

Individuals may value learning something but may not be motivated to pursue the processes used. Many students are motivated to learn when they first encounter a topic but do not maintain that motivation.

Processes must elicit, enhance, and maintain motivation so that students stay mobilized. Programs must be designed to maintain, enhance, and expand intrinsic motivation for pursuing current learning activities and also for involving students in learning activities that go beyond the immediate lesson and extend beyond the schoolhouse door.

Negative motivation and avoidance reactions and any conditions likely to generate them must be circumvented or at least minimized. Of particular concern are activities students perceive as unchallenging, uninteresting, overdemanding, or overwhelming. We all react against structures that seriously limit our range of options or that are overcontrolling and coercive. Examples of conditions that can have a negative impact on a person's motivation are sparse resources, excessive rules, and a restrictive day-in, day-out emphasis on drill and remediation.

Students with learning, behavior, and/or emotional problems usually have extremely negative perceptions of and avoidance tendencies toward teachers and activities that look like "the same old thing." Major changes in approach must be made if such students are to change these perceptions. Ultimately, success may depend on the degree to which the students view the adults at school and in the classroom as supportive, rather than indifferent or controlling, and the program as personally valuable and obtainable.

3. School Staff Not Only Need to Try to Increase Motivation—Especially Intrinsic Motivation—But Also to Avoid Practices That Decrease It

Although students may learn a specific lesson (e.g., some basic skills) at school, they may have little or no interest in using newly acquired knowledge and skills outside of the classroom.

Increasing intrinsic motivation requires focusing on students' thoughts, feelings, and decisions. In general, the intent is to use procedures that can reduce negative and increase positive feelings, thoughts, and coping strategies. With learning and behavior problems, it is especially important to identify and minimize experiences that maintain or may increase avoidance motivation. Of particular concern is the need to avoid overreliance on extrinsics to entice and reward, since such strategies can decrease intrinsic motivation.

The point is to enhance stable, positive, intrinsic attitudes that mobilize the ongoing pursuit of desired ends in the classroom, throughout the school, and away from school. Developing intrinsic attitudes is basic to increasing the type of motivated practice, for example, reading for pleasure, that is essential for mastering and assimilating what has just been learned.

Clearly, personalization's emphasis on motivation has fundamental intervention implications. In particular, it calls for offering a broad range of content, outcomes, and procedural *options*, including a personalized structure to facilitate learning. With real options come real opportunities for *involving learners in decision making.* The focus on motivation also stresses the importance of developing nonthreatening ways to provide *ongoing information about learning and performance.* We have more to say about these matters later in the chapter.

Personalization First; Add Special Assistance if Necessary

A sequential and hierarchical framework can guide efforts to provide a good match and determine the least intervention needed for individuals with learning and behavior problems (see Guide 5.2). The first step focuses on changing regular classrooms if they are not designed to personalize instruction. The changes are meant to create a caring context for learning and introduce personalized instruction so that the program is highly responsive to learner differences in motivation and development. With this in place, the next step involves providing special assistance as needed. That is, Step 2 is introduced only if learners continue to have problems. As outlined in Guide 5.2, this second step involves three levels. These are discussed in Chapter 6.

SOME KEY FEATURES OF A PERSONALIZED CLASSROOM

While the framework looks linear, we all know that learning is an ongoing, dynamic, and transactional process. As students change, we must recognize the changes and ensure that practices are a good match. We view this in terms of a set of procedural objectives.

For example, a primary procedural objective in teaching is to establish and maintain an appropriate working relationship with students. This is done by creating a sense of trust and caring, open communication, and providing support and guidance as needed. A basic aspect is clarifying the purpose of learning activities and processes (especially those designed to help correct specific problems) and why processes will be effective.

Guide 5.2   Teaching Sequence and Levels

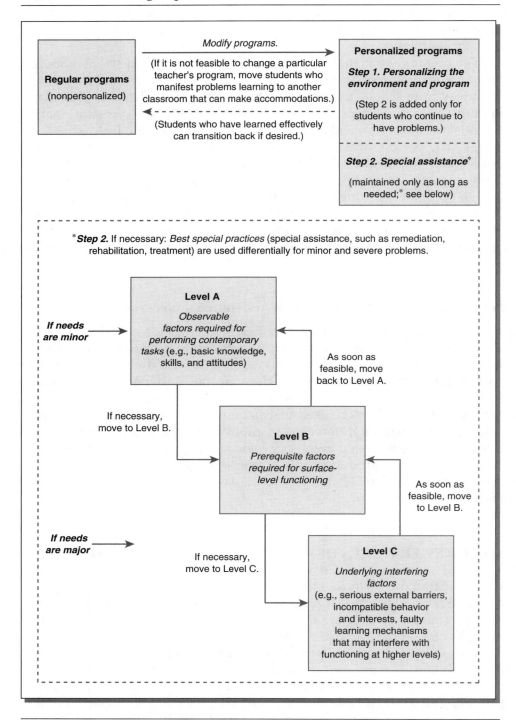

SOURCE: Adapted from H. S. Adelman and L. Taylor (1993).

Examples of other procedural objectives are to

- Clarify the nature and purpose of evaluative processes and apply them in ways that de-emphasize feelings of failure (e.g., explaining to students the value of feedback about learning and performance; providing feedback in ways that minimize any negative impact).
- Guide and support motivated practice (e.g., by suggesting and providing opportunities for meaningful applications and clarifying ways to organize practice).
- Provide opportunities for continued application and generalization (e.g., so learners can pursue additional, self-directed learning in the area or can arrange for additional support and direction).

Classroom teaching, of course, requires focusing on more than one procedure at a time. In general, procedures and content are tightly interwoven means to an end. And with advanced technology (e.g., computers, video), many new means are available for blending content and process into personalized activities.

Providing Personalized Structure for Learning

In talking about classroom structure, some people seem to see it as all or nothing—structured or unstructured. The tendency also is to equate structure simply with limit setting and social control. Such practices tend to produce vicious cycles. The emphasis on control can have a negative impact on students' motivation (e.g., producing psychological reactance), which makes it harder to teach and control them. As long as students do not value the classroom, the teacher, and the activities, poor learning and inappropriate behavior are likely outcomes. This increasingly can lead school staff to push, prod, and punish. Such a cycle results in the whole enterprise of schooling taking on a negative tone for students and staff.

The view of structure as social control is particularly prevalent in responding to student misbehavior. In such cases, it is common for observers to say that youngsters need "more structure." Sometimes the phrase used is "clearer limits and consequences," but the idea is the same. Youngsters are seen as being out of control, and the solution—more control.

Most teachers wish it were that easy. Obviously, it is not possible to facilitate the learning of youngsters who are out of control. Also obvious is the reality that some procedures used to control behavior interfere with efforts to facilitate learning. A teacher cannot teach youngsters sent out of the classroom or suspended from school; students may be less receptive to the teacher upon returning to class.

In general, efforts to use external means to control behavior (e.g., isolating students in a time-out situation, sending them for discipline) are incompatible with developing working relationships that facilitate learning.

Using the term *structure* to describe extreme efforts to control behavior fails to recognize that the objective is to facilitate learning and performance, not just control behavior.

Good teaching involves a definition of structure that goes well beyond how much control a teacher has over students. Structure must be viewed as *the type of support, guidance, and direction provided the learner, and encompasses all efforts to clarify essential information—including communication of limits as necessary.* Structure can be *personalized* by varying it to match learners' current motivation and capabilities with respect to specific tasks and circumstances.

Good support and guidance in the classroom allows for active interactions between students and their environment, and these interactions are meant to lead to relatively stable, positive, ongoing working relationships. How positive the relationships are depends on how learners perceive the communications, support, guidance, direction, and limit setting. Negative perceptions often lead to avoidance behavior and poor working relationships.

Figuring out the best way to provide personalized structure is one of the most important problems a teacher faces in building working relationships with students. The problem is how to make the structure neither too controlling nor too permissive. Good schools do not want to create an authoritarian atmosphere, and no one working in a school wants to be pushed around. Most school staff find that a positive working relationship requires mutual respect; a warm working relationship requires mutual caring and understanding.

Personalizing classroom structure involves providing a great deal of support and guidance for students when they need it and averting a classroom climate that is experienced by students as tight and controlling. For instance, it is clear that when students misbehave, staff must respond immediately—but the emphasis needs to be on enhancing personalized structure rather than simply on punishment. Yes, the students have gone beyond allowable limits; there must be some logical and reasonable consequence. At the same time, a focus simply on reemphasizing limits (e.g., the rules) and enforcing them is counterproductive. Such situations must be handled in ways that do not increase student disengagement with school learning; even better, the goal is to enhance engagement. This requires responding in the most positive and matter-of-fact way.

The process begins by enhancing the amount of support, guidance, and direction provided in ways that keep students focused on learning. As discussed later in the chapter, volunteers, aides, or student support staff can be used to positively engage disruptive students at the first sign of problems. Then, as soon as feasible, offending students can be encouraged to dialogue about *why* the misbehavior occurred and what needs to be done to prevent future occurrences (including decisions about consequences now and in the future). The message is: *We all make mistakes at times; we just need to find a way to make things better.* The tone is: *We can still respect and like each other and work together after we do a bit of problem solving.* (Chapter 6 provides further discussion about responding to behavior problems.)

With respect to staff-student communication in general, it is important not only to keep students informed but also to interact in ways that consistently convey a sense of appropriate and genuine warmth, interest, concern, and respect. The intent is to help students "know their own minds," make their own decisions, and at the same time feel that others like and care about them.

A personalized approach encourages students to take as much responsibility as they can for identifying the types and degree of structure they require. Some request a great amount of support and guidance; others prefer to work autonomously. Some like lots of help on certain tasks but want to be left alone at other times. Many activities can be pursued without help, and should be, if the learners are to attain and maintain independence. Other tasks require considerable help if learning is to occur. Although teachers currently are the primary source of support and guidance in classrooms, new directions for student support call for student support staff teaming with teachers. Such personnel would be invaluable in training aides, other students, and volunteers to provide special support and guidance so that classroom structure can be varied to meet learners' needs.

When a continuum of structure is made available and students are able to indicate their preferences, the total environment appears less confining. The main point of personalizing structure is to provide a high level of support and guidance for students when they need it and to avoid creating a classroom climate that is experienced by students as tight and controlling. Such an approach is a great aid in establishing positive working relationships and provides a basis for turning big classes into smaller units.

GOSH, MRS. THOMPSON, I WAS READY TO LEARN MATH YESTERDAY. TODAY I'M READY TO LEARN TO READ.

Options and Learner Decision Making

From a motivational perspective, a basic instructional concern is the way in which students are involved in making decisions about options. Decision-making processes can lead to perceptions of coercion and control or to perceptions of real choice (being in control of one's destiny, being self-determining). Such differences in perception can affect whether a student is mobilized to pursue or avoid planned learning activities or outcomes.

People who have the opportunity to make decisions among valued and feasible options tend to be committed to follow through. In contrast, people who are not involved in decisions often have little commitment to what is decided. If individuals disagree with a decision that affects them, they may also react with hostility.

Thus, decision-making processes that affect perceptions of choice, value, and probable outcome are essential to programs focusing on motivation. Optimally, teachers hope to maximize perceptions of having a choice from among personally worthwhile options and attainable outcomes. At the very least, they want to minimize perceptions of having no choice, little value, and probable failure (Aregalado, Bradley, & Lane, 1996; Passe, 1996).

> In Ms. Hopkins's classroom, David, Maria, James, and Matt all have reading problems David refuses to have anything to do with reading. Maria wants to improve her reading, but on most days she just doesn't like any of the materials she is given. James indicates he will read about science but nothing else. Matt will try anything if someone will sit and help him with the work.

Students differ in important ways with respect to topics and procedures that currently interest or bore them. Clearly, motivation is a primary consideration in facilitating the learning of David, Maria, James, and Matt. As we have stressed, the place to start generally involves expanding the range of options related to content, processes, outcomes, and support so that these youngsters perceive classroom activity as a good fit with what they value and believe they can do.

Every teacher knows the value of variety. For students with learning and behavior problems, more variety seems necessary than for those without problems. Moreover, among those with problems are a greater proportion of individuals with avoidance or low motivation for learning at school. For these individuals, few currently available options may be appealing.

How much greater the range of options needs to be depends mainly on how strong avoidance tendencies are. In general, however, initial strategies involve expansion of the range of learning options, with a primary emphasis on areas in which the student has made personal and active decisions. And initially, reengaging such students in classroom learning almost always requires accommodation of a wider range of behavior than usually is tolerated.

For students who seem impulsive and easily distracted, enhancing options and decision making are key to determining whether the problem is mostly motivational. True learning disabilities (LD) and ADHD should only be diagnosed when a student is well motivated to learn and perform and is unable to stay focused. We discuss all this in more detail in Chapter 6.

Turning Homework Into Motivated Practice

Most of us have had the experience of wanting to be good at something such as playing a musical instrument or participating in a sport. We soon learned that becoming good at it meant a great deal of practice, and practicing often wasn't fun. In the face of this fact, many of us turned to other pursuits. In some cases, individuals are compelled by parents to labor on, and many of these sufferers grow to dislike the activity. (A few, of course, later may commend their parents for pushing them, but be assured these are a small minority. Ask your friends who were compelled to practice the piano.)

Becoming good at reading, mathematics, writing, and other academic pursuits requires practice outside the classroom. This, of course, is called *homework.* Properly designed, homework can benefit students. Inappropriately designed homework can lead to avoidance, parent-child conflicts, teacher disapproval, and student dislike of various arenas of learning. Well-designed homework involves assignments that emphasize motivated practice.

As with all learning processes that engage students, motivated practice requires designing activities that students perceive as worthwhile and doable with an appropriate amount of effort (National Research Council and the Institute of Medicine, 2004). In effect, the intent is to personalize in-class practice and homework. This does not mean every student has a different practice activity. Good teachers quickly learn what their students find engaging, and they can provide three or four practice options that will be effective for most students in a class.

Motivated practice is especially important in helping students overcome learning and behavior problems. Students with reading deficits, for example, are unlikely to overcome deficits and become good readers if they do not practice.

Facilitating motivated practice minimally requires establishing a variety of task options that are potentially challenging—neither too easy nor too hard. However, as we have stressed, the processes by which tasks are chosen must lead to perceptions on the part of the learner that practice activities, task outcomes, or both are worthwhile, especially as potential sources of personal satisfaction.

The examples in Guide 5.3 illustrate ways in which activities can be varied to provide for motivated learning and practice. Because most people have experienced a variety of reading and writing activities, the focus here is on other types of activity. Students can be encouraged to pursue such activity with classmates and/or family members. Friends

Guide 5.3 Homework and Motivated Practice

Learning and practicing by

1. Doing

- The use of movement and manipulation of objects to explore a topic (e.g., using coins to learn to add and subtract)
- Dramatization of events (e.g., historical, current)
- Role playing and simulations (e.g., learning about democratic vs. autocratic government by trying different models in class; learning about contemporary life and finances by living on a budget)
- Actual interactions (e.g., learning about human psychology through analysis of daily behavior)
- Applied activities (e.g., school newspapers, film and video productions, band, sports)
- Actual work experience (e.g., on-the-job learning)

2. Listening

- Time for reading to students (e.g., to enhance their valuing of literature)
- Audio media (e.g., tapes, records, and radio presentations of music, stories, events)
- Listening games and activities (e.g., Simon Says; imitating rhymes, rhythms, and animal sounds)
- Analysis of actual oral material (e.g., learning to detect details and ideas in advertisements or propaganda presented on radio or television, learning to identify feelings and motives underlying statements of others)

3. Looking

- Direct observation of experts, role models, and demonstrations
- Visual media
- Visual games and activities (e.g., puzzles, reproducing designs, map activities)
- Analysis of actual visual material (e.g., learning to find and identify ideas observed in daily events)

4. Asking

- Information gathering (e.g., investigative reporting, interviewing, and opinion sampling at school and in the community)
- Brainstorming of answers to current problems and puzzling questions
- Inquiry learning (e.g., learning social studies and science by identifying puzzling questions, formulating hypotheses, gathering and interpreting information, generalizing answers, and raising new questions)
- Question-and-answer games and activities (e.g., 20 Questions, provocative and confrontational questions)
- The questioning of everyday events (e.g., learning about a topic by asking people about how it affects their lives)

with common interests can provide positive models and support that enhance productivity and even creativity.

Research on motivation indicates that one of the most powerful factors keeping a person on task is the expectation of feeling some sense of satisfaction when the task is completed. Task persistence results, for example, from the expectation that one will feel smart or competent while performing the task or at least will feel that way after the skill is mastered.

Within some limits, the stronger the sense of potential outcome satisfaction, the more likely practice will be pursued even when practice activities are rather dull. The weaker the sense of potential outcome satisfaction, the more the practice activities must be inherently motivating.

One other point: the most motivated practice stems from a desire to use what one has learned. The reason so many people are good readers probably has less to do with specific teaching approaches than with the fact that they were motivated to read at home. In contrast, youngsters who have reading problems have difficulty overcoming their deficits because their motivation for reading has been dampened and they do not pursue reading away from the classroom. A problem with overrelying on extrinsic motivators in providing special reading assistance to such youngsters is that such strategies don't seem to enhance their intrinsic motivation for reading. As a consequence, they may learn to read twenty new words and various other skills at school and still not go home and use what they have learned, other than perhaps to do some assigned homework task. The result is that they are unlikely to become good readers.

Will you do my homework for me?

No! It wouldn't be right!

That's okay. I don't get them all right either.

Conferencing as a Key Process

The ability to talk *with* rather than *at* a student is critical for successful teaching. Talking *with* involves a true dialogue—which, of course, depends on each participant's truly listening to and hearing the other. Personalized instruction is built on a base that appreciates what each student is thinking and feeling, and carrying on an ongoing dialogue with students offers the best opportunity to learn about such matters.

The mechanism for carrying on dialogues often is called a *conference*. However, the term does not convey the full sense of what is involved and at times, is interpreted in ways contrary to the meaning used here. From a motivational perspective, conferences should be nurturing experiences designed to give, share, and clarify useful information as the teacher or a team member and a student plan the next steps for learning and teaching.

Conferences provide a time and context for

- Exploring progress and problems
- Clarifying and sampling options for pursuing the next steps for learning and solving problems
- Planning and making decisions together
- Modifying previous decisions whenever necessary

The importance of the dialogue as a two-way process cannot be overemphasized. A conference should be a time for persons to say what they need, want, and are hoping for from each other. When problems exist, time should be devoted to problem solving. Conferences vary in length, depending first on how much time is available and then on how much time is needed by a specific student.

Even when a teacher or team member can carve out time, one conference often is insufficient for arriving at a full-blown plan and related decisions. Therefore, the process is ongoing and not always done in a formal manner. Indeed, some of the best dialogues are spontaneous (e.g., occur when a teacher or team member takes time to sit down next to a student during class for an informal chat). For some students, several informal chats need to occur each day backed up by a formal conference every few days. Such impromptu conferences are particularly feasible when the classroom is designed to maximize the use of small-group and independent learning activities.

Some students like to keep *dialogue journals* as an aid for conferencing. Usually, a dialogue journal is a bound composition book in which the student carries on a conversation with the teacher or a team member. They write to each other in a direct and informal manner about matters of mutual concern relevant to making learning in the classroom better. This mechanism not only can facilitate communication, but it also provides motivated practice related to writing and reading. And as with face-to-face conferences, it encourages self-evaluation and critical reflection.

A few ideas and guidelines for conferencing are presented in Guide 5.4.

Participating in conferences can enhance a student's feelings of competence, self-determination, and connectedness to the school's staff. Conferencing is pivotal in enhancing student engagement and reengagement in learning. Through talking with a student, a teacher or team member can convey a sense of positive regard and gain a richer understanding of the status and bases for a student's current levels of motivation and capability. For example, dialogues yield information on motivational factors (e.g., student hopes, goals, desires, interests, attitudes, preferences, expectations,

Guide 5.4   Some Guidelines for Conferencing

---

1. Scheduling

Each day the teacher or another team member can plan to meet formally with about five individuals. The list for the day is generated as a combination of students who request a meeting and students with whom the staff asks to meet. Sometimes a decision may be made to hold a group conference when the focus is on matters that can benefit from a group discussion. Students are asked to sign up for specific times and to take responsibility for preparing for and coming to the designated place for the conference.

Another variation, particularly for the secondary level, uses a "conferencing teacher" for a group of students. Every teacher and student support staff member are assigned a set of students. They conference with these students every two weeks to review how their entire schedule is working out, review work samples (portfolios), and record progress.

2. Involving Parents

Periodically, staff-student conferences should involve parents or parent surrogates. Here too care must be taken to ensure that true dialogues take place and that mutual sharing, planning, and decision making are intended. These conferences can take place at designated times and as needed. Because face-to-face conferences are costly and difficult to arrange, phone and e-mail exchanges need to become the rule rather than the exception. Although not always feasible, conferences with family members should include the student. Indeed, a good idea is that of student-led parent-staff conferences.

3. Some Process Guidelines

- Start out on a positive note: Ask about what the student currently likes at school and in the class and clarify areas of strength. (During first conferences, ask about outside interests, hobbies, areas of success.)
- In exploring current progress, be certain to ask the student about the reasons for his or her successes.
- In exploring current problems, be certain to ask the student about the reasons for the problems (including what aspects he or she doesn't like about school and the class). Clarify details about these matters (e.g., Are assignments seen as too hard? Is the student embarrassed because others will think he or she does not have the ability to do assignments? Are the assignments not seen as interesting? No support at home? Are there problems with peers or at home?).
- When necessary, use some of the time to analyze academic abilities and learning styles (e.g., listen to the student read aloud, review and discuss the work in a student's portfolio).
- Explore what the student thinks can be done to make things better (e.g., different assignments, extra support from a volunteer/peer, etc.).
- Arrive at some mutual agreements that the student values and expects to be able to do with a reasonable amount of effort.

concerns) that should be considered in all planning. Dialogues also provide other information about who the student is as an individual (e.g., personal and family background and/or current life events that have relevance to current behavior and learning).

Properly conducted conferences convey positive regard, valuing of the student's perspective, and belief that the student should play a meaningful role in defining options and making decisions. Conferences also are one of the best contexts for providing feedback in a nurturing way and for conveying the staff's sincere desire to help the student succeed.

Assessment to Plan; Feedback to Nurture

Assessment is used for a variety of purposes in schools. It is used to screen and identify those who need special assistance; it is used to help make decisions about a special placement for a student; it is used to evaluate programs and personnel. But from a teaching perspective, the main use is to help plan instruction and provide feedback in ways that enhance learning.

Planning Instruction

Different views about how to design instruction for specific learners lead to divergent assessment plans. For instance, from the perspective of personalized instruction, student assessments inadequately address motivation and lead to faulty instructional planning.

To clarify the point, *individualization* typically emphasizes detecting a student's deficiencies by monitoring daily performance on learning tasks and then modifying instruction to address the deficiencies. In addition, some approaches, such as dynamic assessment, attempt to assess the best teaching approach for a given child. In most cases, however, a major shortcoming is the overemphasis on developmental deficiencies and the underemphasis on motivation, especially intrinsic motivation. The concept of *personalization*, which encompasses individualization, broadens the focus of assessment to include motivational considerations.

Many experts also caution that among those not doing well in school, poor performance often is due to low motivation or high anxiety. In such cases, assessment findings are "contaminated." It is impossible to know whether failure to demonstrate an ability or skill represents a real deficiency in a particular area of development. Under such circumstances, it is easy to misprescribe what a student needs. It is, for example, not uncommon to assess a problem as due to skill deficiencies and design a program to teach "missing" skills—instead of helping overcome psychological problems interfering with performance.

Given that teachers and support staff should assess both motivation and capabilities, increasing efforts have gone into exploring how to help them do so. One direction focuses on enhancing available tools. As Shepard (cited in Kirst, 1991) notes:

A broader range of assessment tools is needed to capture important learning goals and processes and to more directly connect assessment to ongoing instruction. The most obvious reform has been to devise more open-ended performance tasks to ensure that students are able to reason critically, to solve complex problems, and to apply their knowledge in real-world contexts. . . . In order for assessment to play a more useful role in helping students learn it should be moved into the middle of the teaching and learning process instead of being postponed as only the end-point of instruction. (p. 21)

In terms of broadening the range of tools, Shepard stresses inclusion of observations, interviews, open discussion ("instructional conversations"), reflective journals, projects, demonstrations, collections of student work, and students' self-evaluations.

Beyond tools is the matter of how assessment is pursued. In designing instruction, assessment must reflect student learning, achievement, motivation, and attitudes on instructionally relevant classroom activities. One of the best ways to think about pursuing such assessment is to view it as an *interactive* process. As captured by the notions of "dynamic" and "authentic" assessment, interactive assessment involves not only reviewing products but clarifying, through observation and discussion, learners' responses to specific efforts to guide and support performance and learning. Such concepts and the traditional psychological testing idea of "testing the limits" are the genesis of recommendations for using "response to intervention" as a basis for differential diagnoses of LD and ADHD.

"Authentic" assessment also has been proposed as a special approach to assessing complex performance. The process focuses on performance-based evaluation using such tools as essays, open-ended responses, responses to computer simulations, interview data, and analyses of student journals and work that is accumulated over time in a portfolio. The information garnered from such assessments helps to design the next steps related to both what and how to teach.

Providing Nurturing Feedback

As anyone who has been evaluated knows, feedback can enhance one's sense of well-being, but too often it is devastating. Relatedly, when rewards and punishment are tied to feedback, they can complicate the situation greatly. In both cases, the impact can be negative (e.g., too great an emphasis on extrinsic rewards and punishment can be counterproductive to maintaining and enhancing intrinsic motivation). For these reasons, great care must be taken in providing information on progress; procedures that may be perceived as efforts to entice and control should be avoided. As much as feasible, we emphasize success, including feedback on effectiveness in making decisions, and underscore how well the outcomes match the student's intrinsic reasons for pursuing them. And with a view to enhancing positive attitudes, feedback is conveyed in ways that nurture the student's feelings about self, learning, school, and teachers. *Handled well, the information should contribute to the student's feelings of competence, self-determination, and relatedness and should clarify directions for future progress.*

A good context for providing feedback is a student conference, formal or informal. At such times, products and work samples can be analyzed; the appropriateness of current content, outcomes, processes, and structure can be reviewed; agreements and schedules can be evaluated and revised as necessary. Staff-student dialogues and group open discussions often are the easiest and most direct way to find out learners' views of the match between themselves and the program.

Regardless of the format in which feedback is given, the point is to maintain student motivation and feelings of well-being while providing appropriate information to improve learning. For students who make many errors, this means providing support and guidance that anticipates and strives to prevent errors and also gives feedback selectively. In this last respect, the emphasis is on errors that must be reviewed because they are most relevant to planning the next instructional encounter. Others can be ignored until a later time. In all this, student self-monitoring, record keeping, and self-evaluation are especially helpful; close supervision and external rewards are used sparingly.

Many students are ready to evaluate and say what's working well for them and what isn't; others need to develop the ability to do so. This is especially so for those motivated to make excuses, to overstate how well they are doing, or to avoid discussing the matter at all. The presence of students who have trouble with self-evaluation is not a reason to return to procedures that stress close supervision and unilateral adult decision making. When students are not motivated to appropriately self-evaluate and be self-directive, they need opportunities to find out how personally valuable these basic skills can be. Sometimes all they need is to feel it's safe to say what's on their minds. If they already feel safe and just haven't acquired the skills, self-monitoring and regular record keeping provide a good framework for learning such competence.

An example may help further clarify the matter.

Matt wants to improve his spelling. From various options, he has chosen to learn five interesting words each day, which he will pick for himself from his experiences at school or at home. He agrees to bring a list of his five chosen words to school each day.

On the first day, Matt shows up without his list. "I lost it," he explains. The next day, still no list. "We had to go visit my grandmother; she's sick."

Naturally, Ms. Evans, his teacher, is suspicious. She knows that many students with learning problems use elaborate excuses and blame everything but themselves for their poor performance. Her first thought is, Matt is telling tales. He really doesn't want to work on his spelling. He's lazy. Probably I should assign him spelling words.

But then she thinks, Suppose he's telling the truth. And even if he isn't, what will I accomplish by accusing him of lying and by going back to procedures that I know were unsuccessful in working with him before. I must work with what he says and try to help him see that there are other ways to cope besides saying he will do something and then giving excuses for not following through.

Ms. Evans tells Matt, "I want you to think about your program. If you don't want to work on spelling, that's okay. Or if you want to choose another way to work on it, we can figure out a new way. I won't check up on what you do. When we meet, you can just let me know how you're doing and what help you want."

Matt seemed greatly relieved by this. The next day he told Ms. Evans that he'd decided to find his five words at school each day, and he'd like some help in doing so.

About Instructional Techniques to Enhance Learning

As discussed above, some degree of structure is inherent in all planned activities. To enhance student engagement and guide learning and performance, teachers often want to make activities more attractive and accessible and to minimize interfering factors (factors that lead to avoidance and distraction). This is accomplished through various techniques.

Techniques alter the structure provided for an activity. The same activity can be pursued with different degrees of support and direction by varying the amount of cueing and prompting. Some variations are built in when an activity is developed (such as special formatting in published materials); others are added as the activity is pursued. Practice activities present a special concern because they often involve the type of drill that people find dull and prefer to avoid.

From a psychological perspective, techniques are intended to enhance

- Motivation (attitudes, commitment, approach, follow-through)
- Sensory intake (perceptual search and detection)
- Processing and decision making (evaluation and selection)
- Output (practice, application, demonstration)

For our purposes, we group techniques into two sets: (1) techniques to enhance motivation and (2) techniques used to guide performance and learning. All such techniques can enhance a student's feelings of competence, self-determination, and connectedness and minimize threats to such feelings.

Using Techniques to Enhance Motivation

The foundation for enhancing student motivation is establishing a classroom climate that students experience as caring, supportive, and interesting, and as a place where they feel competent, valued, and respected. This involves

- A degree of nurturance on the part of school staff
- Creating an atmosphere that encourages exploration and change
- Ensuring a sense of protection related to such exploration and change

It also involves providing support and guidance that facilitates effectiveness.

In terms of valuing, the focus can be on intrinsics, extrinsics, or both. However, as we have stressed, care must be taken not to overrely on extrinsics. Efforts to enhance relevance (e.g., making tasks authentic, stressing their personal meaning and value) are consistent with an emphasis on intrinsic motivation, as are strategies that emphasize use of novelty to stimulate curiosity. Specific examples of techniques for use in enhancing motivation are listed in Guide 5.5.

Using Techniques to Support and Guide Performance and Learning

In designing curricula and instruction, techniques are used to support and guide performance and learning by enhancing *sensory intake, processing, decision making,* and *output.* All this is accomplished through techniques that (a) stress meaning, (b) provide appropriate structure, (c) encourage active contact and use, and (d) offer appropriate feedback. Specific examples are highlighted in Guide 5.6.

The concept of *scaffolding* provides a good example of combining several techniques to guide and support student performance and learning (Hogan & Pressley, 1997). Scaffolding requires awareness of students' capabilities and cognitive and affective states of being. The objective is to

Guide 5.5 Some Techniques That Nurture and Encourage Exploration for Learning

---

1. Nurturing Learning (including positive regard, acceptance and validation of feelings, appropriate reassurance, praise, and satisfaction)

Specific examples:

- Eliciting and listening to problems, goals, and progress
- Making statements intended to reassure students that change is possible
- Increasing the number of interpersonal but nonauthoritarian and nonsupervisory interactions
- Increasing the frequency of positive feedback and positive public recognition
- Reducing criticism, especially related to performance
- Avoiding confrontations

2. Creating an Atmosphere for Exploration and Change (including encouragement and opportunity)

Specific examples:

- Increasing availability of valued opportunities
- Establishing and clarifying appropriate expectations
- Modeling expression of affect (self-disclosing) when relevant
- Encouraging pursuit of choices and preferences
- Reducing demand characteristics such as expanding behavioral and time limits, reducing the amount to be done

3. Ensuring a Sense of Protection for Exploration and Change (including principles and guidelines—rights and rules—to establish "safe" conditions)

Specific examples:

- Reducing exposures to negative appraisals
- Providing privacy and support for risk taking
- Making statements intended to reassure learners when risk taking is not successful
- Reducing exposure to negative interactions with significant others through eliminating inappropriate competition and providing privacy
- Establishing nondistracting and safe work areas
- Establishing guidelines, consistency, and fairness in rule application
- Advocating rights through statements and physical actions

Also important, of course, are techniques that provide support and guidance to facilitate effectiveness. Such techniques are outlined in Guide 5.6.

---

create a good match with learner capabilities and motivation. Scaffolding uses explanations, invites student participation (often using a Socratic style of interaction), verifies and clarifies student understandings, models and coaches thinking processes and desired behaviors, invites students to contribute clues through use of cues and prompts, and provides feedback

Guide 5.6 Some Techniques That Help Guide and Support Learning

*1. Meaning (including personal valuing and
association with previous experiences)*

    Specific examples:

- Using stimuli of current interest and meaning
- Introducing stimuli through association with meaningful materials, such as analogies and pictorial representation of verbal concepts, stressing emotional connections
- Presenting novel stimuli
- Participating in decision making

*2. Structure (including amount, form, sequencing
and pacing, and source of support and guidance)*

    Specific examples:

- Presenting small amounts (discrete units) of material and/or information
- Increasing vividness and distinctiveness of stimuli through physical and temporal figure-ground contrasts (patterning and sequencing), such as varying context, texture, shading, outlining, use of color
- Varying the levels of abstraction and complexity
- Using multisensory presentation
- Providing models to emulate, such as demonstrations, role models
- Encouraging self-selection of stimuli
- Using prompts, cues, and hints, such as color coding, directional arrows, step-by-step directions
- Using verbally mediated "self"-direction ("stop, look, and listen")
- Grouping material
- Using formal coding/decoding strategies such as mnemonic devices, word analysis and synthesis
- Applying rote use of specified study skill and decision-making sequences
- Allowing responses to be idiosyncratic with regard to rate, style, amount, and quality
- Reducing criteria for success
- Using mechanical devices for display, processing, and production, such as projectors, tape recorders, and other audiovisual media, typewriters, calculators, computers
- Using person resources such as teachers, aides, parents, peers to aid in displaying, processing, and producing

*3. Active Contact and Use (including amount, form,
and sequencing, and pacing of interaction with relevant stimuli)*

    Specific examples:

- Using immediate and frequent review
- Allowing for self-pacing
- Encouraging overlearning

- Using small increments in level of difficulty, such as in "errorless training"
- Using play, games, and other personally valued opportunities for practice
- Incorporating role playing and role taking
- Using formal reference aids, such as dictionaries, multiplication charts
- Using mechanical devices and person resources to aid in interactions

4. Feedback (including amount, form, sequencing and pacing, and source of information/rewards)

Specific examples:

- Providing feedback in the form of information/rewards
- Providing immediate feedback related to all processes and/or outcomes or provided on a contingency basis (reinforcement schedules or need)
- Using peer and/or self-evaluation
- Using mechanical monitoring and scoring

in ways that nurture students and encourages them to summarize what they have learned and to self-evaluate progress. Clearly, scaffolding is a tool for improving the match (enhancing fit, working in the "zone of proximal development"), thereby enabling personalized instruction.

CONCLUDING COMMENTS

As a leading writer of the 20th century, John Steinbeck (1955) was asked to address a convention of teachers. What follows is part of what he said to them:

> School is not easy and it is not for the most part very much fun, but then, if you are very lucky, you may find a teacher. Three real teachers in a lifetime is the very best of luck. My first was a science and math teacher in high school, my second a professor of creative writing at Stanford and my third was my friend and partner, Ed Rickets.
>
> I have come to believe that a great teacher is a great artist and that there are as few as there are any other great artists. It might even be the greatest of the arts since the medium is the human mind and spirit.
>
> My three had these things in common—they all loved what they were doing. They did not tell—they catalyzed a burning desire to know. Under their influence, the horizons sprung wide and fear went away and the unknown became knowable. But most important of all, the truth, that dangerous stuff, became beautiful and very precious.

It is well to acknowledge that great teaching rises to the level of art. At the same time, we all want to understand as much about the process as can be learned through daily practice, theory, and sound research.

Regardless of curriculum content, the process of teaching starts with mobilizing the learner. This involves providing for (a) a broad range of content, outcomes, and procedural options—including personalized structure, (b) learner decision making, and (c) ongoing information about learning and performance. These are all encapsulated into personalized instruction.

What does it take to personalize a classroom? First of all, we must expect and value individual differences in students' motivation, as well as their capacities. We must also be willing to engage students in a dialogue about their expectations and what interests them and then help them make decisions about a learning agenda that they perceive as a good match. And as new information is acquired about what is and isn't a good match, we must be willing to change the agenda.

Beyond having potential for preventing and correcting a full range of learning and behavior problems, the personalized, sequential, and hierarchical approach outlined here and in the next chapter is seen as having promise for identifying different types of learning and behavior problems and for detecting errors in diagnosis. For example, when only personalized instruction is needed to correct a learning and/or behavior problem, it seems reasonable to suggest that the individual does not have a learning *disability* or ADHD. At the same time, when a highly mobilized individual still has extreme difficulty in learning, the hypothesis that the person has a disability seems safer. Thus, we suggest that personalization is a necessary first step in facilitating valid identification of different types of learning and behavior problems. We now turn to the second step, providing special assistance.

We just missed the school bus.

Don't worry. I heard the principal say no child will be left behind!

REFLECTION AND STIMULUS FOR DISCUSSION

Key Insights About "Personalizing Learning"

Based on what you learned so far,

> *Define (and discuss) what the term* personalized instruction
> *means and outline the key features of a personalized classroom.*

If there is an opportunity for group discussion, you may find the following group process guidelines helpful:

- Start by identifying someone who will facilitate the group interchange.
- Take a few minutes to make a few individual notes on a worksheet.
- Be sure all major points are compiled for sharing with other groups.
- Ask someone else to watch the time so that the group doesn't bog down.

ACTIVITY

- Make a list of what you would want to have in a classroom so that students would find it an appealing place to learn.
- Make another list of the types of activities, materials, resources, and personnel you would want to have available for students to engage them in learning at school.
- What about at home and what about homework?

Father (in a helpful tone): James, don't forget that 4 o'clock is homework time.

James: Okay, but if I don't remember, go ahead without me.

REFERENCES

Adelman, H. S., & Taylor, L. (1993). *Learning problems and learning disabilities: Moving forward.* Pacific Grove, CA: Brooks/Cole.

Adelman, H. S., & Taylor, L. (1994). *On understanding intervention in psychology and education.* Westport, CT: Praeger.

Aregalado, R. J., Bradley, R. C., & Lane, P. S. (1996). *Learning for life: Creating classrooms for self-directed learning.* Thousand Oaks, CA: Corwin Press.

Hogan, K., & Pressley, M. (Eds.). (1997). *Scaffolding student learning: Instructional approaches and issues.* Cambridge, MA: Brookline Books.

Kirst, M. W. (1991). Interview on assessment issues with Lorrie Shepard. *Educational Researcher, 20,* 21–23, 27.

National Research Council and the Institute of Medicine. (2004). *Engaging schools: Fostering high school students' motivation to learn.* Washington, DC: National Academies Press.

Passe, J. (1996). *When students choose content: A guide to increasing motivation, autonomy, and achievement.* Thousand Oaks, CA: Corwin Press.

Steinbeck, J. (1955). Like captured fireflies. *California Teachers Association Journal, 51,* 7.

*Chapter 14 contains a list of special resources related
to the above matters available at no cost from the national
Center for Mental Health in Schools, which is at UCLA and is
directed by the authors of this book. Go to http://smhp.psych.ucla.edu.*

Special Assistance to Address Specific Problems

6

A youngster told his new teacher: I have a note for you from my old teacher. It's not on paper though; it's in my head. She wanted me to tell you how lucky you are to have me in class!

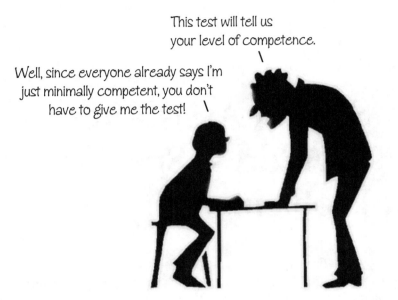

ORIENTING QUESTIONS

? When is special assistance needed?
? What are the three hierarchical levels of special assistance?
? What is the optimal way for a school to address behavior problems?

If we learn from our mistakes, then today should have made me pretty smart.

When personalized classroom instruction is not enough to enable learning, some form of special assistance is necessary.[1] Special assistance combines with personalized instruction as a second step in a sequential approach to addressing learning, behavior, and emotional problems (see Guide 5.2 again). Using effective special assistance is fundamental to reducing misbehavior, suspensions, expulsions, grade retention, referrals to special education, and dropouts.

Special assistance is an essential aspect of revamping classroom systems to address the needs of *all* learners. The assistance often is just an extension of general strategies; sometimes, however, more specialized interventions are needed. In either case, the process objectives are the same—to improve the match between the program and a learner's motivation and capabilities.

Special assistance is provided in the classroom and in some instances outside the classroom. Any student who is not learning as well as *most* others in the classroom is a candidate for special assistance.

The first criteria for offering special assistance are straightforward indications of learning, behavior, and emotional problems. There is little difficulty identifying those who are extremely poor learners. It is particularly poignant to see a student who is working hard but learning little, retaining less, and clearly needs special help. A bit harder to identify may be those doing mostly satisfactory work but not quite performing up to standards in one area of instruction. Students who are disruptive or harmful to self and/or others almost always are readily identified, as are those who appear to be extremely disinterested and disengaged.

Most teachers and many parents have little difficulty identifying students who need special assistance. More difficult is determining what type of assistance to provide and how to provide it.

SPECIAL ASSISTANCE IN AND OUT OF THE CLASSROOM

The ability of school staff to intervene appropriately, of course, depends on the availability and accessibility of an effective array of interventions in and out of the classroom (see Guide 6.1). However, even with a good array, remember that sound practice requires intervening only as necessary and when the benefits significantly outweigh the costs.

As with personalization, special assistance must focus on motivation systematically and comprehensively. This involves (a) assessing motivation about classroom learning and other school-related concerns, (b) overcoming negative attitudes, (c) enhancing motivational readiness for classroom learning, (d) maintaining motivation throughout the learning process, and (e) nurturing the type of intrinsic motivation that results in youngsters' choosing to apply what they have learned. Attending to these matters is the key to maximizing maintenance, generalization, and expansion of learning. Ignoring such matters means intervening with passive (and often hostile) learners. When motivation considerations are given short shrift, assessments and diagnoses are confounded, and intervention may just as readily exacerbate as correct students' problems.

In the classroom, special assistance is an extension of general efforts to facilitate learning. It is the struggle to find an appropriate match for learners having problems and who require special classroom assistance. Because the science base is still limited, a great deal of the process remains a matter of trial and appraisal.

All who are available to work with the youngster in the classroom (e.g., teachers, aides, volunteers, resource teachers, student support staff) must take the time to develop an understanding of students who are not learning well. This encompasses an appreciation of strengths as well as weaknesses (including missing prerequisites and interfering behaviors and attitudes, limitations, likes, dislikes). This is not a matter of requesting formal assessment (e.g., testing).

Guide 6.1   Array of Special Assistance

Level of Concern	In the Classroom	Outside the Classroom
Observable Factors Required for Effective Learning at School Special assistance encompasses what often is called "prereferral" intervention and highly structured instruction. In a broad sense, it encompasses the approach referred to as response to intervention. The instruction remains focused on directly enabling acquisition of the basic knowledge, skills, and interests with which students appear to have difficulty as they pursue age-appropriate life and learning tasks (e.g., reading, writing, inter- and intrapersonal problem solving, positive attitudes).	Where feasible, special assistance should be implemented in the classroom. This may require the addition of an aide or mentor and the use of specialist staff at specific times during the school day. Essentially, at this level, special assistance in the classroom involves reteaching—but not with the same approach that has failed. Alternative strategies must be used for students having difficulty. The approach involves further modification of activities to improve the match with the learners' current levels of motivation and capability. Teachers can use a range of environmental factors to influence the match, as well as techniques that enhance motivation, sensory intake, processing and decision making, and output.	As necessary, added assistance is provided outside class. Special attention is given to both external and internal barriers to learning and performance. Examples at this level include outside tutoring, supportive and stress reduction counseling for the student, and parent training related to supporting student learning and performance.
Missing Prerequisites (i.e., the readiness gap) Special assistance at this level focuses on identifying and directly enabling acquisition of missing prerequisites (knowledge, skills, attitudes) in order to fill the readiness gap.	The more that youngsters have missed key learning opportunities, the more likely they will have gaps in the knowledge, skills, and attitudes needed for succeeding in the current grade. If the readiness gap is not filled, it grows. Thus, it is all too common to have high school students who can barely read. Where a readiness gap exists, teaching staff must be able to take the time to address the gap by identifying missing prerequisites and ensuring that students acquire them. Procedures are the same as those used in facilitating learning related to current life tasks.	Examples at this level also are outside tutoring, supportive and stress reduction counseling for the students, and parent training related to supporting student learning and performance. In addition, students may need additional counseling to restore feelings of competence and efficacy.
Underlying Problems and Interfering Factors Special assistance at this level focuses on identifying and then overcoming underlying deficiencies by directly correcting the problems (if feasible) or indirectly compensating for possible underlying problems interfering with learning and performance (e.g., major motivational problems—including disengagement from classroom learning, serious social and emotional problems, faulty learning mechanisms).	Special assistance in the classroom at this level involves assessment of underlying interfering factors and use of remedial, rehabilitative, and/or compensatory strategies.	At this level, the need is for intensive interventions designed to address barriers related to a host of external and internal risk factors and interventions for promoting healthy development (including a focus on resiliency and protective factors). See examples in text. In extreme cases, full-time outside interventions may be required for a limited period of time.

Before requesting formal assessment, extensive efforts must be made to ensure that students are mobilized to learn and that instruction is appropriately designed to accommodate their capabilities. Accomplishing this requires access to, control over, and willingness to use a wide range of learning options and accommodations. And it may be necessary to reduce levels of abstraction, intensify the way stimuli are presented and acted upon, and increase the amount and consistency of guidance and support.

Prereferral Intervention

Prereferral interventions are a form of special assistance. The intent is to reduce unnecessary referrals for *specialized services,* such as counseling or special education programs. At the same time, students' responses to such interventions provide assessment and diagnostic data about the need for referral. Without a strong emphasis on providing this form of special assistance, referral systems become flooded and help for many students with learning, behavior, and emotional problems grinds to a halt.

Reducing unnecessary referrals requires enhancing the capacity of classroom staff to assess problems and implement special assistance. Student support staff can play critical roles in helping build such capacity and implementing prereferral interventions.

Adding Learning Options and Broadening Accommodations

Everyone knows classroom programs must offer variety to mesh with student interests. And more variety seems necessary for some students. This is especially so for those with low motivation for or negative attitudes about school. For such individuals, few currently available options may be appealing. How much greater the range of options must be depends primarily on the strength of their avoidance tendencies. Determining what will engage them is a major teaching challenge and an immediate focus for prereferral intervention.

Besides adding options, it is imperative to accommodate a wider range of behavior than usually is tolerated. For example, environments can be changed to better account for youngsters who are very active and/or distractible. For some students, initially certain behavioral expectations and standards must be relaxed a bit. This means widening limits for a time so that certain behaviors are not an infringement of the rules. *Accommodative strategies are intended to affect students' motivation by involving them in activities they value and believe are attainable with appropriate effort* (see Guide 6.2).

Remember that, in general, the initial focus in working with students with low motivation or negative attitudes is on ensuring that programs are a good fit. This requires dialoguing with them and facilitating their efforts to

- Identify a range of learning options they perceive of as considerable personal value and as attainable with an appropriate amount of effort (including, as necessary, alternatives to established curriculum content and processes)
- Make personal and active decisions

Guide 6.2   Accommodations

If students seem easily distracted, the following might be used:

- ✓ Identify any specific environmental factors that distract students and make appropriate environmental changes.
- ✓ Have students work with a group that is highly task focused.
- ✓ Let students work in a study carrel or in a space that is private and uncluttered.
- ✓ Designate a volunteer to help whenever students becomes distracted and/or start to misbehave and, if necessary, to help them make transitions.
- ✓ Allow for frequent breaks.
- ✓ Interact with students in ways that will minimize confusion and distractions (e.g., keep conversations relatively short, talk quietly and slowly, use concrete terms, express warmth and nurturance).

If students need more support and guidance, the following might be used:

- ✓ Develop and provide sets of specific prompts, multisensory cues, steps, and so forth using oral, written, and perhaps pictorial and color-coded guides as organizational aids related to specific learning activities, materials, and daily schedules.
- ✓ Ensure that someone checks with students frequently throughout an activity to provide additional support and guidance in concrete ways (e.g., model, demonstrate, coach).
- ✓ Support student efforts related to self-monitoring and self-evaluation and provide nurturing feedback keyed to student progress and next steps.

If students have difficulty finishing tasks as scheduled, try the following:

- ✓ Modify the length and time demands of assignments and tests.
- ✓ Modify the nature of the process and products (e.g., allow use of technological tools and allow for oral, audiovisual, arts and crafts, graphic, and computer-generated products).

A note about learner decision making. Key to the success of prereferral interventions is the involvement of students in making decisions from valued options. Fostering student perceptions of real choice (e.g., being in control of one's destiny, being self-determining) can help counter perceptions of coercion and control. Shifting such perceptions can reduce reactance and enhance engagement in classroom learning.

It is worth reiterating an earlier point here. Before some students will decide to participate in a proactive way, they have to perceive the learning environment as positively different—and quite a bit so—from the one in which they had so much trouble. In specific cases, this may mean *temporarily* putting aside established options and standards and focusing on the most fundamental choice: *Do they want to participate or not?*

Steps to Guide the Process

The following is one example of steps and tasks to guide the prereferral intervention process:

1. Formulate an initial description of the problem. Get youngsters' views of what's wrong and, as feasible, explore the problem with the family. As every teacher knows, the causes of learning, behavior, and emotional problems are hard to analyze. What looks like a learning disability or an attentional problem may be emotionally based. Misbehavior often arises in reaction to learning difficulties. What appears as a school problem may be the result of problems at home. The following can help school staff find out more about the causes of youngsters' problems and what interventions to try.

- Through enhanced personal contacts, build a positive working relationship with youngsters and their families.
- Focus first on assets (e.g., positive attributes, outside interests, hobbies, what youngsters like at school and in class).
- Ask about what youngsters don't like at school.
- Explore the reasons for "dislikes" (e.g., Are assignments seen as too hard? As uninteresting? Are youngsters embarrassed because others will think they don't have the ability to do assignments? Are youngsters picked on? Rejected? Alienated?)
- Clarify other likely causal factors.
- Explore what youngsters and those in the home think can be done to make things better (including extra support from a volunteer, a peer, friend, etc.).
- Discuss some new things youngsters and those in the home would be *willing* to try to make the situation better.

2. Try new strategies in the classroom—based on what has been discovered so far. Enhance student engagement through (a) an emphasis on learning and enrichment options that students indicate they want to and can pursue and (b) a temporary de-emphasis on areas that are not of high interest.

3. Related to the above, it may be important to find ways for students to have special, positive status in class and/or in other arenas around the school or community. (This helps counter a negative image students may

have created among peers and negative feelings about themselves that, in turn, helps work against students' tendencies to pursue negative behaviors.)

4. Enhance the use of aides, volunteers, peer tutors or coaches, mentors, those in the home, and so forth not only to help support student efforts to learn and perform but to enhance students' social support networks.

5. If the new strategies don't work, it is time to reach out for support, including mentoring or coaching, and to request additional staff development for working with such youngsters.

6. After trying all the above, add some tutoring specifically designed to enhance student engagement in learning and to facilitate learning of specific academic and social skills that still appear to be interfering with effective classroom performance and learning.

Only after all this is done and has not worked is it time to use the school's referral processes to ask for additional support services. As such services are added, of course, they must be coordinated with what is going on in the classroom, schoolwide, and at home.

Sequence and Hierarchy

Thinking about intervening sequentially and hierarchically provides a helpful perspective in implementing the principle of least intervention needed. Before providing special assistance on a person-by-person basis, the logical first step is to ensure that general environmental causes of problems are addressed and that the environment is enriched. In regular classrooms, this first step usually requires some redesign to personalize instruction (again see Guide 5.2). Where redesign is unlikely, students experiencing problems should be moved to classrooms where instruction is personalized.

By improving the fit between classroom instruction and individual differences in motivation and capability, most students should be mobilized to try harder. A few, however, may continue to have significant learning and behavior problems (e.g., those whose difficulties are the result of interfering internal factors such as specific vulnerabilities or a major disability). The second step involves providing these students with special assistance, perhaps including specialized practices, but only for as long as necessary.

As discussed above, special assistance is provided in the classroom and in some instances outside the classroom. Depending on problem severity and pervasiveness, the assistance involves one (or more) of three levels of intervention (outlined in Guide 5.2, the relevant portions of which are noted below).

- Level A focuses on *observable factors* required for learning effectively at school (direct assistance with immediate problems related to successful pursuit of age-appropriate life and learning tasks).

- Level B focuses on *missing prerequisites* necessary for pursuing age-appropriate tasks.
- Level C is concerned with *underlying problems* and factors that interfere with classroom learning (major external and internal "barriers"). As discussed in Part I, these barriers may be related to neighborhood, home, school, peer, and personal factors. Personal factors include disabling conditions, avoidance motivation, and serious interfering behaviors sometimes related to emotional disorders.

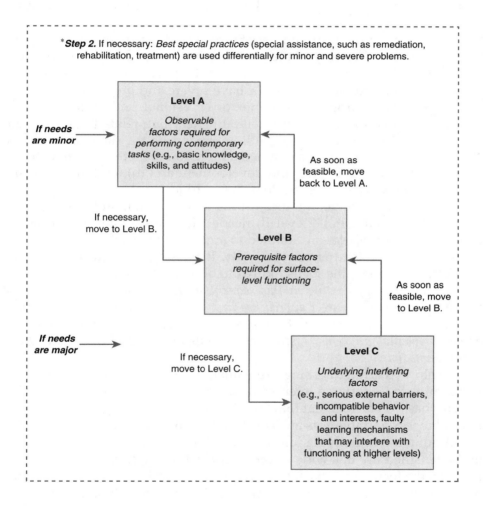

*Step 2. If necessary: *Best special practices* (special assistance, such as remediation, rehabilitation, treatment) are used differentially for minor and severe problems.

Level A

Observable factors required for performing contemporary tasks (e.g., basic knowledge, skills, and attitudes)

If needs are minor

As soon as feasible, move back to Level A.

If necessary, move to Level B.

Level B

Prerequisite factors required for surface-level functioning

As soon as feasible, move to Level B.

If needs are major

If necessary, move to Level C.

Level C

Underlying interfering factors (e.g., serious external barriers, incompatible behavior and interests, faulty learning mechanisms that may interfere with functioning at higher levels)

The concept of using the least intervention needed applies to decisions about intervening at Level A, B, or C. The point is to ensure that the right amount of assistance is provided so that, first and foremost, students' needs are addressed. At the same time, the idea is to keep interventions from becoming too intrusive and to ensure that the costs and benefits are appropriately balanced.

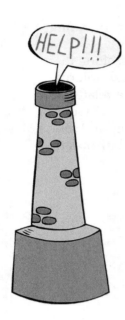

Specific needs are determined initially and on an ongoing basis by assessing students' responses to intervention efforts, supplemented with formal assessment instruments if necessary. The initial level of intervention and changes in level are determined by assessing external and internal factors that can interfere with student learning. *Specific objectives* at any level are formulated initially through dialogue with the learners (and key family members) to identify processes and outcomes that students value and perceive as attainable. All changes result from ongoing dialogues that are informed by analyses of task performance.

When special assistance is indicated, the teacher may focus on any of the three levels. However, the sequence and level differ depending on whether students have minor and occasional problems or have severe and pervasive problems. For learners with minor or occasional problems, the initial focus is on directly facilitating learning related to immediate tasks and interests and on expanding the range of interests. The procedures involve (a) continued adaptation of methods to match and enhance levels of motivation and development and (b) reteaching specific skills and knowledge when students have difficulty.

If problems continue, the focus shifts to assessment and development of missing prerequisites (Level B) needed for functioning at the higher level. Again, procedures are adapted to improve the match, and reteaching is used when the learner has difficulty. If missing prerequisites are successfully developed, the focus returns to observable factors (Level A).

The intent in proceeding in this sequential and hierarchical way is to use the simplest and most direct approaches first whenever problems appear minor. However, if available data indicate the presence of severe and pervasive motivation or developmental problems, instruction for missing prerequisites (Level B) is begun immediately.

If help in learning missing prerequisites (Level B) is not effective, the focus shifts to underlying interfering factors (Level C). Only at this level is the emphasis on factors that may interfere with functioning (i.e., incompatible behaviors and interests and/or dysfunctional learning mechanisms).

In pursuing underlying interfering factors (Level C), there is increased and intensified use of a wide range of instructional techniques. As soon as feasible, the focus shifts back to prerequisites (Level B) and then on to current tasks and interests (Level A). The special strategies are used whenever and as long as necessary.[2]

Remediation

As discussed, a significant number of learning and behavior problems may be corrected and others prevented through optimal, nonremedial intervention. There does come a time, however, when remediation is necessary for some individuals.

Remediation is not synonymous with all special assistance, special education, or special placements. For our purposes, remediation fits under the term *special assistance*. Concerns include the following: *Do staff have the ability to personalize instruction, structure teaching, and provide special assistance in ways that account for the range of individual differences and disabilities? Are they accounting for differences in both motivation and capability and implementing special practices when necessary? Does the student-staff ratio ensure the necessary time required for personalizing instruction, implementing special assistance, and providing enrichment? Is there a full array of programs and services designed to address factors interfering with learning and teaching? Is there an appropriate curriculum—one that attends to students' strengths and weaknesses and not only addresses potentially unlearned prerequisites and underlying factors that may interfere with learning but also offers enrichment opportunities?*

Remediation generally is used when students have difficulty learning or retaining what they have learned. Most of these students will not have learning problems in all areas. Therefore, most of their instruction can continue to use nonremedial approaches.

Techniques and materials designated as remedial often appear quite different from those used in regular teaching. However, the differences may not be as great as appearance suggests. Some remedial practices are simply adaptations of regular procedures. This is even the case with some packaged programs and materials especially developed for problem populations.

A great many regular and remedial procedures draw on the same instructional models and basic principles. Thus, the question is frequently asked: *What makes remedial instruction different?* The answer involves the following factors:

- *Sequence of Application.* Remedial practices are pursued after the best available nonremedial practices prove inadequate.

- *Level of Intervention Focus.* Specialized psychoeducational procedures to facilitate learning may be applied at any of three levels noted above.

- *Staff Competence and Time.* Probably the most important feature differentiating remedial from regular practices is the need for a competent professional who has time to provide one-to-one intervention. While special training does not necessarily guarantee such competence, remediation usually is done by staff who have special training. Establishing an appropriate match for learners with problems is difficult and involves a great deal of trial and appraisal. Additional time is essential in developing an understanding of the learner (strengths, weaknesses, limitations, likes, dislikes).

- *Content and Outcomes.* Along with basic skills and knowledge, special assistance often adds other content and outcome objectives. These are aimed at overcoming missing prerequisites, faulty learning mechanisms, or interfering behaviors and attitudes.

- *Instructional and Other Intervention Processes.* Remediation usually stresses an extreme application of instructional principles. Such applications may include reductions in levels of abstraction, intensification of the way stimuli are presented and acted upon, and increases in the amount and consistency of direction and support—including added reliance on other resources. This may include in-classroom use of paid aides, resource personnel, and volunteer and peer tutors. (Again, we stress that use of special settings outside regular classrooms is a last resort.) There must also be access to a wide range of other intervention options for addressing barriers to learning.

- *Resource Costs.* Because of the factors described above, remediation is more costly than regular teaching (allocations of time, personnel, materials, space, etc.).

- *Psychological Impact.* The features of remediation are highly visible to students, teachers, and others. Chances are that such features are seen as "different" and stigmatizing. Thus, the psychological impact of remediation can have a negative component. The sensitive nature of remediation is another reason it should be implemented only when necessary and in ways that strive to produce positive perceptions all around.

Case Examples

The experiences of Larry and Joan may clarify matters a bit more. In Larry's case, the need was to address a minor reading problem. Joan's problem was somewhat more severe.

Mr. Johnston's first efforts to help Larry improve his reading skills involved a variety of reteaching strategies. The activity focused on current reading tasks in which Larry had indicated an interest. The reteaching strategies were not simply a matter of trying more of the same—more drill, for example. He tried alternative procedures ranging from commonly used explanations, techniques, and materials (such as another example or analogy, a concrete demonstration, a memorization strategy) to less common, specialized, *remedial* techniques (such as a multisensory method). After working on this level for a week, Mr. Johnston found that over the preceding years, Larry had not learned a number of prerequisites widely viewed as reading-readiness skills. For example, Larry had difficulty following directions involving more than one point at a time, and he had problems ordering and sequencing events described to him. He also seemed to have little awareness of the relationship between the spoken and the printed word. As he assessed these problems in his daily work with Larry, Mr. Johnston pointed them out, and they agreed to include them as a major focus of instruction. As had happened with other students, Mr. Johnston found that once the missing prerequisites were learned, Larry had little problem learning basic reading skills.

Joan's situation, however, proved to be more difficult. Because her problem was more severe, Mr. Johnston focused from the start on absent reading prerequisites. As he worked with her over a period of several weeks, he found she had trouble learning most of the prerequisites he taught her and retained only a small amount of what she learned. Thus, he moved on to try to detect any dysfunctional learning mechanisms that might be interfering with her learning. Over a period of weeks, it became clear that Joan was having widespread difficulty discriminating sounds and was continuing to have severe trouble recalling what she had learned the day before. Rather than have her continue to experience failure, Mr. Johnston shifted the focus of instruction. The time usually spent on reading instruction was devoted to helping overcome factors interfering with her learning. Activities she wanted to do were identified; as she had trouble, he worked with her using techniques that stressed multisensory involvement. To improve her retention, he encouraged her to take smaller amounts, and together they identified a variety of interesting activities with which she could immediately apply and practice what she was learning. At first, Joan was hesitant to try things that she had failed at previously. Mr. Johnston did not push. He followed her lead and, at the same time, increasingly encouraged her to risk exploring new things. It should be noted that one of Mr. Johnston's goals with Joan was to help her increase her feelings of competence. When he first began working with her, however, she perceived the special help as another sign of her lack of competence, and this made her feel worse. Such a reaction is common. In the end, as was usually the case with such students, Mr. Johnston found Joan's progress to be slow but steady.

In sum, what makes remedial strategies appear different is their rationale, the extreme degree and consistency with which they must be applied, and their application on levels of functioning other than current life tasks. What may make a remedial procedure work is how different it is from practices students have already experienced and found ineffective. Novel procedures can have motivational and attention-inducing value.

In most instances, however, learning and behavior problems and LD and ADHD aren't corrected by a specific teaching method or technique. Teachers and support staff must draw on a wide range of materials and techniques and be imaginative and flexible in using them to personalize instruction and provide special assistance.

A Cautionary Note

Too many schools tend to redefine and constrict the curriculum for individuals identified as needing special assistance. For example, remedial programs often focus primarily on students' deficits. Always working on one's problems and trying to catch up can be grueling. Students must be tremendously motivated to keep working on their "problems" day in and day out.

Concerns arise particularly about research applications that encourage an overemphasis on assessing and remedying students' problems. For example, applied ideas for assessing and fostering development of language and cognitive abilities (e.g., phonological, executive function, writing, and mathematics skills) are appropriate and invaluable; however, an overemphasis on remedying these areas of development could have the same unfortunate consequences as the historic overemphasis on remedying problems related to visual-spatial abilities. When specific areas for remediation are overstressed, other areas tend to be de-emphasized, resulting in a narrowing of curriculum and a fragmentation of instruction.

Limiting the focus to special assistance presumes that the learner cannot learn when motivated to do so, and it risks making the whole curriculum rather deadening. Broadening the focus to an increased range of developmental tasks and enrichment activities not only can balance the picture but also may be key to finding better ways to help individuals overcome their problems.

A comprehensive curriculum also is essential to minimizing delays in the degree to which students accomplish major developmental tasks not affected by the factors causing them problems. Even among those with pervasive and severe problems, areas are likely in which their learning problems are not severely handicapping. In these areas, learning can proceed without special assistance, or at least the focus can be on missing prerequisites or observable factors. In such cases, individuals pursue learning at several levels at once.

Learning Supports Outside the Classroom

One reason out-of-the-classroom assistance is requested so often is because so many individuals with learning problems also manifest behavior problems. Such individuals are frequently described not only as having LD but as hyperactive, distractible, impulsive, emotionally and behaviorally disordered, and so forth. Their behavior patterns can interfere with efforts to remedy their learning problems. When this is the case, the interfering behavior must be eliminated or minimized in order to pursue remediation. In addition to direct behavior control, programs are used to alter deviant and devious behavior by improving impulse control, selective attention, sustained attention and follow-through, perseverance, frustration tolerance, and social awareness and skills.

Added assistance outside class must be provided whenever necessary, but only when necessary. Special attention is given to both external and internal barriers to learning and performance (again see Guide 6.1). Examples include outside tutoring, supportive and stress reduction counseling for the student, and training for parents to support student learning and performance. If prerequisites are missing, students also may be offered counseling to restore feelings of competence and efficacy. For underlying interfering factors, intensive interventions  address barriers related to a host of external and internal risk factors (including a focus on resiliency and protective factors). In extreme cases, full-time outside interventions are provided for a limited period of time.

DEVELOPING PREREQUISITES

Some students may not have acquired certain "readiness" skills or attitudes that are prerequisites for effectively learning to read, do math, understand science, and negotiate other subjects. Individuals who have not learned to order and sequence events, follow learning directions, and so forth need to develop such skills to enable success with basic academics. Similarly, if students don't see much point in learning the three R's or other school subjects, motivational readiness must be engendered.

Guide 6.3 outlines a set of prerequisites relevant to the process of teaching basic academics. Special assistance at this level remains necessary only for the time required to facilitate acquisition of specific missing prerequisites. Another set of prerequisites needed to engage students in positive classroom learning and enhance their progress, of course, includes factors interfering with learning. We turn to this topic now.

Guide 6.3 Prerequisites for Classroom Learning

In general, individuals should have the following important prerequisites if they are to benefit appropriately from instruction in the three R's.

Language

1. *Expressive.* Working vocabulary and ability to speak clearly and plainly enough to be understood

2. *Receptive.* Ability to understand what is said

3. *Use.* Ability to use at least simple sentences and to express ideas, thoughts, and feelings; understanding of the relationship between spoken and written language

Perception

1. *Visual Discrimination.* Ability to discriminate differences and similarities in letters, words, numbers, and colors and to see the relationship of a part to a whole

2. *Auditory Discrimination.* Ability to discriminate differences and similarities in sounds of letters

Cognition and Motivation (including Attentional, Memory, and Conceptual Skills)

1. Interest in what is being taught

2. Ability and desire to follow simple directions

3. Ability and desire to stay at one's desk for sufficient periods of time to complete a simple classroom task

4. Ability and desire to remember simple facts

5. Ability and desire to answer questions about a simple story

6. Ability and desire to tell a story from a picture (i.e., associate symbols with pictures, objects, and facts)

7. Ability and desire to stay focused on material (pictures, letters, words) presented to the class by the teacher

8. Ability and desire to solve simple task-oriented problems

9. Ability and desire to tolerate failure sufficiently to persist on a task

10. Ability and desire to make transitions from one activity to another

11. Ability and desire to carry on with a task over several days

12. Ability and desire to accept adult direction without objection or resentment

13. Ability and desire to work without constant supervision or reminders

14. Ability and desire to respond to normal classroom routines

15. Ability and desire to suppress tendencies to interrupt others

ADDRESSING FACTORS INTERFERING WITH LEARNING

If individuals have trouble learning and behaving appropriately in a personalized learning environment even after special assistance has engaged them and missing prerequisites are addressed, it is time to explore the possibility of major interfering problems. Of concern are addressing any external and/or internal barriers interfering with classroom learning and performance.

At this level of intervention, the focus shifts to more intensive special assistance designed to help individuals overcome underlying problems. These include, for example, clinical remediation, psychotherapy and behavior change strategies, and/or social services. Clearly, the complexity of this type of work is great and can only be touched on here.

Basically, efforts to deal with interfering factors involve

- Direct actions to address major external/internal barriers to learning and behaving
- Helping students strengthen themselves in areas where they have weaknesses or vulnerabilities
- Helping students learn ways to compensate, as necessary, when confronted with barriers or areas of weaknesses
- Special accommodations

For school staff, direct action at this level mainly encompasses a continuous process of trial and appraisal to find the best ways to help. This includes working with involved others such as family members, peers, and other school staff—counseling them away from actions that interfere with students' progress and guiding them to helpful strategies. Compensatory approaches may be used. These involve efforts to both enhance students' (families') motivation for addressing barriers and teaching specific strategies for circumventing barriers that can't be overcome.

In addition to direct and systematic teaching and behavior management, intervention strategies may draw on a variety of other teaching models and learning principles, as well as on psychotherapeutic principles. Practices encompass rapport building to reduce anxiety and increase positive involvement, mastery learning, instruction in using cognitive and general learning strategies, use of multisensory approaches, greater use of specific techniques to enhance engagement and guide and support learning, greater emphasis on facilitating social interactions, and so forth.

Technology can help in many ways. In particular, computers are a major compensatory tool for many students. Using a keyboard to write, for example, compensates for poor handwriting, which is especially important for students with weak fine-motor abilities; various software programs help compensate for poor language skills.

Experienced practitioners often pursue "clinical teaching." This day-by-day process involves (a) assessment to provide information for planning the day's work, (b) formulation of the day's plan, (c) carrying it out, and (d) evaluating the effects (positive and negative). Evaluation findings are supplemented with additional assessment if necessary, and these data provide much of the bases for planning the next session. Over time, staff using this cycle acquire an appreciation of what is likely to work or will not work with a specific individual.

As discussed earlier in this chapter, accommodations help establish a good match for learning. For students with significant learning, behavior, and emotional problems, interveners use many special accommodations. In fact, federal law (Section 504 of the Rehabilitation Act of 1973) encourages schools to pursue a range of such accommodations when students' symptoms significantly interfere with school learning but do not qualify them for special education (see Guide 6.4).

Guide 6.4   Section 504 Accommodation Checklist

Various organizations concerned with special populations circulate lists of 504 accommodations. The following is one that was downloaded from the Web site of a group concerned with fetal alcohol syndrome (see www.come-over.to/FAS/IDEA504.htm).

Physical Arrangement of Room

- Seating student near the teacher
- Seating student near a positive role model
- Standing near student when giving directions/presenting lessons
- Avoiding distracting stimuli (air conditioner, high traffic area)
- Increasing distance between desks

Lesson Presentation

- Writing key points on the board
- Providing peer tutoring
- Providing visual aids, large print, films
- Providing peer note taker
- Making sure directions are understood
- Including a variety of activities during each lesson
- Repeating directions to student after they are given to the class: then have the student repeat and explain directions to teacher
- Providing written outline
- Allowing student to tape-record lessons
- Having child review key points orally

- Teaching through multisensory modes, visual, auditory, kinesthetics, olfactory
- Using computer-assisted instruction
- Accompanying oral directions with written directions for child to refer to blackboard or paper
- Providing model to help students, posting the model, referring to it often
- Providing cross-age peer tutoring
- Assisting the student in finding the main idea by underlining, highlighting, cue cards, and so forth
- Breaking longer presentations into shorter segments
- Pairing students to check work

Assignments/Worksheets

- Giving extra time to complete tasks
- Simplifying complex directions
- Handing worksheets out one at a time
- Reducing the reading level of the assignments
- Requiring fewer correct responses to achieve grade (quality vs. quantity)
- Allowing student to tape-record assignments/homework

- Providing a structured routine in written form
- Providing study skills training/learning strategies
- Giving frequent short quizzes and avoiding long tests
- Shortening assignments; breaking work into smaller segments
- Allowing typewritten or computer-printed assignments prepared by the student or dictated by the student and recorded by someone else if needed
- Using self-monitoring devices
- Reducing homework assignments
- Not grading handwriting
- Not allowing student to use cursive or manuscript writing
- Not marking reversals and transpositions of letters and numbers wrong; reversals or transpositions should be pointed out for corrections
- Not requiring lengthy outside reading assignments
- Monitoring by teacher of student's self-paced assignments (daily, weekly, biweekly)
- Making arrangements for homework assignments to reach home with clear, concise directions
- Recognizing and giving credit for student's oral participation in class

Test Taking

- Allowing open-book exams
- Giving exam orally
- Giving take-home tests
- Using more objective items (fewer essay responses)
- Allowing student to give test answers on tape recorder
- Giving frequent short quizzes, not long exams
- Allowing extra time for exam
- Reading test item to student
- Avoiding placing student under pressure of time or competition

Organization

- Providing peer assistance with organizational skills
- Assigning volunteer homework buddy
- Allowing student to have an extra set of books at home
- Sending daily/weekly progress reports home
- Developing a reward system for in-school work and homework completion
- Providing student with a homework assignment notebook

Behaviors

- Using timers to facilitate task completion
- Structuring transitional and unstructured times (recess, hallways, lunchroom, locker room, library, assembly, field trips, etc.)
- Praising specific behaviors
- Using self-monitoring strategies
- Giving extra privileges and rewards
- Keeping classroom rules simple and clear
- Making "prudent use" of negative consequences
- Allowing for short breaks between assignments
- Cueing student to stay on task (nonverbal signal)
- Marking student's correct answers, not his or her mistakes
- Implementing a classroom behavior management system
- Allowing student time out of seat to run errands and so forth
- Ignoring inappropriate behaviors not drastically outside classroom limits
- Allowing legitimate movement
- Contracting with the student
- Increasing the immediacy of rewards
- Implementing time-out procedures

The concept of "looping" illustrates another form of accommodation some schools employ (Burke, 1997). Looping involves the teacher's moving with students from one grade to the next for one or more years. The intent is to enhance teacher and student opportunities to work together in addressing learning, behavior, and emotional problems. This accommodation can reduce student apprehension about a new school year, and it enables schools to provide more time for slower students, which counters the need for retention. And it ensures more time for relationship and community building and bonding between teachers and students and teachers and parents and among students. Both academic and social benefits are reported for this practice.

ADDRESSING BEHAVIOR PROBLEMS

Because of the frequency with which students may be misbehaving, teachers often feel that they must deal directly with the behavior problem before they can work on engagement and accommodation. A closer look at this matter is in order.

As we have suggested, in their effort to deal with deviant and devious behavior and create safe environments, teachers and other school staff increasingly have adopted social control practices. These include some *discipline* and *classroom management* practices that model behaviors that foster (rather than counter) development of negative values.

As discussed in Chapter 3, many school staff are moving beyond overreliance on punishment. From a prevention viewpoint, there is widespread awareness that application of consequences is an insufficient step in preventing future misbehavior. It also is recognized that program improvements can reduce behavior and learning problems significantly.

From both a prevention and corrective perspective, prevailing interventions include an ongoing emphasis on *social skills training*, programs for *character education, emotional "intelligence" training*, and positive behavior support initiatives. More fundamentally, a growing group believes that behavior problems will diminish markedly by transforming classroom and school climate through enhancing caring, cooperative learning, and a sense of community that embraces a holistic and family-centered orientation.

Desired student outcomes include enhancing personal responsibility (social and moral), integrity, self-regulation or self-discipline, a work ethic, appreciation of diversity, and positive feelings about self and others (Sapon-Shevin, 1996; Slavin, 1994). Embedded throughout are calls for more home involvement, with emphasis on enhanced parent responsibility for their children's behavior and learning.

With all this in mind, interventions for misbehavior are outlined in Guide 6.5 in terms of

- Efforts to prevent and anticipate misbehavior
- Actions to be taken during misbehavior
- Steps to be taken afterward

Guide 6.5   Dealing With Misbehavior

I. Preventing Misbehavior
  A. Expand social programs.
    1. Increase economic opportunity for low income groups.
    2. Augment health and safety prevention and maintenance (encompassing parent education and direct child services).
    3. Extend quality day care and early education.
  B. Improve schooling.
    1. Personalize classroom instruction (e.g., accommodating a wide range of motivational and developmental differences).
    2. Provide status opportunities for nonpopular students (e.g., special roles as assistants and tutors).
    3. Identify and remedy skill deficiencies early.
  C. Follow up all occurrences of misbehavior to remedy causes.
    1. Identify the underlying motivation for misbehavior.
    2. For unintentional misbehavior, strengthen the student's coping skills (e.g., social skills, problem-solving strategies).
    3. If misbehavior is intentional but reactive, work to eliminate the conditions that produce reactions (e.g., conditions that make the student feel incompetent, controlled, or unrelated to significant others).
    4. For proactive misbehavior, offer appropriate and attractive alternative ways the student can pursue a sense of competence, control, and relatedness.
    5. Equip the individual with acceptable steps to take instead of misbehaving (e.g., options to withdraw from a situation or to try relaxation techniques).
    6. Enhance the individual's motivation and skills for overcoming behavior problems (including altering negative attitudes toward school).

II. Anticipating Misbehavior
  A. Personalize the classroom structure for high-risk students.
    1. Identify the underlying motivation for misbehavior.
    2. Design curricula to consist primarily of activities that are a good match with the identified individual's intrinsic motivation and developmental capability.
    3. Provide extra support and direction so the identified individual can cope with difficult situations (including steps that can be taken instead of misbehaving).
  B. Develop consequences for misbehavior that are perceived by the student as logical (i.e., that are perceived by the student as reasonable and fair, and nondenigrating reactions that do not reduce one's sense of autonomy).

III. During Misbehavior
  A. Try to base a response on an understanding of the underlying motivation (if uncertain, start with the assumption that the misbehavior is unintentional).
  B. Reestablish a calm and safe atmosphere.
    1. Use an understanding of the student's underlying motivation for misbehaving to clarify what occurred (if feasible, involve participants in a discussion of the events).
    2. Validate each participant's perspective and feelings.
    3. Indicate how the matter will be resolved, emphasizing the use of previously agreed-upon logical consequences that have been personalized in keeping with an understanding of the underlying motivation.

(Continued)

(Continued)

    4. If the misbehavior continues, revert to a firm but nonauthoritarian statement.
    5. As a last resort, use crises backup resources.
        a. If appropriate, ask the student's friends to help.
        b. Call for help from identified backup personnel.
    6. Throughout the process, keep others calm by dealing with the situation with a calm and protective demeanor.

IV. After Misbehavior
    A. Implement discipline: logical consequences/punishment.
        1. Objectives in using consequences
            a. Deprive the student of something he or she wants.
            b. Make the student experience something he or she doesn't want.
        2. Forms of consequences
            a. Removal/deprivation (e.g., loss of privileges, removal from activity)
            b. Reprimands (e.g., public censure)
            c. Reparations (e.g., of damaged or stolen property)
            d. Recantations (e.g., apologies, plans for avoiding future problems)
    B. Discuss the problem with the parents.
        1. Explain how they can avoid exacerbating the problem.
        2. Mobilize them to work preventively with the school.
    C. Work toward prevention of further occurrences (see I & II).

Discipline in the Classroom

As stressed in Chapter 3, misbehavior disrupts; it may be hurtful; it may disinhibit others. When a student misbehaves, a natural reaction is to want that youngster to experience and other students to see the consequences of misbehaving. A hope is that public awareness of consequences will deter subsequent problems. As a result, schools spend considerable time and resources on *discipline*—sometimes embedding it all in the broader concept of *classroom management*. Guide 6.6 includes an overview of prevailing discipline practices.

It is worth noting that a large literature points to the negative impact of various forms of parental discipline on internalization of values and of early harsh discipline on child aggression and formation of a maladaptive social information processing style. And a significant correlation is found between corporal punishment of adolescents and depression, suicide, alcohol abuse, and domestic violence. Yet many people still see punishment as the primary recourse in dealing with misbehavior. They use the most potent negative consequences available to them in a desperate effort to control someone and make it clear to others that acting in such a fashion is not tolerated.

In schools, short of suspending the individual, punishment essentially takes the form of a decision to do something to students that they do not

Guide 6.6   Defining and Categorizing Discipline Practices

The two mandates that shape much of current practice are (1) schools must teach self-discipline to students and (2) teachers must learn to use disciplinary practices effectively to deal with misbehavior.

Knoff (1987) offers three definitions of discipline as applied in schools:

(a) . . . punitive intervention; (b) . . . a means of suppressing or eliminating inappropriate behavior, of teaching or reinforcing appropriate behavior, and of redirecting potentially inappropriate behavior toward acceptable ends; and (c) . . . a process of self-control whereby the (potentially) misbehaving student applies techniques that interrupt inappropriate behavior, and that replace it with acceptable behavior. (p. 119)

In contrast to the first definition, which specifies discipline as punishment, Knoff sees the other two as nonpunitive or, as he calls them, "positive, best-practices approaches" (p. 119).

Hyman, Flanagan, and Smith (1982) categorize models shaping disciplinary practices into five groups: psychodynamic-interpersonal models, behavioral models, sociological models, eclectic-ecological models, and human-potential models.

Wolfgang and Glickman (1986) group disciplinary practices in terms of a process-oriented framework:

- Relationship-listening models (e.g., Gordon's Teacher Effectiveness Training, values clarification approaches, transactional analysis)
- Confronting-contracting models (e.g., Dreikurs's approach, Glasser's Reality Therapy)
- Rules/rewards-punishment (e.g., Canter's Assertive Discipline)

Bear (1995) offers three categories in terms of the goals of the practice—with a secondary nod to processes, strategies, and techniques used to reach the goals:

- Preventive discipline models (e.g., models that stress classroom management, prosocial behavior, moral/character education, social problem solving, peer mediation, affective education, and communication models)
- Corrective models (e.g., behavior management, Reality Therapy)
- Treatment models (e.g., social skills training, aggression replacement training, parent management training, family therapy, behavior therapy)

want done. In addition, a demand for future compliance usually is made, along with threats of harsher punishment if compliance is not forthcoming. And the discipline may be administered in ways that suggest that a student is an undesirable person. As students get older, suspension increasingly comes into play. Indeed, suspension remains one of the most common disciplinary responses for the transgressions of secondary students.

As with many emergency procedures, the benefits of using punishment may be offset by many negative consequences. These include increased negative attitudes toward school and school personnel that often lead to behavior problems, antisocial acts, and various mental health problems. Disciplinary procedures also are associated with dropping out of school. It is not surprising, then, that some concerned professionals refer to extreme disciplinary practices as "pushout" strategies.

Most school guidelines for managing misbehavior emphasize that discipline should be reasonable, fair, and nondenigrating. This suggests that the practices should be experienced by recipients as legitimate reactions that neither denigrate their sense of worth nor reduce their sense of autonomy. Given such a perspective, classroom management practices usually stress the use of *logical consequences*. This idea is generalized from situations with naturally occurring consequences (e.g., touch a hot stove, get burned).

Logical Consequences

In classrooms, there may be little ambiguity about the rules; unfortunately, the same often cannot be said about "logical" penalties. Even when the consequence for rule infraction is specified ahead of time, the logic may be more in the mind of the school staff than in the eyes of the students. In the recipient's view, any act of discipline may be experienced as punitive—unfair, unreasonable, denigrating, disempowering.

Consequences run the gamut from depriving students of things they want to making them experience something they don't want. Consequences take the form of (a) removal or deprivation (e.g., loss of privileges, exclusion from an activity, suspension from school), (b) reprimands (e.g., public censure), (c) reparations (e.g., to compensate for losses caused by misbehavior), and (d) recantations (e.g., apologies, plans for avoiding future problems).

For instance, teachers commonly deal with acting-out behavior by removing a student from an activity. Often described as "time-out," such a response may be a logical way to stop students from disrupting others by isolating them, or the logic may be that students sometimes need a cooling-off period. It may be reasoned that (a) by misbehaving, students show they do not deserve the privilege of participating (assuming the activity is liked) and (b) the loss will lead to improved behavior in order to avoid future deprivation. Students we talk to seldom perceive time-out in this way. Neither do those of us concerned with reengaging students in classroom learning perceive it as the best way to reduce misbehavior.

Most people have little difficulty explaining their reasons for using a consequence. However, if the intent really is to have students perceive consequences as logical and nondebilitating, it seems logical to determine whether recipients perceive the discipline as a legitimate response to their misbehavior. Moreover, it is well to recognize the difficulty of administering consequences in a way that minimizes the negative impact on students' perceptions of self. Although the intent usually is to stress how bad the misbehavior and its impact are, students can too easily experience the process as characterizing them as bad people.

Organized sports such as youth basketball and soccer offer a proto-type of an established and accepted set of consequences administered, with recipients' perceptions given major consideration. In these arenas, referees are able to use the rules and related criteria to identify inappro-priate acts and apply penalties; moreover, they are expected to do so with positive concern for maintaining youngsters' dignity and engendering respect for all.

If discipline is to be perceived as a logical consequence, steps must be taken to convey that a response is not a personally motivated act of power (e.g., an authoritarian action) and, indeed, is a rational and socially agreed-upon reaction. Also, if the intent is long-term reduction in future misbe-havior, it probably is necessary to take time to help students learn right from wrong, to respect others' rights, to accept responsibility, and to reen-gage with valued learning opportunities.

From a motivational perspective, logical consequences must reflect an understanding of students' perceptions and be used in ways that minimize negative repercussions. To these ends, (a) consequences that are established publicly are more likely to be experienced as socially just (e.g., reasonable, firm, but fair), and (b) such consequences should be administered in ways that allow students to maintain a sense of integrity, dignity, and autonomy. All this is best achieved under conditions where students are empowered to make improvements and avoid future misbehavior and have opportuni-ties for positive involvement and reputation building at school.

Being Just and Fair

In responding to misbehavior, school staff must be just and fair. But what does that mean? Fair to whom? Fair according to whom? Fair using what criteria and procedures? What is fair for one person may cause an inequity for another.

Should staff treat everyone the same? Should they respond in ways that consider cultural and individual differences and needs? Should past performance be a consideration?

When students have similar backgrounds and capabilities, the tendency is to argue that an egalitarian principle of distributive justice should guide efforts to be fair. However, when there are significant disparities in background and capability, different principles may apply. Students who come from a different culture, students who have significant emotional and/or learning problems, young versus older students, students who have a history of good behavior—all these matters suggest that fairness involves consideration of individual differences, special needs, and specific circumstances.

Sometimes fairness demands that two students who break the same rule should be handled differently. To do otherwise with a student who has significant learning, behavior, and emotional problems may result in worsening the student's problems and eventually pushing the student out of school.

If our aim is to *help* all students have an equal opportunity to succeed at school, then we must avoid the trap of pursuing the all-too-simple *socialization* solutions of "no exceptions" and "zero tolerance" when enforcing rules. Society's obligation is to do more than exert power to control and punish. Social institutions, such as schools, must balance socialization interventions with interventions that help individuals in need. It is unfortunate whenever a school's role in socializing the young comes into conflict with the school's role in helping students who have problems.

In adopting a broad set of principles to guide fairness, the opportunity arises for teaching all students why there are exceptions. A caring school community teaches by example and by ensuring that the principles being modeled are well understood. Staff in a caring school go beyond exercising social control and socialization training. They integrate a comprehensive focus on promoting healthy social and emotional development in all their interactions with every student (see Chapters 11 and 12).

In discussing her early frustrations with the need to discipline students, one teacher, Margaret Metzger (2002), notes that it was helpful to keep in mind her own experiences as a student.

> If I was going to stay in education, I knew I had to get past the discipline issues. . . . I wrote down what I liked and hated about my own teachers. . . . I remembered how much I wanted the teachers I adored to like or notice me; I remembered how criticism bruised my fragile ego; I remembered how I resented teacher power plays. Mostly, I remembered how much I hated the infantilizing nature of high school. . . . I reminded myself that I already know a lot—just from the student side of the desk. If I could keep remembering, I could convey genuine empathy and have honest interactions.

Is the Answer Social Skills Training?

Suppression of undesired acts does not necessarily lead to desired behavior. How about social skills training? After all, poor social skills are identified as a symptom (a correlate) and contributing factor in a wide range of educational, psychosocial, and mental health problems.

Programs to improve social skills and interpersonal problem solving are described as having promise both for prevention and correction. However, reviewers of research over the past few decades are only cautiously optimistic. Conclusions stress that individual studies show effectiveness, but outcomes continue to lack generalizability and external validity. The range of skills acquired remains limited, and generalizability and maintenance of outcomes are poor. This is the case for training of specific skills (e.g., what to say and do in a specific situation), general strategies (e.g., how to generate a wider range of interpersonal problem-solving options), as well as efforts to develop cognitive-affective orientations (e.g., empathy training). While the focus of studies generally is on social skills training for students with emotional and behavior disorders, the above conclusions hold for most populations.[3]

Specific discipline practices and social skills training programs ignore the broader picture that all school staff must keep in mind. The immediate objective of stopping misbehavior must be accomplished in ways that maximize the likelihood that students engage/reengage in instruction and positive learning.

Addressing Underlying Motivation

Beyond discipline and skills training is a need to address the roots of misbehavior, especially the underlying motivational bases. Consider students who spend most of the day trying to avoid all or part of the instructional program. An intrinsic motivational interpretation of the avoidance behavior of many of these youngsters is that it reflects their perception that school is not a place where they experience a sense of competence, autonomy, and/or relatedness to others. Over time, these perceptions develop into strong motivational dispositions and related patterns of misbehavior.

Remember: misbehavior can reflect *approach* or *avoidance motivation.* Noncooperative, disruptive, and aggressive behavior patterns that are *proactive* tend to be rewarding and satisfying because the behavior itself is exciting or because the behavior leads to desired outcomes (e.g., peer recognition, feelings of competence or autonomy). Intentional negative behavior stemming from approach motivation can be viewed as the pursuit of deviance.

Misbehavior in the classroom also often is *reactive*, stemming from avoidance motivation. That is, the behavior may be a protective reaction stemming from motivation to avoid and protest against situations in which the student is coerced to participate or cannot cope effectively. For students with learning, behavior, and emotional problems, teaching and therapy situations may be perceived in this way. Under such circumstances, individuals can be expected to react by trying to protect themselves from the unpleasant thoughts and feelings the situations stimulate (e.g., feelings of incompetence, loss of autonomy, negative relationships). In effect, the misbehavior reflects efforts to cope and defend against aversive experiences. The actions may be direct or indirect and include defiance, physical and psychological withdrawal, and diversionary tactics.

Interventions for reactive and proactive behavior problems begin with major program changes. From a motivational perspective, the aims are to (a) prevent and overcome negative attitudes toward school and learning, (b) enhance motivational readiness for learning and overcoming problems, (c) maintain intrinsic motivation throughout learning and problem solving, and (d) nurture continuing motivation so students engage in activities away from school that foster maintenance, generalization, and expansion of learning and problem solving. *Failure to attend to motivational concerns in a comprehensive, normative way results in approaching passive and often hostile students with practices that instigate and exacerbate problems.*

After making broad programmatic changes to the degree feasible, intervention with a misbehaving student involves remedial steps directed at underlying factors. For instance, with intrinsic motivation in mind, the following assessment questions arise:

- Is the misbehavior unintentional or intentional?
- If it is intentional, is it reactive or proactive?
- If the misbehavior is reactive, is it a reaction to threats to self-determination, competence, or relatedness?
- If it is proactive, are there other interests that might successfully compete with the satisfaction derived from deviant behavior?

In general, intrinsic motivational theory suggests that corrective interventions for those misbehaving reactively require steps designed to reduce reactance and enhance positive motivation for participating in an intervention. For youngsters highly motivated to pursue deviance (e.g., those who proactively engage in criminal acts), even more is needed. Intervention might focus on helping these youngsters identify and follow through on a range of valued, socially appropriate alternatives to deviant activity. Such alternatives must be capable of producing greater feelings of self-determination, competence, and relatedness than usually result from the youngsters' deviant actions. To these ends, motivational analyses of the problem can point to corrective steps for implementation by teachers, clinicians, parents, or students themselves.

CONCLUDING COMMENTS

As the world around us is changing at an exponential rate, so must the way we approach problems in school. Every day, our society is called upon to do something about the many individuals who have trouble learning academic skills and whose behavior is disruptive. In responding to this call, we must be prepared to go beyond the narrow perspective of direct instruction of observable skills and related assessment practices.

Those concerned with improving interventions for learning, behavior, and emotional problems must at the very least broaden their view of teaching; optimally, they need to expand their view beyond teaching. It is time for school staff to enhance their focus on motivation as a primary intervention concern and personalized instruction as a foundation upon which to engage and reengage students in classroom learning. When more is needed, a sequential and hierarchical approach to special assistance is indicated. In all cases, the process objectives are the same—to improve the match with a primary emphasis on motivational concerns.

A FEW REFERENCES RELATED TO PROVIDING SPECIAL ASSISTANCE IN THE CLASSROOM

In addition to the references already cited, the following is intended as a beginning resource list to guide you to books that can help in designing classrooms to be a better match for the full range of learners who are enrolled.

I. Classrooms for All Students

A. Encouraging Learning Autonomy

Casteel, J. D., & Stahl, R. J. (1996). *Doorways to decision making: A handbook for teaching decision-making strategies.* Waco, TX: Prufrock Press.

Johnson, D. W., Johnson, R. W., & Holubec, E. J. (1994). *Cooperative learning in the classroom*. Alexandria, VA: Association for Supervision & Curriculum Development.

Manel, S. M. (2003). *Cooperative work groups: Preparing students for the real world*. Thousand Oaks, CA: Corwin Press.

Meichenbaum, D., & Biemiller, A. (1998). *Nurturing independent learners: Helping students take charge of their learning*. Boston: Brookline Books,

Scharle, A., Szabo, A., & Ur, P. (Eds.). (2000). *Learner autonomy: A guide to developing learner responsibility*. Cambridge: Cambridge University Press.

Slavin, R. E. (1994). *Cooperative learning: Theory, research, and practice* (2nd ed.). Boston: Allyn & Bacon.

Tomlinson, C. A., Kaplan, S. N., Renzulli, J. S., Purcell, J., Leppien, J., & Burns, D. (2002). *The parallel curriculum: A design to develop high potential and challenge high-ability learners*. Thousand Oaks, CA: Corwin Press.

Weimer, M. (2002). *Learner-centered teaching: Five key changes to practice*. San Francisco: Jossey-Bass.

B. Appreciating Diversity

Banks, J. A. (2001). *An introduction to multicultural education* (3rd ed.). Boston: Allyn & Bacon.

Bray, M., Brown, A., & Green, T. D. (2004). *Technology for the diverse learner: A guide to classroom practice*. Thousand Oaks, CA: Corwin Press.

Jesness, J. (2004). *Teaching English language learners K–12: A quick-start guide for the new teacher*. Thousand Oaks, CA: Corwin Press.

Kottler, E., & Kottler, J. A. (2002). *Children with limited English: Teaching strategies for the regular classroom* (2nd ed.). Thousand Oaks, CA: Corwin Press.

McGregor, G., & Vogelsberg, R. T. (1999). *Inclusive schooling practices: Pedagogical and research foundations: A synthesis of the literature that informs best practice about inclusive schooling* (spiral ed.). Baltimore: Paul H. Brookes.

Slavin, R. E., & Calderon, M. (Eds.). (2001). *Effective programs for Latino students*. Mahwah, NJ: Lawrence Erlbaum.

Stone, R. (2004). *Best teaching practices for reaching all learners: What award-winning classroom teachers do*. Thousand Oaks, CA: Corwin Press.

Temple, C. A., Ogle, D., Crawford, A., & Freppon, P. (2003). *All children read: Teaching for literacy in today's diverse classrooms*. Boston: Allyn & Bacon.

Tileston, D. W. (2004). *What every teacher should know about special learners*. Thousand Oaks, CA: Corwin Press.

C. Addressing Problems

Beaudoin, M. N., & Taylor, M. (2004). *Breaking the culture of bullying and disrespect, grades K–8: Best practices and successful strategies*. Thousand Oaks, CA: Corwin Press.

Belvel, P., & Jordan, M. M. (2003). *Rethinking classroom management: Strategies for prevention, intervention, and problem solving.* Thousand Oaks, CA: Corwin Press.

Bender, W. N. (2004). *Differentiating instruction for students with learning disabilities.* Thousand Oaks, CA: Corwin Press.

Crone, D. A., & Horner, R. (2003). *Building positive behavior support systems in schools: Functional behavioral assessment.* New York: Guilford Press.

Karten, T. J. (2004). *Inclusion strategies that work! Research-based methods for the classroom.* Thousand Oaks, CA: Corwin Press.

Koegel, L. K., Koegel, R. L., & Dunlap, G. (Eds.). (1996). *Positive behavioral support: Including people with difficult behavior in the community.* Baltimore: Paul H. Brookes.

Lerner, J. (2003). *Learning disabilities: Theories, diagnosis & teaching strategies* (9th ed.). Boston: Houghton Mifflin.

Mercer, C. D., & Mercer, A. R. (2000). *Teaching students with learning problems* (6th ed.). Upper Saddle River, NJ: Prentice Hall.

Queen, J. A. (2002). *The block scheduling handbook.* Thousand Oaks, CA: Corwin Press.

Smith, C. R. (1997). *Learning disabilities: The interaction of learner, task, and setting* (4th ed.). Needham Heights, MA: Allyn & Bacon.

Thomas, A., & Grimes, J. (Eds.). (2002). *Best practices in school psychology-IV.* Washington, DC: National Association of School Psychologists.

Villa, R. A., Thousand, J. S., & Nevin, A. I. (2004). *A guide to co-teaching: Practical tips for facilitating student learning.* Thousand Oaks, CA: Corwin Press.

Walker, H. M., Colvin, G., & Ramsey, E. (1995). *Antisocial behavior in schools: Strategies and best practices.* Pacific Grove, CA: Brooks/Cole.

Wilkinson, P. F., McHutt, M. A., & Friedman, E. S. (2003). *Practical teaching methods K–6: Sparking the flame of learning.* Thousand Oaks, CA: Corwin Press.

Winebrenner, S. (2002). *Teaching kids with learning difficulties in the regular classroom.* Minneapolis, MN: Free Spirit.

II. Methods for Specific Areas of School Functioning

Some of the above basic texts provide overviews of each area. The following offer more depth.

A. Reading and Language

Chapman, C., & King, R. (2003). *Differentiated instructional strategies for reading in the content areas.* Thousand Oaks, CA: Corwin Press.

Chapman, C., & King, R. (2003). *Differentiated instructional strategies for writing in the content areas.* Thousand Oaks, CA: Corwin Press.

Cowen, J. E. (2003). *A balanced approach to beginning reading instruction: A synthesis of six major U.S. research studies.* Newark, DE: International Reading Association.

Guthrie, J. T., & Wigfield, A. (Eds.). (1997). *Reading engagement: Motivating readers through integrated instruction.* Newark, DE: International Reading Association.

McEwan, E. K. (2002). *Teach them all to read.* Thousand Oaks, CA: Corwin Press.

Stahl, S. A. (1998). Teaching children with reading problems to decode: Phonics and "not-phonics" instruction. *Reading and Writing Quarterly, 14,* 165–188.

Strong, R. W., Perini, M. J., Silver, H. F., & Tuculescu, G. M. (2002). *Reading for academic success: Powerful strategies for struggling, average, & advanced readers, grades 7–12.* Thousand Oaks, CA: Corwin Press.

B. Math

Baroody, A. J., & Coslick, R. T. (1998). *Fostering children's mathematical power: An investigative approach to K–8 mathematics instruction.* Mahwah, NJ: Laurence Erlbaum.

Bley, N. S., & Thorton, C. A. (2001). *Teaching mathematics to students with learning disabilities* (4th ed.). Austin, TX: PRO-ED.

Muschla, J. A., & Muschla, G. R. (2002). *Math smart! Over 220 ready-to-use activities to motivate & challenge students, grades 6–12.* San Francisco: Jossey-Bass.

Rivera, D. P. (1998). *Mathematics education for students with learning disabilities: Theory to practice.* Austin, TX: PRO-ED.

Wright, R. J., Martland, J., Stafford, A. K., & Stanger, G. (2002). *Teaching number: Advancing children's skills and strategies.* Thousand Oaks, CA: Corwin Press.

C. Cognitive Prerequisites, Learning Strategies, and Higher Order Thinking

Algozzine, B., & Kay, P. (Eds.). (2002). *Preventing problem behaviors: A handbook of successful prevention strategies.* Thousand Oaks, CA: Corwin Press.

Alvarado, A. E., & Herr, P. R. (2003). *Inquiry-based learning using everyday objects: Hands-on instructional strategies that promote active learning in grades 3–8.* Thousand Oaks, CA: Corwin Press.

Bloom, P. (2002). *How children learn the meanings of words (learning, development, and conceptual change).* Cambridge, MA: MIT Press.

Bowerman, M., & Levinson, S. C. (Eds.). (2001). *Language acquisition and conceptual development.* Cambridge, UK: Cambridge University Press.

D. Social and Emotional Functioning, Motivation, and Interfering Behavior

Deci, E. L., & Ryan, R. M. (1985). *Intrinsic motivation and self-determination in human behavior.* New York: Plenum Press.

Deshler, D. D., Ellis, E. S., & Lenz, B. K. (2003). *Teaching adolescents with learning disabilities* (3rd ed.). Denver, CO: Love Publishing.

Erickson, H. L. (2002). *Concept-based curriculum and instruction: Teaching beyond the facts.* Thousand Oaks, CA: Corwin Press.

Goleman, D. (1995). *Emotional intelligence.* New York: Bantam Books.

Hartman, H. J., & Glasgow, N. A. (2002). *Tips for the science teacher: Research-based strategies to help students learn.* Thousand Oaks, CA: Corwin Press.

Jones, S. J. (2003). *Blueprint for student success: A guide to research-based teaching practices K–12.* Thousand Oaks, CA: Corwin Press.

Lambros, A. (2002). *Problem-based learning in K–8 classrooms: A teacher's guide to implementation.* Thousand Oaks, CA: Corwin Press.

Lambros, A. (2004). *Problem-based learning in middle and high school classrooms: A teacher's guide to implementation.* Thousand Oaks, CA: Corwin Press.

National Research Council. (2004). *Engaging schools: Fostering high school students' motivation to learn.* Washington, DC: Author.

Novick, B., Kress, J. S., & Elias, M. J. (2002). *Building learning communities with character: How to integrate academic, social, and emotional learning.* Arlington, VA: Association for Supervision and Curriculum Development.

Stefanich, G. P., & Egelston-Dodd, J. (Eds.). (1995). *Improving science instruction for students with disabilities.* Proceedings of the Working Conference on Science for Persons With Disabilities. Anaheim, CA. (ERIC Document Reproduction Service No. ED399724)

Stipek, D. J. (1998). *Motivation to learn: From theory to practice* (3rd ed.). Boston: Allyn & Bacon.

Tileston, D. W. (2004). *What every teacher should know about media and technology.* Thousand Oaks, CA: Corwin Press.

Tileston, D. W. (2004). *What every teacher should know about student motivation.* Thousand Oaks, CA: Corwin Press.

Vitto, J. M. (2003). *Relationship-driven classroom management: Strategies that promote student motivation.* Thousand Oaks, CA: Corwin Press.

Zionts, P., Zionts, L., & Simpson, R. L. (2002). *Emotional and behavioral problem: A handbook for understanding and handling students.* Thousand Oaks, CA: Corwin Press.

E. Motoric Development

Capon, J., & Alexander, F. (1998). *Perceptual-motor lesson plans, Level 1: Basic and "practical" lesson plans for perceptual-motor program in preschool and elementary grades.* Discovery Bay, CA: Front Row Experience.

Cheatum, B. A., & Hammond, A. A. (2000). *Physical activities for improving children's learning and behavior.* Champaign, IL: Human Kinetics.

Missiuna, C. (2001). *Children with developmental coordination disorder: Strategies for success.* Binghamton, NY: Haworth Press.

Zelaznik, H. N. (Ed.). (1996). *Advances in motor learning and control.* Champaign, IL: Human Kinetics.

III. Assessment

Center for Mental Health in Schools at UCLA. (2001). *Resource aid packet on screening/assessing students: Indicators and tools.* Retrieved from http://smhp.psych.ucla.edu.

Center for Mental Health in Schools at UCLA. (2003). *Introduction packet on assessing to address barriers to learning.* Retrieved from http://smhp .psych.ucla.edu.

Chapman, C., & King, R. (2004). *Differentiated assessment strategies: One tool doesn't fit all.* Thousand Oaks, CA: Corwin Press.

Costoa, A. L., & Kallick, B. (2004). *Assessment strategies for self-directed learning.* Thousand Oaks, CA: Corwin Press.

DuPaul, G. J., & Stoner, G. D. (2004). *ADHD in the schools: Assessment and intervention strategies* (2nd ed.). New York: Guilford Press.

Goodwin, A. L. (1997). *Assessment for equity and inclusion: Embracing all our children.* London: Routledge.

Johnson, D. W., & Johnson, R. T. (2004). *Assessing students in groups: Promoting group responsibility and individual accountability.* Thousand Oaks, CA: Corwin Press.

Kaufmann, A. S., & Kaufmann, N. L. (Eds.). (2001). *Specific learning disabilities and difficulties in children and adolescents: Psychological assessment and evaluation.* Cambridge: Cambridge University Press.

Nitko, A. J. (2002). *Educational assessment of students* (3rd ed.). Englewood Cliffs, NJ: Prentice Hall College Division.

Salvia, J., & Ysseldyke, J. E. (2001). *Assessment.* Boston: Houghton Mifflin.

Sternberg, R. J., & Grigorenko, E. L. (2002). *Dynamic testing: The nature and measurement of learning potential.* Cambridge, UK: Cambridge University Press.

Thurlow, M. L., Elliott, J. L., & Ysseldyke, J. E. (2002). *Testing students with disabilities: Practical strategies for complying with district and state requirements.* Thousand Oaks, CA: Corwin Press.

Tileston, D. W. (2004). *What every teacher should know about student assessment.* Thousand Oaks, CA: Corwin Press.

REFLECTION AND STIMULUS FOR DISCUSSION

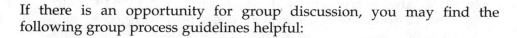

*Key Insights About "Special
Assistance to Address Specific Problems"*

Based on what you learned so far,

> *Define (and discuss) what the term* special assistance *means and outline
> the key features of pursuing such an approach in and out of the classroom.*

If there is an opportunity for group discussion, you may find the
following group process guidelines helpful:

- Start by identifying someone who will facilitate the group
  interchange.
- Take a few minutes to make a few individual notes on a worksheet.
- Be sure all major points are compiled for sharing with other groups.
- Ask someone else to watch the time so that the group doesn't bog
  down.

ACTIVITY

Read the following and then observe a classroom that is for students who need special assistance. Note the degree to which the points discussed are borne out.

> A tendency has been noted in some quarter for curriculum to be redefined and constricted once an individual is identified as needing special assistance. For example, remedial programs may focus primarily on a limited range of factors related to basic skills and pay relatively little attention to other opportunities that enhance learning. Always working on one's problems and trying to catch up can be a grueling experience. One has to be tremendously motivated (and perhaps a bit masochistic) to keep working on fundamentals and problem areas day in and day out.
>
> Limiting the focus to special assistance presumes that the learner cannot learn when motivated to do so and risks making the whole curriculum rather deadening. Broadening the focus to an increased range of developmental tasks and enrichment activities not only can balance the picture a bit but also may prove to be the key to finding better ways to help an individual overcome his or her problems. A comprehensive curriculum also is essential to minimize the degree to which students are delayed in accomplishing major developmental tasks that are not affected by factors interfering with learning.
>
> Even among those with pervasive and severe problems, there are likely to be some areas in which their learning problems are not severely handicapping. These are areas in which learning can proceed without special assistance or, at least, in which the focus can be on other levels. In such cases, an individual would be pursuing learning at several levels at once.

NOTES

1. Use of special assistance is *not* the same as inappropriately adopting a deficit view of the learner. And because the term *remediation* has become controversial in recent years, it is important to understand that the term is used in this chapter to refer to forms of special assistance that may be necessary to enable productive learning.

2. For a discussion of classroom strategies at each level, see the continuing education document prepared by the Center for Mental Health in Schools at UCLA titled *Enhancing Classroom Approaches for Addressing Barriers to Learning: Classroom-Focused Enabling.* This can be downloaded from the Center's Web site at http://smhp.psych.ucla.edu.

3. All this is to be contrasted with programs designed to foster social and emotional development. For specific information on curriculum content areas and research related to such programs, see Collaborative for Academic, Social and Emotional Learning (CASEL) at www.casel.org.

REFERENCES

Bear, G. G. (1995). Best practices in school discipline. In A. Thomas & J. Grimes (Eds.), *Best practices in school psychology—III.* Washington, DC: National Association of School Psychologists.

Burke, D. (1997). *Looping: Adding time, strengthening relationships.* (ERIC Digest, ERIC No. ED414098)

Hyman, I., Flanagan, D., & Smith, K. (1982). Discipline in the schools. In C. R. Reynolds & T. B. Gutkin (Eds.), *The handbook of school psychology* (pp. 454–480). New York: Wiley.

Knoff, H. M. (1987). School-based interventions for discipline problems. In C. A. Maher & J. E. Zins (Eds.), *Psychoeducational interventions in the schools* (pp. 118–140). New York: Pergamon.

Metzger, M. (2002). Learning to discipline. Retrieved from *Phi Delta Kappan online* at www.pdkintl.org/kappan/k0209met.htm.

Sapon-Shevin, M. (1996). Celebrating diversity, creating community: Curriculum that honors and builds on differences. In S. B. Stainback & W. C. Stainback (Eds.), *Inclusion: A guide for educators.* Baltimore: Paul H. Brookes.

Slavin, R. E. (1994). *Cooperative learning: Theory, research, and practice* (2nd ed.). Boston: Allyn & Bacon.

Wolfgang, C. H., & Glickman, C. D. (1986). *Solving discipline problems: Strategies for classroom teachers* (2nd ed.). Boston: Allyn & Bacon.

Chapter 14 contains a list of special resources related
to the above matters available at no cost from the national
Center for Mental Health in Schools, which is at UCLA and is
directed by the authors of this book. Go to http://smhp.psych.ucla.edu.

PART III

Learning Supports
Beyond the Classroom

I find the great thing in this world is not so much where we stand, as in which direction we are moving.

—Oliver W. Holmes

In Part I, we clarified that although some youngsters have disabilities, few start out with internal factors that cause learning, behavior, or emotional problems. Even those who do usually have strengths and protective buffers (assets) that can counter deficits and contribute to success. The majority of student problems seen in schools stem from situations where *external barriers* are not addressed and *learner differences* that require some degree of personalized instruction are not accounted for. And the problems are aggravated as youngsters internalize the debilitating effects of performing poorly at school and interacting negatively with adults and peers. All this is particularly exacerbated in large urban and poor rural schools where so many students are having difficulties. As also stressed in Parts I and II, schools need to address such concerns in the classroom and schoolwide.

We turn now schoolwide—to learning supports beyond the classroom. The matters explored are ones to which the school improvement agenda has given short shrift. This is unfortunate, given how profoundly the lives of teachers, student support staff, students, and families are affected by what goes on schoolwide and in the neighborhood. Such neglect has contributed to the difficulty in closing the achievement gap, reducing bullying, reversing the rate of student (and teacher) dropouts, and many of the other ills that have made public schools the target of staggering criticism.

Schoolwide learning supports are especially important where large numbers of students are affected and at any school that is not yet paying adequate attention to equity and diversity. No one concerned with improving public education can afford to ignore the entire context and climate that students and school staff experience during every school day. Anyone whose current or future well-being is linked with schools must understand what a schoolwide and community focus on learning supports should look like. Then they must play a role in advocating for and helping develop a total approach that ensures that *all* students have an equal opportunity to learn and *all* teachers have the capacity to teach effectively.

In Chapter 2, we discussed an *Enabling* or *Learning Supports Component* as a comprehensive approach for addressing barriers that interfere with learning and teaching. For many students and thus for their teachers, establishment of such a component is fundamental to ensuring success at school; it is absolutely essential to the commitment to leave no child behind.

In Chapter 7, we provide more detailed discussion of matters introduced in Chapter 2. The emphasis is on outlining ways teachers, student support staff, administrators, students, families, and community stakeholders can work together to rethink, reform, and restructure learning supports to create a comprehensive, multifaceted, and cohesive component for classrooms and throughout a school.

Because development of a comprehensive approach requires effective ways to connect families and communities to schools, we explore what this involves in Chapter 8. The increasing interest in *school-community collaborations* provides a useful foundation for understanding what works and what doesn't.

By asking you to play a role in shaping what goes on outside the classroom, we hope to counter the prevailing tendency for school improvement efforts to focus almost exclusively on instructional practices. If schools are to close the achievement gap and leave no child behind, we all truly must think outside the classroom box. Those who work in schools need integrated systems of learning supports

> We must indeed all hang together, or most assuredly we shall all hang separately.
>
> —Benjamin Franklin

that proactively enable student learning and student and staff well-being inside and outside the classroom. All school staff must act as a team to make it so. To do any less is to maintain a very unhappy status quo.

Can you tell me what "status quo" means?

Sure. It's a fancy name for the mess we're in.

Establishing a Schoolwide Learning Supports Component

7

As for the future, our task is not to foresee, but to enable it.

—Antoine de Saint-Exupery

We were pleased to see that the Council of Chief State School Officers (CCSSO) revamped their mission statement in 2002 to clarify that the aim is to achieve the vision of "an American education system that enables *all children to succeed in school, work, and life."*

—CCSSO News Release, February 19, 2002; italics added

Needed: A Program and Policy Shift to Better
   Address Barriers to Learning
      Moving From a Two- to a Three-component Reform
        Framework
      Guidelines for a Component to Address Barriers to Learning
      A Framework for a Learning Supports Component at a School
      Keeping Mutual Support, Caring, and a Sense of Community
        in Mind
      Welcoming and Ongoing Social Support
      Collaboration and Teaming
Getting Started at a School
      Systemic Changes at the School Level
      School Infrastructure for a Learning Supports Component
      A Learning Supports Resource Team
      A Resource-oriented Mechanism for a Family of Schools
Concluding Comments

School staff deserve more credit.

Sure they do, but they wouldn't need it if we paid them more.

ORIENTING QUESTIONS

? Why should teachers be involved in shaping schoolwide learning supports?

? Why is a program and policy shift needed?

? What types of infrastructure mechanisms are needed to get a Learning Supports Component started at a school?

If we replace anonymity with community, sorting with support, and bureaucracy with autonomy, we can create systems of schools that truly help all students achieve.

—Tom Vander Ark (2002)

Why don't schools do a better job in addressing learning, behavior, and emotional problems? As we stressed in Chapter 2, the root of the problem is that learning supports are *marginalized* in school policy and daily practice. As a result, most programs, services, and special projects at a school and districtwide are treated as supplementary (often referred to as support or auxiliary services) and operate on an ad hoc basis. Staff tend to function in relative isolation of each other and other stakeholders, with a great deal of the work oriented to discrete problems and with an overreliance on specialized services for individuals and small groups. In some schools, the deficiencies of current policies give rise to such aberrant practices as assigning a student identified as at risk for grade retention, dropout, and substance abuse to three counseling programs operating independently of each other. Such fragmentation not only is costly, but it also works against cohesiveness and maximizing results.

For the most part, community involvement at schools also remains a token and marginal concern, and the trend toward fragmentation is compounded by most school-linked services initiatives. This happens because such initiatives focus primarily on coordinating *community* services and *linking* them to schools using a co-location model, rather than integrating such services with the ongoing efforts of school staff.

The marginalized status and the associated fragmentation of efforts to address student problems are maintained at schools because of the failure of educational reforms to restructure the work of student support professionals. Currently, most school improvement plans do not focus on using such staff to develop the type of comprehensive, multifaceted, and integrated approaches necessary to address the many overlapping barriers to learning and development. At best, most reformers have offered the notions of *family resource centers* and *full-service schools* to link community resources to schools (e.g., school-linked services) and enhance coordination of services. Much more fundamental changes are needed.

Also mediating against developing schoolwide approaches to address factors interfering with learning and teaching is the marginalized, fragmented, and flawed way in which these matters are handled in providing on-the-job education. Almost none of a teacher's inservice training focuses on improving classroom and schoolwide approaches for dealing effectively with mild-to-moderate behavior, learning, and emotional problems. Paraprofessionals, aides, and volunteers working in classrooms or with special school projects and services receive little or no formal training or supervision before or after they are assigned duties. And little or no attention is paid to inservice for student support staff.

NEEDED: A PROGRAM AND POLICY SHIFT TO BETTER ADDRESS BARRIERS TO LEARNING

As we have stressed throughout this volume, ultimately, addressing barriers to student learning and enhancing healthy development must be viewed from a societal perspective and require fundamental systemic reforms. From this viewpoint, policy is needed to develop a comprehensive continuum of community and school programs for local schools and neighborhoods. Such policy and program shifts can happen only if teachers, student support staff, and administrators share a vision and act together to make it a reality.

Moving From a Two- to a Three-component Reform Framework

In Chapter 2, we introduced the idea that a basic policy shift is needed. Guide 7.1 presents another way of illustrating the inadequacy of the status quo. Painfully clear is the fact that the pressure to increase performance on

Guide 7.1 The Prevailing Two-component Model for School Reform and Restructuring

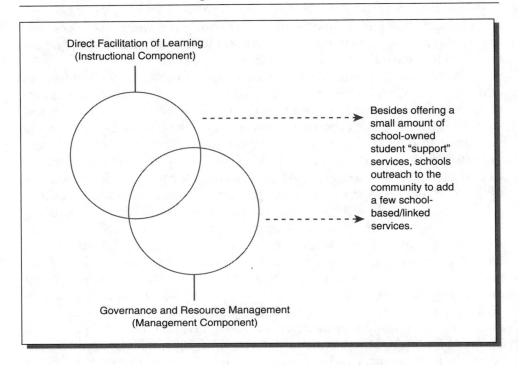

Direct Facilitation of Learning
(Instructional Component)

Besides offering a small amount of school-owned student "support" services, schools outreach to the community to add a few school-based/linked services.

Governance and Resource Management
(Management Component)

academic tests has concentrated attention *mainly* on direct strategies to improve instruction. All efforts to address barriers to learning, development, and teaching are on the margins. In effect, current policy pursues reform using a two- rather than a three-component model.

To fill gaps in current reform and restructuring initiatives, a basic policy shift must occur. To this end, we use the concept of an Enabling Component as a unifying policy-oriented notion to encompass efforts to address barriers to development, learning, and teaching. The concept provides an umbrella for responding to a wide range of psychosocial and mental health factors interfering with students' learning and performance. Adoption of such an inclusive concept is seen as pivotal in convincing policymakers to move to a position that recognizes the *essential* nature of activity to enable learning. As illustrated in Guide 7.2, a three-component model elevates efforts to address barriers to development, learning, and teaching to the level of one of three fundamental, essential, overlapping, and complementary facets of school improvement.

Emergence of a cohesive Enabling or Learning Supports Component requires policy reform and operational restructuring. The emphasis is on weaving together what exists at a school; expanding this through

Guide 7.2   A Three-component Model for School Reform and Restructuring

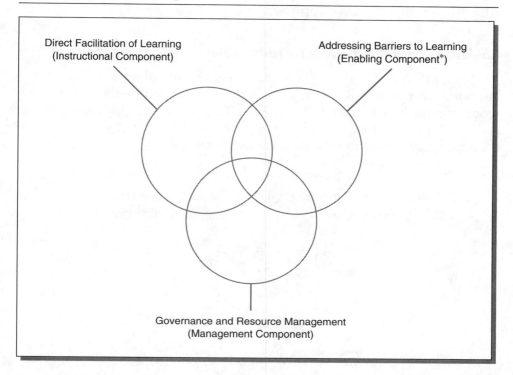

Direct Facilitation of Learning
(Instructional Component)

Addressing Barriers to Learning
(Enabling Component*)

Governance and Resource Management
(Management Component)

*A component that is treated as primary and essential and that weaves together school and community resources to develop comprehensive, multifaceted approaches to addressing barriers.

integrating school, community, and home resources; and enhancing access to community resources through appropriate linkages to the school.

Central to all this is extensive restructuring of school-owned learning supports, such as pupil services and special and compensatory education programs. Mechanisms must be developed to coordinate and eventually integrate school and community-owned resources. And restructuring also must ensure that the Enabling or Learning Supports Component is well integrated with the other two components.

Evidence of the value of rallying around a broad unifying concept for addressing barriers is seen in pioneering initiatives across the country. Schools, districts, and states are exploring the value of enhancing efforts to develop a comprehensive, multifaceted, and integrated approach to addressing barriers to student learning. One example is seen in Hawaii, where the entire state has adopted and begun to implement a *Comprehensive Student Support System* (CSSS). The state of Iowa is pursuing a similar approach, calling it a *Learning Supports Component.* Various other state education agencies, districts, and schools are in the process of adopting and adapting a comprehensive approach.

Guidelines for a Component to Address Barriers to Learning

The outline in Guide 7.3 provides a set of guidelines for a Learning Supports Component. Clearly, no school currently offers the nature and scope of what is embodied in the outline. In essence, the guidelines define a vision for student support designed to address barriers to learning in a comprehensive, multifaceted, and cohesive manner.

A Framework for a Learning Supports Component at a School

Operationalizing an Enabling or Learning Supports Component requires first formulating a framework consisting of a delimited set of basic programmatic areas. Then the focus turns to creating an infrastructure to rethink resource use.

As noted in Chapter 2, we have done an extensive analysis of activity used across school districts to address barriers and support learning. We find that such activity can be framed nicely into six interrelated areas. These are highlighted below and outlined more fully in the series of self-study surveys in Chapter 12. The research base related to the six areas is highlighted in Chapter 13.

1. *Classroom-focused Enabling and Reengaging Students in Classroom Learning.* This arena is designed to enhance teacher capacity for addressing problems and for fostering social, emotional, intellectual, and behavioral development. It provides a fundamental example not only of how an Enabling or Learning Supports Component overlaps regular instructional

Guide 7.3   Guidelines for a Student/Learning Supports Component

1. Major Areas of Concern Related to Barriers to Student Learning

1.1. Addressing common educational and psychosocial problems (e.g., learning problems; language difficulties; attention problems; school adjustment and other life transition problems; attendance problems and dropouts; social, interpersonal, and familial problems; conduct and behavior problems; delinquency and gang-related problems; anxiety problems; affect and mood problems; sexual and/or physical abuse; neglect; substance abuse; psychological reactions to physical status and sexual activity; physical health problems)

1.2. Countering external stressors (e.g., reactions to objective or perceived stress, demands, crises, or deficits at home, school, and in the neighborhood; inadequate basic resources such as food, clothing, and a sense of security; inadequate support systems; hostile and violent conditions)

1.3. Teaching, serving, and accommodating disorders/disabilities (e.g., learning disabilities; attention-deficit/hyperactivity disorder; school phobia; conduct disorder; depression; suicidal or homicidal ideation and behavior; posttraumatic stress disorder; anorexia and bulimia; special education designated disorders such as emotional disturbance and developmental disabilities)

2. Timing and Nature of Problem-oriented Interventions

2.1. Primary prevention

2.2. Intervening early after the onset of problems

2.3. Interventions for severe, pervasive, and/or chronic problems

3. General Domains for Intervention in Addressing Students' Needs and Problems

3.1. Ensuring academic success and also promoting healthy cognitive, social, emotional, and physical development and resilience (including promoting opportunities to enhance school performance and protective factors; fostering development of assets and general wellness; enhancing responsibility and integrity, self-efficacy, social and working relationships, self-evaluation and self-direction, personal safety and safe behavior, health maintenance, effective physical functioning, careers and life roles, creativity)

3.2. Addressing external and internal barriers to student learning and performance

3.3. Providing social/emotional support for students, families, and staff

4. Specialized Student and Family Assistance (Individual and Group)

4.1. Assessment for initial (first level) screening of problems, as well as for diagnosis and intervention planning (including a focus on needs and assets)

4.2. Referral, triage, and monitoring/management of care

4.3. Direct services and instruction (e.g., primary prevention programs, including enhancement of wellness through instruction, skills development, guidance counseling, advocacy, schoolwide programs to foster safe and caring climates, and liaison connections between school and home; crisis intervention and assistance, including psychological and physical first aid; preferral interventions; accommodations to allow for differences and disabilities; transition and follow-up programs; short- and longer-term treatment, remediation, and rehabilitation)

(Continued)

(Continued)

4.4. Coordination, development, and leadership related to school-owned programs, services, resources, and systems—toward evolving a comprehensive, multifaceted, and integrated continuum of programs and services

4.5. Consultation, supervision, and inservice instruction with a transdisciplinary focus

4.6. Enhancing connections with and involvement of home and community resources (including but not limited to community agencies)

5. Ensuring Quality of Intervention

5.1. Systems and interventions are monitored and improved as necessary.

5.2. Programs and services constitute a comprehensive, multifaceted continuum.

5.3. Interveners have appropriate knowledge and skills for their roles and functions and provide guidance for continuing professional development.

5.4. School-owned programs and services are coordinated and integrated.

5.5. School-owned programs and services are connected to home and community resources.

5.6. Programs and services are integrated with instructional and governance/management components at schools.

5.7. Program/services are available, accessible, and attractive.

5.8. Empirically supported interventions are used when applicable.

5.9. Differences among students/families are appropriately accounted for (e.g., diversity, disability, developmental levels, motivational levels, strengths, weaknesses).

5.10. Legal considerations are appropriately accounted for (e.g., mandated services, mandated reporting and its consequences).

5.11. Ethical issues are appropriately accounted for (e.g., privacy and confidentiality, coercion).

5.12. Contexts for intervention are appropriate (e.g., office, clinic, classroom, home).

6. Outcome Evaluation and Accountability

6.1. Short-term outcome data

6.2. Long-term outcome data

6.3. Reporting to key stakeholders and using outcome data to enhance intervention quality

SOURCE: Adapted from *Mental Health in Schools: Guidelines, Models, Resources, and Policy Considerations,* a document developed by the Policy Leadership Cadre for Mental Health in Schools. Available from the Center for Mental Health in Schools at UCLA. Downloadable from the Center's Web site at http://smhp.psych.ucla.edu.

efforts but also how it adds value to prevailing efforts to improve instruction. Classroom-based efforts to enable learning can (a) prevent problems, (b) facilitate intervening as soon as problems are noted, (c) enhance intrinsic motivation for learning, and (d) reengage students who have become disengaged from classroom learning. This is accomplished by increasing teachers' effectiveness so they can account for a wider range of individual differences, foster a caring context for learning, and prevent and handle a wider range of problems when they arise. Effectiveness is enhanced through personalized staff development and opening the classroom door to others who can help. One objective is to provide teachers with the knowledge and skills to develop a classroom infrastructure that transforms a big class into a set of smaller ones. Such a focus increases the effectiveness of regular classroom instruction, supports inclusionary policies, and reduces the need for specialized services.

Guide 7.4   Classroom-based Approaches

Classroom-based Approaches encompass

- Opening the classroom door to bring in available supports (e.g., peer tutors, volunteers, aides trained to work with students-in-need; resource teachers and student support staff work in the classroom as part of the teaching team)
- Redesigning classroom approaches to enhance teacher capability to prevent and handle problems and reduce need for out-of-class referrals (e.g., personalized instruction, special assistance as necessary, developing small-group and independent learning options, reducing negative interactions and overreliance on social control, expanding the range of curricular and instructional options and choices, systematic use of prereferral interventions)
- Enhancing and personalizing professional development (e.g., creating a learning community for teachers; ensuring opportunities to learn through coteaching, team teaching, and mentoring; teaching intrinsic motivation concepts and their application to schooling)
- Curricular enrichment and adjunct programs (e.g., varied enrichment activities that are not tied to reinforcement schedules; visiting scholars from the community)
- Classroom and schoolwide approaches used to create and maintain a caring and supportive climate

Emphasis at all times is on enhancing feelings of competence, self-determination, and relatedness to others at school and reducing threats to such feelings.

Work in this arena requires programmatic approaches and systems designed to personalize professional development of teachers and support staff, develop the capabilities of paraeducators and other paid assistants and volunteers, provide temporary out-of-class assistance for students, and enhance resources. For example, personalized help is provided to increase a teacher's array of strategies for accommodating, as well as teaching students to compensate for, differences, vulnerabilities, and disabilities. Teachers learn to focus the work of paid assistants, peer tutors, and volunteers in targeted ways to enhance social and academic support.

As appropriate, support *in the classroom* also is provided by resource and itinerant teachers and student support staff. This involves restructuring and redesigning the roles, functions, and staff development of resource and itinerant teachers, counselors, and other pupil service personnel so they are able to work closely with teachers and students in the classroom and on regular activities.

2. *Crisis Assistance and Prevention.* Schools must respond to, minimize the impact of, and prevent school and personal crises. This requires schoolwide and classroom-based systems and programmatic approaches. Such activity focuses on (a) emergency and crisis response at a site, throughout a school complex, and communitywide (including a focus on ensuring follow-up care), (b) minimizing the impact of crises, and (c) prevention at school and in the community to address school safety and violence reduction, suicide prevention, child abuse prevention, and so forth.

Desired outcomes of crisis assistance include ensuring immediate emergency and follow-up care so students are able to resume learning without too much delay. Prevention outcome indices reflect a safe and productive environment where students and their families display the type of attitudes and capacities needed to deal with violence and other threats to safety.

A key mechanism in this arena often is the development of a crisis team. Such a team is trained in emergency response procedures, physical and psychological first aid, aftermath interventions, and so forth. The team also can take the lead in planning ways to prevent some crises by facilitating the development of programs to mediate and resolve conflicts, enhance human relations, and promote a caring school culture.

Guide 7.5   Crisis Assistance and Prevention

Crisis Assistance and Prevention encompasses

- Ensuring immediate assistance in emergencies so students can resume learning
- Providing follow-up care as necessary (e.g., brief and longer-term monitoring)
- Forming a school-focused crisis team to formulate a response plan and take leadership for developing prevention programs
- Mobilizing staff, students, and families to anticipate response plans and recovery efforts
- Creating a caring and safe learning environment (e.g., developing systems to promote healthy development and prevent problems; bullying and harassment abatement programs)
- Working with neighborhood schools and community to integrate planning for response and prevention
- Capacity building to enhance crisis response and prevention (e.g., staff and stakeholder development, enhancing a caring and safe learning environment)

3. *Support for Transitions.* This arena is designed to enhance school capacity to handle the variety of transition concerns confronting students and their families. Students and their families are regularly confronted with a variety of transitions: changing schools, changing grades, and encountering other daily hassles and major life demands. Many of these interfere with productive school involvement. A comprehensive focus on transitions requires schoolwide and classroom-based systems and programs to (a) enhance successful transitions, (b) prevent transition problems, and (c) use transition periods to reduce alienation and increase positive attitudes toward school and learning. Examples of programs include schoolwide and classroom-specific activities for welcoming new arrivals (students, their families, staff) and rendering ongoing social support; counseling and articulation strategies to support grade-to-grade and school-to-school transitions and moves to and from special education, college, and postschool living and work; and beforeschool and afterschool and intersession activities to enrich learning and provide recreation in a safe environment.

Anticipated overall outcomes are reduced alienation and enhanced motivation and increased involvement in school and learning activities. Examples of early outcomes include reduced tardies resulting from participation in beforeschool programs and reduced vandalism, violence, and crime at school and in the neighborhood resulting from involvement in afterschool activities. Over time, articulation programs can reduce school avoidance and dropouts, as well as enhancing the number who make successful transitions to higher education and postschool living and work. It is also likely that a caring school climate can play a significant role in reducing student transiency.

Guide 7.6   Support for Transitions

Support for Transitions encompasses

- Welcoming and social support programs for newcomers (e.g., welcoming signs, materials, and initial receptions; peer buddy programs for students, families, staff, volunteers)
- Daily transition programs (e.g., beforeschool, breaks, lunch, afterschool)
- Articulation programs (e.g., grade to grade: new classrooms, new teachers; elementary to middle school; middle to high school; in and out of special education programs)
- Summer or intersession programs (e.g., catch-up, recreation, and enrichment programs)
- School-to-career/higher education (e.g., counseling, pathway, and mentor programs; broad involvement of stakeholders in planning for transitions; students, staff, home, police, faith groups, recreation, business, higher education)
- Broad involvement of stakeholders in planning for transitions (e.g., students, staff, home, police, faith groups, recreation, business, higher education)
- Capacity building to enhance transition programs and activities

4. *Home Involvement in Schooling.* This arena expands concern for parent involvement to encompass anyone in the home influencing the student's life. In some cases, grandparents, aunts, or older siblings have assumed the parenting role. Older brothers and sisters often are the most significant influences on a youngster's life choices. Thus, schools and communities must go beyond focusing on parents in their efforts to enhance home involvement.

This arena includes schoolwide and classroom-based efforts designed to strengthen the home situation, enhance family problem-solving capabilities, and increase support for student well-being. Accomplishing all this requires a range of schoolwide and classroom-based systems and programs to (a) address the specific learning and support needs of adults in the home, such as offering ESL, literacy, vocational, and citizenship classes, enrichment and recreational opportunities, and mutual support groups, (b) help those in the home improve how basic student obligations are met, such as providing guidance related to parenting and how to help with schoolwork, (c) improve forms of basic communication that promote the well-being of the student, family, and school, (d) enhance the home-school connection and sense of community, (e) foster participation in making decisions essential to a student's well-being, (f) facilitate home support of

Guide 7.7   Home Involvement in Schooling

Home Involvement in Schooling encompasses

- Addressing specific support and learning needs of family (e.g., support services for those in the home to assist in addressing basic survival needs and obligations to the children; adult education classes to enhance literacy, job skills, English as a second language, citizenship preparation)
- Improving mechanisms for communication and connecting school and home (e.g., opportunities at school for family networking and mutual support, learning, recreation, enrichment, and for family members to receive special assistance and to volunteer to help; phone calls and/or e-mail from teacher and other staff with good news; frequent and balanced conferences—student-led when feasible; outreach to attract hard-to-reach families—including student dropouts)
- Involving homes in student decision making (e.g., families prepared for involvement in program planning and problem solving)
- Enhancing home support for learning and development (e.g., family literacy, family homework projects, family field trips)
- Recruiting families to strengthen school and community (e.g., volunteers to welcome and support new families and help in various capacities; families prepared for involvement in school governance)
- Capacity building to enhance home involvement

student learning and development, (g) mobilize those at home to problem solve related to student needs, and (h) elicit help (support, collaborations, and partnerships) from those at home with respect to meeting classroom, school, and community needs. The context for some of this activity may be a *parent or family center* if one has been established at the site. Outcomes include indices of family member learning, student progress, and community enhancement specifically related to home involvement.

5. *Community Outreach for Involvement and Support (including a focus on volunteers).* This arena is designed to outreach to the community to build linkages and collaborations. Schools can do their job better when they are an integral and positive part of the community. For example, it is a truism that learning is limited neither to what is formally taught nor to time spent in classrooms. It occurs whenever and wherever the learner interacts with the surrounding environment. All facets of the community (not just the school) provide learning opportunities. *Anyone in the community who wants to facilitate learning might be a contributing teacher.* This includes aides, volunteers, parents, siblings, peers, mentors in the community, librarians, recreation staff, college students, and so forth. They all constitute what can be called *the teaching community.* When a school successfully joins with its surrounding community, everyone has the opportunity to learn and to teach.

Another key facet of community involvement is opening up school sites as places where families and other community residents can engage in learning, recreation, and enrichment and find the services they need. This encompasses community outreach to collaborate in directly strengthening youngsters, families, and neighborhoods. In this respect, increasing attention is paid to interventions to promote healthy development, resiliency, and assets.

For schools to be seen as an integral part of the community, steps must be taken to create and maintain linkage and collaboration. The intent is to maximize mutual benefits, including better student progress, an enhanced sense of community, community development, and more. In the long run, the aims are to strengthen students, schools, families, and neighborhoods. Outreach focuses on public and private agencies, organizations, universities, colleges, and facilities; businesses and professional organizations and groups; and volunteer service programs, organizations, and clubs. Greater volunteerism on the part of families, peers, and others from the community can break down barriers and increase home and community involvement in schools and schooling. Over time, this arena can include systems and programs designed to (a) recruit a wide range of community involvement and support, (b) train, screen, and maintain volunteers, (c) reach out to families and students who don't come to school regularly—including truants and dropouts, (d) connect school and community efforts to promote child and youth development, and (e) enhance community-school connections and sense of community.

Guide 7.8   Community Outreach for Involvement and Support

Community Outreach for Involvement and Support encompasses

- Planning and implementing outreach to recruit a wide range of community resources (e.g., public and private agencies; colleges and universities; local residents; artists and cultural institutions, businesses and professional organizations; service, volunteer, and faith-based organizations; community policy and decision makers)
- Systems to recruit, screen, prepare, and maintain community resource involvement (e.g., mechanisms to orient and welcome, enhance the volunteer pool, maintain current involvements, enhance a sense of community)
- Reaching out to students and families who don't come to school regularly—including truants and dropouts
- Connecting school and community efforts to promote child and youth development and a sense of community
- Capacity building to enhance community involvement and support (e.g., policies and mechanisms to enhance and sustain school-community involvement, staff/stakeholder development on the value of community involvement, "social marketing")

---

6. *Student and Family Assistance.* Specialized assistance for students and their families is designed for the relatively few problems that cannot be handled without adding special interventions. The emphasis is on providing special services in a personalized way to assist with a broad range of needs. To begin with, social, physical, and mental health assistance available in the school and community is used. As community outreach brings in other resources, these are linked to existing activity in an integrated manner. Additional attention is paid to enhancing systems for triage, case and resource management, direct services for immediate needs, and referral for special services and special education as appropriate. Ongoing efforts are made to expand and enhance resources. While any office or room can be used, a valuable context for providing such services is a center facility, such as a family, community, health, or parent resource center.

A programmatic approach in this arena requires systems designed to provide special assistance in ways that increase the likelihood that a student will be more successful at school while also reducing the need for teachers to seek special programs and services. The work encompasses providing all stakeholders with information clarifying available assistance and how to access help, facilitating requests for assistance, handling referrals, providing direct service, implementing case and resource management, and interfacing with community outreach to assimilate additional resources into current service delivery. It also involves ongoing analyses of requests for services as a basis for working with school colleagues to design strategies that can reduce inappropriate reliance on special assistance. Thus, major outcomes are enhanced access to special assistance as needed, indices of effectiveness, *and* the reduction of inappropriate referrals for such assistance.

Specialized assistance for students and family should be reserved for the relatively few problems that cannot be handled without adding special interventions. In effect, this area encompasses most of the services and related systems that are the focus of integrated service models.

Guide 7.9   Student and Family Assistance

Student and Family Assistance encompasses

- Providing extra support as soon as a need is recognized and doing so in the least disruptive ways (e.g., prereferral interventions in classrooms; problem-solving conferences with parents; open access to school, district, and community support programs)
- Timely referral interventions for students and families with problems based on response to extra support (e.g., identification/screening processes, assessment, referrals, and follow-up—school-based, school-linked)
- Enhancing access to direct interventions for health, mental health, and economic assistance (e.g., school-based, school-linked, and community-based programs and services)
- Care monitoring, management, information sharing, and follow-up assessment to coordinate individual interventions and check whether referrals and services are adequate and effective
- Mechanisms for resource coordination and integration to avoid duplication, fill gaps, garner economies of scale, and enhance effectiveness (e.g., braiding resources from school-based and -linked interveners, feeder pattern/family of schools, community-based programs; linking with community providers to fill gaps)
- Enhancing stakeholder awareness of programs and services
- Capacity building to enhance student and family assistance systems, programs, and services

---

A well-designed and supported *infrastructure* is needed to establish, maintain, and evolve a comprehensive approach. Such an infrastructure includes mechanisms for coordinating activity, for enhancing resources by developing direct linkages between school and community programs, for moving toward increased integration of school and community resources, and for integrating the three major components. We discuss infrastructure considerations later in this chapter and in Chapter 8.

Keeping Mutual Support, Caring, and a Sense of Community in Mind

In clarifying each area for learning supports, there is the danger of losing the big picture (see Exhibit 7.1). Ultimately, within the school context, a Learning Supports Component must blend with the instructional and management components in ways that create a schoolwide atmosphere encouraging mutual support, caring, and a sense of community. The degree to which a school can create such an atmosphere seems highly related to its capacity to prevent and ameliorate learning, behavior, and emotional problems. And an obvious connection exists between all this and sustaining morale and minimizing burnout. For these reasons, in developing a Learning Supports Component, a constant focus is on ensuring an increasingly supportive and caring context for learning and working together.

Exhibit 7.1   What Might a Fully Functioning Enabling or Learning Supports Component Look Like at a School?

The following is adapted from a description developed for use by Hawaii's Comprehensive Student Support System (CSSS).

A school with an Enabling or Learning Supports Component integrates the component as a primary and essential facet of school improvement. The aim is to ensure that the school develops a comprehensive, multifaceted, and cohesive approach to address barriers to learning and promote healthy development. Given limited resources, such a component is established by deploying, redeploying, and weaving all existing learning support resources together.

The school has redesigned its infrastructure to establish an administrative leader who guides the component's development and is accountable for daily implementation, monitoring, and problem solving. There is a team (e.g., a learning supports resource team) focused on ensuring that all relevant resources are woven together to install a comprehensive, multifaceted, and integrated continuum of interventions over a period of years. The team maps and analyzes available resources, sets priorities, and organizes work groups to plan program development. As illustrated in Guide 2.1, the goal is to establish effective

1. Systems for promoting healthy development and preventing problems

2. Systems for responding to problems as soon after onset as is feasible

3. Systems for providing specialized assistance and care

And the work involves creating the continuum in keeping with the content or "curriculum" framework the school has adopted for its enabling or Learning Supports Component (e.g., see the six areas illustrated in Guide 2.4).

While the focus of the team is on resource use and program development, it also ensures that effective mechanisms are in operation for responding rapidly when specific students are identified as having mild to moderate learning, behavior, and emotional problems. For most students, the problems are resolved through relatively straightforward situational and program changes and problem-solving strategies. Based on analyses of their response to such interventions, additional assistance *in the classroo*m is provided to those for whom these first methods are insufficient. Those whose problems persist are referred for additional and sometimes specialized assistance. Before such interventions are set in motion, in-depth analyses are made of the reasons for their problems in order to ensure that appropriate assistance is planned. All special interventions are carefully monitored and coordinated. Through a sequential strategy that begins with the least intervention needed and that gauges students' responses to intervention at every stage, there is a significant reduction in the number requiring intensive help and referral for specialized assistance.

Because there is an emphasis on programs and activities that create a schoolwide culture of caring and nurturing, students, families, staff, and the community feel the school is a welcoming and supportive place, accommodating of diversity, and committed to promoting equal opportunities for all students to succeed at school. When problems arise, they are responded to positively, quickly, and effectively. Morale is high.

The following should be understood as examples of the types of interventions that might be used with any student who experiences barriers to learning. Remember that the point is to ensure that a full continuum is available at schools so that the least intervention-needed strategies are implemented and students' responses to intervention can be used to gauge whether more intensive help and referrals for specialized assistance are required. When such a sequential approach is followed, schools can expect a significant reduction in the flow of referrals for specialized assistance.

Example 1: Focusing on Helping the Teacher With Student Reengagement, Rather Than Overemphasizing Discipline and Referral for Services

Matt, a third grader, has not been doing well at school. He often is in trouble on the school playground before school and during lunch. Before the Learning Supports Component was established, his teacher constantly had to discipline him and send him to the principal's office. He had been referred to the student success team but was just one of a long list in line to be reviewed. Now the focus is on how to enhance what goes on in the classroom and on schoolwide changes that minimize negative encounters; this minimizes the need for classroom management, discipline, and referral for expensive special services.

(Continued)

(Continued)

The focus on enhancing teacher capacity to reengage students in daily learning activities is helping Matt's teacher learn more about matching his individual interests and skills and how to design the instructional day to provide additional supports from peers and community volunteers. Rather than seeing the solution in terms of discipline, she learns how to understand what is motivating Matt's problem and is able to provide more of a personalized approach to instruction and extra in-classroom support that will reengage Matt in learning. Over time, all student support staff (all professional staff who are not involved in classroom instruction) will be trained to go into the classroom to help the teacher learn and implement new approaches designed not just for Matt but for all students who are not well engaged in classroom learning.

At the same time, the focus on enhancing support for transition times (such as before school and lunch) increases the recreational and enrichment opportunities available for all students so that they have positive options for interaction. Staff involved in playground supervision are specifically asked to work with Matt to help him engage in an activity that interests him (e.g., a sports tournament, an extramural club activity). They will monitor his involvement to ensure that he is truly engaged, and they, along with one of the student support staff (e.g., school psychologist, counselor, social worker, nurse), will use the opportunity to help him and other students learn any interpersonal skills needed to interact well with peers.

Newcomers: One Example of Support for Transitions and Home Involvement

To increase family involvement in schooling, special attention is placed on enhancing welcoming and social support strategies for new students and families. Student support staff work with office staff to develop welcoming programs and establish social support networks (e.g., peer buddy systems for students; parent-parent connections). As a result, newcomers (and all others) are greeted promptly and with an inviting attitude when they come into the school. Those without correct enrollment records are helped to access what they need. Parents are connected with another parent who helps them learn about school and neighborhood resources. Upon entering the new classroom, teachers connect newcomers with trained peer buddies who will stick with the newcomers for a few weeks while they learn the ropes.

Support staff work with each teacher to identify any student who hasn't made a good transition. Together they will determine why and work with the family to turn things around.

Crisis Prevention

To reduce the number of crises, student support staff analyze what is preventable (usually related to human relations problems) and then design a range of schoolwide prevention approaches. Among these are strategies for involving all school personnel (credentialed and classified) in activities that promote positive interactions and natural opportunities for learning prosocial behavior and mutual respect.

Fewer Referrals, Better Response

As the in-classroom and schoolwide approaches emerge, the need for out-of-classroom referrals declines. This allows for rapid and early response when a student is having problems, and it enables student support staff to work more effectively in linking students up with community services when necessary.

Example 2: Here's What a Family Might Experience When Their Children Have a Problem

Clara, a third grader, finds reading difficult. Her teacher asks one of the many community volunteers to work with Clara to improve her skills, motivation, and confidence. Clara and the volunteer, a local college student, go to the school library, where she is encouraged to choose books on subjects that interest her, and they read together. Clara also writes stories on topics she likes. To further improve her skills, her family is encouraged to have her read the stories to them at home.

As Clara's skills improve, she also begins reading to her younger sister, Emma. Emma needs help in getting ready for kindergarten. She is enrolled in Head Start. Her family, including her grandmother who lives with them, comes to parent meetings to learn ways to enrich Emma's readiness skills.

When the family's oldest child, Tommy, got into trouble for fighting at school, his behavior was reviewed by a student support staff member and the youngster's teacher, who then met with the family and Tommy to explore the causes of his behavior problems and planned some solutions. At subsequent meetings, they reviewed the plan's effectiveness. One of the strategies called for Tommy's becoming a peer buddy to help provide social support for new students. When the next new family enrolled, Tommy spent several days showing the new student around the school, and they both got involved in some extracurricular activities. Tommy's behavior problems quickly turned around, and he soon was able to assume a leadership role during various school events.

In the middle of the year, the grandmother got sick and went to the hospital. Support staff at each of the children's schools were sensitive to the disruption in the home. When Tommy and Clara regressed a bit, they arranged for some extra support and explored ways to assist the family's efforts to cope. The work with the family and the two schools that were involved was coordinated through a "care monitoring" mechanism developed by a multisite council that focuses regularly on common concerns of all schools in the neighborhood.

Being together is no guarantee of feeling a sense of belonging or feeling responsible for a collective mission. In too many schools, teachers, student support staff, students, and other stakeholders feel isolated.

Perceptions of support, care, and community are shaped by daily experiences. Initially, they may be engendered if individuals feel welcomed, supported, nurtured, respected, liked, and connected in reciprocal relationships. Throughout a school and in each classroom, a psychological sense of community exists when a critical mass of stakeholders is committed to each other *and* to the setting's goals and values, *and* they exert effort to achieve the goals and maintain positive relationships. Such situations are the antithesis of those that breed burnout.

Maintaining a sense of community over time requires that a critical mass of stakeholders feel like valued members who are contributing to the collective identity, destiny, and vision and also are committed to being and working together in supportive and efficacious ways. The aim is to promote feelings of competence, self-determination, and connectedness. Such feelings and attitudes are engendered by ensuring that there are mechanisms and strategies that effectively provide support, promote self-efficacy, and foster positive relationships.

Welcoming and Ongoing Social Support

Classrooms and schools can do their job better if students, their families, and staff feel they are truly welcome and have a range of social supports. For students, the process of building a sense of community and caring begins when they (and their families) first arrive at a school or move from grade to grade. A key facet of welcoming new students is effectively connecting them with peers and adults who can provide ongoing social support and advocacy.

As discussed in Part II, efforts to create a caring classroom climate are facilitated through the use of personalized instruction and providing special assistance as necessary. The focus is on using each opportunity to nurture and support, including regular student conferences, cooperative learning, peer tutoring, and any activity designed to foster social and emotional development.

Schoolwide, a caring culture pays special attention to assisting and advocating for students and staff. For example, a caring school pays special attention to students who have difficulty making friends or who get into trouble. Some of these students need just a bit of support to overcome a problem (e.g., a few suggestions, a couple of special opportunities). Some, however, need much more help. They may be overly shy, lacking in social skills, or may act in negative ways. Efforts to assist these youngsters include strategies that facilitate establishing friendships, mentoring, counseling, mediation, conflict resolution, and programs to enhance human relations. A range of school staff, including teachers, classroom or yard aides, student support and resource staff, and parents, can work together to address the problems.

For instance, a "peer buddy" may be brought into the picture. This can be a student with similar interests and temperament and/or one who can be understanding and is willing to reach out to someone who needs a friend. Regular opportunities may be created for students to work with others on shared activities or projects at and away from school. A special relationship may be established with almost anyone on the staff who is willing to help students feel positively connected at school. For youngsters who really don't know how to act like a friend, specific guidelines and social skills also can be taught.

Given the importance of home involvement in schooling, creating a caring atmosphere for family members also warrants enhanced attention. Increased home involvement is more likely if families feel welcome and have access to social support at school. To these ends, school staff can establish a program that effectively welcomes and connects families to staff and other families for the purpose of ongoing social support and greater home involvement with the school.

And don't forget that school staff also need to feel truly welcome and socially supported. Rather than leaving this to chance, a caring school develops and institutionalizes a program to welcome and connect new staff to colleagues. Moreover, this is done in ways that effectively incorporate newcomers into the organization and build their capacity to function effectively (see Exhibit 7.2).

Collaboration and Teaming

In discussing burnout, many writers have emphasized that too often, teaching is carried out under highly stressful working conditions and without much of a collegial and social support structure. Teachers must feel good about themselves if classrooms and schools are to be caring environments. Teaching is one of society's most psychologically demanding jobs, yet few schools have programs designed specifically to counter job stress and enhance staff feelings of well-being. Recommendations to redress this deficiency usually factor down to strategies that reduce environmental stressors, increase personal capabilities, and enhance job and social supports. However, most schools simply do not have adequate mechanisms in place to plan for and implement such recommendations.

Fundamental to dealing with the above concerns and to improving instruction are approaches that enable teachers to work closely with other teachers, student support staff, and other school personnel, as well as with parents, professionals-in-training, volunteers, and so forth. In particular, systemic promotion of collaboration and teaming are key facets of addressing barriers to learning. Such approaches allow teachers to

Exhibit 7.2   Why Should a School Be the Heart of a Community
and a Classroom Be a Student's Home Away From Home?

Schools Often Seem Apart From the Community

Most schools could do their job better if they were experienced as an integral and positive part of the community—perhaps even as the heart of the community. Schools and classrooms often are seen as separate from the community in which they reside. This contributes to a lack of connection between school staff and parents, students, other community residents, and community agency personnel. Development of a caring, learning community requires creating positive connections between school and community.

School-Community Partnerships

For schools to be seen as an integral part of the community, steps must be taken to create and maintain collaborative partnerships between school and community with respect to weaving together (blending) learning opportunities, programs, services, and use of facilities, personnel, and other resources.

Opening Up Use of the School Site

Besides increasing home involvement in schools and schooling, schools must facilitate increased use of school sites as places where parents, families, and other community residents can engage in learning, recreation, and enrichment and can connect with services they need.

Welcoming and Social Support for Students

Most classrooms can do their job better if students feel they are truly welcome and have a range of social supports. Thus, a major focus for school-community collaborative partnership is the establishment of a program that effectively welcomes and connects new students with peers and adults at school who can provide social support and advocacy. In some cases, the concept of the *moving diamond* can be adapted to these ends.

Welcoming and Social Support for Parents/Families

Increased home involvement in school is more likely if families feel they are truly welcome and have a range of social supports. Thus, a major focus for school-community collaborative partnership is establishment of a program that effectively welcomes and connects newly enrolled families with other families, with school staff, and with ongoing social support and home involvement programs.

Volunteers

Parents, peers, and other volunteers help break down the barriers between school and community. Thus, a major focus for school-community collaborative partnership is establishment of a program that effectively recruits, screens, trains, and nurtures volunteers.

Helping Students Feel a Sense of Interpersonal Connection

Personalized instruction and regular student conferencing, cooperative learning strategies, curriculum focused on fostering social and emotional development, opportunities to have special status, peer tutoring, peer counseling and mediation, human relations and conflict resolution programs, moving diamonds—all can contribute to students' feeling positively connected to the classroom.

broaden the resources and strategies available in and out of the classroom to enhance learning and performance.

As Hargreaves (1994) cogently notes, the way to relieve the uncertainty and open-endedness that characterizes classroom teaching is to create "communities of colleagues who work collaboratively [in cultures of shared learning and positive risk-taking] to set their own professional limits and standards, while still remaining committed to continuous improvement. Such communities can also bring together the professional and personal lives of teachers in a way that supports growth and allows problems to be discussed without fear of disapproval or punishment" (p. 156). Collaboration and collegiality are basic to enhancing morale and work satisfaction and to transforming classrooms into caring contexts for learning. Collegiality, however, cannot be demanded. As Hargreaves also stresses, when collegiality is *mandated*, it can produce what is called *contrived collegiality*, which tends to breed inflexibility and inefficiency. Contrived collegiality is compulsory, implementation-oriented, regulated administratively, fixed in time and space, and predictable. In contrast, *collaborative cultures* foster working relationships that are voluntary, development-oriented, spontaneous, pervasive across time and space, and unpredictable.

Collaborative cultures also can foster a school's efforts to organize itself into a learning community that personalizes inservice teacher education. Such "organizational learning" requires an organizational structure "where people continually expand their capabilities to understand complexity, clarify vision and improve shared mental models (Senge, 1990) by engaging in different tasks, acquiring different kinds of expertise, experiencing and expressing different forms of leadership, confronting uncomfortable organizational truths, and searching together for shared solutions" (Hargreaves, 1994, p. 66).

Finally, collaborative cultures recognize the need to build capacity for dealing with working relationship problems. Despite the best of intentions, relationships often go astray—especially when staff become frustrated and angry because students don't respond in desired ways or seem not to be trying. To minimize relationship problems, inservice education must foster an understanding of interpersonal dynamics and barriers to working relationships, and sites must establish effective problem-solving mechanisms to eliminate or at least minimize such problems.

GETTING STARTED AT A SCHOOL

Development of a comprehensive schoolwide approach is easy to call for and hard to accomplish. Anyone who has been involved in systemic reform can describe the difficulties in terms of lack of time, insufficient budget, lack of space, disgruntled stakeholders, inadequate capacity building, and on and on. Such difficulties and various strategies for dealing with them are well discussed in the literature on systemic change. At this point, we simply want to highlight a few fundamentals for those who work in schools, with the caveat that each facet described carries with it a myriad of implementation difficulties.

Systemic Changes at the School Level

> Overheard in the hall:
>
> With all the budget problems, we have to do everything on a shoestring.
>   Wow—are you saying you still have a shoestring?

As we have noted, the *development* of comprehensive schoolwide approaches requires shifts in prevailing policy and new models for practice. In addition, for significant systemic change to occur, policy and program commitments must be backed with resources. Given sparse resources, this means that finances, personnel, time, space, equipment, and other necessary resources must be redeployed.

Existing infrastructure mechanisms also must be modified. Infrastructure changes are needed to ensure matters such as integration, quality improvement, accountability, and self-renewal related to all three components illustrated in Guide 7.2. And let's not forget about infrastructure mechanisms linking schools together to maximize use of limited resources. When a "family of schools" in a geographic area collaborates to address barriers, they can share programs and personnel in many cost-effective ways. Also, in connecting with community resources, a group of schools can maximize the distribution of limited resources in ways that are efficient, effective, and equitable.

Well-designed infrastructure mechanisms ensure local ownership, a critical mass of committed stakeholders, processes that overcome barriers to stakeholders effectively working together, and strategies that mobilize and maintain proactive effort so that changes are implemented and there is renewal over time. *Institutionalization* of comprehensive, multifaceted approaches requires the restructuring of mechanisms associated with at least six basic infrastructure concerns. These encompass processes for daily (1) governance, (2) leadership, (3) planning and implementation of specific organizational and program objectives, (4) coordination and integration for cohesion, (5) management of communication and information, and (6) capacity building.

From the perspective of redeploying resources and changing infrastructure, the importance of creating an atmosphere that encourages mutual support, caring, and collegiality takes on another dimension. New directions for student support call for new collaborative arrangements and some redistribution of authority (power). Key stakeholders and their leadership must understand and commit to the changes. New directions obviously not only require resources but also support, initially and over time. These include appropriate incentives and safeguards for individuals as they become enmeshed in the complexities of systemic change.

The process begins with activity designed to create readiness for the necessary changes by enhancing a climate or culture for change. The steps include

1. Building interest and consensus for establishing a comprehensive, multifaceted component to address barriers to learning and teaching

2. Introducing basic concepts to relevant groups of stakeholders

3. Establishing a policy framework that recognizes that such a component is a primary and essential facet of the institution's activity

4. Appointing leaders for the component, who are of equivalent status to the leaders for the instructional and management facets, to ensure that commitments are carried out

Overlapping the efforts to create readiness are processes to develop an organizational structure for start-up and phase-in. Encompassed in this are the establishment of mechanisms and procedures to guide reforms, such as a steering group and leadership training and formulation of specific start-up and phase-in plans.

Although many of the above points about systemic change seem self-evident, their profound implications are widely ignored. Relatively little work has been done to build conceptual models and develop specific interventions for dealing with the processes and problems associated with introducing, sustaining, and scaling up reforms in schools. As a result, it is not surprising that so many efforts to improve schools fail.

School Infrastructure for a Learning Supports Component

At schools, obviously the administrative leadership is one key to ending the marginalization of efforts to address learning, behavior, and emotional problems. Another key is establishment of a mechanism that focuses specifically on how resources are used at the school to address barriers to learning. As noted in Chapter 2, in some schools as much as 30 percent of the budget may be going to problem prevention and correction. Every school is expending resources to enable learning; few have a mechanism to ensure appropriate use of existing resources and enhance current efforts. Such a mechanism contributes to the cost efficacy of learner support activity by ensuring that all such activity is planned, implemented, and evaluated in a coordinated and increasingly integrated manner. It also provides another means for reducing marginalization. Creation of such a mechanism enables braiding together existing school and community resources and encouraging services and programs to function in an increasingly cohesive way. When this mechanism is created in the form of a "team," it also is a vehicle for building working relationships and can play a role in solving turf and operational problems.

One of the primary tasks a resource-oriented mechanism undertakes is that of enumerating school and community programs and services that are in place to support students, families, and staff. A comprehensive "gap" assessment is generated as resource mapping is compared with surveys of the unmet needs of and desired outcomes for students, their families, and school staff. Analyses of what is available, effective, and needed provide a sound basis for formulating priorities and developing strategies to link with additional resources at other schools, district sites, and in the community, and they enhance the use of existing resources. Such analyses also can guide efforts to improve cost-effectiveness.

In a similar fashion, a resource-oriented team for a complex or family of schools (e.g., a high school and its feeder schools) and a team at the district level provide mechanisms for analyses on a larger scale. This can lead to strategies for cross-school, communitywide, and districtwide cooperation and integration to enhance intervention effectiveness and garner economies of scale. For those concerned with school reform, such resource-oriented mechanisms are a key facet of efforts to transform and restructure school support programs and services.

A Learning Supports Resource Team

Early in our work, we called the school-level resource-oriented mechanism a *resource coordinating team*. However, coordination is too limited a descriptor of the team's role and functions. So we now use the term *learning supports resource team*.

We initially piloted such teams in the Los Angeles Unified School District, and now the concept is being introduced in many schools across the country. Properly constituted, such a team works with the school's administrators to expand on-site leadership for efforts to address barriers comprehensively and ensures the maintenance and improvement of a multifaceted and integrated approach.

When we mention a learning supports resource team, some school staff quickly respond, *We already have one!* When we explore this with them, we usually find that what they have is a *case-oriented team*—that is, a team that focuses on individual students who are having problems. Such a team may be called a student study team, student success team, student assistance team, teacher assistance team, and so forth. To help clarify the difference between resource and case-oriented teams, we contrast the functions of each as outlined in Guide 7.10.

Two metaphors help differentiate the two types of mechanisms and the importance of both sets of functions. A *case orientation* fits the *starfish* metaphor.

The day after a great storm had washed up all sorts of sea life far up onto the beach, a youngster set out to throw back as many of the still-living starfish as he could. After watching him toss one after the other into the ocean, an old man approached him and said: *It's no use your doing that, there are too many. You're not going to make any difference.*

The boy looked at him in surprise, then bent over, picked up another starfish, threw it in, and then replied: *It made a difference to that one!*

Guide 7.10   Contrasting Team Functions

A Case-oriented Team	*A Resource-oriented Team*
Focuses on specific *individuals* and discrete *services* to address barriers to learning	Focuses on *all* students and the *resources, programs, and systems* to address barriers to learning AND promote healthy development
Sometimes called	Possibly called
• Child study team • Student study team • Student success team • Student assistance team • Teacher assistance team • IEP team	• Learning supports resource team • Resource coordinating team • Resource coordinating council • School support team
EXAMPLES OF FUNCTIONS:	EXAMPLES OF FUNCTIONS:
• Triage • Referral • Case monitoring/management • Case progress review • Case reassessment	• Aggregating data across students and from teachers to analyze school needs • Mapping resources in school and community • Analyzing resources • Identifying the most pressing program development needs at the school • Coordinating and integrating school resources and connecting with community resources • Establishing priorities for strengthening programs and developing new ones • Planning and facilitating ways to strengthen and develop new programs and systems • Recommending how resources should be deployed and redeployed • Developing strategies for enhancing resources • Social "marketing"

This metaphor, of course, reflects all the important clinical efforts undertaken by staff alone and when they meet together to work on specific cases.

The *resource-oriented* focus is captured by what can be called the *bridge* metaphor.

> In a small town, one weekend a group of school staff went fishing together down at the river. Not long after they got there, a child came floating down the rapids calling for help. One of the group on the shore quickly dived in and pulled the child out. Minutes later, another, then another, and then many more children were coming down the river. Soon everyone in the group was diving in and dragging children to the shore, resuscitating them, and then jumping back. But there were too many. All of a sudden, in the midst of all this frenzy, one of the group stopped jumping in and was seen walking away. Her colleagues were amazed and irate. How could she leave when there were so many children to save? About an hour later, to everyone's relief, the flow of children stopped, and the group could finally catch their breaths.
>
> At that moment, their colleague came back. They turned on her and angrily shouted: *How could you walk off when we needed everyone here to save the children?*
>
> She replied: *It occurred to me that someone ought to go upstream and find out why so many kids were falling into the river. What I found is that the old wooden bridge had several planks missing, and when some children tried to jump over the gap, they couldn't make it and fell through into the river. So I got a team together, and we fixed the bridge.*

Fixing and building better bridges is a good way to think about prevention, and it helps underscore the importance of taking time to improve and enhance resources, programs, and systems.

A resource-oriented team exemplifies the type of mechanism needed for overall cohesion of school support programs and systems. As indicated, its focus is not on specific individuals but on how resources are used.

In pursuing its functions, the team provides what often is a missing link for managing and enhancing programs and systems in ways that integrate, strengthen, and stimulate new and improved interventions. For example, such a mechanism can be used to (a) map and analyze activities and resources to improve their use in preventing and ameliorating problems, (b) build effective referral, case management, and quality assurance systems, (c) enhance procedures for management of programs and information and for communication among school staff and with the home, and (d) explore ways to redeploy and enhance resources—such as clarifying which activities are nonproductive, suggesting better uses for resources, and establishing priorities for developing new interventions, as well as reaching out to connect with additional resources in the school district and community.

Minimally, a resource-oriented team can reduce fragmentation and enhance cost efficacy by assisting in ways that encourage programs to function in a coordinated and increasingly integrated way. For example, the team can coordinate resources, enhance communication among school staff and with the home about available assistance and referral processes, and monitor programs to be certain they are functioning effectively and efficiently. More generally, this group can provide leadership in guiding school personnel and clientele in evolving the school's vision, priorities, and practices for learning supports and enhancing resources.

Although a resource-oriented mechanism might be created solely around psychosocial programs, it is meant to focus on resources related to all major learning supports programs and services. Thus, it tries to bring together representatives of all these programs and services. This might include, for example, school counselors, psychologists, nurses, social workers, attendance and dropout counselors, special education staff, physical educators and afterschool program staff, bilingual and Title I program coordinators, health educators, safe and drug-free school staff, and union reps. It also should include representatives of any community agency that is significantly involved with the school. Beyond these "service" providers, such a team needs a leader from the school's administration and is well advised to add the energies and expertise of regular classroom teachers, noncertificated staff (e.g., front office, food service, custodian, bus driver), parents, and older students.

Properly constituted, trained, and supported, a resource-oriented team complements the work of the site's governance body through providing on-site overview, leadership, and advocacy for all activity aimed at addressing barriers to learning and teaching. Having at least one representative from the resource team on the school's governing and planning bodies ensures infrastructure connections for maintaining, improving, and increasingly integrating learning supports and classroom instruction. And of course, having an administrator on the team provides the necessary link with the school's administrative decision making about allocation of budget, space, staff development time, and other resources.

It is conceivable that one person could start the process of understanding the fundamental resource-oriented functions and delineating an infrastructure to carry them out. It is better, however, if several stakeholders put their heads together. Where creation of "another team" is seen as a burden, existing teams, such as student or teacher assistance teams, school crisis teams, and healthy school teams, have demonstrated the ability to do resource-oriented functions. In adding the resource-oriented functions to another team's work, great care must be taken to structure the agenda so that sufficient time is devoted to the additional tasks. For small schools, a large team often is not feasible, but a two-person team can still do the job.[1]

A Resource-oriented Mechanism for a Family of Schools

Schools in the same geographic or catchment area have a number of shared concerns, and schools in the feeder pattern often interact with students from the same family. Furthermore, some programs and personnel already are or can be shared in strategic ways by several neighboring schools, thereby reducing costs by minimizing redundancy and opening up ways to achieve economies of scale.

A multisite council can provide a mechanism to help ensure cohesive and equitable deployment of resources and also can enhance the pooling of resources. Such a mechanism can be particularly useful for integrating the efforts of high schools and their feeder middle and elementary schools and connecting with neighborhood resources. This clearly is important in addressing barriers with those families who have youngsters attending more than one level of schooling in the same cluster. It is neither cost-effective nor good intervention for each school to contact a family separately in instances where several children from a family are in need of special attention. With respect to linking with community resources, multischool teams are especially attractive to community agencies that often don't have the time or personnel to make independent arrangements with every school.

In general, a group of schools can benefit from a multisite resource mechanism designed to provide leadership, facilitate communication and connection, and ensure quality improvement across sites. For example, a multisite body, or what we call a "learning supports resource council," might consist of a high school and its feeder middle and elementary schools. It brings together one to two representatives from each school's resource team (see Guide 7.11).

The council meets about once a month to help (a) coordinate and integrate programs serving multiple schools, (b) identify and meet common needs with respect to guidelines and staff development, and (c) create linkages and collaborations among schools and with community agencies. In this last regard, it can play a special role in community outreach both to create formal working relationships and to ensure that all participating schools have access to such resources.

More generally, the council provides a useful mechanism for leadership, communication, maintenance, quality improvement, and ongoing development of a comprehensive continuum of programs and services. Natural starting points for councils are the sharing of needs assessments, resource maps, analyses, and recommendations for reform and restructuring. Specific areas of initial focus would be on local, high priority concerns, such as addressing violence and developing prevention programs and safe school and neighborhood plans.

Representatives from learning supports resource councils would be invaluable members of planning groups (e.g., service planning area councils, local management boards). They bring information about specific schools, clusters of schools, and local neighborhoods and do so in ways that reflect the importance of school-community partnerships.

Guide 7.11   Resource-oriented Mechanisms Across a Family of Schools

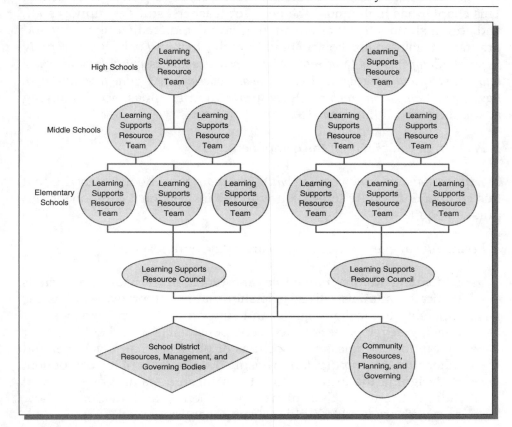

CONCLUDING COMMENTS

Given the tremendous pressure on schools to improve academic indicators, it's not surprising that so much attention centers on direct instructional strategies. For too many students, however, teachers are finding that the educational mission is thwarted because of multifaceted factors that interfere with youngsters' learning and performance. Schoolwide approaches to address barriers to learning and teaching are essential for teachers and students to succeed.

Policymakers do understand that they must invest in learning support programs and services, and they do so. But they do too little to rethink this arena of school activity. Indeed, with the increasing focus on test scores and decreasing budgets, the tendency is to lay off student support staff, rather than understand that such personnel could be used in better ways to enhance learning supports in classrooms and schoolwide. In this chapter, we have tried to lay the foundation for such understanding.

Clearly, establishing new directions for schools requires policy action. This chapter has highlighted the need for teachers, student support staff, and administrators to act as a team in guiding and facilitating policy and program development. Policy should specify that *an Enabling or Learning Supports Component is to be pursued as a primary and essential facet of school improvement and in ways that complement, overlap, and fully integrate with the instructional component.* Developmental guidelines accompanying new policy can outline ways to

1. *Phase in* development of the component.

2. *Expand standards and accountability indicators* for schools to ensure that this component is fully integrated with the instructional component and pursued equitably.

3. *Restructure* at every school and districtwide with respect to

- Redefining administrative roles and functions to ensure that there is dedicated administrative leadership that is authorized and has the capability to facilitate, guide, and support the systemic changes for ongoing development of such a component at every school
- Reframing the roles and functions of pupil services personnel and other student support staff to ensure development of the component
- Redesigning the infrastructure to establish a team at every school and districtwide that plans, implements, and evaluates how resources are used to build the component's capacity

4. *Weave resources into a cohesive continuum of interventions over time.* Specifically, school staff responsible for the component should be mandated to collaborate with families and community stakeholders to evolve systems for

- Promoting healthy development and preventing problems
- Intervening early to address problems as soon after onset as feasible
- Assisting those with chronic and severe problems

In addition, all stakeholders can work together to move

- *Boards of education:* toward establishing a standing subcommittee focused specifically on ensuring effective implementation of the policy for developing a component to address barriers to student learning at each school
- *Preservice and inservice programs* for school personnel: toward including a substantial focus on the concept of an Enabling Component and how to operationalize it at a school in ways that fully integrate with instruction.

With appropriate policy, guidelines, and capacity-building resources aligned, work can advance with respect to *restructuring, transforming,* and *enhancing* learning supports. The long-range aim is to weave all resources together into the fabric of every school and evolve a comprehensive component that effectively addresses barriers to development, learning, and teaching. To these ends, the focus is on *all* school resources, including compensatory and special education, support services, adult education, recreation and enrichment programs, and facility use, and *all* community *resources*—public and private agencies, families, businesses; services, programs, facilities; volunteers, professionals-in-training, and pro bono professional contributions. Once policymakers recognize the essential nature of a Learning Supports Component, it will be easier to braid resources to address barriers and, in the process, elevate the status of programs to enhance healthy development.

When resources are combined properly, the *end product* can be cohesive and potent *school-community connections.* Such connections are fundamental to strengthening schools, neighborhoods, and communities and creating caring and supportive environments that maximize learning and well-being. We return to this topic in Chapter 8.

Education reform is a paradox.

That's right. Everyone is going down the same road in different directions.

REFLECTION AND STIMULUS FOR DISCUSSION

Key Insights About "Establishing a Schoolwide Learning Supports Component"

Based on what you learned so far,

> *Identify (and discuss) what is meant by an Enabling Component, and outline the major arenas the component encompasses.*

If there is an opportunity for group discussion, you may find the following group process guidelines helpful:

- Start by identifying someone who will facilitate the group interchange.
- Take a few minutes to make a few individual notes on a worksheet.
- Be sure all major points are compiled for sharing with other groups.
- Ask someone else to watch the time so that the group doesn't bog down.

ACTIVITY

- Using the matrix on the following page, interview student support staff at a school and map the existing programs and services.
- Note which cells in the matrix are "impoverished."
- What are your conclusions about the school's approach to enabling learning by providing comprehensive learning supports?

Matrix for Reviewing Scope and Content of a Component to Address Barriers to Learning*

Scope of Intervention

		Systems for Promoting Healthy Development & Preventing Problems	Systems for Early Intervention (early after problem onset)	Systems of Care
	Classroom-focused Enabling			
Organizing around the **Content/ "Curriculum"** for addressing barriers to learning & promoting healthy development	Crisis/ Emergency Assistance & Prevention			
	Support for Transitions			
	Home Involvement in Schooling			
	Community Outreach/ Volunteers			
	Student and Family Assistance			

Accommodations for Differences & Disabilities   Specialized Assistance & Other Intensified Interventions (e.g., Special Education & School-based Behavioral Health)

*Note that specific schoolwide and classroom-based activities related to positive behavior support, "prereferral" interventions, and the eight components of the Centers for Disease Control and Prevention's Coordinated School Health Program are embedded into the six content ("curriculum") areas.

NOTE

1. The Center for Mental Health in Schools at UCLA has available hard copy and online resources to guide development of resource-oriented teams and for rethinking how resources are used for learning support. Included are learning supports job descriptions for administrators and staff. For example, see *Developing Resource-oriented Mechanisms to Enhance Learning Supports* (2003) online at http://smhp.psych.ucla.edu/pdfdocs/contedu/developing_resource_oriented-mechanisms.pdf and *Resource-oriented Teams: Key Infrastructure Mechanisms for Enhancing Education Supports* (2001) online at http://smhp.psych.ucla.edu/qf/infrastructure_tt/excerptfromresource_oriented_teams.pdf.

REFERENCES

Hargreaves, A. (1994). *Changing teachers, changing times: Teachers' work and culture in the postmodern age.* New York: Teachers College Press.

Senge, P. M. (1990). *The fifth discipline: The art and practice of the learning organization.* New York: Currency/Doubleday.

Vander Ark, T. (2002). The case for small schools. *Educational Leadership, 59,* 55–59.

*Chapter 14 contains a list of special resources related
to the above matters available at no cost from the national
Center for Mental Health in Schools, which is at UCLA and is
directed by the authors of this book. Go to http://smhp.psych.ucla.edu.*

School-Family-
Community
Connections

8

One of the most important, cross-cutting social policy perspectives to emerge in recent years is an awareness that no single institution can create all the conditions that young people need to flourish.

—Atelia I. Melaville
and Martin Blank (1998)

Can you define "collaboration" for me?

Sure! Collaboration is an unnatural act between nonconsenting adults.

ORIENTING QUESTIONS

? What makes school-community collaboration an imperative?
? What is the range of resources that could be woven into such a collaboration?
? What are the basic dimensions of school-community collaborative arrangements?

Never doubt that a small group of thoughtful, committed people can change the world. Indeed, it is the only thing that ever has.

—Margaret Mead

Recent years have seen an escalating expansion in school-community linkages (Center for Mental Health in Schools, 2002; Honig, Kahne, & McLaughlin, 2001; Southwest Educational Development Laboratory, 2001). Initiatives are sprouting in a rather dramatic and ad hoc manner.

Comprehensive linkages represent a promising direction for generating essential interventions to address barriers to learning, enhance healthy development, and strengthen families and neighborhoods. For schools, such links are seen as a way to provide more support for schools, students, and families. For agencies, connection with schools is seen as providing better access to families and youth and thus as providing an opportunity to reach and have an impact on hard-to-reach clients. The interest in working together is bolstered by concern about widespread fragmentation of school and community interventions. The hope is that integrated resources will have a greater impact on at-risk factors and on promoting healthy development.

While informal school-community linkages are relatively simple to acquire, establishing major long-term connections is complicated. They require vision, cohesive policy, and basic systemic reform. The difficulties are readily seen in attempts to evolve a comprehensive, multifaceted, and integrated continuum of school-community interventions. Such a comprehensive continuum involves more than connecting with the community to enhance resources to support instruction, provide mentoring, and improve facilities. It involves more than school-linked, integrated services and activities. It requires weaving school and community resources together in ways that can be achieved only through connections that are formalized and institutionalized, with major responsibilities shared.

School-community connections often are referred to as collaborations. The intent in forming a collaboration usually is to sustain the connections over time. Optimally, such collaborations formally blend together resources of at least one school and sometimes a group of schools or an entire school district with resources in a given neighborhood or the larger community.

Building an effective collaboration requires an enlightened vision, creative leadership, and new and multifaceted roles for professionals who work in schools and communities, as well as for all who are willing to assume leadership. And in thinking about all this, it is essential not to overemphasize the topics of coordinating community services and co-locating services on school sites. Such thinking ignores the range of resources in a community, including human and social capital, businesses, community-based organizations, postsecondary institutions, faith-based and civic groups, parks and libraries, and facilities for recreation, learning, enrichment, and support. Also, the overemphasis on service agencies downplays the need to also restructure the various education support programs and services that schools own and operate. As we have noted, some policymakers have the mistaken impression that community service agencies can effectively meet the needs of schools in addressing barriers to learning. Even when one adds together community and school assets, the total set of services in impoverished locales is woefully inadequate.

In general, collaboration among schools, families, and communities could improve schools, strengthen families and neighborhoods, and lead to a marked reduction in young people's problems. Poorly implemented collaboration, however, risks becoming another reform that promised a lot, did little good, and even did some harm. With hope for a promising future, this chapter briefly

- Underscores the "why" of school-family-community collaborations
- Highlights their key facets
- Sketches out the state of the art across the country
- Discusses steps for building and maintaining school-community partnerships
- Offers some recommendations for local school and community policymakers and other leaders

WHY CONNECT?

Schools are located in communities, but often are islands with no bridges to the mainland. Families live in neighborhoods, often with little connection to each other or to the schools their youngsters attend. Neighborhood entities such as agencies, youth groups, and businesses have major stakes in the community. All these entities affect each other, for good or bad. Because of this and because they share goals related to the education, socialization, and well-being of the young, schools, homes, and communities must collaborate with each other if they are to minimize problems and maximize results with respect to overlapping goals.

Dealing with multiple and interrelated problems, such as poverty, child development, education, violence, crime, safety, housing, and employment, requires multiple and interrelated solutions. Interrelated solutions require collaboration. Promoting well-being, resilience, and protective factors and empowering families, communities, and schools also require the concerted effort of all stakeholders. All stakeholders means *all*, not just service providers. As important as health and human services are, such services remain only one facet of a comprehensive, cohesive approach for strengthening families and neighborhoods. The community side of school-community collaboratives must encompass more than representatives of service agencies. The school side must include more than student support staff. Teachers and families, in particular, have a major stake in school-community connections.

It seems evident that when schools are an integral and positive part of the community, they are better positioned to address barriers to learning; enhance opportunities for learning, development, and academic performance; reduce discipline problems; expand home involvement; increase staff morale; and improve use of resources. Indeed, *leaving no child behind is only feasible through well-designed collaborative efforts.*

Similarly, working with schools, families, and other community entities can enhance parenting and socialization, address psychosocial problems, and strengthen the fabric of family and community well-being and community self-sufficiency. Agencies, for example, can make services more accessible to youth and families by linking with schools and can connect better with and have an impact on hard-to-reach clients.

Interest in working together also is bolstered by concern about widespread fragmentation of school and community interventions. Clearly, appropriate and effective school-community collaboration should be part of any strategy for developing comprehensive, multifaceted, and integrated approaches to promote well-being and address barriers. Strong school-community connections are critical in impoverished communities where schools often are the largest piece of public real estate and resources and also may be the single largest employer.

Comprehensive collaboration represents a promising direction for generating essential interventions to address barriers to learning, enhance healthy development, and strengthen families and neighborhoods. This is accomplished by weaving together a critical mass of resources and strategies that enables effective teaching and learning by supporting all youth, their families, and teachers.

> It is only those who don't care about where they end up who can afford not to be involved in which way they are going.

DEFINING COLLABORATION AND ITS PURPOSES

As we have noted, some wit defined collaboration as "an unnatural act between nonconsenting adults." This captures the reality that establishing a collaborative is a snap compared to the task of turning the group into an effective, ongoing mechanism. Collaboration involves more than simply working together, and a collaborative is more than a process to enhance cooperation and coordination. Thus, teachers who team are not a collaborative; they are a teaching team. Professionals who work as a multidisciplinary team to coordinate treatment are not a collaborative; they are a treatment team. Interagency teams established to enhance coordination and communication across agencies are not collaboratives; they are coordinating teams.

A collaborative is a form of collaboration that involves establishing an infrastructure for *working together to accomplish specific functions* related to developing and enhancing interventions and systems in arenas where the participants' agendas overlap. One hallmark of authentic collaboration is a *formal agreement* among participants to establish mechanisms and processes to accomplish *mutually desired results*—usually outcomes that would be difficult to achieve by any of the stakeholders alone. Thus, while participants may have a primary affiliation elsewhere, they commit to working together under specified conditions to pursue a shared vision and common set of goals.

Effective collaboratives are built with vision, policy, leadership, infrastructure, and capacity building. A collaborative structure requires shared governance (power, authority, decision making, accountability) and weaving together an adequate set of resources. It also requires establishing well-defined and effective *working* relationships that enable participants to overcome their agendas. If this cannot be accomplished, the intent of pursuing a shared agenda and achieving a collective vision is jeopardized.

Growing appreciation of human and social capital has resulted in collaboratives expanding to include a wide range of stakeholders (people, groups, formal and informal organizations). Many who at best were silent partners in the past now are finding their way to the collaborative table and becoming key players. The political realities of local control have expanded collaborative bodies to encompass local policymakers, representatives of families, nonprofessionals, and volunteers. Families, of course, have always provided a direct connection between school and community, but now they are seeking a greater decision-making role. In addition, advocates for students with special needs have opened the way for increased parent and youth participation in forums making decisions about interventions. Clearly, any effort to connect home, community, and school resources must embrace a wide spectrum of stakeholders.

In the context of a collaborative, collaboration is both a desired process and an outcome. That is, the intent is to work together to establish strong working relationships that are enduring. However, family, community, and school collaboration is not an end in itself. It is a turning point meant to enable participants to pursue increasingly potent strategies for strengthening families, schools, and communities.

Effective collaboratives, then, attempt to weave the responsibilities and resources of participating stakeholders together to create a new form of unified entity. For our purposes here, any group designed to connect a school, families, and other entities from the surrounding neighborhood is referred to as a "school-community" collaborative. Such collaboratives may include entities focused on providing programs for education, literacy, youth development, the arts, health and human services, juvenile justice, vocational education, economic development, and more. They may include various sources of human, social, and economic capital, including teachers; student support staff; youth; families; community-based and -linked organizations, such as public and private health and human service agencies; civic groups; businesses; faith-based organizations; and institutions of postsecondary learning.

Operationally, a collaborative is defined by its *functions*. That is, a collaborative is about accomplishing functions, not about establishing and maintaining a "collaborative" body. Major examples of functions include the following:

- Facilitating communication, cooperation, coordination, integration
- Operationalizing the vision of stakeholders into desired functions and tasks
- Enhancing support for and developing a policy commitment to ensure that the necessary resources are dispensed for accomplishing desired functions
- Advancing advocacy, analysis, priority setting, governance, planning, implementation, and evaluation related to desired functions
- Aggregating data from schools and neighborhood to analyze system needs

- Mapping, analyzing, managing, redeploying, and braiding available resources to enable accomplishment of desired functions
- Establishing leadership and institutional and operational mechanisms (e.g., infrastructure) for guiding and managing the accomplishment of desired functions
- Defining and incorporating new roles and functions into job descriptions
- Building capacity for planning, implementing, and evaluating desired functions, including ongoing stakeholder development for continuous learning and renewal and for bringing new arrivals up to speed
- Defining standards and ensuring accountability
- Promoting social marketing

Functions encompass specific tasks, such as mapping and analyzing resources; exploring ways to share facilities, equipment, and other resources; expanding opportunities for community service, internships, jobs, recreation, and enrichment; developing pools of nonprofessional volunteers and professional pro bono assistance; making recommendations about priorities for use of resources; raising funds and pursuing grants; and advocating for appropriate decision making.

> Much of the emerging theory and practice of family and community connections with schools encourages a rethinking of our understanding of how children develop and how the various people and contexts fit together to support that development.
>
> —Southwest Educational Development Laboratory (2001)

In organizing a collaborative, the fundamental principle is *structure follows function.* Based on clear functions, a differentiated infrastructure must be developed to enable the accomplishment of functions and related tasks. Minimally, the need is for infrastructure mechanisms to steer and do work on a regular basis. And since the work almost always overlaps with that of others, a collaborative needs to establish connections with other bodies.

COLLABORATION: A GROWING MOVEMENT

Most of us know how hard it is to work effectively with a group. In fact, we all can point to committees and teams that drain our time and energy to little avail.

Nevertheless, the fact remains that no organization can be truly effective if too many staff work in isolation. The same is true when school and community entities do not work together. Thus, calls for collaboration have increased, and initiatives for school-community collaboration and collaborative bodies are springing up everywhere. Moreover, increased federal funding for afterschool programs at school sites is enhancing opportunities for collaboration by expanding recreation, enrichment, academic supports, and child care programs.

Various levels and forms of school, community, and family collaboration are being tested, including statewide initiatives. Some cataloguing has begun, but there is no complete picture of the scope of activity.

From what is known, it is clear that many efforts to collaborate have not taken the form of a collaborative. Many demonstration projects are mainly efforts to incorporate health, mental health, and social services into *centers* (including health centers, family centers, parent centers). These centers are established at or near a school and use terms such as *school-linked* or *school-based services, coordinated services, wrap-around services, one-stop shopping, full-service schools, systems of care,* and *community schools.*[1]

When collaborations and collaboratives are developed as part of funded projects, the aims generally are to improve coordination and eventually integrate many programs and enhance their linkages to school sites. Scope varies. Most of the projects want to improve access to health services (including immunizations, prevention programs, substance abuse, asthma, and pregnancy) and access to social service programs (including foster care, family preservation, and child care). In addition or as a primary focus, some are concerned with (a) expanding afterschool academic, recreation, and enrichment, including tutoring, youth sports and clubs, art, music, and museum programs, (b) building systems of care, including case management and specialized assistance, (c) reducing delinquency, including truancy prevention, conflict mediation, and violence reduction, (d) enhancing transitions to work, career, and postsecondary education, including mentoring, internships, career academies, and job shadowing and job placement programs, and (e) strengthening schools and community connections through adopt-a-school programs, use of volunteers and peer supports, and neighborhood coalitions.

Projects have been stimulated by diverse initiatives:

- Some are driven by school reform.
- Some are connected to efforts to reform community health and social service agencies.
- Some stem from the community school and youth development movements.
- A few stem from community development endeavors.

Currently, only a few projects are driven by school reform. Most stem from efforts to reform community health and social services with the aim of reducing redundancy and increasing access and effectiveness. These tend to focus narrowly on "services." Projects initiated by schools are connecting schools and communities to enhance school-to-career opportunities, develop pools of volunteers and mentors, and expand afterschool recreation and enrichment programs.

The community school and youth development movements have spawned school-community collaborations that clearly go beyond a narrow service emphasis. They encourage a view of schools not only as community centers where families can access services but as hubs for communitywide learning and activity. In doing so, they encompass concepts and practices aimed at promoting protective factors, asset building, wellness, and empowerment. Included are efforts to establish full-fledged community schools, programs for community and social capital mobilization, and initiatives to establish community policies and structures that enhance youth support, safety, recreation, work, service, and enrichment. Their efforts, along with adult education and training at neighborhood schools, are changing the old view that schools close when the youngsters leave. The concept of a "second shift" at a school site to respond to community needs is beginning to spread.

While data are sparse, a reasonable inference from available research is that school-community collaboration can be successful and cost-effective over the long run. Moreover, school-community collaborations not only have the potential for improving access to and co-ordination of interventions, but they encourage schools to open their doors and enhance opportunities for community and family involvement.

Currently, as portrayed in the top section of Guide 8.1, schools and community entities usually function as separate agents, with a few discrete linkages designed to address highly circumscribed matters. Often the linkages are encouraged by and/or directed at parents of school-age children. The

---

How many members of a collaborative does it take to change a lightbulb?

- 14 to share similar experiences of changing lightbulbs and how the lightbulb could have been changed differently
- 7 to caution about the dangers of changing lightbulbs
- 27 to point out spelling/grammar errors in posts about changing lightbulbs
- 53 to flame the spelling/grammar critics
- 1 to correct the spelling and grammar in the spelling/grammar flames
- 6 to argue whether it's "lightbulb" or "lightbulb"

Family and Citizen Involvement

For various reasons, many collaboratives around the country consist mainly of professionals. Family and other citizen involvement may be limited to a few representatives of powerful organizations or to token participants who are expected to sign off on decisions.

Genuine involvement of a wide range of representative families and citizens requires a deep commitment of collaborative organizers to recruiting and building the capacity of such stakeholders so that they can competently participate as enfranchised and informed decision makers.

Collaboratives that proactively work to ensure that a broad range of stakeholders are participating effectively can establish an essential democratic base for their work. This also helps buffer against inevitable mobility that results in participant turnover. Such an approach not only enhances family and community involvement, but it may be essential to sustaining collaborative efforts over the long run.

immediate goal of many school-family-community collaboratives is to bring the entities together to work in more cooperative ways and where feasible to integrate resources and activities when they are dealing with overlapping concerns (see middle section of Guide 8.1). Ultimately, some argue that it is all about community, that families should be understood and nurtured as the heart of any community, and that schools should be completely embedded and not seen as a separate agent (see bottom section of Guide 8.1).

Guide 8.1   School-Community Relationships: Current Situation and Goals for the Future

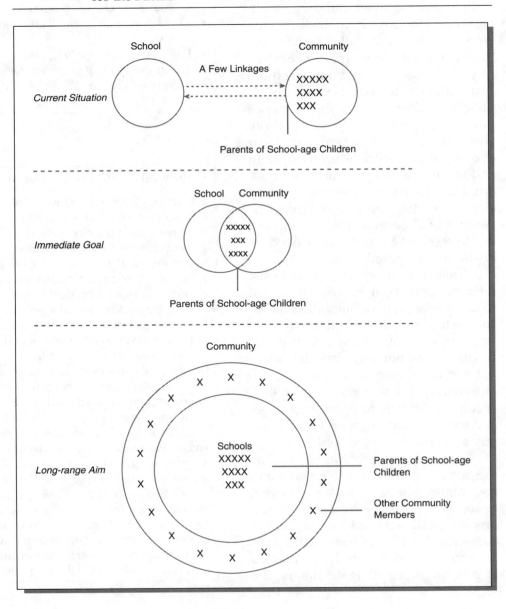

UNDERSTANDING KEY FACETS
OF SCHOOL-COMMUNITY CONNECTIONS

As should be evident by now, school-community connections differ in terms of purposes adopted and functions pursued. They also differ in terms of a range of other dimensions. For example, they may vary in their degree of formality, time commitment, breadth of the connections, as well as the amount of systemic change required to carry out their functions and achieve their purposes.

Key Dimensions

Because family, community, and school collaboration can differ in so many ways, it is helpful to think in terms of categories of key factors relevant to such arrangements (see Guide 8.2).

Range of Resources

Guide 8.3 highlights the wealth of community resources that should be considered in establishing family, community, and school connections.

BARRIERS TO COLLABORATION

Collaboration is a developing process. It must be continuously nurtured, facilitated, and supported, and special attention must be given to overcoming institutional and personal barriers.

Years ago, former surgeon general Jocelyn Elders noted: "We all say we want to collaborate, but what we really mean is that we want to continue doing things as we have always done them while others change to fit what we are doing." More recently, some advocates for collaboration have cautioned that some collaborations amount to little more than groups of people sitting around engaging in "collabo-babble."

Barriers to collaboration arise from a variety of institutional and personal factors. A fundamental institutional barrier to family-community-school collaboration is the degree to which efforts to establish such connections are *marginalized* in policy and practice. The extent to which this is the case can be seen in how few resources most schools deploy to build effective collaboratives.

Institutional barriers are seen when existing policy, accountability, leadership, budget, space, time schedules, and capacity-building agenda do not address the effective and efficient use of collaborative arrangements to accomplish desired results. This may simply be a matter of benign neglect. More often, it reflects a lack of understanding, commitment, and/or capability related to establishing and maintaining a potent infrastructure for working together and for sharing resources. Occasionally, active forces are at work that mean to undermine collaboration.

Guide 8.2   Some Key Dimensions Relevant to Family-Community-School Collaborative Arrangements

I.   Initiation
   A. School-led
   B. Community-driven

II. Nature of Collaboration
   A. Formal
      • Memorandum of understanding
      • Contract
      • Organizational/operational mechanisms
   B. Informal
      • Verbal agreements
      • Ad hoc arrangements

III. Focus
   A. Improvement of program and service provision
      • For enhancing case management
      • For enhancing use of resources
   B. Major systemic changes
      • To enhance coordination
      • For organizational restructuring
      • For transforming system structure/function

IV. Scope of Collaboration
   A. Number of programs and services involved (from just a few—up to a comprehensive, multifaceted continuum)
   B. Horizontal collaboration
      • Within a school/agency
      • Among schools/agencies
   C. Vertical collaboration
      • Within a catchment area (e.g., school and community agency, family of schools, two or more agencies)
      • Among different levels of jurisdictions (e.g., community/city/county/ state/federal)

V.   Scope of Potential Impact
   A. *Narrow-band.* A small proportion of youth and families can access what they need.

B. *Broadband.* All in need can access what they need.

VI. Ownership and Governance of Programs and Services
   A. Owned and governed by school
   B. Owned and governed by community
   C. Shared ownership and governance
   D. Public-private venture; shared ownership and governance

VII. Location of Programs and Services
   A. Community-based, school-linked
   B. School-based

VIII. Degree of Cohesiveness Among Multiple Interventions Serving the Same Student/Family
   A. Unconnected
   B. Communicating
   C. Cooperating
   D. Coordinated
   E. Integrated

IX. Level of Systemic Intervention Focus
   A. Systems for promoting healthy development
   B. Systems for prevention of problems
   C. Systems for early-after-onset of problems
   D. Systems of care for treatment of severe, pervasive, and/or chronic problems
   E. Full continuum including all levels

X.   Arenas for Collaborative Activity
   A. Health (physical and mental)
   B. Education
   C. Social services
   D. Work/career
   E. Enrichment/recreation
   F. Juvenile justice
   G. Neighborhood/community improvement

Guide 8.3   A Range of Community Resources That Could Be Part of a Collaboration

County Agencies and Bodies

(e.g., depts. of health, mental health, children and family services, public social services, probation, sheriff, office of education, fire, service planning area councils, recreation and parks, library, courts, housing)

Municipal Agencies and Bodies

(e.g., parks and recreation, library, police, fire, courts, civic event units)

Physical and Mental Health and Psychosocial Concerns Facilities and Groups

(e.g., hospitals, HMOs, clinics, guidance centers, Planned Parenthood, Aid to Victims, MADD, "Friends of" groups, family crisis and support centers, help lines, hotlines, shelters, mediation and dispute resolution centers, private practitioners)

Mutual Support/Self-help Groups

(e.g., for almost every problem and many other activities)

Child Care/Preschool Centers

Postsecondary Education Institutions/Students

(e.g., community colleges, state universities, public and private colleges and universities, vocational colleges; specific schools within these such as schools of law, education, nursing, dentistry)

Service Agencies

(e.g., PTA/PTSA, United Way, clothing and food pantry, Visiting Nurses Association, Cancer Society, Catholic Charities, Red Cross, Salvation Army, volunteer agencies, legal aid society)

Service Clubs and Philanthropic Organizations

(e.g., Lions Club, Rotary Club, Optimists, Assistance League, men's and women's clubs, League of Women Voters, veteran's groups, foundations)

Youth Agencies and Groups

(e.g., Boys and Girls Clubs, Y's, scouts, 4-H, Woodcraft Rangers)

Sports/Health/Fitness/Outdoor Groups

(e.g., sports teams, athletic leagues, local gyms, conservation associations, Audubon Society)

Community-based Organizations

(e.g., neighborhood and homeowners' associations, Neighborhood Watch, block clubs, housing project associations, economic development groups, civic associations)

Faith Community Institutions

(e.g., congregations and subgroups, clergy associations, Interfaith Hunger Coalition)

Legal Assistance Groups and Practitioners

(e.g., public counsel, schools of law)

Ethnic Associations

(e.g., Committee for Armenian Students in Public Schools, Korean Youth Center, United Cambodian Community, African American, Latino, Asian Pacific, Native American Organizations)

Special Interest Associations and Clubs

(e.g., Future Scientists and Engineers of America, pet owner and other animal-oriented groups)

Artists and Cultural Institutions

(e.g., museums, art galleries, zoos, theater groups, motion picture studios, TV and radio stations, writers' organizations, instrumental/choral, drawing/painting, technology-based arts, literary clubs, collector's groups)

Businesses/Corporations/Unions

(e.g., neighborhood business associations, chambers of commerce, local shops, restaurants, banks, AAA, Teamsters, school employee unions)

Media

(e.g., newspapers, TV and radio, local access cable)

Family Members, Local Residents, Senior Citizens Groups

Examples of institutional barriers include

- Policies that mandate collaboration but do not enable the process (e.g., a failure to reconcile differences among participants with respect to the outcomes for which they are accountable; inadequate provision for braiding funds across agencies and categorical programs)
- Policies for collaboration that do not provide adequate resources and time for leadership and stakeholder training and for overcoming barriers to collaboration
- Leadership that does not establish an effective infrastructure, especially mechanisms for steering and accomplishing tasks on a regular, ongoing basis
- Differences in the conditions and incentives associated with participation, such as the fact that meetings usually are set during the workday, which means that community agency and school personnel are paid participants, while family members are expected to volunteer their time

At the personal level, barriers mostly stem from practical deterrents, negative attitudes, and deficiencies of knowledge and skill. These vary for different stakeholders but often include problems related to work schedules, transportation, child care, communication skills, understanding of differences in organizational culture, and accommodations for language and cultural differences.

Other barriers arise because of inadequate attention to factors associated with systemic change. How well an innovation such as a collaborative is implemented depends to a significant degree on the personnel doing the implementing and the motivation and capabilities of participants. Sufficient resources and time must be redeployed so they can learn and carry out new functions effectively. And when newcomers join, well-designed procedures must be in place to bring them up to speed.

When schools and community agencies are at the same table, it is a given that problems will arise related to the differences in organizational mission, functions, cultures, bureaucracies, and accountabilities. Considerable effort will be required to teach each other about these matters. When families are at the table, power differentials are common, especially when low income families are involved and are confronted with credentialed and titled professionals. And if the collaborative is not well conceived and carefully developed, this generates additional barriers.

In too many instances, so-called school-community partnerships have amounted to little more than co-location of community agency staff on school campuses. Services continue to function in relative isolation from each other, focusing on discrete problems and specialized services for individuals and small groups. Too little thought is given to the importance of meshing, as contrasted with simply linking, community services and programs with existing school-owned and -operated activity. The result is that a small number of youngsters are provided services that they may not otherwise have received, but little connection is made with families, teachers, and other school staff and related programs. Because of this, a new form of fragmentation is emerging as community and school professionals engage in a form of parallel play at school sites.

Moreover, when outside professionals are brought into schools, district student support staff may view the move as discounting their skills and threatening their jobs. On the other side, the outsiders often feel unappreciated. Conflicts arise over turf, use of space, confidentiality, and liability. School professionals tend not to understand the culture of community agencies; agency staff are rather naive about the culture of schools.

Working collaboratively requires overcoming barriers. Participants must be sensitive to a variety of human and institutional differences, and learn strategies for dealing with them. These include differences in sociocultural and economic background and current lifestyle, primary language spoken, skin color, sex, motivation, and capability. In addition, there are differences related to power, status, orientation, and organizational culture.

Differences can be complementary and helpful—as when staff from different disciplines work with and learn from each other. Differences become a barrier in collaboratives when negative attitudes and inappropriate competition are allowed to prevail. Interpersonally, the result generally is conflict and poor communication. For example, many individuals who have been treated unfairly, been discriminated against, or been deprived of opportunity and status at school, on the job, and in society use whatever means they can to seek redress and sometimes to strike back. Such an individual may promote conflict in hopes of correcting power imbalances or at least to call attention to injustice and inequality. However, because power differentials are so institutionalized, it is common for individual action to have little impact. This engenders growing frustration and a tendency to fight with anyone who seems to represent institutionalized power. Such fighting usually begins with words such as "you don't understand," or worse, "you probably don't want to understand." Underlying all this may be the message "you are my enemy."

It is unfortunate when barriers arise between those we are trying to help; it is a travesty when such barriers interfere with helpers' working together effectively. The problem for a collaborative is how to keep such conflict from becoming counterproductive. Too much conflict among collaborative members interferes with accomplishing goals and contributes in a major way to burnout.

> Heard at a collaborative meeting where a member was talking on and on about too little.
> "Has he finished yet?"
> "Long ago, but he won't stop talking."

Overcoming barriers is easier to do when all stakeholders are committed to learning to do so. It means moving beyond naming problems to careful analysis of why the problem has arisen and then moving on to creative problem solving (see Guide 8.4). Without dedicated commitment to creative problem solving, school-community collaboration bogs down and fades away.

Guide 8.4   Overcoming Barriers Related to Differences

Although workshops and presentations may be offered in an effort to increase specific cultural awareness, what can be learned in this way is limited, especially when one is in a community of many cultures. There also is a danger in prejudgments based on apparent cultural awareness. It is desirable to have the needed language skills and cultural awareness; it is also essential not to rush to judgment.

There are no easy solutions to overcoming deeply embedded negative attitudes. Certainly, a first step is to understand that the problem is not differences per se, but negative perceptions stemming from the politics and psychology of the situation. Such perceptions lead to (a) prejudgments that a person is bad because of an observed difference and (b) the view that there is little to be gained from working with that person.

In general, the task of overcoming negative attitudes interfering with a particular working relationship involves finding ways to counter negative prejudgments (e.g., to establish the credibility of those who have been prejudged) and demonstrate that there is something of value to be gained from working together.

In facilitating effective working relationships, collaborative leaders should

- Encourage all participants to defer negative judgments about those with whom they will be working.
- Enhance expectations that working together will be productive, with particular emphasis on establishing the value added by each participant in pursuing mutually desired outcomes.
- Ensure that there is appropriate time for making connections.
- Establish an infrastructure that provides support and guidance for effective task accomplishment.
- Provide active, task-oriented meeting facilitation that minimizes ego-oriented behavior.
- Ensure regular celebration of positive outcomes resulting from working together.

On a personal level, it is worth teaching participants that building relationships and effective communication involve the willingness and ability to

- *Convey empathy and warmth:* as a way of communicating understanding and appreciation of what others are thinking and feeling and transmitting a sense of liking
- *Convey genuine regard and respect:* as a way of transmitting real interest and enabling others to maintain a feeling of integrity and personal control
- *Talk with, not at, others:* as a way of conveying that one is a good listener who avoids prejudgment, doesn't pry, and shares experiences only when appropriate and needed

BUILDING AND MAINTAINING EFFECTIVE COLLABORATIONS

It is commonly said that collaboration is about building relationships. That's fine, as long as the aim is to build potent, synergistic, *working* relationships, not simply to establish positive personal connections.

Collaboratives built mainly on personal connections are vulnerable to the mobility of participants that characterizes many such groups and to the exclusion of folks who are not already in the inner circle. The intent must be to establish stable and sustainable working relationships and to recruit and involve all who are willing to contribute their talents. Remember: *It's not about having a collaborative—it's about collaborating to be effective. It involves more than meeting and talking. It's about working together in ways that produce effective interventions.*

Effective collaboration requires ensuring that participants have the training, time, support, and authority that enable them to carry out their roles and functions. Participants need well-delineated functions and defined tasks, clear roles, responsibilities, and an institutionalized infrastructure, including well-designed mechanisms for

> **You know you are an education leader if**
>
> - You want to slap the next person who says, "Must be nice to work 8 to 3:20 and have summers free."
> - You've ever had your profession slammed by someone who would "never DREAM" of doing your job.
> - You think caffeine should be available in intravenous form.

performing tasks, solving problems, and mediating conflict. Also needed are respected leaders and thoughtful, skilled, and content-focused facilitation.

In the absence of careful attention to the above matters, collaboratives rarely live up to hopes and expectations. Participants often start out with great enthusiasm. But poorly facilitated working sessions quickly degenerate into another ho-hum meeting, lots of talk but little action, another burden, and a waste of time. Meeting and meeting but going nowhere are particularly likely to happen when the emphasis is mainly on the unfocused mandate to "collaborate." Stakeholders must do more than embrace an important vision and mission. They need an infrastructure that ensures that effective work is done with respect to carefully defined functions and tasks.

An optimal approach to building a school-community collaborative involves formally weaving together resources of at least one school and sometimes a group of schools or an entire school district with local family and community resources. The intent is to sustain connections over time. As indicated in Guide 8.3, the range of entities in a community can be extensive. Developing a comprehensive approach to shared school and community concerns requires expanding participation in a strategic manner and with a commitment to inclusion.

From a policy perspective, policymakers and other leaders must establish a foundation for building collaborative bridges connecting school, family, and community. Policy must be translated into authentic agreements. Although all of this takes considerable time and other resources, the importance of building such bridges cannot be overemphasized. Failure to establish and successfully maintain effective collaboratives probably is attributable in great measure to the absence of clear, high-level, and long-term policy support. For example, the primary agenda of community agencies in working with schools usually is to have better access to clients; this is a marginal item in the school accountability agenda for raising test scores and closing the achievement gap. Policy and leadership are needed to address the disconnect in ways that integrate what the agency and school can contribute to each other's mission and to elevate school-community collaboration to a high priority.

When all major parties are committed to building an effective collaboration, the next step is to ensure that they understand that the process involves significant systemic changes and that they have the ability to facilitate such changes. Leaders in this situation must have both a vision for change and an understanding of how to effect and institutionalize the type of systemic changes needed to build an effective collaborative infrastructure. This encompasses changes related to governance, leadership, planning, implementation, sustainability, scale-up, and accountability. For example:

- Existing governance must be modified over time. The aim is shared decision making involving school and community agency staff, families, students, and other community representatives. This involves equalizing power and sharing leadership so that decision making appropriately reflects and accounts for all stakeholder groups.
- High-level leadership assignments must be designated to facilitate essential systemic changes and build and maintain family-community-school connections.
- Mechanisms must be established and institutionalized for analyzing, planning, coordinating, integrating, monitoring, evaluating, and strengthening collaborative efforts. All participants must share in the workload—pursuing clear functions.

Evidence of appropriate policy support is seen in the adequacy of funding for *capacity building* to accomplish desired system changes and ensure that the collaborative operates effectively over time. Accomplishing systemic changes requires establishment of temporary facilitative mechanisms and providing incentives, supports, and training to enhance commitment to and capacity for essential changes. Ensuring effective collaboration requires institutionalized mechanisms, long-term capacity building, and ongoing support.

About Building From Localities Outward

Collaborations can be organized by any group of stakeholders. Connecting the resources of families and the community through collaboration with schools is essential for developing comprehensive, multifaceted programs and services. At the multilocality level, efficiencies and economies of scale are achieved by connecting a complex (or family) of schools, such as a high school and its feeder schools. In a small community, such a complex often is the school district. Conceptually, it is best to think in terms of building from the local outward, but in practice, the process of establishing the initial collaboration may begin at any level.

As suggested in Chapter 7, developing an effective collaborative requires an infrastructure of organizational and operational mechanisms at all relevant levels for oversight, leadership, capacity building, and ongoing support. Such mechanisms are used to (a) make decisions about priorities and resource allocation, (b) maximize systematic planning, implementation, maintenance, and evaluation, (c) enhance and redeploy existing resources and pursue new ones, and (d) nurture the collaborative. At each level, such tasks require pursuing a proactive agenda.

Guide 8.5 provides a simplified illustration of the basic infrastructure needed. Guide 8.6 provides a more detailed picture.

Guide 8.5   About Basic Collaborative Infrastructure

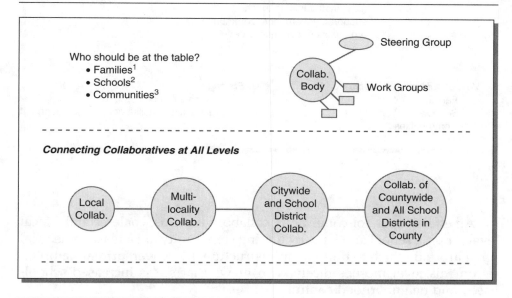

---

[1] *Families.* It is important to ensure that all who live in an area are represented—including, but not limited to, representatives of organized family advocacy groups. The aim is to mobilize all the human and social capital represented by family members and other home caretakers of the young.

[2] *Schools.* This encompasses all institutionalized entities that are responsible for formal education (e.g., pre-K, elementary, secondary, higher education). The aim is to draw on the resources of these institutions.

[3] *Communities.* This encompasses all the other resources (public and private money, facilities, human and social capital) that can be brought to the table at each level, such as health and social service agencies; businesses and unions; recreation, cultural, and youth development groups; libraries; juvenile justice and law enforcement; faith-based community institutions; service clubs; and media. As the collaborative develops, additional steps must be taken to outreach to disenfranchised groups.

Guide 8.6   Comprehensive Collaborative Infrastructure

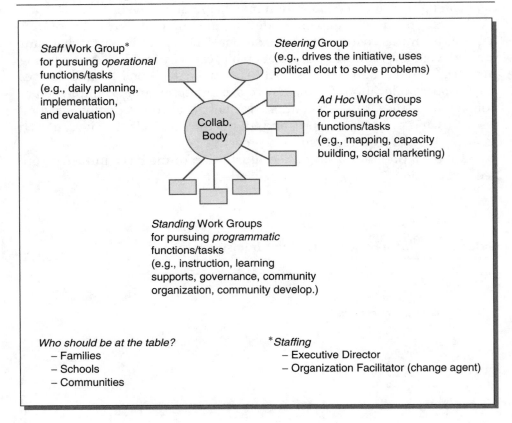

Staff Work Group*
for pursuing *operational*
functions/tasks
(e.g., daily planning,
implementation,
and evaluation)

Steering Group
(e.g., drives the initiative, uses
political clout to solve problems)

Collab.
Body

Ad Hoc Work Groups
for pursuing *process*
functions/tasks
(e.g., mapping, capacity
building, social marketing)

Standing Work Groups
for pursuing *programmatic*
functions/tasks
(e.g., instruction, learning
supports, governance, community
organization, community develop.)

Who should be at the table?
– Families
– Schools
– Communities

*Staffing
– Executive Director
– Organization Facilitator (change agent)

An effective school-community collaborative must coalesce at the local level. Thus, a school and its surrounding community are a reasonable focal point around which to build an infrastructure. Moreover, primary emphasis on this level meshes nicely with views that stress increased school-based and neighborhood control.

To maintain the focus on evolving a comprehensive continuum of intervention that plays out in an effective manner in *every locality*, it is a good idea to conceive the process from the local level outward. That is, first the focus is on mechanisms at the school-neighborhood level. Based on analyses of what is needed to facilitate and enhance efforts at a locality, mechanisms are conceived that enable several school-neighborhood collaboratives to work together for increased efficiency, effectiveness, and economies of scale. Then systemwide mechanisms can be (re)designed to provide support for what each locality is trying to develop.

About Capacity Building

As noted, oversight, leadership, resource development, and ongoing support are required at all levels. With each of these functions in mind, specific mechanisms and their interrelationship with each other and with other planning groups can be developed. A well-designed infrastructure provides ways to (a) arrive at decisions about resource allocation, (b) maximize systematic and integrated planning, implementation, maintenance, and evaluation, (c) outreach to create formal working relationships with all concerned stakeholders, and (d) regularly upgrade and renew the collaborative.

A special concern of school-community partnerships involves what often is called diffusion, replication, roll-out, or scale-up. The process of scale-up requires a separate capacity-building emphasis (see discussion in Chapter 9).

A Few Lessons Learned

The following are lessons we learned the hard way and that should be kept in mind by those who establish collaboratives. First, an obvious point: a collaborative needs financial support. The core operational budget can be direct funding and in-kind contributions from the resources of stakeholder groups. A good example is the provision of space for the collaborative. A school or community entity or both should be asked to contribute the necessary space. As specific functions and initiatives are undertaken that reflect overlapping arenas of concern for schools and community organizations, such as safe schools and neighborhoods, some portion of their respective funding streams can be braided together. Over time, there will be opportunities to supplement the budget with extramural grants.

A caution here is to avoid pernicious funding. That is, it is important not to pursue funding for projects that will distract the collaborative from vigorously pursuing its vision in a cohesive (nonfragmented) manner. A related concern has been the trend to try to expand resources through providing services that can be reimbursed through third-party payments, such as Medicaid funds. This often results in further limiting the range of interventions offered and who receives them. Moreover, payments from third-party sources often do not adequately cover the costs of services rendered, and as the numbers receiving services increases markedly, third-party payers seek ways to cap costs.

A second lesson relates to how agreements are made. In marketing new ideas, it is tempting to accentuate their promising attributes and minimize complications. For instance, in negotiating agreements for school connections, decision makers frequently are asked simply to sign a memorandum of understanding, rather than involving them in processes that lead to a comprehensive, informed commitment. Sometimes their motivation mainly is to obtain extra resources; sometimes they are motivated by a desire to be seen by constituents as doing *something* to improve things. In both instances, the result may be premature implementation that produces the form rather than the substance of change.

Third, without careful planning, implementation, and capacity building, collaborative efforts rarely live up to the initial hope. For example, formal arrangements for working together often take the form of meetings. To be effective, such sessions require thoughtful and skillful facilitation. Even when they begin with great enthusiasm, poorly facilitated working sessions quickly degenerate into another meeting, more talk but little action, another burden, and a waste of time. This is particularly likely to happen when the primary emphasis is on the unfocused mandate to "collaborate," rather than on moving an important vision and mission forward through effective working relationships and well-defined functions and tasks.

Finally, given how hard it is to work effectively in a group, steps must be taken to ensure that work groups are formed in ways that maximize their effectiveness. This includes providing them with the training, time, support, and authority to carry out their role and functions. It also requires effective meeting facilitation.

SOME POLICY RECOMMENDATIONS

Any school-community collaborative agenda that addresses barriers to learning and development must focus on evolving a comprehensive, multifaceted, and cohesive approach. The agenda must encompass addressing the complex needs of all youngsters, their families, the participating schools, and the surrounding neighborhood.

The work must be resource-oriented so that existing resources are used in the most cost-effective manner. This includes braiding together many public and private resources.

To these ends, a cohesive, high-priority policy commitment is required. This encompasses revisiting current policies to reduce redundancy and redeploy school and community resources that are used ineffectively.

Policy must be operationalized in ways that (a) support the strategic development of comprehensive approaches by weaving together school and community resources, (b) sustain partnerships, and (c) generate renewal. In communities, the need is for better ways of connecting agency and other resources to each other and to schools. In schools, there is a need for restructuring to combine parallel efforts supported by general funds, compensatory and special education entitlement, safe and drug-free school grants, and specially funded projects. This includes enhancing efficiency and effectiveness by connecting families of schools.

With all this in mind, Guides 8.7 and 8.8 outline some policy and practice guidelines for those concerned with development of effective school-community collaboratives.

Guide 8.7   Recommendations to Enhance and Sustain School-Community
Collaboratives

Effective school-community collaboratives require policies and leadership to

- Establish collaborative *governance* in ways that move toward shared decision making, with appropriate degrees of local control and private-sector involvement; a key facet of this is guaranteeing roles and providing incentives, supports, and training for effective involvement of all concerned stakeholders.
- Delineate high-level *leadership assignments* and underwrite essential *leadership/ management training* regarding vision for outcomes and collaboration, how to effect and institutionalize changes, and how to generate ongoing renewal.
- Establish *institutionalized mechanisms* (e.g., work groups) to carry out collaborative functions and tasks (e.g., analyzing, planning, coordinating, integrating, monitoring, evaluating, and strengthening ongoing efforts).
- Provide adequate funds for *capacity building* of collaborative participants to enhance operational quality over time; a key facet of this is a major investment in stakeholder recruitment and development using well-designed and technologically sophisticated strategies for dealing with the problems of frequent turnover and diffusing information updates; another facet is an investment in technical assistance at all levels and for all aspects and stages of the work.
- Encourage use of some braided funds to hire two staff members to carry out the daily activities stemming from work group activity (e.g., an executive director and someone with organization facilitator/change agent capabilities).
- Require a sophisticated approach to *accountability* that calls for data that can help develop effective collaboration through initial focus on short-term benchmarks and evolves into evaluation on long-range indicators of impact.

Such strengthened policy focus would allow collaborative participants to build the continuum of interventions needed to make a significant impact in addressing learning, behavior, emotional, and health concerns through strengthening youngsters, families, schools, and neighborhoods.

CONCLUDING COMMENTS

Interest in connecting schools, communities, and families is growing at an exponential rate. Collaboratives often are established because of the desire to address a local problem or in the wake of a crisis. In the long run, however, school-community connections must be driven by a comprehensive vision about strengthening youngsters, families, schools, and neighborhoods. This encompasses a focus on safe schools and neighborhoods; positive development and learning; personal, family, and economic well-being; and more.

While it is relatively simple to make informal linkages, establishing major long-term collaborations is complicated. The complications are readily seen in any effort to develop a comprehensive, multifaceted, and

Guide 8.8   Some Ways to Begin or Reinvigorate a Collaborative

1. Adopt a Comprehensive Vision for the Collaborative

Collaborative leadership builds consensus that the aim of those involved is to help weave together community and school resources to develop a comprehensive, multifaceted, and integrated continuum of interventions so that no child is left behind.

2. Write a Brief to Clarify the Vision

Collaborative establishes a writing team to prepare a brief concept paper, executive summary, and a set of talking points clarifying the vision by delineating the rationale and frameworks that will guide development of a comprehensive, multifaceted, and integrated approach.

3. Establish a Steering Committee to Move the Initiative Forward and Monitor Process

Collaborative identifies and empowers a representative subgroup that will be responsible and accountable for ensuring that the vision (the "big picture") is not lost and the momentum of the initiative is maintained through establishing and monitoring ad hoc work groups that are asked to pursue specific tasks.

4. Start a Process for Translating the Vision Into Policy

Steering committee establishes a work group to prepare a campaign geared to key local and state school and agency policymakers that focuses on (a) establishing a policy framework for the development of a comprehensive, multifaceted, and integrated approach and (b) ensuring that such policy has a high enough level of priority to end the current marginalized status such efforts have at schools and in communities.

5. Develop a Five-year Strategic Plan

Steering committee establishes a work group to draft a five-year strategic plan that delineates (a) the development of a comprehensive, multifaceted, and integrated approach and (b) the steps to be taken to accomplish the required systemic changes (the strategic plan will cover such matters as use of formulation of essential agreements about policy, resources, and practices; assignment of committed leadership; change agents to facilitate systemic changes; infrastructure redesign; enhancement of infrastructure mechanisms; resource mapping, analysis, and redeployment; capacity building; standards, evaluation, quality improvement, and accountability; social marketing).

- Steering committee circulates draft of plan (a) to elicit suggested revisions from key stakeholders and (b) as part of a process for building consensus and developing readiness for proceeding with its implementation.
- Work group makes relevant revisions based on suggestions.

6. Move the Strategic Plan to Implementation

Steering committee

- Ensures that key stakeholders finalize and approve strategic plan
- Submits plan on behalf of key stakeholders to school and agency decision makers to formulate formal agreements (e.g., MOUs, contracts) for start-up, initial implementation, and ongoing revisions that can ensure institutionalization and periodic renewal of a comprehensive, multifaceted, and integrated approach
- Establishes work group to develop action plan for start-up and initial implementation (action plan identifies general functions and key tasks to be accomplished, necessary systemic changes, and how to get from here to there in terms of who, how, by when, who monitors, etc.)

integrated approach to promoting healthy development and addressing barriers to development and learning. Such efforts necessitate major systemic changes involving formal and institutionalized sharing of a wide spectrum of responsibilities and resources. The nature and scope of change require stakeholder readiness, an enlightened vision, cohesive policy, creative leadership, basic systemic reforms, and new and multifaceted roles for professionals who work in schools and communities, as well as for family and other community members assuming leadership.

It is unwise to limit school-community connections to coordinating community services, recreation, and enrichment activities and co-locating some on school sites. As we have stressed, this tends to downplay the need also to restructure the various education support programs and services that schools own and operate, and it has led some policymakers to the mistaken impression that community resources can effectively meet the needs of schools in addressing barriers to learning. Policymakers must realize that increasing access to services is only one facet of any effort to establish a comprehensive, cohesive approach for strengthening students, schools, families, and neighborhoods.

Clearly, the myriad political and bureaucratic difficulties involved in making major institutional changes, especially with sparse financial resources, leads to the caution that such changes are not easily accomplished without a high degree of commitment and relentlessness of effort. Also, it should be remembered that systemic change rarely proceeds in a linear fashion. The work of establishing effective school-community connections emerges in overlapping and spiraling ways.

The success of school-community connections is first and foremost in the hands of policymakers. For increased connections to be more than another desired but underachieved aim of reformers, policymakers must understand the nature and scope of what is involved. They must deal with the problems of marginalization and fragmentation. They must support development of appropriately comprehensive and multifaceted school-community collaboratives. They must revise policy related to school-linked services, because such initiatives are a grossly inadequate response to the many complex factors that interfere with development, learning, and teaching.

Focusing primarily on linking community services to schools downplays the role of existing school and other community and family resources. This perpetuates an orientation that overemphasizes individually prescribed services, results in further fragmentation of interventions, and undervalues the human and social capital indigenous to every neighborhood. And all this is incompatible with developing the type of comprehensive approaches needed for statements such as *We want all children to succeed* and *No child left behind* to become more than rhetoric.

REFLECTION AND STIMULUS FOR DISCUSSION

Key Insights About "School-Family-Community Connections"

Based on what you learned so far,

> *Define (and discuss) what the term* collaboration
> *means; why school, family, and community collaboration is*
> *essential; and what is involved in building such a collaboration.*

As an aid, see the attached list, which reflects the main categories of a self-study survey related to school-community collaboration (see Chapter 12).

If there is an opportunity for group discussion, you may find the following group process guidelines helpful:

- Start by identifying someone who will facilitate the group interchange.
- Take a few minutes to make a few individual notes on a worksheet.
- Be sure all major points are compiled for sharing with other groups.
- Ask someone else to watch the time so that the group doesn't bog down.

Tool for Reflection Activity: From Adelman and Taylor's Self-study Survey on School-Community (Including Family) Collaboration

Which of the following are matters on
which a collaborative might need to focus?

A. Improving the school?

For example:

1. The instructional component of schooling

2. The governance and management of schooling

3. Financial support for schooling

4. Stakeholder development

5. School-based programs and services to address barriers to learning

B. *Improving the neighborhood and strengthening families?*

For example:

1. Youth development programs

2. Youth and family recreation and enrichment opportunities

3. Physical health services

4. Mental health services

5. Programs to address psychosocial problems

6. Basic living needs services

7. Work/career programs

8. College prep programs

9. Social services

10. Crime and juvenile justice programs

11. Legal assistance

12. Support for development of neighborhood organizations

13. Economic development programs

C. *Which of the following might be important*
in establishing an effective school-community collaboration?

1. A stated policy for enhancing school-community partnerships

2. A designated leader or leaders for enhancing school-community partnerships

3. Specific persons designated formally as representatives to meet with each other

4. Leadership that monitors and evaluates the collaborative process and plans next steps

5. A plan for capacity building of the collaborative and its members

6. A written description to give all stakeholders regarding the collaboration's vision, purpose, current goals, and processes

ACTIVITY

By yourself and/or in a group, brainstorm about the following topic:

What makes a school a supportive and caring learning community?

Then discuss:

How do you think families, communities, and schools can work together to create a supportive and caring learning community?

NOTE

1. In practice, the terms *school-linked* and *school-based* encompass two separate dimensions: (1) where programs/services are *located* and (2) who *owns* them. Taken literally, school-based should indicate activity carried out on a campus, and school-linked should refer to off-campus activity with formal connections to a school site. In either case, services may be owned by schools or a community-based organization or in some cases may be co-owned. As commonly used, the term *school-linked* refers to community-owned on- and off-campus services and is strongly associated with the notion of coordinated services.

REFERENCES

Center for Mental Health in Schools. (2002). *School-community partnership: A guide.* Los Angeles: Center for Mental Health in Schools at UCLA.

Honig, M. I., Kahne, J., & McLaughlin, M. W. (2001) School-community connections: Strengthening opportunity to learn and opportunity to teach. In V. Richardson (Ed.), *Handbook of research on teaching* (4th ed.). Washington, DC: American Educational Research Association.

Melaville, A., & Blank, M. J. (1998). *Learning together: The developing field of school-community initiatives.* Flint, MI: Mott Foundation.

Southwest Educational Development Laboratory. (2001). *Emerging issues in school, family, & community connections: Annual synthesis.* Austin, TX: Author.

Chapter 14 contains a list of special resources related
to the above matters available at no cost from the national
Center for Mental Health in Schools, which is at UCLA and is
directed by the authors of this book. Go to http://smhp.psych.ucla.edu.

Coda

9

Moving Schools Forward

The Parable of the Lamppost

It was a dark and stormy night.

I left the building and started to run across the street to the parking lot. As I reached the curb, I bumped into a somewhat dazed acquaintance who was down on his hands and knees searching for something.

"What did you lose?" I asked.

"My keys," he said.

He looked so frazzled I just had to help. A half hour later, soaked to the skin and frustrated, I said, "We need to do this more systematically. Tell me just where you think you dropped them."

"Oh," he said, "across the road in the parking lot."

"What!" I screamed. "Then why are we looking over here?"

"Well," he said, looking a bit sheepish, "the light is so much better here under this lamppost."

> ***Moral:*** *Where there's light, there may be hope,*
> *but solving problems requires looking in the right place.*

No more prizes for predicting rain.   Prizes only for building arks.

> *Ultimately, only three things matter about educational reform. Does it have depth: does it improve important rather than superficial aspects of students' learning and development? Does it have length: can it be sustained over long periods of time instead of fizzling out after the first flush of innovation? Does it have breadth: can the reform be extended beyond a few schools, networks or showcase initiatives to transform education across entire systems or nations?*
>
> —Andy Hargreaves and Dean Fink (2000)

Some people believe that the reason they are good readers is because they were taught by a phonetic approach. Others believe they are good readers because they were taught with a language experience or a combination approach. Indeed, most good readers seem to advocate for whatever method they think worked for them.

Our reading of the research literature, however, indicates that almost every method has *not* worked for a significant number of people. For a *few*, their reading problems stem from unaccommodated disabilities, vulnerabilities, and individual developmental differences. For many, the problems stem from socioeconomic inequities that affect readiness to learn at school and the quality of schools and schooling.

If our society truly means to provide the opportunity for all students to succeed at school, fundamental changes are needed so that teachers can personalize instruction, and teachers along with other school staff can address barriers to learning. Policymakers can call for higher standards and greater accountability, improved curricula and instruction, increased discipline, reduced school violence, and on and on. None of it means much if the reforms enacted do not ultimately result in substantive changes in the classroom and throughout a school site. Moreover, such reforms have to be sustained over time. And if the intent is to leave no child behind, then such reforms have to be replicated in all schools in a district.

THE PROBLEMS OF PROTOTYPE
IMPLEMENTATION AND SCALE-UP

Guide 9.1 outlines what we see as major matters that must be considered in moving schools forward. This tool can be used as a framework for thinking about basic considerations in planning, implementing, sustaining, and going-to-scale. It also can be used as a template for establishing benchmarks for purposes of formative evaluation.

As outlined, changes may encompass introducing one or more interventions, developing a demonstration at a specific site, or replicating a prototype on a large scale. Whatever the nature and scope of focus, all the *key facets* outlined come into play.

Guide 9.1 New Initiatives: Considerations Related to Planning, Implementing, Sustaining, and Going-to-Scale

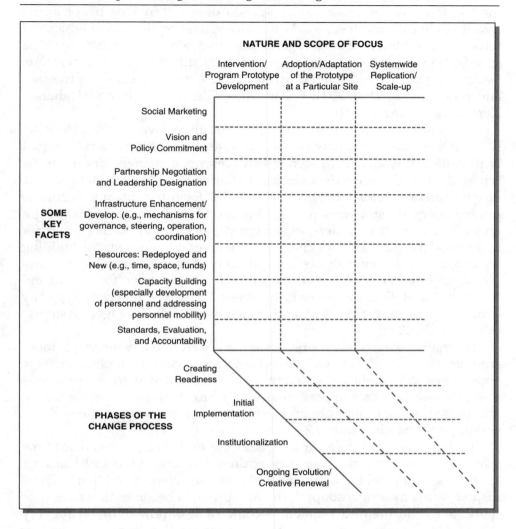

As illustrated, the focus related to an initiative to improve schools begins with the prototype for an improved approach. Such a prototype usually is developed and initially implemented as a pilot demonstration at one or more sites. Efforts to reform schooling, however, require much more than implementing demonstrations at a few sites. Improved approaches are only as good as a school district's ability to develop and institutionalize them on a large scale. This process often is called diffusion, replication, roll-out, or scale-up (Adelman & Taylor, 2003).

For the most part, education researchers and reformers have paid little attention to the complexities of large-scale diffusion. This is evident from the fact that the nation's research agenda does not include major initiatives to delineate and test models for widespread replication of education reforms. In addition, change agents are used who have relatively little specific training in facilitating large-scale systemic changes. Furthermore, leadership training has given short shrift to the topic of scale-up processes and problems (Elmore, 2004; Fullan, 2005; Glennan, Bodilly, Galegher, & Kerr, 2004; Thomas, 2002).

It is not surprising, then, that the pendulum swings characterizing shifts in the debate over how best to improve schools are not accompanied with sufficient resources to accomplish prescribed changes throughout a school district. Common deficiencies are failure to address the four phases of the change process outlined in Guide 9.1. Examples include failure to pursue adequate strategies for creating motivational readiness among a critical mass of stakeholders, especially principals and teachers, and for accommodating assignment changes. Moreover, time frames for building the capacity to accomplish desired institutional changes usually are unrealistic. As Tom Vander Ark, executive director of education for the Bill and Melinda Gates Foundation, wisely notes: "Effective practices typically evolve over a long period in high-functioning, fully engaged systems" (Vander Ark, 2002).

For many years, our work revolved mainly around developing demonstration programs. Then we moved into the world of replicating new approaches to schooling on a large scale. Confronted with the problems and processes of scale-up, we analyzed a broad range of psychological and organizational literature and delineated the working framework for scale-up outlined in Guide 9.2.

To appreciate the point, think about the best model around for how schools can improve the way they address barriers to student learning. Assuming the model has demonstrated cost-effectiveness and that a school district wants to adopt/adapt it, the first problem becomes that of how to replicate it, and the next problem becomes that of how to do so at every school. Or in common parlance, the question is: *How do we get from here to there?*

Whether the focus is on establishing a prototype at one site or replicating it at many, the systemic changes can be conceived in terms of four overlapping phases: (1) *creating readiness*—increasing a climate/culture for change through enhancing the motivation and capability of a critical mass of stakeholders, (2) *initial implementation*—change is carried out in stages using a well-designed infrastructure to provide guidance and support, (3) *institutionalization*—accomplished by ensuring that there is an infrastructure to maintain and enhance productive changes, and (4) *ongoing evolution*—through use of mechanisms to improve quality and provide continuing support in ways that enable stakeholders to become a community of learners and experience periodic creative renewal.

Guide 9.2 Prototype Implementation and Scale-up: Phases and Parallel and Linked Tasks

Phase I **Creating** **Readiness** Enhancing the Climate/Culture for Change	*System Change* **Staff** Disseminates the prototype to create interest (promotion and marketing) Evaluates indications of interest Makes in-depth presentations to build stakeholder consensus Negotiates a policy framework and conditions of engagement with sanctioned bodies Elicits ratification and sponsorship by stakeholders	Implementation **Team** works at site with **Organization** **Leadership** to Redesign the organizational and programmatic infrastructure Clarify need to add temporary mechanisms for the implementation process Restructure time (the school day, time allocation over the year) Conduct stakeholder foundation-building activity	
Phase II **Initial** **Implementation** Adapting and Phasing in the Prototype With Well- designed Guidance and Support		Establish temporary mechanisms to facilitate the implementation process Design appropriate prototype adaptations Develop site-specific plan to phase in prototype	**Team** works at site with appropriate **Stakeholders** Plans and implements ongoing stakeholder development/empower- ment programs Facilitates day-by-day prototype implementation Establishes formative evaluation procedures
Phase III **Institutionalization** Ensuring That the Infrastructure Maintains and Enhances Productive Changes	*System* **Change Staff** continues contact with **Organization** **Leadership** Facilitates expansion of the formative evaluation system (in keeping with summative evaluation needs) Clarifies ways to improve the prototype	Institutionalize ownership, guidance, and support Plan and ensure commitment to ongoing leadership Plan and ensure commitment to maintain mechanisms for planning, implementation, and coordination Plan for continuing education and technical assistance to maintain and enhance productive changes and generate renewal (including programs for new arrivals)	
Phase IV **Ongoing Evolution**	Compiles information on outcome efficacy		**Organization** **Leadership** works with **Stakeholders** in evolving the prototype

SOURCE: Adapted from H. S. Adelman & L. Taylor (1997).

As indicated in Guide 9.2, a change *mechanism* is needed. One way to conceive such a mechanism is in terms of a *system implementation staff.* Such staff provide a necessary organizational base and skilled personnel for disseminating a prototype, negotiating decisions about replication, and dispensing the expertise to facilitate implementation of a prototype and eventual scale-up. They can dispense expertise by sending out a *team* consisting of personnel who, for designated periods of time, travel to the location in which the prototype is to be implemented/replicated. A core team of perhaps two to four staff works closely with a site throughout the process. The team is augmented whenever a specialist is needed to assist in replicating a specific element of the prototype design. Implementation and scaling up of a comprehensive prototype almost always requires *phased-in* change and the addition of *temporary infrastructure mechanisms* to facilitate changes.

Guides 9.1 and 9.2 briefly highlight key facets and specific tasks related to the four phases of prototype implementation and eventual scale-up. Note in particular the importance of

- Promoting ongoing social marketing
- Articulating a clear, shared vision for the work
- Ensuring that there is a major policy commitment from all participating partners
- Negotiating partnership agreements
- Designating leadership
- Enhancing/developing an infrastructure based on a clear articulation of essential functions (e.g., mechanisms for governance and priority setting, steering, operations, resource mapping and coordination; strong facilitation related to all mechanisms)
- Redeploying resources and establishing new ones
- Building capacity (especially personnel development and strategies for addressing personnel and other stakeholder mobility)
- Establishing standards, evaluation processes, and accountability procedures

Each facet and task requires careful planning based on sound intervention fundamentals. This means paying special attention to the problem of the match between intervention and those who are to change.

We do not mean to belabor all this. Our point simply is to make certain that there is a greater appreciation for and more attention paid to the problems of systemic change. Those who set out to change schools and schooling are confronted with two enormous tasks. The first is to develop prototypes; the second involves large-scale replication. One without the other is insufficient. Yet considerably more attention is paid to developing and validating prototypes than to delineating and testing scale-up processes. Clearly, it is time to correct this deficiency.

IT'S ABOUT WHAT HAPPENS AT THE
SCHOOL AND IN THE CLASSROOM

Finally, we want to end Part III by stressing a simple truth: if it doesn't play out at a school and in the classroom, it doesn't mean much. Improving test scores and closing the achievement gap require replication of good practices for every school in a district. Moreover, the type of innovations we have outlined requires avoiding the mistakes of past "district-centric" planning and resource allocation. For too long there has been a terrible disconnect between central office policy and operations and how programs and services evolve in classrooms and schools.

The time is opportune for schools and classrooms to truly become the center and guiding force for all planning. That is, planning should begin with a clear image of what the classroom and school must do to teach all students effectively. Then the focus can move to planning how a family of schools and the surrounding community can complement each other's efforts and achieve economies of scale. With all this clearly in perspective, central staff and state and national policy can be reoriented to the role of developing the best ways to support local efforts *as defined locally.*

At the same time, it is essential not to create a new mythology suggesting that every classroom and school are unique. There are fundamentals that permeate all efforts to improve schools and schooling and that should continue to guide policy, practice, research, and training. For example:

- The curriculum in every classroom must include a major emphasis on acquisition of basic knowledge and skills. However, such basics must be understood to involve more than the old three R's and cognitive development. There are many important areas of human development and functioning, and each contains basics that individuals may need help in acquiring. Moreover, any individual may require special accommodation in any of these areas.
- Every classroom must address student motivation as an antecedent, process, and outcome concern.
- Special assistance must be *added* to instructional programs for certain individuals, but only after the best nonspecialized procedures for facilitating learning have been tried. Moreover, such procedures must be designed to build on strengths and must not supplant continued emphasis on promoting healthy development.
- Beyond the classroom, schools must have policy, leadership, and mechanisms for developing schoolwide programs to address barriers to learning. Some of the work will need to be in partnership with other schools, some will require weaving school and community resources together. The aim is to evolve a comprehensive, multifaceted, and integrated continuum of programs and services ranging from primary prevention through early intervention to treatment of

serious problems. Our work suggests that at a school this will require evolving programs to (a) enhance the ability of the classroom to enable learning, (b) provide support for the many transitions experienced by students and their families, (c) increase home involvement, (d) respond to and prevent crises, (e) offer special assistance to students and their families, and (f) expand community involvement (including volunteers).

- Leaders for education reform at all levels are confronted with the need to foster effective scale-up of promising reforms. This encompasses a major research thrust to develop efficacious demonstrations and effective models for replicating new approaches to schooling.
- Relatedly, policymakers at all levels must revisit current policy using the lens of addressing barriers to learning with the intent of both realigning existing policy to foster cohesive practices and enacting new policies to fill critical gaps.

CONCLUDING COMMENTS

Clearly, there is ample direction for improving how schools address barriers to learning and teaching. The time to do so is now. Unfortunately, too many school professionals and researchers are caught up in the day-by-day pressures of their current roles and functions. Everyone is so busy "doing" that there is no time to introduce better ways. One is reminded of Winnie the Pooh, who was always going down the stairs, bump, bump, bump, on his head behind Christopher Robin. He thinks it is the only way to go down the stairs. Still, he reasons, there might be a better way if only he could stop bumping long enough to figure it out.

> Do not follow where the path may lead.
> Go instead where there is no path and leave a trail.
>
> —Anonymous

REFERENCES

Adelman, H. S., & Taylor, L. (1997). Toward a scale-up model for replicating new approaches to schooling. *Journal of Educational and Psychological Consultation, 8,* 197–230.

Adelman, H. S., & Taylor, L. (2003). On sustainability of project innovations as systemic change. *Journal of Educational and Psychological Consultation, 14,* 1–25.

Elmore, R. F. (2004). *School reform from the inside out: Policy, practice, and performance.* Cambridge, MA: Harvard Educational Publishing Group.

Fullan, M. (2005). *Leadership & sustainability: System thinkers in action.* Thousand Oaks, CA: Corwin Press.

Glennan, T. K., Bodilly, S. J., Galegher, J., & Kerr, K. A. (Eds.). (2004). *Expanding the reach of education reforms: Perspectives from leaders in the scale-up of educational interventions.* Santa Monica, CA: RAND.

Hargreaves, A., & Fink, D. (2000). The three dimensions of reform. *Educational Leadership, 57,* 30–34.

Taylor, L., Nelson, P., & Adelman, H. S. (1999). Scaling-up reforms across a school district. *Reading and Writing Quarterly, 15,* 303–326.

Thomas, R. M. (2002). *Overcoming inertia in school reform: How to successfully implement change.* Thousand Oaks, CA: Corwin Press.

Vander Ark, T. (2002). Toward success at scale. *Phi Delta Kappan, 84,* 322–326.

*Chapter 14 contains a list of special resources
related to the above matters available at no cost from the
national Center for Mental Health in Schools, which is at UCLA
and is directed by the authors of this book. Go to http://smhp.psych.ucla.edu.*

PART IV

Resources

Besides the resources included throughout the volume, we wanted to provide a few others that folks around the country have found useful. Included here are

- "Guide to Using Natural Opportunities to Promote Social-Emotional Learning and Well-being" (Chapter 10)
- "Guide to Active Learning" (Chapter 11)
- "Surveying How a School Is Addressing Barriers to Student Learning" (Chapter 12)
- "Research Base for Addressing Barriers to Learning" (Chapter 13)
- "Our Published Works and Center-produced Resources on Addressing Barriers to Learning" (Chapter 14)
- "Internet Sites for a Sampling of Major Agencies and Organizations to Support Learning" (Chapter 15)

For more resources that we have helped to develop and for links to even more, go to the Quick Find Online Clearinghouse for the Center for Mental Health in Schools at UCLA, http://smhp.psych.ucla.edu.

Guide to Using Natural Opportunities to Promote Social-Emotional Learning and Well-being

10

I n some form or another, every school has goals that emphasize a desire to enhance students' personal and social functioning. Such goals reflect an understanding that social and emotional growth plays an important role in

- Enhancing the daily smooth functioning of schools and the emergence of a safe, caring, and supportive school climate
- Facilitating students' holistic development
- Enabling student motivation and capability for academic learning
- Optimizing life beyond schooling

With all this in mind, efforts to enhance classroom and schoolwide practices can and need to do much more to (a) capitalize on *natural* opportunities at schools to promote social and emotional development and (b) minimize transactions that interfere with positive growth in these areas. This brief resource highlights a range of such natural opportunities

WHAT ARE NATURAL OPPORTUNITIES?

In effect, natural opportunities are one of the most authentic examples of "teachable moments." Guide 10.1 offers examples of natural opportunities at schools for promoting personal and social growth. They are grouped into four categories:

1. Daily opportunities

2. Yearly patterns

3. Transitions

4. Early after the onset of student problems

Appreciation of what needs attention can be garnered readily by looking at the school day and school year through the lens of goals for personal and social functioning. Is instruction carried out in ways that strengthen or hinder development of interpersonal skills and connections and student understanding of self and others? Are cooperative learning and sharing promoted? Is counterproductive competition minimized? Are interpersonal conflicts mainly suppressed, or are they used as learning opportunities? Are roles provided for all students to be positive helpers throughout the school and community?

Pay particular attention to

- *Daily Opportunities.* Schools are social milieus. Each day in the classroom and around the school, students interact with their peers and various adults in formal and informal ways. Every encounter, positive and negative, represents a potential learning experience. All school staff, and especially teachers, can be taught ways to capitalize on these to enhance social-emotional learning and minimize transactions that work against positive growth.

- *Yearly Patterns.* The culture of most schools yields fairly predictable patterns over the course of the year. The beginning of the school year, for example, typically is a period of hope. As the year progresses, a variety of stressors are encountered. Examples include homework assignments that are experienced as increasingly difficult, interpersonal conflicts, and testing and grading pressures. There also are special circumstances associated with holidays, social events, sports, grade promotions, and graduation.

Each month strategies can be implemented that encourage school staff to enhance coping and minimize stressors through social-emotional learning and shared problem solving. The point is to establish a focus each month and build the capacity of school staff to evolve the school culture in ways that reduce unnecessary stressors and naturally promote social and emotional development. (Monthly themes are readily generated. One set of examples is listed in Guide 10.1. For resources to pursue these monthly themes, go to the Center for Mental Health in Schools at UCLA—http:// smhp.psych.ucla.edu.)

- *Transitions.* As is evident, students are regularly confronted with a variety of transitions—changing schools, changing grades, and encountering

Guide 10.1   Examples of *Natural* Opportunities at School to *Promote* Social-Emotional Learning

---

I. Using Natural Daily Opportunities

   A. In the classroom (e.g., as students relate to each other and to staff during class and group instruction; as essential aspects of cooperative learning and peer sharing and tutoring; as one facet of addressing interpersonal and learning problems)

   B. Schoolwide (e.g., providing roles for all students to be positive helpers and leaders throughout the school and community; engaging students in strategies to enhance a caring, supportive, and safe school climate; as essential aspects of conflict resolution and crisis prevention)

II. In Response to Yearly Patterns

   Schools have a yearly rhythm, changing with the cycle and demands of the school calendar. The following are examples of monthly themes the Center for Mental Health in Schools at UCLA has developed for schools to draw upon and go beyond. The idea is to establish focal points for minimizing potential problems and pursuing natural opportunities to promote social-emotional learning.

   September: *Getting Off to a Good Start*

   October: *Enabling School Adjustment*

   November: *Responding to Referrals in Ways That Can Stem the Tide*

   December: *Reengaging Students: Using a Student's Time Off in Ways That Pay Off!*

   January: *New Year's Resolutions—A Time for Renewal; A New Start for Everyone*

   February: *The Midpoint of a School Year—Report Cards and Conferences—Another Barrier or a Challenging Opportunity*

   March: *Reducing Stress; Preventing Burnout*

   April: *Spring Can Be a High-Risk Time for Students*

   May: *Time to Help Students and Families Plan Successful Transitions to a New Grade or School*

   June: *Summer and the Living Ain't Easy*

   July: *Using Downtime to Plan Better Ways to Work Together in Providing Learning Supports*

   August: *Now Is the Time to Develop Ways to Avoid Burnout*

III. During Transitions

   A. Daily (e.g., capturing opportunities before school, during breaks, at lunch, after school)

   B. Newcomers (e.g., as part of welcoming and social support processes; in addressing school adjustment difficulties)

   C. Grade-to-grade (e.g., preparing students for the next year; addressing adjustment difficulties as the year begins)

IV. At the First Indication That a Student Is Experiencing Problems

   Enhancing social and emotional functioning is a natural focus of early-after-onset interventions for learning, behavior, and emotional problems.

a range of other minor and major transitory demands. Every transition can exacerbate problems or be used to promote positive learning and attitudes and reduce alienation. However, institutionalized efforts to support students through such transitions often are neglected. Examples of schoolwide and classroom-specific opportunities to address transitions proactively include a focus on welcoming new arrivals (students, their families, staff); providing ongoing social supports as students adjust to new grades, new schools, new programs; and using beforeschool and afterschool and intersession activities as times for ensuring generalization and enrichment of such learning.

• *Early After a Problem Arises.* Stated simply, every student problem represents a need and an opportunity for learning—and often what needs to be learned falls into the social-emotional arena. A theme throughout this volume has been that whatever the first response, the second response to such problems should be a focus on promoting personal and social growth.

Guide to Active Learning

11

Teaching strategies must always have as their primary concern producing effective *learning*. Effective learning requires ensuring that the student is truly engaged. This is especially important in preventing learning, behavior, and emotional problems, and essential at the first indications of such problems. A key aspect in all this is *active learning*. This guide offers examples of instructional approaches that are designed to enhance activity and motivation to learn.

Active learning is *learning by doing, listening, looking, and asking;* but it is not just being active that counts. It is the mobilization of the student to seek out and learn (see Exhibit 11.1).

There are many examples of ways to promote active learning at all grade levels: interactive class discussions; authentic learning; problem-based, discovery, and project-based learning; involvement in learning centers; experiences outside the classroom; independent learning experiences in or out of school. Specific activities are designed to capitalize on students' interests and curiosity, involve them in problem solving and guided inquiry, and elicit their thinking through reflective discussions and specific products. Moreover, the activities are designed to do all this in ways that (a) enhance feelings of competence, self-determination, and relatedness to others and (b) minimize threats to such feelings.

And active learning does much more than motivate learning of subject matter and academic skills. Students also learn how to cooperate with others, share responsibility for planning and implementation, and develop understanding and skills related to conflict resolution and mediation. Such formats also provide a context for collaboration among teachers and school staff and with a variety of volunteers.

Active learning methods can be introduced gradually so that students can be taught how to benefit from them and so that they can be provided appropriate support and guidance. Below are brief overviews of a variety of interactive instruction, authentic learning, problem-based and discovery learning, project-based learning, learning centers, and enrichment activity.

Exhibit 11.1   What Is Active Learning?

As discussed by Newmann, Marks, and Gamoran (1996), active learning is "students actively constructing meaning grounded in their own experience rather than simply absorbing and reproducing knowledge transmitted from subject-matter fields."

Examples are

- Small-group discussions
- Cooperative learning tasks
- Independent research projects
- Use of hands-on manipulatives, scientific equipment, and arts and crafts materials
- Use of computer and video technology
- Community-based projects such as surveys, oral histories, and volunteer service

Components of Active Learning in the Classroom are

- *Higher-order Thinking.* Instruction involves students in manipulating information and ideas by synthesizing, generalizing, explaining, hypothesizing, or arriving at conclusions that produce new meanings and understandings for them.
- *Substantive Conversation.* Students engage in extended conversational exchanges with the teacher and/or their peers about subject matter in a way that builds an improved and shared understanding of ideas or topics.
- *Deep Knowledge.* Instruction addresses central ideas of a topic or discipline with enough thoroughness to explore connections and relationships and to produce relatively complex understandings.
- *Connections to the World Beyond the Classroom.* Students make connections between substantive knowledge and either public problems or personal experiences.

INTERACTIVE INSTRUCTION

One of the most direct ways teachers try to engage students is through class discussion and sharing of insights about what is being learned, often bringing in their own experiences and personal reactions. Discussion not only helps students practice and assimilate, but it adds opportunities to enhance skills (such as organizing and orally presenting one's ideas) and to learn more (e.g., from teacher clarifications and peer models). It also can provide an impetus for further independent learning.

For students just learning to engage in discussion or who have an aversion to such a format, it is important to keep discussions fairly brief and use a small-group format. If students want to participate but are having trouble doing so, individual interaction away from the group can help them develop essential readiness skills, such as listening, organizing one's thoughts, and interacting appropriately with another. Whole-class discussion is reserved for occasions when the topic affects all the students. These can be invaluable opportunities to enhance a sense of community.

Suggested guidelines for effective discussions include

- Using material and concepts familiar to the students
- Using a problem or issue that does not require a particular response
- Stressing that opinions must be supported
- Providing some sense of closure as the discussion ends, such as a summary of what was said, insights and solutions generated, any sense of consensus, and implications for the students' lives now and in the future

AUTHENTIC LEARNING

Authentic learning (sometimes called genuine learning) facilitates active learning by connecting content, process, and outcomes to real-life experiences. The concept encompasses student learning in authentic contexts outside the classroom, such as around the school, in the neighborhood, and at home, including classroom, schoolwide, or community service or action projects and internships.

The emphasis is on learning activities that have genuine purpose. The intent is to enhance student valuing of the curriculum through working on somewhat complex problems and tasks/projects they naturally experience or that they will experience later in their lives.

For example, by focusing on current problems or controversies affecting them, students work on projects and create products they value. Tasks range from simple activities, such as groups' writing letters to the local newspaper, to more complex projects, such as cross-subject thematic instruction, science and art fairs, major community service projects, and a variety of on-the-job experiences. Specific examples include developing a classroom newspaper or multimedia newscast on a controversial topic, carrying out an ecological project, developing a school Web site or specific sections of the school's Web site, and creating a display for the school regarding the neighborhood's past, present, and future.

The key to properly implementing authentic learning activity is to minimize busywork and ensure that the major learning objectives are being accomplished. Good authentic tasks involve

- Locating, gathering, organizing, and synthesizing
- Making collaborative decisions and interpreting information and resources
- Solving problems

- Elaborating
- Explaining
- Evaluating

The process also usually involves a public exhibition of products and related presentations to others outside the class.

Properly implemented, authentic learning activity helps develop

- Inquiry (learning to ask relevant questions and search for answers)
- Critical and divergent thinking and deep understanding
- Judgment
- General decision-making and problem-solving capability
- Performance and communication skills

Such an approach also can contribute to enhancing a sense of community.

PROBLEM-BASED AND DISCOVERY LEARNING

Problem-based and discovery learning processes overlap with the concept of authentic learning. They are built around a series of active problem-solving investigations. The intent is that with appropriate guidance and support, students will be motivated by the defined problem and by the process of discovery and use their capabilities to make pertinent observations, comparisons, inferences, and interpretations and to arrive at new insights.

In general, the approach begins with the teacher's raising a question or series of questions and leading a discussion to identify a problem worth exploring. Students decide ways to investigate the problem and work individually and/or in small groups conducting "investigations." For example, they manipulate phenomena, make observations, gather and interpret data, and draw inferences. Then they draw conclusions and make generalizations (see Exhibit 11.2).

Project-based Learning

This problem-based and discovery learning approach also draws on the motivational benefits of having students engage in meaningful investigation of interesting problems and work and learn cooperatively. Because of the scope of such projects, students must first learn how to work in a cooperative learning group, share and communicate learning strategies and background knowledge, and then how to share accomplishments across groups. With respect to the implementation of project-based learning, various writers stress that students should be involved in choosing a topic, and the topic should be multifaceted enough to maintain student engagement over an extended period of time (see Exhibits 11.3 and 11.4).

Exhibit 11.2 Problem-based Learning I

Problem-based learning (PBL) is a term that some have adopted for one type of authentic learning. It is described by the Maricopa Center for Learning and Instruction (2004) as a "total approach to education. . . . PBL is both a curriculum and a process. The curriculum consists of carefully selected and designed problems that demand from the learner acquisition of critical knowledge, problem-solving proficiency, self-directed learning strategies, and team participation skills. The process replicates the commonly used systemic approach to resolving problems or meeting challenges that are encountered in life and career. . . .

"In problem-based learning, the traditional teacher and student roles change. The students assume increasing responsibility for their learning, giving them more motivation and more feelings of accomplishment, setting the pattern for them to become successful life-long learners. The faculty in turn become resources, tutors, and evaluators, guiding the students in their problem-solving efforts (p. 1)."

Exhibit 11.3 Problem-based Learning II

As stated by Ferretti & Okolo (1996), "Project-based learning offers an intrinsically interesting and pedagogically promising alternative to an exclusive reliance on textbooks. When students have the opportunity to engage in meaningful investigation of interesting problems for the purpose of communicating their findings to others, their interest in learning is enhanced. . . . Increased interest can yield significant cognitive benefits, including improved attention, activation and utilization of background knowledge, use of learning strategies, and greater effort and persistence. . . . Moreover, during project-based learning activities, students have the opportunity to cooperate and collaborate with peers" (p. 452).

Ferretti and Okolo outline five essential features of project-based instruction:

1. An authentic question or problem provides a framework for organizing concepts and principles.

2. Students engage in investigations that enable them to formulate and refine specific questions, locate data sources or collect original data, analyze and interpret information, and draw conclusions.

3. These investigations lead to the development of artifacts that represent students' proposed solutions to problems, reflect their emerging understanding about the domain, and are presented for the critical consideration of their colleagues.

4. Teachers, students, and other members of the community of learners collaborate to complete their projects, share expertise, make decisions about the division of labor, and construct a socially mediated understanding of their topic.

5. Cognitive tools, such as multimedia technology, are used to extend and amplify students' representational and analytic capacities.

Exhibit 11.4 More on Problem-based Learning

Katz & Chard (1998) stress that

> a main aim of project work in the early years is to strengthen children's dispositions to be interested, absorbed, and involved in in-depth observation, investigation, and representation of some worthwhile phenomena in their own environments. (p. 2)

From their perspective, among the factors to consider in selecting and implementing projects are (a) characteristics of the particular group of children, (b) the geographic context of the school, (c) the school's wider community, (d) the availability of relevant local resources, (e) the topic's potential contribution to later learning, and (f) the teacher's own knowledge of the topic.

Criteria for Choosing Projects

- It is directly observable in the children's own environment (real world).
- It is within most children's experiences.
- First-hand direct investigation is feasible and not potentially dangerous.
- Local resources (field sites and experts) are favorable and readily accessible.
- It has good potential for representation in a variety of media (e.g., role play, construction, writing, multidimensional, graphic organizers).
- Parental participation and contributions are likely, and parents can become involved.
- It is sensitive to the local culture as well as culturally appropriate in general.
- It is potentially interesting to many of the children, or represents an interest that adults consider worthy of developing in children.
- It is related to curriculum goals and standards of the school or district.
- It provides ample opportunity to apply basic skills (depending on the age of the children).
- It is optimally specific: not too narrow and not too broad.

Learning Centers

Learning centers are an especially useful strategy for mobilizing and maintaining student engagement. The format goes well with the concept of authentic learning and processes such as discovery and problem-based learning. As McCarthy (1977) noted decades ago,

> Many problems of motivation can be attributed to the fact that children are bored because the class is moving too slowly or too quickly. Also, some behavior problems arise because children are restless when they are required to sit still for long periods of time. These problems can be reduced by supplementing the regular classroom

program with learning-center activities. . . . The learning center tries to deal with the reality that pupils learn at different rates, have different interests and needs, and are motivated when they are permitted to make choices based on these unique needs and interests. Learning centers are not a panacea for all the problems that confront education today, but well-planned centers can enhance the learning environment. (pp. 292–293)

The following are some ways learning centers are used:

1. *Total Learning Environment.* The entire instructional program is personalized. Youngsters engage in small-group and individual activities at various learning stations throughout the room. Teacher-conducted learning activities are kept at a minimum.

2. *Remedial Work.* Students who have not mastered basic skills go to learning centers focused on those skills. They work with audiovisual materials and individualized instruction programs or help one another as peer tutors.

3. *Practice.* To reinforce knowledge or skills learned in regular classroom instruction, students go to learning centers equipped with materials for motivated practice to enhance recent learning and challenge them to go beyond what they have learned.

4. *Enrichment Activities.* At specific times during the day, students choose to engage in activities they enjoy, such as arts and crafts, games, puzzles, science experiments, or cooking. These also provide a change of pace when students get bored.

Learning center activities can be designed to meet the unique needs of a student. Although learning centers are usually associated with self-directed activities, one or more stations may be teacher directed. Also, paraprofessionals, volunteers, or pupils who have specific talents can direct centers at various times.

Examples of Types of Centers

Single-subject Centers
1. Reading center
2. Math center
3. Science/health center
4. Writing/spelling/handwriting center
5. Social studies center
6. Foreign language center

Remedial Learning Centers
7. Any of the subjects listed above

Enrichment Centers
8. Library center
9. Computer center
10. Art/music center
11. Activities and game center
12. Listening center

Independent Study Centers
13. Research center
14. Discovery center
15. Invention center

THE IMPORTANCE OF ENRICHMENT ACTIVITIES

The richer the environment, the more likely students will discover new interests, information, and skills. Enrichment comprises opportunities for exploration, inquiry, and discovery related to topics and activities that are not part of the usual curriculum. Opportunities are offered but need not be taken. No specific learning objectives are specified. Equally as important as what is learned is the experience of feeling value and joy in pursuing knowledge.

Enrichment activities often are more attractive and intriguing than those offered in the developmental curriculum. In part, this is because they are not required, and individuals can seek out those that match their interests and abilities. Enrichment activities also tend to be responsive to students; whatever doesn't keep their attention is replaced.

Because so many people think of enrichment as a frill, it is not surprising that such activities may be overlooked—especially for youngsters who manifest learning and behavior problems. After all, these persons are seen as needing all the time that is available for catching up. This view is unfortunate. The broader the curriculum, the better the opportunity for creating a good motivational match and for facilitating learning throughout an important range of developmental tasks and remedial needs.

> ### Example of One School's Way of Organizing Enrichment Offerings
>
> 1. *Arts:* stained glass, raku, ceramics, pottery, painting, junk art, mask making, puppetry, jewelry making, basket weaving, air brushing, silk screening, photography, drama, street dancing, line dancing, folk dancing, hula, creative movement, video/film-making, card making, tile mosaics
> 2. *Science/Math:* dissection, kitchen physics, kitchen chemistry, marine biology, rocketry, robotics, Knex, string art, math games and puzzles, science and toys, boat making, Hawaiian ethnobotany, and laser/holography
> 3. *Computer:* computer graphics, Internet, computer simulations, computer multimedia, and computer Lego logo
> 4. *Athletics:* basketball, baseball, volleyball, football, soccer, juggling, unicycling, golf
> 5. *Others:* cooking, magic, clowning around, French culture, Spanish culture, Japanese culture, board games

Enrichment should be an integral part of daily classroom time. It should be part of schoolwide opportunities during the day and after school. Afterschool programs not only enable schools to stay open longer to provide academic support and safe havens, drug and violence prevention, and various services such as counseling, but they also provide opportunities for youngsters to participate in supervised recreation, chorus, band, the arts, and using the Internet. All this allows youngsters to learn skills that often are not part of the school's curricula, such as athletic and artistic performance skills. In some cases, these experiences lead to lifelong interests or careers. But perhaps just as important, youngsters are able to enhance their sense of competence and affiliation.

ACTIVE LEARNING: YES, BUT . . .

The push for an increased emphasis on direct instruction to make quick gains related to basic academic skills (e.g., reading, math) narrows thinking about active learning. The nature and scope of activity described in this book requires devoting more time to the learning process. This is good for learning but may be thought of as slowing down the pace for increasing elementary school achievement test gains with respect to the three R's. This is an either/or form of thinking we see as a false dichotomy. Nevertheless, this mind-set, paired with accountability pressure for rapid test score increases, is working against appropriate use of active learning. In reaction, growing concerns are voiced about the likelihood that the foundation for higher-order learning and future engagement in learning at school is being sacrificed to allow for short-term, and usually modest, achievement test gains.

> **A Few Other Examples of Activities That Can Be Used Regularly to Engage Learners and Enrich Learning**
>
> - Library activities; music/art/drama; student exhibitions and performances; outside speakers and performers; field trips
> - Mentoring and service learning; clubs; special interest groups; recreation and similar organized activities; schoolwide activities such as student council and other leadership opportunities
> - Athletics; school environment projects (e.g., mural painting, gardening, school cleanup and beautification); poster/essay contests; sales events (e.g., candy, T-shirts)
> - Book fairs; health fairs; student newspapers/magazines

As motivational theorists (Deci & Flaste, 1995) emphasize:

> It is all quite ironic. Parents, politicians, and school administrators, all want students to be creative problem-solvers and to learn material at a deep, conceptual level. But in their eagerness to achieve these ends, they pressure teachers to produce. The paradox is that the more they do that, the more controlling the teachers become, which, as we have seen so many times, undermines intrinsic motivation, creativity, and conceptual understanding in the students. The harder the teachers are pushed to get results, the less likely it is that the important results will be forthcoming. (p. 158)

REFERENCES

Deci, E. L., with Flaste, R. (1995). *Why we do what we do.* New York: Penguin Books.

Ferretti, R., & Okolo, C. (1996). Authenticity in learning: Multimedia design projects in the social studies for students with disabilities. *Journal of Learning Disabilities, 29,* 450–460.

Katz, L., & Chard, S. (1998). Issues in selecting topics for projects. *ERIC Digest.* (ERIC No. ED424031)

Maricopa Center for Learning and Instruction. (2004). *PBL overview.* Retrieved from http://www.mcli.dist.maricopa.edu/pbl/info.html.

McCarthy, M. M. (1977). The how and why of learning centers. *Elementary School Journal, 77,* 292–299.

Newmann, F., Marks, H., & Gamoran, A. (1996). Authentic pedagogy and student performance. *American Journal of Education, 104,* 280–312.

Surveying How a School Is Addressing Barriers to Student Learning

12

Throughout the book, we stress the following points:

- In their effort to raise test scores, school leaders usually have pursued intensive instruction as the primary route. While improved instruction is necessary, for too many youngsters it is not sufficient. Students who arrive at school on any given day lacking motivational readiness and/or certain abilities need something more. That something more involves developing comprehensive, multifaceted, and integrated approaches to address barriers to student learning and promote healthy development.
- Schools already have a variety of programs and services to address barriers and promote development. These range from Title I programs, through extra help for low-performing students, to accommodations for special education students. In some places, the personnel and programs to support learning may account for as much as 25%–30% of the resources expended by a school. However, because school leaders have been so focused on instruction, too little attention is paid to the need for and potential impact of rethinking how these resources can be used to enable student learning.

Critical steps in enhancing learning supports involve (a) taking stock of the resources already being expended and (b) considering how these valuable resources can be used to the greatest effect. These matters involve a variety of functions and tasks we encompass under the theme of mapping, analyzing, and enhancing resources.

MAPPING, ANALYZING, AND ENHANCING RESOURCES

In most schools and community agencies, there is redundancy stemming from ill-conceived policies and lack of coordination. These facts do not translate into evidence that there are pools of unneeded personnel and programs; they simply suggest that there are resources that can be used in different ways to address unmet needs. Given that additional funding is hard to come by, redeployment of resources is the primary answer to the ubiquitous question: *Where will we find the funds?* A primary and essential task in improving the current state of affairs, therefore, is to enumerate (map) school and community programs and services already in place. Such mapping is followed by analyses of what is available, effective, and needed. The analyses provide a sound basis for formulating strategies to link with additional resources at other schools, district sites, and in the community, and to enhance the use of existing resources. Such analyses can also guide efforts to improve cost-effectiveness. In a similar fashion, mapping and analyses of a complex or family of schools provide information that can guide strategies for cooperation and integration to enhance intervention effectiveness and garner economies of scale.

Carrying out the functions and tasks related to mapping, analyzing, and managing resources is, in effect, an intervention that underscores the need for systemic change. For example:

- A focus on these matters highlights the reality that the school's current infrastructure probably requires some revamping to ensure that there is a mechanism focusing on resources and ongoing development of a comprehensive approach to addressing barriers to learning.
- By identifying and analyzing existing resources (e.g., personnel, programs, services, facilities, budgeted dollars, social capital), awareness is heightened of their value and potential for playing a major role in helping students engage and reengage in learning at school.
- Analyses also lead to sophisticated recommendations for deploying and redeploying resources to improve programs, enhance cost-effectiveness, and fill programmatic gaps in keeping with well-conceived priorities.
- The products from mapping can be invaluable for "social marketing" efforts designed to show teachers, parents, and other community stakeholders all that the school is doing to address barriers to learning and promote healthy development.

Enhanced appreciation of the importance of resource mapping, analysis, and management may lead to a desire to move too quickly in doing the tasks in order to get on with the "real business." This is unwise. Resource mapping and management is real business, and the tasks are ongoing.

Generally speaking, mapping usually is best done in stages, and the information requires constant updating and analysis. Most schools find it convenient to do the easiest forms of mapping first and then build the capacity to do in-depth mapping over a period of months. Similarly, initial analyses and management of resources focus mostly on enhancing an understanding of what exists and coordinating resource use. Over time, the focus is on spreadsheet-type analyses, priority recommendations, and braiding resources to enhance cost-effectiveness and fill programmatic gaps. Guide 12.1 outlines matters related to mapping and managing resources. More on this topic is available in *Resource Mapping and Management to Address Barriers to Learning: An Intervention for Systemic Change* (a technical assistance packet developed by the Center for Mental Health in Schools at UCLA).[1]

SOME TOOLS TO AID MAPPING

A gap analysis is generated when surveys of unmet needs of students, their families, and school staff are paired with resource mapping. The following set of self-study surveys were developed to aid school staff in mapping and analyzing current programs, services, and systems (see Guides 12.2–12.9). These surveys provide a starter tool kit to aid in mapping.

- The first survey provides an overview of system status (see Guide 12.2).
- This is followed by a set of surveys related to each of the six content areas of an Enabling or Learning Supports Component: (1) classroom-based approaches to enable and reengage students in classroom learning (Guide 12.3), (2) crisis assistance and prevention (Guide 12.4), (3) support for transitions (Guide 12.5), (4) home involvement in schooling (Guide 12.6), (5) outreach to develop greater community involvement and support—including recruitment of volunteers (Guide 12.7), and (6) prescribed student and family assistance (Guide 12.8).
- Finally, included is a survey focusing specifically on school-community collaboration (Guide 12.9).

The items on any of the surveys can help clarify

- What is currently being done and whether it is being done well
- What else is desired

Guide 12.1 About Resource Mapping and Management

A. Why Mapping Resources Is So Important

- To function well, every system has to fully understand and manage its resources. Mapping is a first step toward enhancing essential understanding, and done properly, it is a major intervention in the process of moving forward with enhancing systemic effectiveness.

B. Why Mapping Both School and Community Resources Is So Important

- Schools and communities share
  - Goals and problems with respect to children, youth, and families
  - The need to develop cost-effective systems, programs, and services to meet the goals and address the problems
  - Accountability pressures related to improving outcomes
  - The opportunity to improve effectiveness by coordinating and eventually integrating resources to develop a full continuum of systemic interventions

C. What Are Resources?

- Programs, services, real estate, equipment, money, social capital, leadership, infrastructure mechanisms, and more

D. What Do We Mean by Mapping, and Who Does It?

- A representative group of informed stakeholders is asked to undertake the process of identifying
  - What currently is available to achieve goals and address problems
  - What else is needed to achieve goals and address problems

E. What Does This Process Lead To?

- Analyses to clarify gaps and recommend priorities for filling gaps related to programs and services and deploying, redeploying, and enhancing resources
- Identifying needs for making infrastructure and systemic improvements and changes
- Clarifying opportunities for achieving important functions by forming and enhancing collaborative arrangements
- Social marketing

F. How to Do Resource Mapping

- Do it in stages (start simple and build over time).
  - A first step is to clarify people/agencies who carry out relevant roles/functions.
  - Next, clarify specific programs, activities, services (including information on how many students/families can be accommodated).
  - Identify the dollars and other related resources (e.g., facilities, equipment) that are being expended from various sources.
  - Collate the various policies that are relevant to the endeavor.
- At each stage, establish a computer file, and in the later stages create spreadsheet formats.
- Use available tools (see following examples).

G. Use Benchmarks to Guide Progress Related to Resource Mapping

At schools, this type of self-study is best done by teams. However, it is *not* about having another meeting and/or getting through a task. It is about moving on to better outcomes for students through (a) working together to understand what is and what might be and (b) clarifying gaps, priorities, and next steps. For example, a group of school staff (teachers, support staff, administrators) could use the items to discuss how the school currently addresses any or all of the areas. Members of a team initially might work separately in responding to survey items, but the real payoff comes from group work.

The purposes of the group's work are to

- Analyze whether certain activities should no longer be pursued (because they are not effective or not as high a priority as some others that are needed).
- Decide about what resources can be redeployed to enhance current efforts that need embellishment.
- Identify gaps with respect to important areas of need.
- Establish priorities, strategies, and timelines for filling gaps.

Done right, mapping and analysis of resources can

- Counter fragmentation and redundancy.
- Mobilize support and direction.
- Enhance linkages with other resources.
- Facilitate effective systemic change.
- Integrate all facets of systemic change and counter marginalization of the component to address barriers to student learning.

Ongoing attention to all this provides a form of quality review.

- Now review the set of surveys and think about how to use them to enhance learning supports.
- See Guide 12.10 for a tool that can be used to facilitate priority setting and follow-up actions.

Guide 12.2 Survey of Learning Supports System Status

As a school sets out to enhance the usefulness of learning supports designed to address barriers to learning, it helps to clarify what you have in place as a basis for determining what needs to be done. You will want to pay special attention to

- Clarifying what resources already are available
- How the resources are organized to work in a coordinated way
- What procedures are in place for enhancing resource usefulness

This survey provides a starting point.

The first form provides a template that you can fill in to clarify the people and their positions at your school who provide services and programs related to addressing barriers to learning. This also is a logical group of people to bring together in establishing a resource-oriented team for learning supports at the school.

Following this is a survey designed to help you review how well systems for learning supports have been developed and are functioning.

Learning Supports Staff at the School

In a sense, each staff member is a special resource for every other. A few individuals are highlighted here to underscore some special functions.

Administrative Leader for Learning Supports _____

School Psychologist _____

Times at the school _____

- Provides assessment and testing of students for special services. Counseling for students and parents. Support services for teachers. Prevention, crisis, conflict resolution, program modification for special learning and/or behavioral needs

School Nurse _____

Times at the school _____

- Provides immunizations, follow-up, communicable disease control, vision and hearing screening and follow-up, health assessments and referrals, health counseling and information for students and families

Pupil Services and Attendance Counselor

_____

Times at the school _____

- Provides a liaison between school and home to maximize school attendance, provide transition counseling for returnees, enhance attendance improvement activities.

Social Worker _____

Times at the school _____

- Assists in identifying at-risk students and provides follow-up counseling for students and parents. Refers families for additional services if needed.

Counselor _____

Times at the school _____

Counselor _____

Times at the school _____

- General and special counseling/ guidance services. Consultation with parents and school staff

Dropout Prevention Program Coordinator

_____

Times at the school _____

- Coordinates activity designed to promote dropout prevention

Title I and Bilingual Coordinators

_____

_____

- Coordinate categorical programs, provide services to identified Title I students, implement bilingual master plan (supervising the curriculum, testing, and so forth)

Resource and Special Education Teachers

_____

_____

_____

Times at the school _____

- Provide information on program modifications for students in regular classrooms as well as provide services for special education

Other Important Resources:

School-based Crisis Team (list by name/title)

_____ / _____

_____ / _____

_____ / _____

_____ / _____

_____ / _____

School Improvement Program Planners

_____ / _____

_____ / _____

_____ / _____

Community Resources

- Providing school-linked or school-based interventions and resources

Who	What they do	When
_____ /	_____ /	_____
_____ /	_____ /	_____
_____ /	_____ /	_____
_____ /	_____ /	_____
_____ /	_____ /	_____
_____ /	_____ /	_____

Survey of Learning Supports System Status

Items 1–9 ask about what processes are in place.

Use the following ratings in responding to these items.

DK = Don't know
1 = Not yet
2 = Planned
3 = Just recently initiated
4 = Has been functional for a while
5 = Well institutionalized (well established with a commitment to maintenance)

1. Is someone at the school designated as the administrative leader for activity designed to address barriers to learning (e.g., learning supports, health and social services, the Enabling Component)? 　DK 1 2 3 4 5

2. Is there a time and place when personnel involved in activity designed to address barriers to learning meet together? 　DK 1 2 3 4 5

3. Is there a resource-oriented team (e.g., a Learning Supports Resource Team), as contrasted to a case-oriented team? 　DK 1 2 3 4 5
   a. Does the team analyze data trends at the school with respect to
      - Attendance? 　DK 1 2 3 4 5
      - Dropouts? 　DK 1 2 3 4 5
      - Achievement? 　DK 1 2 3 4 5
   b. Does the team map learning supports programs to determine whether
      - Identified priorities are being addressed adequately? 　DK 1 2 3 4 5
      - Program quality is up to standards? 　DK 1 2 3 4 5
      - Gaps have been identified, and priorities for the future are set? 　DK 1 2 3 4 5
   c. Which of the following areas of learning support are reviewed regularly?
      - Classroom-based Approaches to Enable and Reengage Students in Classroom Learning (see Guide 12.3) 　DK 1 2 3 4 5
      - Crisis Assistance and Prevention (see Guide 12.4) 　DK 1 2 3 4 5
      - Support for Transitions (see Guide 12.5) 　DK 1 2 3 4 5
      - Home Involvement in Schooling (see Guide 12.6) 　DK 1 2 3 4 5
      - Community Outreach for Involvement and Support (see Guide 12.7) 　DK 1 2 3 4 5
      - Student and Family Assistance Programs and Services (see Guide 12.8) 　DK 1 2 3 4 5

4. Are there *written descriptions* of learning supports programs available to give to
   a. Staff? 　DK 1 2 3 4 5
   b. Families? 　DK 1 2 3 4 5
   c. Students? 　DK 1 2 3 4 5
   d. Community stakeholders? 　DK 1 2 3 4 5

5. Are there case-oriented systems in place for
   a. Concerned parties to use in making referrals? 　DK 1 2 3 4 5
   b. Triage (to decide how to respond when a referral is made)? 　DK 1 2 3 4 5
   c. Case monitoring and management? 　DK 1 2 3 4 5
   d. A student review team? 　DK 1 2 3 4 5
   e. A crisis team? 　DK 1 2 3 4 5

6. Are there *written descriptions* available to give
   to staff and others about
   a. How to make referrals?   DK 1 2 3 4 5
   b. The triage process?   DK 1 2 3 4 5
   c. The process for case monitoring and management?   DK 1 2 3 4 5
   d. The process for student review?   DK 1 2 3 4 5

7. Are there systems in place to support staff wellness?   DK 1 2 3 4 5

8. Are there processes by which staff and families learn
   a. What is available in the way of programs/services at school? DK 1 2 3 4 5
   b. How to access programs/services they need?   DK 1 2 3 4 5

9. Has someone at the school been designated as a representative DK 1 2 3 4 5
   to meet with the other schools in the feeder pattern to enhance
   coordination and integration of learning supports among the schools
   and with community resources?

The following items ask about the effectiveness of existing processes.

Use the following ratings in responding to these items.

   DK = Don't know
    1 = Hardly ever effective
    2 = Effective about 25% of the time
    3 = Effective about half the time
    4 = Effective about 75% of the time
    5 = Almost always effective

10. How effective are the processes for
    a. Planning, implementing, and evaluating learning   DK 1 2 3 4 5
       supports system improvements?
    b. Enhancing learning supports resources (e.g., through budget DK 1 2 3 4 5
       decisions and staff development, developing or bringing new
       programs/services to the site, making formal linkages with
       programs/services in the community)?

11. How effective are the processes for ensuring that
    a. Resources are properly allocated and coordinated?   DK 1 2 3 4 5
    b. Community resources linked with the school are effectively DK 1 2 3 4 5
       coordinated/integrated with related school activities?

12. How effective are the processes for ensuring that resources   DK 1 2 3 4 5
    available to the whole feeder pattern of schools are properly
    allocated and shared/coordinated?

13. How effective is the
    a. Referral system?   DK 1 2 3 4 5
    b. Triage system?   DK 1 2 3 4 5
    c. Case monitoring and management system?   DK 1 2 3 4 5
    d. Student review team?   DK 1 2 3 4 5
    e. Crisis team?   DK 1 2 3 4 5

14. List community resources with which you have formal relationships.
    a. Those that bring program(s) to the school site
    b. Those not at the school site but which have made a special
       commitment to respond to the school's referrals and needs

Guide 12.3   Classroom-based Approaches to Enable and Reengage
Students in Classroom Learning: A Self-study Survey

This arena provides a fundamental example not only of how learning supports overlap regular instructional efforts but how they add value to prevailing efforts to improve instruction. Classroom-based efforts to enable learning can (a) prevent problems, (b) facilitate intervening as soon as problems are noted, (c) enhance intrinsic motivation for learning, and (d) reengage students who have become disengaged from classroom learning. This is accomplished by increasing teachers' effectiveness so they can account for a wider range of individual differences, foster a caring context for learning, and prevent and handle a wider range of problems when they arise. Effectiveness is enhanced through personalized staff development and opening the classroom door to others who can help. One objective is to provide teachers with the knowledge and skills to develop a classroom infrastructure that transforms a big class into a set of smaller ones. Such a focus is essential for increasing the effectiveness of regular classroom instruction, supporting inclusionary policies, and reducing the need for specialized services.

Work in this arena requires programmatic approaches and systems designed to personalize the professional development of teachers and support staff, develop the capabilities of paraeducators and other paid assistants and volunteers, provide temporary out-of-class assistance for students, and enhance resources. For example, personalized help is provided to increase a teacher's array of strategies for accommodating, as well as teaching students to compensate for, differences, vulnerabilities, and disabilities. Teachers learn to use paid assistants, peer tutors, and volunteers in targeted ways to enhance social and academic support.

As appropriate, support *in the classroom* also is provided by resource and itinerant teachers and counselors. This involves restructuring and redesigning the roles, functions, and staff development of resource and itinerant teachers, counselors, and other pupil service personnel so they are able to work closely with teachers and students in the classroom and on regular activities.

Classroom-based Approaches

Indicate all items that apply.

	Yes	Yes, but more of this is needed.	No	If no, is this something you want?
I. Opening the Classroom Door				
A. Are others invited into the classroom to assist in enhancing classroom approaches?				
1. Aides (e.g., paraeducators, other paid assistants)?	___	___	___	___
2. Older students?	___	___	___	___
3. Other students in the class?	___	___	___	___
4. Volunteers?	___	___	___	___
5. Parents?	___	___	___	___
6. Resource teacher?	___	___	___	___
7. Specialists?	___	___	___	___
8. Other? (specify) _____	___	___	___	___
B. Are there programs to train aides, volunteers, and other "assistants" who come into the classrooms to work with students who need help?	___	___	___	___
II. Redesigning Classroom Approaches to Enhance Teacher Capability to Prevent and Handle Problems and Reduce Need for Out-of-Class Referrals				
A. Is instruction personalized (i.e., designed to match each student's motivation and capabilities)?	___	___	___	___
B. When needed, is in-classroom special assistance provided?	___	___	___	___
C. Are there small-group and independent learning options?	___	___	___	___
D. Are behavior problems handled in ways designed to minimize a negative impact on student attitudes toward classroom learning?	___	___	___	___
E. Is there a range of curricular and instructional options and choices?	___	___	___	___
F. Are prereferral interventions used?	___	___	___	___
G. Are materials and activities upgraded to				
1. Ensure that there are enough basic supplies in the classroom?	___	___	___	___
2. Increase the range of high-motivation activities (keyed to the interests of students in need of special attention)?	___	___	___	___
3. Include advanced technology?	___	___	___	___
4. Other? (specify) _____	___	___	___	___
H. Are regular efforts to foster social and emotional development supplemented?	___	___	___	___
I. Which of the following can teachers request as special interventions?				
1. Family problem-solving conferences?	___	___	___	___
2. Exchange of students to improve student-teacher match and for a fresh start?	___	___	___	___

	Yes	Yes, but more of this is needed.	No	If no, is this something you want?
3. Referral for specific services?	___	___	___	___
4. Other? (specify) _____	___	___	___	___
J. What programs are there for temporary out-of-class help?				
1. A family center providing student and family assistance?	___	___	___	___
2. Designated problem remediation specialists?	___	___	___	___
3. A time-out situation?	___	___	___	___
4. Other? (specify) _____	___	___	___	___
K. What is done to assist a teacher who has difficulty with limited-English-speaking students?				
1. Is the student reassigned?	___	___	___	___
2. Does the teacher receive professional development related to working with limited-English-speaking students?	___	___	___	___
3. Does a bilingual coordinator offer consultation?	___	___	___	___
4. Is a bilingual aide assigned to the class?	___	___	___	___
5. Are volunteers brought in to help (e.g., parents, peers)?	___	___	___	___
6. Other? (specify) _____	___	___	___	___

III. Enhancing and Personalizing Professional Development

	Yes	Yes, but more of this is needed.	No	If no, is this something you want?
A. Are teachers clustered for support and staff development?	___	___	___	___
B. Are demonstrations provided?	___	___	___	___
C. Are workshops and readings offered regularly?	___	___	___	___
D. Is consultation available from persons with special expertise such as				
1. Learning supports staff (e.g., psychologist, counselor, social worker, nurse)?	___	___	___	___
2. Resource specialists and/or special education teachers?	___	___	___	___
3. Members of special committees?	___	___	___	___
4. Bilingual and/or other coordinators?	___	___	___	___
5. Other? (specify) _____	___	___	___	___
E. Is there a formal mentoring program?	___	___	___	___
F. Is team teaching or coteaching used as an opportunity for teachers to learn on the job?	___	___	___	___
G. Is the school creating a learning community?	___	___	___	___
H. Is there staff social·support?	___	___	___	___
I. Is there formal conflict mediation/resolution for staff?	___	___	___	___
J. Is there a focus on learning how to integrate intrinsic motivation into teaching and classroom management?	___	___	___	___
K. Is there assistance in learning to use advanced technology?	___	___	___	___
L. Other? (specify) _____	___	___	___	___

	Yes	Yes, but more of this is needed.	No	If no, is this something you want?

IV. Curricular Enrichment and Adjunct Programs

A. What types of technology are available to the classroom?

1. Are there computers in the classroom?
2. Is there a computer lab?
3. Is computer-assisted instruction offered?
4. Are there computer literacy programs?
5. Are computer programs used to address ESL needs?
6. Does the classroom have video recording capability?
7. Is instructional TV used in the classroom?
8. Is there a multimedia lab?
9. Other? (specify) _____

B. What curricular enrichment and adjunct programs do teachers use?

1. Are library activities used regularly?
2. Is music/art used regularly?
3. Is health education a regular part of the curriculum?
4. Are student performances regular events?
5. Are there several field trips a year?
6. Are there student council and other leaders opportunities?
7. Are there school environment projects such as
   a. Mural painting?
   b. Horticulture/gardening?
   c. School cleanup and beautification?
   d. Other? (specify) _____
8. Are there special schoolwide events such as
   a. Sports?
   b. Clubs and similar organized activities?
   c. Publication of a student newspaper?
   d. Sales events?
   e. Poster contests?
   f. Essay contests?
   g. A book fair?
   h. Pep rallies/contests?
   i. Attendance competitions?
   j. Attendance awards/assemblies?
   k. Other? (specify) _____
9. Are guest contributors used (e.g., outside speakers/performers)?
10. Other? (specify) _____

V. Classroom and Schoolwide Approaches Used to Create and Maintain a Caring and Supportive Climate

A. Are there schoolwide approaches for

1. Creating and maintaining a caring and supportive climate?

	Yes	Yes, but more of this is needed.	No	If no, is this something you want?
2. Supporting high standards for positive behavior?	_____	_____	_____	_____
3. Other? (specify) _____	_____	_____	_____	_____
B. Are there classroom approaches for				
1. Creating and maintaining a caring and supportive climate?	_____	_____	_____	_____
2. Supporting high standards for positive behavior?	_____	_____	_____	_____
3. Other? (specify) _____	_____	_____	_____	_____

VI. Capacity Building for Classroom-based Approaches

	Yes	Yes, but more of this is needed.	No	If no, is this something you want?
A. Are there programs to enhance broad stakeholder involvement in classroom-based approaches?	_____	_____	_____	_____
B. Programs used to meet the educational needs of personnel related to classroom-based approaches	_____	_____	_____	_____
1. Is there ongoing training for learning supports staff with respect to classroom-based approaches?	_____	_____	_____	_____
2. Is there ongoing training for others involved in providing classroom-based approaches (e.g., teachers, peer buddies, office staff, administrators)?	_____	_____	_____	_____
3. Other? (specify) _____	_____	_____	_____	_____
C. Which of the following topics are covered in educating stakeholders?				
1. How others can work effectively in the classroom	_____	_____	_____	_____
2. Reengaging students who have disengaged from classroom learning	_____	_____	_____	_____
3. Personalizing instruction	_____	_____	_____	_____
4. Addressing learning, behavior, and emotional problems	_____	_____	_____	_____
5. Enriching options and facilitating student and family involvement in decision making	_____	_____	_____	_____

D. Indicate below other things you want the school to do to assist a teacher's efforts to address barriers to students' learning.

Other matters relevant to classroom-based approaches are found in the surveys on

- Support for Transitions (Guide 12.5)
- Home Involvement in Schooling (Guide 12.6)
- Community Involvement and Support (Guide 12.7)

Guide 12.4   Crisis Assistance and Prevention: A Self-study Survey

Schools must respond to, minimize the impact of, and prevent school and personal crises. This requires schoolwide and classroom-based systems and programmatic approaches. Such activity focuses on (a) emergency/crisis response at a site, throughout a school complex, and communitywide (including a focus on ensuring follow-up care), (b) minimizing the impact of crises, and (c) prevention at school and in the community to address school safety and violence reduction, suicide prevention, child abuse prevention, and so forth.

Desired outcomes of crisis assistance include ensuring immediate emergency and follow-up care so students are able to resume learning without too much delay. Prevention outcome indices reflect a safe and productive environment where students and their families display the type of attitudes and capacities needed to deal with violence and other threats to safety.

A key mechanism in this arena often is development of a crisis team. Such a team is trained in emergency response procedures, physical and psychological first aid, aftermath interventions, and so forth. The team also can take the lead in planning ways to prevent some crises by facilitating development of programs to mediate and resolve conflicts, enhance human relations, and promote a caring school culture.

Crisis Assistance and Prevention

Indicate all items that apply.

	Yes	Yes, but more of this is needed.	No	If no, is this something you want?

I. Ensuring Immediate Assistance in Emergencies/Crises

A. Is there a plan that details a coordinated response

1. For all at the school site? _____ _____ _____ _____

2. With other schools in the complex? _____ _____ _____ _____

3. With community agencies? _____ _____ _____ _____

B. Are emergency/crisis plans updated appropriately with regard to

1. Crisis management guidelines (e.g., flowcharts, checklists)? _____ _____ _____ _____

2. Plans for communicating with homes/community? _____ _____ _____ _____

3. Media relations guidelines? _____ _____ _____ _____

C. Are stakeholders regularly provided with information about emergency response plans? _____ _____ _____ _____

D. Is medical first aid provided when crises occur? _____ _____ _____ _____

E. Is psychological first aid provided when crises occur? _____ _____ _____ _____

F. Other? (specify) _____ _____ _____ _____ _____

II. Providing Follow-up Assistance as Necessary

A. Are there programs for *short-term* follow-up assistance? _____ _____ _____ _____

B. Are there programs for *longer-term* follow-up assistance? _____ _____ _____ _____

C. Other? (specify) _____ _____ _____ _____ _____

III. Crisis Team to Formulate Response and Prevention Plans

A. Is there an active crisis team? _____ _____ _____ _____

B. Is the crisis team appropriately trained? _____ _____ _____ _____

C. Does the team focus on prevention of school and personal crises? _____ _____ _____ _____

IV. Mobilizing Staff, Students, and Families to Anticipate Response Plans and Recovery Efforts

With respect to planning and training for crisis response and recovery, are there programs to involve and integrate

A. Learning supports staff? _____ _____ _____ _____

B. Teachers? _____ _____ _____ _____

C. Other school staff? _____ _____ _____ _____

	Yes	Yes, but more of this is needed.	No	If no, is this something you want?
D. Students?	___	___	___	___
E. Families?	___	___	___	___
F. Other schools in the vicinity?	___	___	___	___
G. Other concerned parties in the community?	___	___	___	___

V. Creating a Caring and Safe Learning Environment Through Programs to Enhance Healthy Development and Prevent Problems

A. Are there programs for

	Yes	Yes, but more	No	If no
1. Promoting healthy development?	___	___	___	___
2. Bullying and harassment abatement?	___	___	___	___
3. School and community safety/violence reduction?	___	___	___	___
4. Suicide prevention?	___	___	___	___
5. Child abuse prevention?	___	___	___	___
6. Sexual abuse prevention?	___	___	___	___
7. Substance abuse prevention?	___	___	___	___
8. Other? (specify) _____	___	___	___	___

B. Is there an ongoing emphasis on enhancing a caring and safe learning environment

1. Schoolwide?	___	___	___	___
2. In classrooms?	___	___	___	___

VI. Capacity Building to Enhance Crisis Response and Prevention

A. Is there an ongoing emphasis on enhancing a caring and safe learning environment through programs to enhance the capacity of

1. Learning supports staff?	___	___	___	___
2. Teachers?	___	___	___	___
3. Other school staff?	___	___	___	___
4. Students?	___	___	___	___
5. Families?	___	___	___	___
6. Other schools in the feeder pattern?	___	___	___	___
7. Other concerned parties in the community?	___	___	___	___

B. Is there ongoing training for learning supports staff with respect to the area of crisis assistance and prevention? — ___ ___ ___ ___

C. Is there ongoing training for others involved in crisis response and prevention (e.g., teachers, office staff, administrators)? — ___ ___ ___ ___

D. Which of the following topics are covered in educating stakeholders?

1. Anticipating emergencies	___	___	___	___
2. How to respond when an emergency arises	___	___	___	___
3. How to access assistance after an emergency (including watching for posttraumatic psychological reactions)	___	___	___	___

	Yes	Yes, but more of this is needed.	No	If no, is this something you want?
4. Indicators of abuse and potential suicide and what to do	_____	_____	_____	_____
5. How to respond to concerns related to death, dying, and grief	_____	_____	_____	_____
6. How to mediate conflicts and minimize violent reactions	_____	_____	_____	_____
7. Other (specify) _____	_____	_____	_____	_____
E. Indicate below other things you want the school to do in responding to and preventing crises.	_____	_____	_____	_____

Other matters relevant to crises response are found in the survey on Student and Family Assistance (Guide 12.8).

Guide 12.5   Support for Transitions: A Self-study Survey

Students and their families are regularly confronted with a variety of transitions—changing schools, changing grades, encountering a range of other daily hassles and major life demands. Many of these can interfere with productive school involvement. A comprehensive focus on transitions requires schoolwide and classroom-based systems and programs designed to (a) enhance successful transitions, (b) prevent transition problems, and (c) use transition periods to reduce alienation and increase positive attitudes toward school and learning. Examples of programs include schoolwide and classroom-specific activities for welcoming new arrivals (students, their families, staff) and rendering ongoing social support; counseling and articulation strategies to support grade-to-grade and school-to-school transitions and moves to and from special education, college, and postschool living and work; and beforeschool and afterschool and intersession activities to enrich learning and provide recreation in a safe environment.

Anticipated overall outcomes are reduced alienation and enhanced motivation and increased involvement in school and learning activities. Examples of early outcomes include reduced tardies resulting from participation in beforeschool programs and reduced vandalism, violence, and crime at school and in the neighborhood resulting from involvement in afterschool activities. Over time, articulation programs can reduce school avoidance and dropouts, as well as enhance the number who make successful transitions to higher education and postschool living and work. It is also likely that a caring school climate can play a significant role in reducing student transiency.

Support for Transitions

Indicate all items that apply.

	Yes	Yes, but more of this is needed.	No	If no, is this something you want?

I. Programs Establishing a Welcoming and Socially Supportive School Community

  A. Supportive welcoming

1. Are there welcoming materials and a welcoming decor? ____ ____ ____ ____
2. Are there welcome signs? ____ ____ ____ ____
3. Are welcoming information materials used? ____ ____ ____ ____
4. Is a special welcoming booklet used? ____ ____ ____ ____
5. Are materials translated into appropriate languages? ____ ____ ____ ____
6. Is advanced technology used as an aid (e.g., a video or computerized introduction to the school and staff)? ____ ____ ____ ____

  B. Orientation and follow-up "induction"

1. Are there orientation programs? ____ ____ ____ ____
2. Are there introductory tours? ____ ____ ____ ____
3. Are introductory presentations made? ____ ____ ____ ____
4. Are new arrivals introduced to special people such as the principal and teachers? ____ ____ ____ ____
5. Are special events used to welcome recent arrivals? ____ ____ ____ ____
6. Are different languages accommodated? ____ ____ ____ ____

  C. Is special assistance available to those who need help registering? ____ ____ ____ ____

  D. Social supports

1. Are social support strategies and mechanisms used? ____ ____ ____ ____
2. Are peer buddies assigned? ____ ____ ____ ____
3. Are peer parents assigned? ____ ____ ____ ____
4. Are special invitations used to encourage family involvement? ____ ____ ____ ____
5. Are special invitations used to encourage students to join in activities? ____ ____ ____ ____
6. Are advocates available when new arrivals need them? ____ ____ ____ ____

  E. Other (specify) _____ ____ ____ ____ ____

II. Daily Transition Programs for Before and After School and Lunch and Breaks

  A. Which of the following are available?

1. Subsidized food program ____ ____ ____ ____
2. Recreation program ____ ____ ____ ____
3. Sports program ____ ____ ____ ____
4. Drill team ____ ____ ____ ____
5. Student and family assistance program ____ ____ ____ ____

	Yes	Yes, but more of this is needed.	No	If no, is this something you want?
6. Youth groups such as				
a. Interest groups (e.g., music, drama, career)	____	____	____	____
b. Service clubs	____	____	____	____
c. Organized youth programs (Y, Scouts)	____	____	____	____
d. Cadet Corps	____	____	____	____
e. Other (specify) _____	____	____	____	____
7. Academic support in the form of				
a. Tutors	____	____	____	____
b. Homework club	____	____	____	____
c. Study hall	____	____	____	____
d. Homework phone line	____	____	____	____
e. E-mail and Web assistance	____	____	____	____
f. Homework center	____	____	____	____
g. Other (specify) _____	____	____	____	____

III. Articulation Programs

Which of the following transition programs are in use for grade-to-grade and program-to-program articulation?

	Yes	Yes, but more of this is needed.	No	If no, is this something you want?
A. Are orientations to the new situation provided?	____	____	____	____
B. Is transition counseling provided?	____	____	____	____
C. Are students taken on warm-up visits?	____	____	____	____
D. Is there a "survival" skill training program?	____	____	____	____
E. Is information available from previous teachers?	____	____	____	____
F. Is the new setting primed to accommodate the individual's needs?	____	____	____	____
G. Other? (specify) _____	____	____	____	____

IV. Vacation and Intersession Programs

Which of the following programs are offered during vacation and/or intersession?

	Yes	Yes, but more of this is needed.	No	If no, is this something you want?
A. Recreation	____	____	____	____
B. Sports	____	____	____	____
C. Student and family assistance	____	____	____	____
D. Youth groups	____	____	____	____
E. Academic support	____	____	____	____
F. Enrichment opportunities (including classes)	____	____	____	____
G. Other (specify) _____	____	____	____	____

V. Transitions to Higher Education/Career

Which of the following are used to facilitate transition to higher education and postschool living?

	Yes	Yes, but more of this is needed.	No	If no, is this something you want?
A. Vocational counseling	____	____	____	____
B. College counseling	____	____	____	____
C. A mentoring program	____	____	____	____
D. College prep courses and related activity	____	____	____	____
E. Job training	____	____	____	____
F. Job opportunities on campus	____	____	____	____
G. A work-study program	____	____	____	____
H. Life skills counseling	____	____	____	____
I. Other (specify) _____	____	____	____	____

	Yes	Yes, but more of this is needed.	No	If no, is this something you want?
VI. Capacity Building to Enhance Support for Transitions				
A. Are there programs to enhance broad stakeholder involvement in transition activity?	____	____	____	____
B. With respect to programs used to meet the educational needs of personnel related to support for transitions,				
1. Is there ongoing training for learning supports staff with respect to providing supports for transitions?	____	____	____	____
2. Is there ongoing training for others involved in providing supports for transitions (e.g., teachers, peer buddies, office staff, administrators)?	____	____	____	____
3. Other? (specify) _____	____	____	____	____
C. Which of the following topics are covered in educating stakeholders?				
1. Understanding how to create a psychological sense of community	____	____	____	____
2. Developing systematic social supports for students, families, and staff	____	____	____	____
3. How to ensure successful transitions	____	____	____	____
4. The value of and strategies for creating beforeschool and afterschool programs	____	____	____	____
5. Other (specify) _____	____	____	____	____
D. Indicate below other things you want the school to do in providing support for transitions.				

Other matters relevant to support for transitions are found in the surveys on

- Classroom-based Approaches (Guide 12.3)
- Home Involvement in Schooling (Guide 12.6)
- Community Involvement and Support (Guide 12.7)

Guide 12.6 Home Involvement in Schooling: A Self-study Survey

This arena expands concern for parent involvement to encompass anyone in the home who is influencing the student's life. In some cases, grandparents, aunts, or older siblings have assumed the parenting role. Older brothers and sisters often are the most significant influences on a youngster's life choices. Thus, schools and communities must go beyond focusing on parents in their efforts to enhance home involvement.

This arena includes schoolwide and classroom-based efforts designed to strengthen the home situation, enhance family problem-solving capabilities, and increase support for student well-being. Accomplishing all this requires schoolwide and classroom-based systems and programs to (a) address the specific learning and support needs of adults in the home, such as offering them ESL, literacy, vocational, and citizenship classes, enrichment and recreational opportunities, and mutual support groups, (b) help those in the home improve how basic student obligations are met, such as providing guidance related to parenting and how to help with schoolwork, (c) improve forms of basic communication that promote the well-being of student, family, and school, (d) enhance the home-school connection and sense of community, (e) foster participation in making decisions essential to a student's well-being, (f) facilitate home support of student learning and development, (g) mobilize those at home to problem solve related to student needs, and (h) elicit help (support, collaborations, and partnerships) from those at home with respect to meeting classroom, school, and community needs. The context for some of this activity may be a *parent or family center* if one has been established at the site. Outcomes include indices of parent learning, student progress, and community enhancement specifically related to home involvement.

Home Involvement in Schooling

Indicate all items that apply.

	Yes	Yes, but more of this is needed.	No	If no, is this something you want?

I. Addressing Specific Learning and Support Needs of the Family

   A. Does the site offer adult classes focused on

      1. English as a Second Language (ESL)? _____ _____ _____ _____

      2. Basic literacy skills? _____ _____ _____ _____

      3. GED preparation? _____ _____ _____ _____

      4. Job preparation? _____ _____ _____ _____

      5. Citizenship preparation? _____ _____ _____ _____

      6. Other? (specify) _____ _____ _____ _____ _____

   B. Are there groups for

      1. Mutual support? _____ _____ _____ _____

      2. Discussion? _____ _____ _____ _____

   C. Are adults in the home offered assistance in accessing outside help for personal needs? _____ _____ _____ _____

   D. Which of the following are available to help those in the home meet basic survival needs and basic obligations to the student?

      1. Is help provided for addressing special family needs for

         a. Food? _____ _____ _____ _____

         b. Clothing? _____ _____ _____ _____

         c. Shelter? _____ _____ _____ _____

         d. Health and safety? _____ _____ _____ _____

         e. School supplies? _____ _____ _____ _____

         f. Other? (specify) _____ _____ _____ _____ _____

      2. Are education programs offered on

         a. Child-rearing/parenting? _____ _____ _____ _____

         b. Creating a supportive home environment for students? _____ _____ _____ _____

         c. Reducing factors that interfere with a student's school learning and performance? _____ _____ _____ _____

      3. Are guidelines provided for helping a student deal with homework? _____ _____ _____ _____

      4. Other? (specify) _____ _____ _____ _____ _____

II. Improve Mechanisms for Communication and Connecting School and Home

   A. Are there periodic general announcements and meetings such as

      1. Advertising for incoming students? _____ _____ _____ _____

      2. Orientation for incoming students and families? _____ _____ _____ _____

      3. Bulletins/newsletters? _____ _____ _____ _____

	Yes	Yes, but more of this is needed.	No	If no, is this something you want?
4. Web site?	_____	_____	_____	_____
5. Back-to-school night/open house?	_____	_____	_____	_____
6. Parent-teacher conferences?	_____	_____	_____	_____
7. Other? (specify) _____	_____	_____	_____	_____
B. Is there a system to inform the home on a regular basis (e.g., regular letters, newsletters, e-mail, computerized phone messages, Web site)				
1. About general school matters?	_____	_____	_____	_____
2. About opportunities for home involvement?	_____	_____	_____	_____
3. Other? (specify) _____	_____	_____	_____	_____
C. To enhance home involvement in the student's program and progress, are interactive communications used, such as				
1. Sending notes home regularly?	_____	_____	_____	_____
2. A computerized phone line?	_____	_____	_____	_____
3. E-mail?	_____	_____	_____	_____
4. Frequent in-person conferences with the family?	_____	_____	_____	_____
5. Other? (specify) _____	_____	_____	_____	_____
D. Which of the following are used to enhance the home-school connection and sense of community?				
1. Does the school offer orientations and open houses?	_____	_____	_____	_____
2. Does the school have special receptions for new families?	_____	_____	_____	_____
3. Does the school regularly showcase students to the community through	_____	_____	_____	_____
a. Student performances?	_____	_____	_____	_____
b. Award ceremonies?	_____	_____	_____	_____
c. Other? (specify) _____	_____	_____	_____	_____
4. Does the school offer the community				
a. Cultural and sports events?	_____	_____	_____	_____
b. Topical workshops and discussion groups?	_____	_____	_____	_____
c. Health fairs?	_____	_____	_____	_____
d. Family preservation fairs?	_____	_____	_____	_____
e. Work fairs?	_____	_____	_____	_____
f. Newsletters?	_____	_____	_____	_____
g. Community bulletin boards?	_____	_____	_____	_____
h. Community festivals and celebrations?	_____	_____	_____	_____
i. Other? (specify) _____	_____	_____	_____	_____
5. Is there outreach to families that are hard to involve, such as				
a. Making home visits?	_____	_____	_____	_____
b. Offering support networks?	_____	_____	_____	_____
c. Other? (specify) _____	_____	_____	_____	_____
d. Other? (specify) _____	_____	_____	_____	_____

	Yes	Yes, but more of this is needed.	No	If no, is this something you want?
III. Involving Homes in Making Decisions Essential to the Student				
A. Are families invited to participate through personal				
1. Letters?	____	____	____	____
2. Phone calls?	____	____	____	____
3. E-mail?	____	____	____	____
4. Other? (specify) _____	____	____	____	____
B. Are families informed about schooling choices through				
1. Letters?	____	____	____	____
2. Phone calls?	____	____	____	____
3. E-mail?	____	____	____	____
4. Conferences?	____	____	____	____
5. Other? (specify) _____	____	____	____	____
C. Are families taught skills to participate effectively in decision making?	____	____	____	____
D. With respect to mobilizing problem solving at home related to student needs,				
1. Is instruction provided to enhance family problem-solving skills (including increased awareness of resources for assistance)?	____	____	____	____
2. Is good problem solving modeled at conferences with the family?	____	____	____	____
E. Other? (specify) _____	____	____	____	____
IV. Enhancing Home Support for Student Learning and Development				
A. Are families instructed on how to provide opportunities for students to apply what they are learning?	____	____	____	____
B. Are families instructed on how to use enrichment opportunities to enhance youngsters' social and personal and academic skills and higher-order functioning?	____	____	____	____
C. Are family field trips organized?	____	____	____	____
D. Are families provided space and facilitation for meeting together as a community of learners?	____	____	____	____
E. Are family literacy programs available?	____	____	____	____
F. Are family homework programs offered?	____	____	____	____
G. Other? (specify) _____	____	____	____	____
V. Recruiting Families to Strengthen School and Community				
A. For which of the following are those in the home recruited and trained to help meet school/community needs?				
1. Improving schooling for students by assisting				
a. Administrators	____	____	____	____
b. Teachers	____	____	____	____
c. Other staff	____	____	____	____

	Yes	Yes, but more of this is needed.	No	If no, is this something you want?
d. Others in the community	___	___	___	___
e. With lessons or tutoring	___	___	___	___
f. On class trips	___	___	___	___
g. In the cafeteria	___	___	___	___
h. In the library	___	___	___	___
i. In computer labs	___	___	___	___
j. With homework help lines	___	___	___	___
k. The front office, to welcome visitors and new enrollees and their families	___	___	___	___
l. With phoning/e-mailing home regarding absences	___	___	___	___
m. Outreach to the home	___	___	___	___
n. Other (specify) _____	___	___	___	___
2. Improving school operations by assisting with				
a. School and community upkeep and beautification	___	___	___	___
b. Improving school-community relations	___	___	___	___
c. Fundraising	___	___	___	___
d. PTA	___	___	___	___
e. Enhancing public support by increasing political awareness about the contributions and needs of the school	___	___	___	___
f. School governance	___	___	___	___
g. Advocacy for school needs	___	___	___	___
h. Advisory councils	___	___	___	___
i. Program planning	___	___	___	___
j. Other (specify) _____	___	___	___	___
3. Establishing home-community networks to benefit the community	___	___	___	___
4. Other (specify) _____	___	___	___	___

VI. Capacity Building to Enhance Home Involvement

	Yes	Yes, but more of this is needed.	No	If no, is this something you want?
A. Are there programs to enhance broad stakeholder involvement in efforts to enhance home involvement in schools?	___	___	___	___
B. With respect to programs used to meet the educational needs of personnel related to home involvement,				
1. Is there ongoing training for learning supports staff with respect to enhancing home involvement?	___	___	___	___
2. Is there ongoing training for others involved in enhancing home involvement (e.g., teachers, parent peer buddies, office staff, administrators)?	___	___	___	___
3. Other? (specify) _____	___	___	___	___
C. Which of the following topics are covered in educating stakeholders?				
1. How to facilitate family participation in decision-making meetings	___	___	___	___
2. Designing an inclusionary parent center	___	___	___	___

	Yes	Yes, but more of this is needed.	No	If no, is this something you want?
3. Overcoming barriers to home involvement	_____	_____	_____	_____
4. Developing group-led mutual support groups	_____	_____	_____	_____
5. Developing families as a community of learners	_____	_____	_____	_____
6. Available curriculum for parent education	_____	_____	_____	_____
7. Teaching parents to be mentors and leaders at the school	_____	_____	_____	_____
8. Other (specify) _____	_____	_____	_____	_____
D. Indicate below other things you want the school to do to enhance home involvement.	_____	_____	_____	_____

Other matters relevant to home involvement are found in the surveys on

- Classroom-based Approaches (Guide 12.3)
- Support for Transitions (Guide 12.5)
- Community Involvement and Support (Guide 12.7)
- Student and Family Assistance (Guide 12.8)

Guide 12.7   Community Outreach for Involvement and Support:
A Self-study Survey

Schools can do their job better when they are an integral and positive part of the community. For example, it is a truism that learning is neither limited to what is formally taught nor to time spent in classrooms. It occurs whenever and wherever the learner interacts with the surrounding environment. All facets of the community (not just the school) provide learning opportunities. *Anyone in the community who wants to facilitate learning might be a contributing teacher.* This includes aides, volunteers, parents, siblings, peers, mentors in the community, librarians, recreation staff, college students, and so forth. They all constitute what can be called *the teaching community.* When a school successfully joins with its surrounding community, everyone has the opportunity to learn and to teach.

Another key facet of community involvement is opening up school sites as places where parents, families, and other community residents can engage in learning, recreation, and enrichment and can find services they need. This encompasses an outreach to the community to collaborate and enhance the engagement of young people to directly strengthen youngsters, families, and neighborhoods. In this respect, increasing attention is paid to interventions to promote healthy development, resiliency, and assets.

For schools to be seen as an integral part of the community, outreach steps must be taken to create and maintain linkages and collaborations. The intent is to maximize mutual benefits, including better student progress, an enhanced sense of community, community development, and more. In the long run, the aims are to strengthen students, schools, families, and neighborhoods. Outreach focuses on public and private agencies, organizations, universities, colleges, and facilities; businesses and professional organizations and groups; and volunteer service programs, organizations, and clubs. Greater volunteerism on the part of parents, peers, and others from the community can break down barriers and increase home and community involvement in schools and schooling. Over time, this area can include systems and programs designed to (a) recruit a wide range of community involvement and support, (b) train, screen, and maintain volunteers, (c) reach out to students and families who don't come to school regularly—including truants and dropouts, (d) connect school and community efforts to promote child and youth development, and (e) enhance community-school connections and sense of community.

Community Outreach for Involvement and Support

Indicate all items that apply.

	Yes	Yes, but more of this is needed.	No	If no, is this something you want?
I. Planning and Implementing Outreach to Recruit a Wide Range of Community Resources				
A. From which of the following sources are participants recruited?				
1. Public community agencies, organizations, facilities, and providers	_____	_____	_____	_____
2. Private community agencies, organizations, facilities, and providers	_____	_____	_____	_____
3. Business sector	_____	_____	_____	_____
4. Professional organizations and groups	_____	_____	_____	_____
5. Volunteer service programs, organizations, and clubs	_____	_____	_____	_____
6. Universities and colleges	_____	_____	_____	_____
7. Other (specify) _____	_____	_____	_____	_____
B. Indicate current types of community involvement at the school.				
1. Mentoring for students and families	_____	_____	_____	_____
2. Volunteer functions	_____	_____	_____	_____
3. A community resource pool that provides expertise as requested, such as				
a. Artists	_____	_____	_____	_____
b. Musicians	_____	_____	_____	_____
c. Librarians	_____	_____	_____	_____
d. Health and safety programs	_____	_____	_____	_____
e. Other (specify) _____	_____	_____	_____	_____
4. Formal agency and program linkages that result in community health and social services providers coming to the site, such as				
a. Afterschool programs coming to the site	_____	_____	_____	_____
b. Services programs providing direct access to referrals from the site	_____	_____	_____	_____
c. Other (specify) _____	_____	_____	_____	_____
5. Formal arrangements that involve community agents in				
a. School governance	_____	_____	_____	_____
b. Advocacy for the school	_____	_____	_____	_____
c. Advisory functions	_____	_____	_____	_____
d. Program planning	_____	_____	_____	_____
e. Fundraising	_____	_____	_____	_____
f. Sponsoring activity (e.g., adopt-a-school)	_____	_____	_____	_____
g. Creating awards and incentives	_____	_____	_____	_____
h. Providing job-shadowing opportunities	_____	_____	_____	_____

	Yes	Yes, but more of this is needed.	No	If no, is this something you want?
i. Creating jobs	_____	_____	_____	_____
j. Other (specify) _____	_____	_____	_____	_____
6. Formal arrangements that connect school and community for enhancing child and youth development	_____	_____	_____	_____
C. With specific respect to volunteers,				
1. What types of volunteers are used at the site?	_____	_____	_____	_____
a. Nonprofessionals				
b. Parents	_____	_____	_____	_____
c. College students	_____	_____	_____	_____
d. Senior citizens	_____	_____	_____	_____
e. Businesspeople	_____	_____	_____	_____
f. Peer and cross-age tutors	_____	_____	_____	_____
g. Peer and cross-age counselors	_____	_____	_____	_____
h. Paraprofessionals	_____	_____	_____	_____
i. Professionals-in-training (specify) _____	_____	_____	_____	_____
j. Professionals (pro bono) (specify) _____	_____	_____	_____	_____
k. Other (specify) _____	_____	_____	_____	_____
2. Who do volunteers assist?				
a. Administrators	_____	_____	_____	_____
b. Teachers	_____	_____	_____	_____
c. Other staff	_____	_____	_____	_____
d. Others (specify) _____	_____	_____	_____	_____
3. In which of the following ways do volunteers participate?				
a. Providing general classroom assistance	_____	_____	_____	_____
b. Assisting with targeted students	_____	_____	_____	_____
c. Assisting after school	_____	_____	_____	_____
d. Providing special tutoring	_____	_____	_____	_____
e. Helping students with attention problems	_____	_____	_____	_____
f. Helping with bilingual students	_____	_____	_____	_____
g. Helping to address other diversity matters	_____	_____	_____	_____
h. Helping in the cafeteria	_____	_____	_____	_____
i. Helping in the library	_____	_____	_____	_____
j. Helping in the computer lab	_____	_____	_____	_____
k. Helping on class trips	_____	_____	_____	_____
l. Helping with homework help lines	_____	_____	_____	_____
m. Working in the front office	_____	_____	_____	_____
n. Helping to welcome visitors	_____	_____	_____	_____
o. Helping to welcome new enrollees and their families	_____	_____	_____	_____
p. Phoning or e-mailing home about absences	_____	_____	_____	_____
q. Outreaching to the home	_____	_____	_____	_____
r. Acting as mentors or advocates for students, families, staff	_____	_____	_____	_____
s. Assisting with school upkeep and beautification efforts	_____	_____	_____	_____

	Yes	Yes, but more of this is needed.	No	If no, is this something you want?
t. Helping enhance public support by increasing political awareness about the contributions and needs of the school	_____	_____	_____	_____
u. Other (specify) _____	_____	_____	_____	_____

II. Systems to Recruit, Screen, Prepare, and Maintain Community Resource Involvement

A. Are there systems and programs specifically designed to	_____	_____	_____	_____
1. Recruit community stakeholders?	_____	_____	_____	_____
2. Orient and welcome community stakeholders who have been recruited for school involvement and support?	_____	_____	_____	_____
3. Enhance the volunteer pool?	_____	_____	_____	_____
4. Screen volunteers?	_____	_____	_____	_____
5. Train volunteers?	_____	_____	_____	_____
6. Maintain volunteers?	_____	_____	_____	_____

III. Reaching Out to Students and Families Who Don't Come to School Regularly, Including Truants and Dropouts

A. Which of the following are used to enhance school involvement of hard-to-involve students and families?

1. Home visits to assess and plan ways to overcome barriers to				
a. Student attendance	_____	_____	_____	_____
b. Family involvement in schooling	_____	_____	_____	_____
2. Support networks connecting hard-to-involve				
a. Students with peers and mentors	_____	_____	_____	_____
b. Families with peers and mentors	_____	_____	_____	_____
3. Special incentives for				
a. Students	_____	_____	_____	_____
b. Families	_____	_____	_____	_____
4. Other (specify) _____	_____	_____	_____	_____

IV. Connecting School and Community Efforts to Promote Child and Youth Development and a Sense of Community

A. Which of the following are used to enhance community-school connections and sense of community?

1. Orientations and open houses for				
a. Newly arriving students	_____	_____	_____	_____
b. Newly arriving families	_____	_____	_____	_____
c. New staff	_____	_____	_____	_____
2. Student performances for the community	_____	_____	_____	_____
3. School-sponsored				
a. Cultural and sports events for the community	_____	_____	_____	_____
b. Community festivals and celebrations	_____	_____	_____	_____
c. Topical workshops and discussion groups	_____	_____	_____	_____
d. Health fairs	_____	_____	_____	_____

	Yes	Yes, but more of this is needed.	No	If no, is this something you want?

     e. Family preservation fairs

     f. Work fairs

    4. Other (specify) _____

V. Capacity Building to Enhance Community Involvement and Support

  A. Are there programs to enhance broad stakeholder involvement in enhancing community involvement and support?

  B. With respect to programs used to meet the educational needs of personnel related to community involvement and support,

    1. Is there ongoing training for learning supports staff with respect to enhancing community involvement and support?

    2. Is there ongoing training for others involved in enhancing community involvement and support (e.g., teachers, administrators, volunteers)?

    3. Other? (specify) _____

  C. Which of the following topics are covered in educating stakeholders?

    1. Understanding the local community: culture, needs, resources

    2. How to recruit, train, and retain community resources and volunteers

      a. In general

      b. For special roles

    3. How to move toward collaborations with community resources

    4. How to outreach to hard-to-involve students and families

    5. Understanding how to create a psychological sense of community

    6. Developing systematic social supports for students, families, and staff

    7. Other (specify) _____

  D. Indicate below other things you want the school to do in enhancing community involvement and support.

Other matters relevant to enhancing community involvement and support are found in the surveys on

- Classroom-based Approaches (Guide 12.3)
- Home Involvement in Schooling (Guide 12.6)
- School-Community Collaboration (Guide 12.9)

Guide 12.8   Student and Family Assistance Programs and Services:
A Self-study Survey

Specialized assistance for students and their families is for the relatively few problems that cannot be handled without adding special interventions. The emphasis is on providing special services in a personalized way to assist with a broad range of needs. To begin with, social, physical, and mental health assistance available in the school and community is used. As community outreach brings in other resources, these are linked to existing activity in an integrated manner. Additional attention is paid to enhancing systems for triage, case and resource management, direct services for immediate needs, and referral for special services and special education as appropriate. Ongoing efforts are made to expand and enhance resources. While any office or room can be used, a valuable context for providing such services is a center facility, such as a family, community, health, or parent resource center.

A programmatic approach in this arena requires systems designed to provide special assistance in ways that increase the likelihood that a student will be more successful at school while also reducing the need for teachers to seek special programs and services. The work encompasses providing all stakeholders with information clarifying available assistance and how to access help, facilitating requests for assistance, handling referrals, providing direct service, implementing case and resource management, and interfacing with community outreach to assimilate additional resources into current service delivery. It also involves ongoing analyses of requests for services as a basis for working with school colleagues to design strategies that can reduce inappropriate reliance on special assistance. Thus, major outcomes are enhanced access to special assistance as needed, indices of effectiveness, *and* the reduction of inappropriate referrals for such assistance.

Student and Family Assistance Programs and Services

Indicate all items that apply.

	Yes	Yes, but more of this is needed.	No	If no, is this something you want?

I. Providing Extra Support as Soon as a Need Is Recognized and Doing So in the Least Disruptive Ways

  A. Are there classroom-based approaches to reduce the need for teachers to seek special programs and services (e.g., prereferral interventions in classrooms; problem-solving conferences with parents; open access to school, district, and community support programs—see the Survey on Classroom-based Approaches, Guide 12.3)?

II. Timely Referral Interventions for Students and Families With Problems Based on Response to Extra Support

  A. What activity is there to facilitate and evaluate requests for assistance?

    1. Does the site have a directory that lists services and programs?

    2. Is information circulated about services/programs?

    3. Is information circulated clarifying how to make a referral?

    4. Is information about services, programs, and referral procedures updated periodically?

    5. Is a triage process used to assess

      a. Specific needs?

      b. Priority for service?

    6. Are procedures in place to ensure the use of prereferral interventions?

    7. Do inservice programs focus on teaching the staff ways to prevent unnecessary referrals?

    8. Other? (specify) _____

III. Enhancing Access to Direct Interventions for Health, Mental Health, and Economic Assistance

  A. After triage, how are referrals handled?

    1. Is detailed information provided about available services (e.g., is an annotated community resource system available)?

    2. Is there a special focus on facilitating effective decision making?

    3. Are students/families helped to take the necessary steps to connect with a service or program to which they have been referred?

    4. Is there a process to ensure referral follow-through?

	Yes	Yes, but more of this is needed.	No	If no, is this something you want?

B. What types of direct interventions are provided?

1. Which medical services and programs are provided?
   a. Immunizations
   b. First aid and emergency care
   c. Crisis follow-up medical care
   d. Health and safety education and counseling
   e. Health and safety prevention programs
   f. Screening for vision problems
   g. Screening for hearing problems
   h. Screening for health problems (specify) _____
   i. Screening for dental problems (specify) _____
   j. Treatment of some acute problems (specify) _____
   k. Medication monitoring
   l. Medication administration
   m. Home outreach
   n. Other (specify) _____

2. Which psychological services and programs are provided?
   a. Psychological first aid
   b. Crisis follow-up counseling
   c. Crisis hotlines
   d. Conflict mediation
   e. Alcohol and other drug abuse programs
   f. Pregnancy prevention program
   g. Programs for pregnant and parenting students
   h. Gang prevention program
   i. Gang intervention program
   j. Dropout prevention program
   k. Physical and sexual abuse prevention and response
   l. Individual counseling
   m. Group counseling
   n. Family counseling
   o. Mental health education
   p. Home outreach
   q. Other (specify) _____

3. Which of the following are provided to meet basic survival needs?
   a. Emergency food
   b. Emergency clothing
   c. Emergency housing
   d. Transportation support
   e. Welfare services
   f. Language translation
   g. Legal aid

	Yes	Yes, but more of this is needed.	No	If no, is this something you want?
h. Protection from physical abuse	_____	_____	_____	_____
i. Protection from sexual abuse	_____	_____	_____	_____
j. Child care	_____	_____	_____	_____
k. Employment assistance	_____	_____	_____	_____
l. Other (specify) _____	_____	_____	_____	_____

4. Which of the following special education, Special Eligibility, and independent study programs and services are provided?

	Yes	Yes, but more of this is needed.	No	If no, is this something you want?
a. Early education program	_____	_____	_____	_____
b. Special day classes (specify) _____	_____	_____	_____	_____
c. Speech and language therapy	_____	_____	_____	_____
d. Adaptive PE	_____	_____	_____	_____
e. Occupational and physical therapy	_____	_____	_____	_____
f. Special assessment	_____	_____	_____	_____
g. Resource Specialist Program	_____	_____	_____	_____
h. Title I	_____	_____	_____	_____
i. School Readiness Language Development Program	_____	_____	_____	_____
j. Other (specify) _____	_____	_____	_____	_____

5. Which of the following adult education programs are provided?

	Yes	Yes, but more of this is needed.	No	If no, is this something you want?
a. ESL	_____	_____	_____	_____
b. Citizenship classes	_____	_____	_____	_____
c. Basic literacy skill	_____	_____	_____	_____
d. Parenting	_____	_____	_____	_____
e. Helping children do better at school	_____	_____	_____	_____
f. Other (specify) _____	_____	_____	_____	_____
6. Are services and programs provided to enhance school readiness? (specify) _____	_____	_____	_____	_____

7. Which of the following are provided to address attendance problems?

	Yes	Yes, but more of this is needed.	No	If no, is this something you want?
a. Absence follow-up	_____	_____	_____	_____
b. Attendance monitoring	_____	_____	_____	_____
c. First-day calls	_____	_____	_____	_____
8. Are discipline proceedings carried out regularly?	_____	_____	_____	_____
9. Other? (specify) _____	_____	_____	_____	_____

IV. Care Monitoring, Management, Information Sharing, and Follow-up Assessment

	Yes	Yes, but more of this is needed.	No	If no, is this something you want?
	_____	_____	_____	_____
A. Which of the following are used to manage cases and resources?	_____	_____	_____	_____
1. Is a student information system used?	_____	_____	_____	_____
2. Is a system used to trail the progress of students and their families?	_____	_____	_____	_____
3. Is a system used to facilitate communication for				
a. Case management?	_____	_____	_____	_____
b. Resource and system management?	_____	_____	_____	_____

	Yes	Yes, but more of this is needed.	No	If no, is this something you want?

4. Are there follow-up systems to determine
   a. Referral follow-through?
   b. Consumer satisfaction with referrals?
   c. The need for more help?
5. Other? (specify) _____

B. Which of the following are used to help enhance the quality and quantity of services and programs?
   1. Is a quality improvement system used?
   2. Is a mechanism used to coordinate and integrate services/programs?
   3. Is there outreach to link up with community services and programs?
   4. Is a mechanism used to redesign current activity as new collaborations are developed?
   5. Other? (specify) _____

V. Mechanisms for Resource Coordination and Integration

A. Is there a resource-oriented mechanism (e.g., a Learning Supports Resource Team) that focuses on
   1. Coordinating and integrating resources?
   2. Braiding resources?
   3. Pursuing economies of scale?
   4. Filling gaps?
   5. Linking with community providers (e.g., to fill gaps)?

B. Is there a special facility to house student and family assistance programs and services (e.g., health center, family or parent center, counseling center)?

VI. Enhancing Stakeholder Awareness of Programs and Services

A. Are there *written descriptions* of available learning supports programs?

B. Are there written descriptions about
   1. How to make referrals?
   2. The triage process?
   3. The process for case monitoring and management?
   4. The process for student review?

C. Are there communication processes that inform stakeholders about available learning supports programs and how to navigate the systems?

VII. Capacity Building to Enhance Student and Family Assistance

A. Are there programs to enhance broad stakeholder involvement in enhancing student and family assistance?

B. With respect to programs used to meet the educational needs of personnel related to student and family assistance,

	Yes	Yes, but more of this is needed.	No	If no, is this something you want?
1. Is there ongoing training for learning supports staff with respect to student and family assistance?	_____	_____	_____	_____
2. Is there ongoing training for others involved in enhancing student and family assistance (e.g., teachers, administrators, volunteers)?	_____	_____	_____	_____
3. Other? (specify) _____	_____	_____	_____	_____
C. Which of the following topics are covered in educating stakeholders?				
1. Broadening understanding of causes of learning, behavior, and emotional problems	_____	_____	_____	_____
2. Broadening understanding of ways to ameliorate (prevent, correct) learning, behavior, and emotional problems	_____	_____	_____	_____
3. Developing systematic academic supports for students in need	_____	_____	_____	_____
4. What classroom teachers and the home can do to minimize the need for special interventions	_____	_____	_____	_____
5. Enhancing resource quality, availability, and scope	_____	_____	_____	_____
6. Enhancing the referral system and ensuring effective follow-through	_____	_____	_____	_____
7. Enhancing the case management system in ways that increase service efficacy	_____	_____	_____	_____
8. Other (specify) _____	_____	_____	_____	_____
D. Indicate below other things you want the school to do in providing student and family assistance.				

Other matters relevant to enhancing student and family assistance are found in the surveys on

- Learning Supports System Status (Guide 12.2)
- Home Involvement in Schooling (Guide 12.6)
- School-Community Collaboration (Guide 12.9)

Guide 12.9   School-Community Collaboration: A Self-study Survey

Formal efforts to create school-community collaboration to improve schools and neighborhoods encompass building formal relationships to connect resources involved in pre-K–12 schooling and resources in the community. (This includes collaboration among formal and informal organizations such as (a) schools, (b) the home, (c) agencies involved in providing health and human services, religion, policing, justice, economic development, fostering youth development, recreation, and enrichment, (c) businesses, (e) unions, (f) governance bodies, and (g) institutions of higher education.)

As you work toward enhancing such collaboration, it helps to clarify what you have in place as a basis for determining what needs to be done. You will want to pay special attention to

- The mechanisms used to enhance collaboration
- Clarifying what resources already are available
- How the resources are organized to work together
- What procedures are in place for enhancing resource usefulness

The following survey is designed as a self-study instrument related to school-community collaboration. Stakeholders can use such surveys to map and analyze the current status of their efforts.

This type of self-study is best done by teams. For example, a group of stakeholders could use the items to discuss how well specific processes and programs are functioning and what's not being done. Members of the team initially might work separately in filling out the items, but the real payoff comes from discussing them as a group. The instrument also can be used as a form of program quality review.

In analyzing the status of their school-community collaboration, the group may decide that some existing activity is not a high priority and that the resources should be redeployed to help establish more important programs. Other activity may be seen as needing to be embellished so that it is effective. Finally, decisions may be made regarding new desired activities, and since not everything can be added at once, priorities and timelines can be established.

I. List Current School-Community Collaboration

Make two lists:

    1. Activity and collaborators that are focused on improving the *school* and

    2. Those focused on improving the *neighborhood* (through enhancing links with the school, including use of school facilities and resources)

II. Overview: Areas for School-Community Collaboration

Indicate the status of collaboration between a given school or family of schools and community with respect to each of the following areas.

Indicate all items that apply.

	Yes	Yes, but more of this is needed.	No	If no, is this something you want?
A. Improving the school (name of school(s): _____)				
1. The instructional component of schooling	_____	_____	_____	_____
2. The governance and management of schooling	_____	_____	_____	_____
3. Financial support for schooling	_____	_____	_____	_____
4. Stakeholder development	_____	_____	_____	_____
5. School-based programs and services to address barriers to learning	_____	_____	_____	_____
B. Improving the neighborhood (through enhancing linkages with the school, including use of school facilities and resources)	_____	_____	_____	_____
1. Youth development programs	_____	_____	_____	_____
2. Youth and family recreation and enrichment opportunities	_____	_____	_____	_____
3. Physical health services	_____	_____	_____	_____
4. Mental health services	_____	_____	_____	_____
5. Programs to address psychosocial problems	_____	_____	_____	_____
6. Basic living needs services	_____	_____	_____	_____
7. College prep programs	_____	_____	_____	_____
8. Work/career programs	_____	_____	_____	_____
9. Social services	_____	_____	_____	_____
10. Crime and juvenile justice programs	_____	_____	_____	_____
11. Legal assistance	_____	_____	_____	_____
12. Support for development of neighborhood organizations	_____	_____	_____	_____
13. Economic development programs	_____	_____	_____	_____

III. Overview: System Status for Enhancing School-Community Collaboration

Items A–F ask about what processes are in place. Use the following ratings in responding to these items.

DK = Don't know

1 = Not yet

2 = Planned

3 = Just recently initiated

4 = Has been functional for a while

5 = Well institutionalized (well established with a commitment to maintenance)

A. Is there a stated policy for enhancing school-community collaboration (e.g., from the school, community agencies, government bodies)?	DK	1	2	3	4	5
B. Is there a designated leader or leaders for enhancing school-community collaboration?	DK	1	2	3	4	5
C. With respect to each entity involved in the school-community collaboration, have specific persons been designated as representatives to meet with each other?	DK	1	2	3	4	5
D. Do personnel involved in enhancing school-community collaboration meet regularly as a team to evaluate current status and plan next steps?	DK	1	2	3	4	5
E. Is there a written plan for capacity building related to enhancing the school-community collaboration?	DK	1	2	3	4	5
F. Are there written descriptions available to give to all stakeholders regarding current school-community collaboration efforts?	DK	1	2	3	4	5

Use the following ratings in responding to these items.

DK = Don't know

1 = Hardly ever effective

2 = Effective about 25% of the time

3 = Effective about half the time

4 = Effective about 75% of the time

5 = Almost always effective

G. Are there effective processes by which stakeholders learn						
1. What is available in the way of programs/services?	DK	1	2	3	4	5
2. How to access programs/services they need?	DK	1	2	3	4	5
H. In general, how effective are your local efforts to enhance school-community collaboration?	DK	1	2	3	4	5
I. With respect to enhancing school-community collaboration, how effective are each of the following:						
1. Current policy?	DK	1	2	3	4	5
2. Designated leadership?	DK	1	2	3	4	5
3. Designated representatives?	DK	1	2	3	4	5
4. Team monitoring and planning of next steps?	DK	1	2	3	4	5
5. Capacity-building efforts?	DK	1	2	3	4	5

IV. School-Community Collaboration to Improve the School

Indicate the status of collaboration between a given school or family of schools and community
(name of school(s): _____)

Indicate all items that apply.

	Yes	Yes, but more of this is needed.	No	If no, is this something you want?
A. Collaboration to improve *school*				
1. The instructional component of schooling				
a. Kindergarten readiness programs	_____	_____	_____	_____
b. Tutoring	_____	_____	_____	_____
c. Mentoring	_____	_____	_____	_____
d. School reform initiatives	_____	_____	_____	_____
e. Homework hotlines	_____	_____	_____	_____
f. Media/technology	_____	_____	_____	_____
g. Service learning	_____	_____	_____	_____
h. Career mentoring	_____	_____	_____	_____
i. Career academy programs	_____	_____	_____	_____
j. Adult education, ESL, literacy, citizenship classes	_____	_____	_____	_____
k. Others _____	_____	_____	_____	_____
2. The governance and management of schooling				
a. PTA/PTSA	_____	_____	_____	_____
b. Shared leadership	_____	_____	_____	_____
c. Advisory bodies	_____	_____	_____	_____
d. Others _____	_____	_____	_____	_____
3. School-based programs and services to address barriers to learning				
a. Student and family assistance programs/services*	_____	_____	_____	_____
b. Transition programs*	_____	_____	_____	_____
c. Crisis response and prevention programs*	_____	_____	_____	_____
d. Home involvement programs*	_____	_____	_____	_____
e. Community involvement programs*	_____	_____	_____	_____
f. Classroom-based approaches*	_____	_____	_____	_____
g. Pre- and inservice staff development programs	_____	_____	_____	_____
h. Others _____	_____	_____	_____	_____
4. Stakeholder development				
a. School staff	_____	_____	_____	_____
b. Staff from community programs and services	_____	_____	_____	_____
c. Family members	_____	_____	_____	_____
d. Others _____	_____	_____	_____	_____

	Yes	Yes, but more of this is needed.	No	If no, is this something you want?

5. Financial support for schooling
   a. Adopt-a-school
   b. Grant programs and funded projects
   c. Donations/fundraising
   d. Others _____

B. Collaboration to improve *neighborhood*
  1. Youth development programs
    a. Home visitation programs
    b. Parent education
    c. Infant and toddler programs
    d. Child care/children's centers/ preschool programs
    e. Community service programs
    f. Public health and safety programs
    g. Leadership development programs
    h. Others _____

  2. Youth and family recreation and enrichment opportunities
    a. Art/music/cultural programs
    b. Park programs
    c. Youth clubs
    d. Scouts
    e. Youth sports leagues
    f. Community centers
    g. Library programs
    h. Faith community activities
    i. Camping programs
    j. Others _____

  3. Physical health services
    a. School-based/linked clinics for primary care
    b. Immunization clinics
    c. Communicable disease control programs
    d. Early Periodic Screening, Diagnosis, and Treatment (EPSDT) programs
    e. Pro bono/volunteer programs
    f. AIDS/HIV programs
    g. Asthma programs
    h. Pregnant and parenting minors programs
    i. Dental services
    j. Vision and hearing services
    k. Referral facilitation
    l. Emergency care
    m. Others _____

  4. Mental health services
    a. School-based/linked clinics with mental health component
    b. EPSDT mental health focus
    c. Pro bono/volunteer programs
    d. Referral facilitation

	Yes	Yes, but more of this is needed.	No	If no, is this something you want?
e. Counseling				
f. Crisis hotlines				
g. Others _____				
5. Programs to address psychosocial problems				
a. Conflict mediation/resolution				
b. Substance abuse				
c. Community/school safe havens				
d. Safe passages				
e. Youth violence prevention				
f. Gang alternatives				
g. Pregnancy prevention and counseling				
h. Case management of programs for high-risk youth				
i. Child abuse and domestic violence programs				
j. Others _____				
6. Basic living needs services				
a. Food				
b. Clothing				
c. Housing				
d. Child care				
e. Transportation assistance				
f. Others _____				
7. Work/career/higher-education programs				
a. College prep programs				
b. Job mentoring				
c. Job shadowing				
d. Job programs and employment opportunities				
e. Others _____				
8. Social services				
a. School-based/linked family resource centers				
b. Integrated services initiatives				
c. Budgeting/financial management counseling				
d. Family preservation and support				
e. Foster care school transition programs				
f. Case management				
g. Immigration and cultural transition assistance				
h. Language translation				
i. Others _____				
9. Crime and juvenile justice programs				
a. Camp returnee programs				
b. Children's court liaison				
c. Truancy mediation				
d. Juvenile diversion programs with school				

		Yes	Yes, but more of this is needed.	No	If no, is this something you want?
e.	Probation services at school	____	____	____	____
f.	Police protection programs	____	____	____	____
g.	Others ____	____	____	____	____
10.	Legal assistance				
a.	Legal aid programs	____	____	____	____
b.	Others ____	____	____	____	____
11.	Support for development of neighborhood organizations				
a.	Neighborhood protective associations	____	____	____	____
b.	Emergency response planning and implementation	____	____	____	____
c.	Neighborhood coalitions and advocacy groups	____	____	____	____
d.	Volunteer services	____	____	____	____
e.	Welcoming clubs	____	____	____	____
f.	Social support networks	____	____	____	____
g.	Others ____	____	____	____	____
12.	Economic development and housing programs				
a.	Empowerment zones	____	____	____	____
b.	Urban village programs	____	____	____	____
c.	Accessing affordable housing	____	____	____	____
d.	Others ____	____	____	____	____

*See surveys for each of these arenas of school intervention.

Guide 12.10 Analyzing Gaps, Reviewing Resources, Planning Action

Based on the mapping you have done, make an analysis of

1. Which programs address barriers that your district/school has identified as the most significant factors interfering with students' learning and teachers' teaching effectively

2. Which of the significant factors are not being addressed (these are gaps to be filled)

3. Your priorities with respect to filling gaps

4. Any programs that you think are not effective and probably should be discontinued so that the resources can be redeployed to fill your high-priority gaps

5. Who in the community you can establish a collaboration with to fill your high priority gaps

6. Other sources of funds available at this time to fill the gaps

7. What steps you will take to act upon the analysis

NOTE

1. This document and the surveys reproduced on the following pages also can be downloaded at no cost from the Web site of the Center for Mental Health in Schools at UCLA at http://smhp.psych.ucla.edu/pdfdocs/Surveys/Set1.pdf.

Research Base for Addressing Barriers to Learning

13

The science base for intervention is an essential building block. However, we must extend it, and we must be careful that we don't limit progress while we do so.

I find myself looking at children and wondering how they'll impact the average score of my class. I sometimes find myself doing calculations where my students are not learners but assets and liabilities toward the class average on a standardized exam.

—Teacher, quoted in *Intrator* (2002)

The first step is to measure whatever can be easily measured. This is okay as far as it goes. The second step is to disregard that which can't be measured or give it an arbitrary quantitative value. This is artificial and misleading. The third step is to presume that what can't be measured easily isn't very important. This is blindness. The fourth step is to say what can't be measured really doesn't exist. This is suicide.

—Attributed to Yankelovich

All professional interveners need data to enhance the quality of their efforts and to monitor their outcomes in ways that promote appropriate accountability. This is especially the case for those who work with youngsters who manifest behavior, learning, and emotional problems. Sound planning, implementation, accountability, and advancement of the field necessitate amassing and analyzing existing information and gathering appropriate new evaluative data. In addition, the field is at a point in time when there is an intensive policy emphasis on the evidence base for instruction and interventions to promote healthy development, prevent problems, intervene early, counsel, collaborate, and so forth.

Commonly heard these days is the shibboleth

In God we trust; from all others, demand data.

Increasingly, policymakers and others who make decisions are demanding,

Show me the data!

With respect to addressing barriers to learning and teaching, the policy emphasis on an evidence base has produced somewhat of a catch-22. Proposals to strengthen student support are consistently met with demands from policymakers for data showing that the additional effort will improve student achievement. The reality is that available direct evidence is sparse, and other relevant data must be appreciated in terms of addressing barriers that interfere with improving student achievement. Because the body of evidence showing a direct and immediate relationship is limited, many school districts shy away from investing in efforts to improve learning supports. And because policymakers do not invest in building the type of learning support systems that can produce, over time, the results they are looking for, it is unlikely that better data will be generated soon.

At this time, the field is a long way from having enough sound research to rely on as the sole basis for building truly comprehensive, multifaceted approaches that match the complexity of the problems we face in schools and communities. Moreover, because the need to address barriers to learning, development, and teaching covers so many different facets of intervention, it is hard even to summarize what has been found to date. Much of the literature focuses on only one facet, such as instruction, prevention, or treatment, and often only on narrow, person-focused interventions. Most collections of practice include a mixture of research projects and home-grown programs. And because schools and collaboratives do not have the resources for extensive data gathering, a great many local program evaluations are methodologically flawed.

The emphasis here is on sharing the results of the Center for Mental Health in Schools at UCLA's effort to draw on the existing research base for support in developing comprehensive, multifaceted approaches to address barriers to learning and promote healthy development. (Note: Because the list of references in this section is so extensive, they are cited by number and included at the end of this chapter.)

A USABLE RESEARCH BASE

As schools evolve their improvement plans in keeping with higher standards and expectations and increased accountability, most planners should recognize the need to include a comprehensive focus on addressing barriers to student learning and promoting healthy development.[1-15] Throughout this book, we have stressed the conceptual base for doing so. In this chapter, we highlight the extensive body of literature that supports the conceptual base. That literature includes a growing volume of research on the value of schools, families, and communities working together to provide supportive programs and services that enable students to learn and teachers to teach.[16-22] Findings include improved school attendance, fewer behavior problems, improved interpersonal skills, enhanced achievement, and increased bonding at school and at home.[23]

Most *formal* studies have focused on specific interventions (see Guide 13.1). This and other bodies of research report positive outcomes for school and society associated with a wide range of interventions. Because of the fragmented nature of the studies, the findings are best appreciated in terms of the whole being greater than the sum of the parts, and implications are best derived from the total theoretical and empirical picture. When such a broad perspective is adopted, schools have a larger science base to draw upon in addressing barriers to learning and enhancing healthy development.[24]

At the outset, we stress that research on comprehensive approaches for addressing barriers to learning is still in its infancy. As we have noted, there are many "natural" experiments underscoring the promise of ensuring that all youngsters have access to a comprehensive, multifaceted continuum of interventions. These natural experiments play out in every school and neighborhood where families are affluent enough to purchase the additional programs and services they feel will maximize their youngsters' well-being. Those who can afford such interventions clearly understand their value. And not surprisingly, most indicators of well-being, including higher achievement test scores, are correlated with socioeconomic status. Available data highlight societal inequities that can be remedied through public financing for comprehensive programs.

The research base supporting development of a comprehensive, multifaceted approach to addressing barriers to learning and teaching is highlighted below. To illustrate the value of a unifying framework, we have organized examples into the six arenas of an Enabling or Learning Supports Component. To reiterate, these are (1) enhancing classroom teachers' capacity for addressing problems and for fostering positive social, emotional, intellectual, behavioral, and physical development, (2) enhancing school capacity to handle transition concerns confronting students and families, (3) responding to, minimizing impact of, and preventing crises, (4) enhancing home involvement, (5) outreaching to the community to build linkages

Guide 13.1   Annotated "Lists" of Empirically Supported/Evidence-based
Interventions for School-age Children and Adolescents

The following table provides a list of lists, with indications of what each list covers, how it was developed, what it contains, and how to access it.

I. Universal Focus on Promoting Healthy Development

A. Safe and Sound. An Educational Leader's Guide to Evidence-based Social & Emotional Learning Programs (2002). The Collaborative for Academic, Social, and Emotional Learning (CASEL).

   1. *How It Was Developed.* Contacts with researchers and literature search yielded 250 programs for screening; 81 programs were identified that met the criteria of being a multiyear program with at least eight lessons in one program year, designed for regular ed classrooms, and nationally available.
   2. *What the List Contains.* Descriptions (purpose, features, results) of the 81 programs.
   3. *How to Access.* CASEL (www.casel.org).

B. Positive Youth Development in the United States: Research Findings on Evaluations of Positive Youth Development Programs (2002). Social Development Research Group, University of Washington.

   1. *How It Was Developed.* Seventy-seven programs that sought to achieve positive youth development objectives were reviewed. Criteria used: research designs employed control or comparison group and had measured youth behavior outcomes.
   2. *What the List Contains.* Twenty-five programs designated as effective based on available evidence.
   3. *How to Access.* Online journal *Prevention & Treatment* (http://journals.apa.org/prevention/volume5/pre0050015a.html).

II. Prevention of Problems; Promotion of Protective Factors

A. Blueprints for Violence Prevention (1998). Center for the Study and Prevention of Violence, Institute of Behavioral Science, University of Colorado, Boulder.

   1. *How It Was Developed.* Review of over 450 delinquency, drug, and violence prevention programs based on a criteria of a strong research design, evidence of significant deterrence effects, multiple site replication, sustained effects.
   2. *What the List Contains.* Ten model programs and 15 promising programs.
   3. *How to Access.* Center for the Study and Prevention of Violence (www.colorado.edu/cspv/blueprints).

B. Exemplary Substance Abuse and Mental Health Programs (SAMHSA).

   1. *How It Was Developed.* These science-based programs underwent an expert consensus review of published and unpublished materials on eighteen criteria (e.g., theory, fidelity, evaluation, sampling, attrition, outcome measures, missing data, outcome data, analysis, threats to validity, integrity, utility, replications, dissemination, cultural/age appropriateness). The reviews have grouped programs as "models," "effective," and "promising" programs.
   2. *What the List Contains.* Prevention programs that may be adapted and replicated by communities.
   3. *How to Access.* SAMHSA (http://www.modelprograms.samhsa.gov).

C. Preventing Drug Use Among Children and Adolescents. Research-based Guide (1997). National Institute on Drug Abuse (NIDA).

1. *How It Was Developed.* NIDA and the scientists who conducted the research developed research protocols. Each was tested in a family/school/community setting for a reasonable period with positive results.
2. *What the List Contains.* Ten programs that are universal, selective, or indicated.
3. *How to Access.* NIDA (www.nida.nih.gov/prevention/prevopen.html).

D. Safe, Disciplined, and Drug-Free Schools Expert Panel Exemplary Programs (2001). U.S. Department of Education Safe & Drug-Free Schools.

1. *How It Was Developed.* Review of 132 programs submitted to the panel. Each program reviewed in terms of quality, usefulness to others, and educational significance.
2. *What the List Contains.* Nine exemplary and 33 promising programs focusing on violence, alcohol, tobacco, and drug prevention.
3. *How to Access.* U.S. Dept. of Education. (www.ed.gov/offices/OERI/ORAD/KAD/expert_panel/drug-free.html).

III. Early Intervention: Targeted Focus on Specific Problems or At-risk Groups

A. The Prevention of Mental Disorders in School-age Children: Current State of the Field (2001). Prevention Research Center for the Promotion of Human Development, Pennsylvania State University.

1. *How It Was Developed.* Review of scores of primary prevention programs to identify those with quasiexperimental or randomized trials and been found to reduce symptoms of psychopathology or factors commonly associated with an increased risk for later mental disorders.
2. *What the List Contains.* Thirty-four universal and targeted interventions that have demonstrated positive outcomes under rigorous evaluation and the common characteristics of these programs.
3. *How to Access.* Online journal *Prevention & Treatment* (http://journals.apa.org/prevention/volume4/pre0040001a.html).

IV. Treatment for Problems

A. American Psychological Association's Society for Clinical Child and Adolescent Psychology, Committee on Evidence-based Practice List.

1. *How It Was Developed.* Committee reviews outcome studies to determine how well a study conforms to the guidelines of the Task Force on Promotion and Dissemination of Psychological Procedures (1996).
2. *What It Contains.* Reviews of the following:
   - *Depression (dysthymia).* Analyses indicate only one practice meets criteria for "well-established treatment" (best supported) and two practices meet criteria for "probably efficacious" (promising).
   - *Conduct/Oppositional Problems.* Two meet criteria for "well-established treatments": videotape modeling parent training programs (Webster-Stratton) and parent training program based on Living With Children (Patterson and Guillion). Ten practices identified as "probably efficacious."
   - *ADHD.* Behavioral parent training, behavioral interventions in the classroom, and stimulant medication meet criteria for "well-established treatments." Two others meet criteria for "probably efficacious."

(Continued)

(Continued)

- *Anxiety Disorders.* For phobias, participant modeling and reinforced practice are well established; filmed modeling, live modeling, and cognitive behavioral interventions that use self-instruction training are "probably efficacious." For anxiety disorders, cognitive-behavioral procedures with and without family anxiety management, modeling, in vivo exposure, relaxation training, and reinforced practice are listed as "probably efficacious."

Caution. Reviewers stress the importance of (a) devising developmentally and culturally sensitive interventions targeted to the unique needs of each child and (b) a need for research informed by clinical practice.

3. *How to Access.* (www.effectivechildtherapy.com).

V. Review/Consensus Statements/Compendia of Evidence-based Treatments

A. School-based Prevention Programs for Children and Adolescents (1995). J. A. Durlak. Sage: Thousand Oaks, CA.

Reports results from 130 controlled outcome studies that support "a secondary prevention model emphasizing timely intervention for subclinical problems detected early. . . . In general, best results are obtained for cognitive-behavioral and behavioral treatments & interventions targeting externalizing problems."

B. Mental Health and Mass Violence.

Evidence-based early psychological intervention for victims/survivors of mass violence. A workshop to reach consensus on best practices (U.S. Departments of Health and Human Services, Defense, Veterans Affairs, and Justice, and American Red Cross). Available at http://www.nimh.nih.gov/publicat/massviolence.pdf.

C. Society of Pediatric Psychology, Division 54, American Psychological Association, Journal of Pediatric Psychology.

Articles on empirically supported treatments in pediatric psychology related to obesity, feeding problems, headaches, pain, bedtime refusal, enuresis, encopresis, and symptoms of asthma, diabetes, and cancer.

D. Preventing Crime: What Works, What Doesn't, What's Promising. A Report to the United States Congress (1997) by L. W. Sherman, Denise Gottfredson et al. Washington, DC: U.S. Department of Justice.

Reviews programs funded by the U.S. Department of Justice's Office of Justice Programs for crime, delinquency, and substance use at www.ncjrs.org/pdffiles/171676.pdf. Also see Denise Gottfredson's book *Schools and Delinquency* (2001). New York: Cambridge University Press.

E. School Violence Prevention Initiative Matrix of Evidence-based Prevention Interventions (1999). Center for Mental Health Services, SAMHSA.

Synthesis of several lists cited above to highlight examples of programs that meet some criteria for a designation of evidence-based for violence prevention and substance abuse prevention (i.e., synthesizes lists from the Center for the Study and Prevention of Violence, Center for Substance Abuse Prevention, Communities that Care, U.S. Departments of Education, Justice, Health and Human Services Health Resources and Services Administration, National Association of School Psychologists) (http://modelprograms .samhsa.gov/).

and collaborations, and (6) providing special assistance to students and families.

Given how extensive the relevant research literature is, obviously the following in no way is meant to be exhaustive. We have chosen examples that make the point. There are many others that can be drawn upon, and many more will be forthcoming in the coming years.

1. Enhancing Teacher Capacity for Addressing Problems and Fostering Healthy Development

When a classroom teacher encounters difficulty in working with a youngster, the first step is to see whether there are ways to address the problem within the classroom and perhaps with added home involvement. It is essential to equip teachers to respond to garden-variety learning, behavior, and emotional problems using more than social control strategies for classroom management. Teachers must be helped to learn many ways to enable the learning of such students, and schools must develop schoolwide approaches to assist teachers in doing this fundamental work. The literature offers many relevant practices. A few prominent examples are prereferral intervention efforts, tutoring and other forms of one-to-one or small-group instruction, enhancing protective factors, and assets building (including use of curriculum-based approaches for promoting social-emotional development). Outcome data related to such matters indicate that they do make a difference. For instance:

- Many forms of *prereferral intervention programs* have shown success in reducing learning and behavior problems and unnecessary referrals for special assistance and special education.[25-31]
- Although only a few *tutoring programs* have been evaluated systematically, available studies report positive effects on academic performance when tutors are trained and appropriately used.[32-40]
- And some *programs that reduce class size* are finding increases in academic performance and decreases in discipline problems.[41-45]

2. Enhancing School Capacity to Handle the Variety of Transition Concerns Confronting Students and Their Families

It has taken a long time for schools to face up to the importance of establishing transition programs. In recent years, a beginning has been made. Transition programs are an essential facet of reducing levels of alienation and increasing levels of positive attitudes toward and involvement at school and in learning. Thus, schools must plan, develop, and maintain a focus on the variety of transition concerns confronting students and their families. Examples of relevant practices are readiness-to-learn programs, beforeschool and afterschool programs to enrich learning and provide recreation in a safe environment, articulation programs for each new step in formal education, vocational and college counseling, and support in moving to and from special education, welcoming and social support programs, school-to-career programs, and programs to support moving to postschool living and work. Interventions to enable successful transitions have made a significant difference in how motivationally ready and able students are to benefit from schooling. For instance:

- Available evidence supports the positive impact of *early childhood programs* in preparing young children for school. The programs are associated with increases in academic performance and may even contribute to decreases in discipline problems in later school years.[46–54]
- There is enough evidence that *beforeschool and afterschool programs* keep kids safe and steer them away from crime, and some evidence suggests that such programs can improve academic performance.[55–59]
- Evaluations show that well-conceived and implemented *articulation programs* can successfully ease students' transition between grades,[60–62] and preliminary evidence suggests the promise of programs that provide *welcoming and social support* for children and families transitioning into a new school.[63, 64]
- Initial studies of programs for transition *in and out of special education* suggest the interventions can enhance students' attitudes about school and self and can improve their academic performance.[65–67]
- Finally, programs providing *vocational training and career education* are having an impact in terms of increasing school retention and graduation and show promise for successfully placing students in jobs following graduation.[68–72]

3. Responding to, Minimizing Impact of, and Preventing Crisis

The need for crisis response and prevention is constant in many schools. Such efforts ensure assistance when emergencies arise, and follow-up care is provided as necessary and appropriate so that students can resume learning without undue delays. Prevention activity stresses creation of a safe and productive environment and development of student and family attitudes about and capacities for dealing with violence and other threats to safety. Examples include (a) systems and programs for emergency/crisis response and follow-up care at a site, throughout a family of schools, and communitywide and (b) prevention programs for school and community to address school safety and violence reduction, child abuse and suicide prevention, and so forth. Examples of relevant practices are the establishment of a crisis team to ensure planning and implementation of crisis response and aftermath interventions, school environment changes and safety strategies, and curriculum approaches to preventing crisis events such as violence, suicide, and physical/sexual abuse prevention. Current trends are stressing schoolwide and communitywide prevention programs. Most research in this area focuses on

- Programs designed to ensure a *safe and disciplined school environment* as a key to deterring violence and reducing injury.
- *Violence prevention and resiliency curriculum* designed to teach children anger management, problem-solving skills, social skills, and conflict resolution.

In both instances, the evidence supports a variety of practices that help reduce injuries and violent incidents in schools.[73–95]

4. Enhancing Home Involvement

In recent years, the trend has been to expand the school's focus on enhancing home involvement. Intervention practices encompass efforts for (a) addressing specific learning and support needs of adults in the home, such as mutual support groups and classes to enhance literacy, job skills, and English as a second language, (b) helping those in the home meet basic obligations to the student, (c) improving systems to communicate about matters essential to student and family, (d) strengthening the home-school connection and sense of community, (e) enhancing participation in making decisions essential to the student's well-being, (f) enhancing home support related to the student's basic learning and development, (g) mobilizing those at home to problem solve related to student needs, and (h) eliciting help from the home to meet classroom, school, and community needs. A few examples illustrate the growing research base for expanded home involvement.

- *Adult education* is a proven commodity in general and is beginning to be studied in terms of its impact on home involvement in schooling and on the behavior and achievement of youngsters in the family. For example, evaluations of adult education in the form of *family literacy* are reporting highly positive outcomes with respect to preschool children, and a summary of findings on family literacy reports highly positive trends into the elementary grades.[96, 97]
- Similarly, evaluations of *parent education* classes indicate the promise of such programs with respect to improving parent attitudes, skills, and problem-solving abilities; parent-child communication; and in some instances the child's school achievement.[98–102] Data also suggest an impact on reducing children's negative behavior.[103–111]
- More broadly, programs to *mobilize the home in addressing students' basic needs* affect a range of behaviors and academic performance.[112, 113]

5. Outreaching to the Community to Build Linkages and Collaborations

Currently, most school outreach to the community is designed to develop greater involvement in schooling and enhance support for efforts to enable learning. Outreach may be made to (a) public and private community agencies, colleges, organizations, and facilities, (b) businesses and professional organizations and groups, and (c) volunteer service programs, organizations, and clubs. Efforts in this area might include (a) programs to recruit and enhance community involvement and support, (b) systems and programs specifically designed to train, screen, and maintain volunteers, (c) outreach programs to hard-to-involve students and families, and (d) programs to enhance community-school connections and sense of community.

The research base for involving the community is growing.

- A popular example are the various *mentoring and volunteer programs.* Available data support their value for both students and those from the community who offer to provide such supports. Student outcomes include positive changes in attitudes, behavior, and academic performance (including improved school attendance, reduced substance abuse, less school failure, improved grades).[114–118]
- Another example are the efforts to outreach to the community to develop *school-community collaborations.* A reasonable inference from available data is that school-community collaborations can be successful and cost-effective over the long run. They not only improve access to services, but they seem to encourage schools to open their doors in ways that enhance recreational, enrichment, and remedial opportunities and family involvement. A few have encompassed concerns for economic development and have demonstrated the ability to increase job opportunities for young people.[119–123]

Another aim of outreach to the community is to collaborate to enhance the engagement of young people to directly strengthen youngsters, families, and neighborhoods. Across the country a dialogue has begun about how to both promote youth development and address barriers to development and learning. In this respect, increasing attention has been paid to interventions to promote healthy development, resiliency, and assets. There is widespread agreement that communities should coalesce resources and strengthen opportunities for healthy, holistic development and learning in responsive environments.

- *Responsive and Caring Environments.* Engagement is fostered if the environment (a) creates an atmosphere where youngsters feel welcome, respected, and comfortable, (b) structures opportunities to develop caring relationships with peers and adults, (c) provides information, counseling, and expectations that enable them to determine what it means to care for themselves and to care for a definable group, and (d) provides opportunities, training, and expectations that encourage contributing to the greater good through service, advocacy, and active problem solving with respect to important matters.[124]

- *Facilitating Holistic Development.* Research has focused on interventions to provide for (a) basic needs: nutrition, shelter, health, and safety, (b) effective parenting and schooling using appropriate structure and expectations, and (c) more opportunities for recreation, enrichment, and creativity and for community, civic, and religious involvement. Findings indicate that features of positive developmental settings include physical and psychological safety, appropriate structure, supportive relationships, opportunities to belong, positive social norms, support for efficacy, opportunities for skill building, and integration of family, school, and community efforts.[125]

After evaluating programs designed to promote youth development, Catalano and his colleagues reported:

Effective programs addressed a range of positive youth development objectives yet shared common themes. All sought to strengthen social, emotional, cognitive and/or behavioral competencies, self-efficacy, and family and community standards for healthy social and personal behavior. . . . The youth competency strategies varied among programs from targeting youth directly with skills training sessions, to peer tutoring conducted by at-risk youth, to teacher training that resulted in better classroom management and instruction. The evidence showed an associated list of important outcomes including better school attendance, higher academic performance, healthier peer and adult interactions, improved decision-making abilities, and less substance use and risky sexual behavior.[126]

6. Providing Special Assistance for Students and Families

Some problems cannot be handled without a few special interventions—thus the need for student and family assistance. The emphasis is on providing special services in a personalized way to assist with a broad range of needs. School-owned, -based, and -linked interventions clearly provide better access for many youngsters and their families. Moreover, as a result of initiatives that enhance school-owned support programs and those fostering school-linked services and school-community connections, more schools have more to offer in the way of student and family assistance.

In current practice, available social, physical, and mental health programs in the school and community are used. Special attention is paid to enhancing systems for prereferral intervention, triage, case and resource management, direct services to meet immediate needs, and referral for special services and special education resources and placements as appropriate. A growing body of data indicates the current contribution and future promise of work in this area. For example:

- The more *comprehensive approaches* not only report results related to ameliorating health and psychosocial problems, but they are beginning to report a range of academic-related improvements, such as increased attendance, improved grades, improved achievement, promotion to the next grade, reduced suspensions and expulsions, fewer dropouts, and increased graduation rates.[127-137]
- A rapidly increasing number of *targeted interventions* are reporting positive results related to the specific problems addressed, including reduced behavior, emotional and learning problems, enhanced positive social-emotional functioning, reduced sexual activity, lower rates of unnecessary referral to special education, fewer visits to hospital emergency rooms, and fewer hospitalizations.[138-143]

Taken as a whole, the research base for initiatives to pursue a comprehensive focus on addressing barriers indicates a range of activity that can enable students to learn and teachers to teach. The findings also underscore that addressing major psychosocial problems one at a time is unwise because the problems are interrelated and require multifaceted and cohesive solutions. In all, the literature both offers content for learning supports and also stresses the importance of coalescing such activity into a comprehensive, multifaceted approach.

CONCLUDING COMMENTS

Gathering good evaluative data is a key to designing a promising future. It is a process that can improve programs, protect consumers, and advance knowledge. Doing so, however, is a difficult process, which many would prefer to avoid. Nevertheless, the need for professionals to improve their practices and be accountable is obvious.

The need to improve current evaluation practices seems equally obvious. Because evaluations can as easily reshape programs in negative as in positive directions, it is essential that such practices be improved and that accountability pressures not inappropriately narrow a program's focus. This is especially the case for programs designed to enable the learning of students who are not doing well at school. If the push for the use of evidence-based practices is done in an unsophisticated way, we worry that it will narrow options for dealing with learning, behavior, and emotional problems. There is also the likelihood of further undermining efforts to deal with complex problems in a comprehensive, multifaceted way. The danger is that resources will be redeployed in ways that favor the current "evidence base"—no matter what its deficits.

Finding out if a program is any good is a necessity. But in doing so, it is wise to recognize that evaluation is not simply a technical process. Evaluation involves decisions about what and how to measure. It involves decisions about what standards to use in making judgments. These decisions are based in great part on values and beliefs.

As a result, limited knowledge, bias, vested interests, and ethical issues are constantly influencing the descriptive and judgmental processes and shape conclusions at the end of the evaluation. While researchers build a better evidence base over the next 20 years, rational judgments must temper the zeal to prematurely claim scientific validation. And everyone concerned about learning, behavior, and emotional problems must increase the efforts to bolster both the scientific and rational bases for enhancing learning supports.

As is increasingly being stressed, we can easily raise standards, but it will mean little for many students if we don't provide essential learning supports that enable students to meet high standards. Schools clearly are being held accountable for higher standards for the academic curriculum. Now the question arises: *When will our schools finally develop a comprehensive, multifaceted, and cohesive approach to addressing barriers to learning and teaching?* Ultimately, the answer to that question will affect not only individuals with learning, behavior, and emotional problems but the entire society.

USABLE RESEARCH BASE REFERENCES

1. Adelman, H. S., & Taylor, L. (1997). Addressing barriers to learning: Beyond school-linked services and full service schools. *American Journal of Orthopsychiatry, 67,* 408–421.

2. Adelman, H. S., & Taylor, L. (1998). Reframing mental health in schools and expanding school reform. *Educational Psychologist, 33,* 135–152.

3. Adelman, H. S., & Taylor, L. (2000). Looking at school health and school reform policy through the lens of addressing barriers to learning. *Children Services: Social Policy, Research, and Practice, 3,* 117–132.

4. Allensworth, D., Wyche, J., Lawson, E., & Nicholson, L. (Eds.). (1997). *Schools and health: Our nation's investment.* Washington, DC: National Academy Press.

5. Carnegie Council on Adolescent Development's Task Force on Education of Young Adolescents. (1989). *Turning points: Preparing American youth for the 21st century.* Washington, DC: Author.

6. Center for Mental Health in Schools. (1998). *Restructuring boards of education to enhance schools' effectiveness in addressing barriers to student learning.* Los Angeles: Author (at UCLA).

7. Center for Mental Health in Schools. (1999). *Policymakers' guide to restructuring student support resources to address barriers to learning.* Los Angeles: Author (at UCLA).

8. Comer, J. (1988). Educating poor minority children. *Scientific American, 259,* 42–48.

9. Dryfoos, J. (1998). *Safe passage: Making it through adolescence in a risky society.* New York: Oxford University Press.

10. Hargreaves, A. (Ed.). (1997). *Rethinking educational change with heart and mind* (1997 ASCD Yearbook). Alexandria, VA: ASCD.

11. Kirst, M. W., & McLaughlin, M. (1990). Rethinking children's policy: Implications for educational administration. In B. Mitchell & L. L. Cunningham (Eds.), *Educational leadership and changing context of families, communities, and schools:*

89th yearbook of the National Society for the Study of Education (Pt. 2, pp. 69–90). Chicago: University of Chicago Press.

12. Knitzer, J., Steinberg, Z., & Fleisch, B. (1990). *At the schoolhouse door: An examination of programs and policies for children with behavioral and emotional problems.* New York: Bank Street College.

13. Marx, E., & Wooley, S. F., with Northrop, D. (Eds.). (1998). *Health is academic: A guide to coordinated school health programs.* New York: Teachers College Press.

14. Schorr, L. B. (1988). *Within our reach: Breaking the cycle of disadvantage.* New York: Doubleday.

15. Schorr, L. B. (1997). *Common purpose: Strengthening families and neighborhoods to rebuild America.* New York: Anchor Press.

16. Adler, L., & Gardner, S. (Eds.). (1994). *The politics of linking schools and social services.* Washington, DC: Falmer Press.

17. Center for Mental Health in Schools. (1999). *School-community partnerships: A guide.* Los Angeles: Author (at UCLA).

18. Center for Mental Health in Schools. (1999). *Policymakers' guide to restructuring student support resources to address barriers to learning.* Los Angeles: Author (at UCLA).

19. Kretzmann, J. (1998). *Community-based development and local schools: A promising partnership.* Evanston, IL: Institute for Policy Research.

20. Lawson, H., & Briar-Lawson, K. (1997). *Connecting the dots: Progress toward the integration of school reform, school-linked services, parent involvement and community schools.* Oxford, OH: Danforth Foundation and Institute for Educational Renewal at Miami University.

21. Melaville, A., & Blank, M. J. (1998). *Learning together: The developing field of school-community initiatives.* Flint, MI: Mott Foundation.

22. Sailor, W., & Skrtic, T. M. (1996). School/community partnerships and educational reform: Introduction to the topical issue. *Remedial and Special Education, 17,* 267–270, 283.

23. Center for Mental Health in Schools. (2000). *A sampling of outcome findings from interventions relevant to addressing barriers to learning.* Los Angeles: Author (at UCLA).

24. Iowa Department of Education. (n.d.). *Developing Iowa's future: Every child matters: Success4.* Des Moines: Author.

25. Bry, B. H. (1982). Reducing the incidence of adolescent problems through preventive intervention: One- and five-year follow-up. *American Journal of Community Psychology, 10,* 265–276.

26. Fuchs, D., Fuchs, L. S., & Bahr, M. W. (1990). Mainstream assistance teams: Scientific basis for the art of consultation. *Exceptional Children, 57,* 128–139.

27. O'Donnell, J., Hawkins, J. D., Catalano, R. F., Abbot, R. D., & Day, E. (1995). Preventing school failure, drug use, and delinquency among low-income children: Long-term intervention in elementary schools. *American Journal of Orthopsychiatry, 65,* 87–100.

28. Nelson, J. R., Carr, B. A., & Smith, D. J. (1997). Managing disruptive behaviors in school settings: The THINK TIME strategy. *Communique, 25,* 24–25.

29. Shure, M. B. (1993). *Interpersonal problem solving and prevention:* Five-year longitudinal study. Prepared for Department of Health and Human Services, Public Health Service, NIMH. Bethesda, MD: National Institute of Mental Health.

30. Smith, L. J., Ross, S. M., & Casey, J. P. (1994). *Special education analyses for success for all in four cities.* Memphis, TN: University of Memphis, Center for Research in Educational Policy.

31. Sugai, G., & Horner, R. H. (1999). Discipline and behavioral support: Preferred processes and practices. *Effective School Practices, 7,* 10–22.

32. Cohen, P. A., Kuklik, J. A., & Kuklik, C.-L. C. (1982). Educational outcomes of tutoring: A meta analysis of findings. *American Educational Research Journal, 19,* 237–248.

33. Cooper, R., Slavin, R. E., & Madden, N. A. (1998). Success for all: Improving the quality of implementation of whole-school change through the use of a national reform network. *Education and Urban Society, 30,* 385–408.

34. Giesecke, D., Cartledge, G., & Gardner, R., III. (1993). Low-achieving students as successful cross-age tutors. *Preventing School Failure, 37,* 34–43.

35. Martino, L. R. (1994). Peer tutoring classes for young adolescents: A cost-effective strategy. *Middle School Journal, 25,* 55–58.

36. Ross, S. M., Nunnery, J., & Smith, L. J. (1996). *Evaluation of Title I reading programs: Amphitheater public schools. Year 1: 1995–96.* Memphis, TN: University of Memphis, Center for Research in Educational Policy.

37. Rossi, R. J. (1995). *Evaluation of projects funded by the School Dropout Demonstration Assistance Program: Final evaluation report: Vol. 1. Findings and recommendations.* Palo Alto, CA: American Institutes for Research.

38. Slavin, R. E., Madden, N. A., Dolan, L., Wasik, B. A., Ross, S. M., Smith, L. J., et al. (1996). Success for all: A summary of research. *Journal of Education for Students Placed at Risk, 1,* 41–76.

39. Baker, S., Gersten, R., & Keating, T. (2000). When less may be more: A 2-year longitudinal evaluation of a volunteer tutoring program requiring minimal training. *Reading Research Quarterly, 35,* 494–519.

40. Invernizzi, M., Rosemary, C., Juel, C., & Richards, H. C. (1997). At-risk readers and community volunteers: A 3-year perspective. *Scientific Studies of Reading, 1,* 277–300.

41. Egelson, P., Harman, P., & Achilles, C. M. (1996). *Does class size make a difference? Recent findings from state and district initiatives.* Washington, DC: ERIC Clearinghouse. (ERIC Document Reproduction Service No. ED398644)

42. Molnar, A., Percy, S., Smith, P., & Zahorik, J. (1998). *1997–98 results of the Student Achievement Guarantee in Education (SAGE) program.* Milwaukee: University of Wisconsin-Milwaukee.

43. Pritchard, I. (1999). *Reducing class size: What do we know?* Washington, DC: National Institute on Student Achievement, Curriculum and Assessment, Office of Educational Research and Improvement, USDOE.

44. Robinson, G. E., & Wittebols, J. H. (1986). *Class size research: A related cluster analysis for decision-making.* Arlington, VA: Education Research Service.

45. Wright, E. N., Stanley, M., Shapson, G. E., & Fitzgerald, J. (1977). *Effects of class size in the junior grades: A study.* Toronto, Canada: Ontario Institute for Studies of Education.

46. Cryan, J., Sheehan, R., Weichel, J., & Bandy-Hedden, I. G. (1992). Success outcomes of full-day kindergarten: More positive behavior and increased achievement in the years after. *Early Childhood Research Quarterly, 7,* 187–203.

47. Gomby, D. S., Larner, M. B., Stevenson, C. S., Lewit, E. M., & Behrman, R. E. (1995). Long-term outcomes of early childhood programs: Analysis and recommendations. *Future of Children, 5,* 6–24.

48. U.S. Department of Education. (n.d.). *Even Start: Evidence from the past and a look to the future. Planning and evaluation service analysis and highlights.* Retrieved from http://www.ed.gov/pubs/EvenStart/highlights.html.

49. Caliber Associates, Ellsworth Associates, Westat, & Mathematica Policy Research. (1997). *First progress report on the Head Start program performance measures.* Prepared for Administration on Children, Youth and Families, Head Start Bureau. Retrieved from http://www2.acf.dhhs.gov/programs/hsb/html/final_report.html.

50. Karweit, N. (1992). The kindergarten experience. *Educational Leadership, 49,* 82–86.

51. Yoshikawa, H. (1995). Long-term effects of early childhood programs on social outcomes and delinquency. *Future of Children, 5,* 51–75.

52. Henderson, A. T., & Mapp, K. L. (Eds.). (2002). *A new wave of evidence: The impact of school, family, and connections on student achievement, annual synthesis 2002.* Austin, TX: National Center for Family & Community Connections With Schools, Southwest Educational Development Laboratory.

53. Brigman, G. A., & Webb, L. D. (2003). Ready to learn: Teaching kindergarten students school success skills. *Journal of Educational Research, 96,* 286–292.

54. Reynolds, A. J., Temple, J. A., Robertson, D. L., & Mann, E. A. (2001). Long-term effects of an early childhood intervention on educational achievement and juvenile arrest. *Journal of the American Medical Association, 285,* 2339–2346.

55. Lattimore, C. B., Mihalic, S. F., Grotpeter, J. K., & Taggart, R. (1998). *Blueprints for violence prevention: Book 4. The Quantum Opportunities Program.* Boulder, CO: Center for the Study and Prevention of Violence.

56. Posner, J. K., & Vandell, D. L. (1994). Low-income children's after-school care: Are there beneficial effects of after-school programs? *Child Development, 65,* 440–456.

57. *Safe and smart: Making afterschool hours work for kids.* (1998). Retrieved from http://www.ed.gov/pubs/SafeandSmart.

58. Seppanen, P. S., et al. (1993). *National study of before- and after-school programs: Final report.* Retrieved from eric-web.tc.columbia.edu/abstracts/ed356043. html.

59. Ferrin, D., & Amick, S. (2002). San Diego's 6 to 6: A community's commitment to out-of-school time. *New Directions for Youth Development, 94,* 109–117.

60. Felner, R. D., Ginter, M., & Primavera, J. (1982). Primary prevention during school transitions: Social support and environmental structure. *American Journal of Community Psychology, 10,* 277–289.

61. Greene, R. W., & Ollendick, T. H. (1993). Evaluation of a multidimensional program for sixth-graders in transition from elementary to middle school. *Journal of Community Psychology, 21,* 162–176.

62. Hellem, D. W. (1990). Sixth grade transition groups: An approach to primary prevention. *Journal of Primary Prevention, 10,* 303–311.

63. Felner, R. D., Brand, S., Adan, A. M., Mulhall, P. F., Flowers, N., Sartain, B., et al. (1993). Restructuring the ecology of the school as an approach to prevention during school transitions: Longitudinal follow-ups and extensions of the School Transitional Environment Project (STEP). In L. A. Jason, K. E. Danner, & K. S. Kurasaki (Eds.), *Prevention and school transitions: Prevention in human services.* New York: Haworth Press.

64. Jason, L. A., Weine, A. M., Johnson, J. H., Danner, K. E., Kurasaki, K. S., & Warren-Sohlberg, L. (1993). The School Transitions Project: A comprehensive preventive intervention. *Journal of Emotional and Behavioral Disorders, 1,* 65–70.

65. Blalock, G. (1996). Community transition teams as the foundation for transition services for youth with learning disabilities. *Journal of Learning Disabilities, 29,* 148–159.

66. Smith, G., & Smith, D. (1985). A mainstreaming program that really works. *Journal of Learning Disabilities, 18,* 369–372.

67. Wang, M. C., & Birch, J. W. (1984). Comparison of a full-time main-streaming program and a resource room approach. *Exceptional Children, 51,* 33–40.

68. Biller, E. F. (1987). *Career decision making for adolescents and young adults with learning disabilities: Theory, research and practice.* Springfield, IL: Charles C Thomas.

69. Hackett, H., & Baron, D. (1995). Canadian action on early school leaving: A description of the national stay-in-school initiative. *ERIC Digest.* (ERIC Document Reproduction Service No. ED399481)

70. Miller, J. V., & Imel, S. (1987). Some current issues in adult, career, and vocational education. In E. Flaxman (Ed.), *Trends and issues in education.* Washington, DC: Council of ERIC Directors, Educational Resources Information Center, Office of Educational Research and Improvement, U.S. Department of Education. (ERIC Reproduction Service No. ED281897)

71. Naylor, M. (1987). Reducing the dropout rate through career and vocational education. Overview. *ERIC Digest.* (ERIC Document Reproduction Service No. ED282094)

72. Renihan, F., Buller, E., Desharnais, W., Enns, R., Laferriere, T., & Therrien, L. (1994). Taking stock: An assessment of the National Stay-In-School Initiative. Hull, Canada: Youth Affairs Branch, Human Resources Development Canada.

73. Altman, E. (1994). *Violence prevention curricula: Summary of evaluations.* Springfield, IL: Illinois Council for the Prevention of Violence.

74. Bureau of Primary Health Care. (n.d.). *Healing fractured lives: How three school-based projects approach violence prevention and mental health care.* Washington, DC: U.S. Department of Health & Human Services.

75. Carter, S. L. (1994). *Evaluation report for the New Mexico Center for Dispute Resolution. Mediation in the Schools Program, 1993–1994 school year.* Albuquerque, NM: Center for Dispute Resolution.

76. Davidson, L. L., Durkin, M. S., Kuhn, L., O'Connor, P., Barlow, B., & Heagarty, M. C. (1994). The impact of the Safe Kids/Health Neighborhoods Injury Prevention Program in Harlem, 1988–1991. *American Journal of Public Health, 84,* 580–586.

77. Embry, D. D., Flannery, D. J., Vazsonyi, A. T., Powell, K. E., & Atha, H. (1996). PeaceBuilders: A theoretically driven, school-based model for early violence prevention. *American Journal of Preventive Medicine. Youth Violence Prevention: Description and Baseline Data from 13 Evaluation Projects (Supp.), 12,* 91–100.

78. Farrell, A. D., Meyer, A. L., & Dahlberg, L. L. (1996). The effectiveness of a school-based curriculum for reducing violence among urban sixth-grade students. *American Journal of Public Health, 87,* 979–984.

79. Farrell, A. D., Meyer, A. L., & Dahlberg, L. L. (1996). Richmond youth against violence: A school-based program for urban adolescents. *American Journal of Preventive Medicine, 12,* 13–21.

80. Meyer, A. L., & Farrell, A. D. (1998). Social skills training to promote resilience in urban sixth grade students: One product of an action research

strategy to prevent youth violence in high-risk environments. *Education and Treatment of Children, 21,* 461–488.

81. Grossman, D. C., Neckerman, H. J., Koepsell, T. D., Liu, P., Asher, K. N., Beland, K., et al. (1997). Effectiveness of a violence prevention curriculum among children in elementary school: A randomized controlled trial. *Journal of the American Medical Association, 277,* 1605–1611.

82. Jason, L. A., & Burrows, B. (1983). Transition training for high school seniors. *Cognitive Therapy and Research, 7,* 79–91.

83. Klingman, A., & Hochdorf, Z. (1993). Coping with distress and self-harm: The impact of a primary prevention program among adolescents. *Journal of Adolescence, 16,* 121–140.

84. Knoff, H. M., & Batsche, G. M. (1995). Project ACHIEVE: Analyzing a school reform process for at-risk and underachieving students. *School Psychology Review, 24,* 579–603.

85. Orbach, I., & Bar-Joseph, H. (1993). The impact of a suicide prevention program for adolescents on suicidal tendencies, hopelessness, ego identity and coping. *Suicide and Life-Threatening Behavior, 23,* 120–129.

86. Poland, S. (1994). The role of school crisis intervention teams to prevent and reduce school violence and trauma. *School Psychology Review, 23,* 175–189.

87. Quinn, M. M., Osher, D., Hoffman, C. C., & Hanley, T. V. (1998). *Safe, drugfree, and effective schools for ALL students: What works!* Washington, DC: Center for Effective Collaboration and Practice, American Institutes for Research.

88. Tolan, P. H., & Guerra, N. G. (1994). *What works in reducing adolescent violence: An empirical review of the field.* Boulder, CO: Center for the Study and Prevention of Violence.

89. Walker, H. M., Colvin, G., & Ramsey, E. (1995). *Anti-social behavior in schools: Strategies and best practices.* Pacific Grove, CA: Brooks/Cole.

90. Walker, H. M., Severson, H. H., Feil, E. G., Stiller, B., & Golly, A. (1997). *First step to success: Intervening at the point of school entry to prevent antisocial behavior patters.* Longmont, CO: Sopris West.

91. Walker, H. M., Kavanagh, K., Stiller, B., Golly, A., Steverson, H. H., & Feil, E. G. (1998). First step to success: An early intervention approach for preventing school antisocial behavior. *Journal of Emotional and Behavioral Disorders, 6,* 66–80.

92. Symons, C. W., Cinelli, B., James, T. C., & Groff, P. (1997). Bridging student health risk and academic achievement through comprehensive school health programs. *Journal of School Health, 67,* 220–227.

93. Nelson, R. J. (2001). Designing schools to meet the needs of students who exhibit disruptive behavior. In H. Walker & M. Epstein (Eds.), *Making schools safer and violence free: Critical issues, solutions, and recommended practices.* Austin, TX: PRO-ED.

94. Johnson, D. W., & Johnson, R. T. (1996). Conflict resolution and peer mediation programs in elementary and secondary schools: Review of the research. *Review of Educational Research, 66,* 459–506.

95. Rollin, S. A., Kaiser-Ulrey, C., Potts, I., & Creason, A. H. (2003). A school-based violence prevention model for at-risk eighth grade youth. *Psychology in the Schools, 40,* 403–415.

96. *Even Start: An effective literacy program helps families grow toward independence.* (1997). Retrieved from National Center for Family Literacy Web site: www .famlit.org/research/research.html.

97. Jordan, G. E., Snow, C. E., & Porche, M. V. (2000). Project EASE: The effect of a family literacy project on kindergarten students' early literacy skills. *Reading Research Quarterly, 35,* 524–546.

98. Dishion, T. J., & Andrews, D. W. (1995). Preventing escalation in problem behaviors with high-risk young adolescents: Immediate and one-year outcomes. *Journal of Consulting and Clinical Psychology, 63,* 538–548.

99. Dishion, T. J., Andrews, D. W., Kavanagh, K., & Soberman, L. H. (1996). Chapter 9, preventive interventions for high-risk youth: The adolescent transitions program. In R. Peteres & R. McMahon (Eds.), *Preventing childhood disorders, substance abuse, and delinquency* (pp. 184–218). Thousand Oaks, CA: Sage.

100. Lally, J. R., Mangione, P. L., & Honig, A. S. (1988). The Syracuse University Family Development Research Program: Long-range impact on an early intervention with low-income children and their families. In D. R. Powell & Irving E. Sigel (Eds.), *Parent education as early childhood intervention: Emerging direction in theory, research, and practice. Annual advances in applied developmental psychology* (Vol. 3). Norwood, NJ: Ablex Publishing.

101. Spoth, R., Redmond, C., Haggerty, K., & Ward, T. (1995). A controlled parenting skills outcome study examining individual differences and attendance effects. *Journal of Marriage and the Family, 57,* 449.

102. Epstein, J. L., Simon, B. S., & Salinas, K. C. (1997). *Involving parents in homework in the middle grades.* Baltimore: Johns Hopkins.

103. Aktan, B. B., Kumpfer, K. L., & Turner, C. (1996). The Safe Haven Program: Effectiveness of a family skills training program for substance abuse prevention with inner city African-American families. *International Journal of the Addictions, 31,* 158–175.

104. Battistich, V., Schaps, E., Watson, M., & Solomon, D. (1996). Prevention effects of the Child Development Project: Early findings from an ongoing multi-site demonstration trial. *Journal of Adolescent Research, 11,* 12–35.

105. Battistich, V., Solomon, D., Kim, D., Watson, M., & Schaps, E. (1995). Schools as communities, poverty levels of student populations, and student' attitudes, motives, and performance: A multilevel analysis. *American Educational Research Journal, 32,* 627–658.

106. Berrueta-Clement, J. R., Schweinhart, L. J., Barnett, W. S., Epstein, A. S., & Weikart, D. P. (1984). *Changed lives: The effects of the Perry Preschool Program on youths through age 19.* Ypsilanti, MI: High/Scope Press.

107. Epstein, A. S. (1993). *Training for quality: Improving early childhood programs through systematic inservice training.* Ypsilanti, MI: High/Scope Press.

108. McDonald, L., Billingham, S., Dibble, N., Rice, C., & Coe-Braddish, D. (1991). Families and Schools Together: An innovative substance abuse prevention program. *Social Work in Education: A Journal of Social Workers in School, 13,* 118–128.

109. O'Donnell, J., Hawkins, J. D., Catalano, R. F., Abbot, R. D., & Day, E. (1995). Preventing school failure, drug use, and delinquency among low-income children: Long-term intervention in elementary schools. *American Journal of Orthopsychiatry, 65,* 87–100.

110. Schweinhart, L. J., Barnes, H. V., & Weikart, D. P. (1993). *Significant benefits: The High/Scope Perry preschool study through age 27.* Monographs of the High/Scope Educational Research Foundation, No 10. Ypsilanti, MI: High/Scope Foundation.

111. Tremblay, R. E., Vitaro, F., Betrand, L., LeBlanc, M., Beauchesne, H., Bioleau, H., & David, L. (1992). Parent and child training to prevent early onset of delinquency: The Montreal longitudinal experimental study. In J. McCord & R. Tremblay (Eds.), *Preventing antisocial behavior: Interventions from birth through adolescence.* New York: Guilford Press.

112. Epstein, J. (1995). School/family/community partnerships: Caring for the children we share. *Phi Delta Kappan, 76,* 701–713.

113. Gorman-Smith, D., Tolan, P. H., Henry, D. B., & Leventhal, A. (2002). Predictors of participation in a family-focused preventive intervention for substance use. *Psychology of Addictive Behaviors, 16*(Suppl. 4), S55.

114. Armstrong, P. M., Davis, P., & Northcutt, C. (1987). *Year-end and final evaluation reports, project years 1985–1986 and 1986–1987.* San Francisco: School Volunteers, San Francisco Unified School District.

115. Carney, J. M., Dobson, J. E., & Dobson, R. L. (1987). Using senior citizen volunteers in the schools. *Journal of Humanistic Education and Development, 25,* 136–143.

116. Grossman, J. B., & Garry, E. M. (1997). *Mentoring—A proven delinquency prevention strategy.* U.S. Department of Justice, Office of Justice Programs, Office of Juvenile Justice and Delinquency Prevention. Retrieved from http://www.ncjrs.org/txtfiles/164834.txt.

117. Davis, N. (1999). *Resilience: Status of the research and research-based programs.* Rockville, MD: U.S. Department of Health and Human Services, Substance Abuse and Mental Health Administration Center for Mental Health Services Division of Program Development, Special Populations & Projects Special Programs Development Branch.

118. Michael, B. (1990). *Volunteers in public schools.* Washington, DC: National Academy Press.

119. Cahill, M., Perry, J., Wright, M., & Rice, A. (1993). *A documentation report of the New York Beacons initiative.* New York: Youth Development Institute.

120. Davis, N. (1999). *Resilience: Status of the research and research-based programs.* Rockville, MD: U.S. Department of Health and Human Services, Substance Abuse and Mental Health Administration Center for Mental Health Services Division of Program Development, Special Populations & Projects Special Programs Development Branch.

121. Melaville, A., & Blank, M. (1998). *Learning together: The developing field of school-community initiatives.* Flint, MI: Mott Foundation.

122. Shames, S. (1997). *Pursuing the dream: What helps children and their families succeed.* Chicago: Coalition.

123. Woodruff, D., Shannon, N., & Efimba, M. (1998). Collaborating for success: Merritt elementary extended school. *Journal of Education for Students Placed at Risk, 1,* 11–22.

124. Pittman, K., Irby, M., Tolman, J., Yohalem, N., & Ferber, T. (2001). *Prevention problems promoting development, encouraging engagement: Competing priorities or inseparable goals?* Washington, DC: Forum for Youth Investment.

125. Eccles, J., & Gootman, J. (Eds.). (2002). *Community programs to promote youth development.* Washington, DC: National Academies Press.

126. Catalano, R., Berglund, M., Tyan, J., Lonczak, H., & Hawkins, J. D. (1998). *Positive youth development in the United States: Research findings on evaluations of positive youth development programs.* Retrieved from http://aspe.hhs.gov/hsp/PositiveYouthDev99.

127. Botvin, G. J., Mihalic, S. F., & Grotpeter, J. K. (1998). *Blueprints for violence prevention, Book 5: Life skills training.* Boulder, CO: Center for the Study and Prevention of Violence.

128. Bureau of Primary Health Care. (1993). *School-based clinics that work.* Washington, DC: Division of Special Populations, Health Resources and Services Administration.

129. Caplan, M., Weissberg, R. P., Grober, J. S., Sivo, P. J., Grady, K., & Jacoby, C. (1992). Social competence promotion with inner-city and suburban young adolescents: Effects on social adjustment and alcohol use. *Journal of Consulting and Clinical Psychology, 60*, 56–63.

130. Bry, B. H., Catalano, R. F., Kumpfer, K. L., Lochman, J. E., & Szapocznik, J. (1998). Scientific findings from family prevention intervention research. In R. S. Ashery, E. B. Robertson, & K. L. Kumpfer (Eds.), *NIDA Research Monograph: Vol. 177. Drug abuse prevention through family interventions* (pp. 103–129). Rockville, MD: National Institute on Drug Abuse.

131. Dryfoos, J. G., Brindis, C., & Kaplan, D. W. (1996). Research and evaluation in school-based health care. *Adolescent Medicine: State of the Art Reviews, 7.*

132. Henggler, S. W. (1998). Mulitsystemic therapy. In D. S. Elliott (Ed.), *Blueprints for violence prevention.* Boulder, CO: Center for the Study and Prevention of Violence.

133. California Department of Education, Healthy Start and After School Partnerships Office. (1999). *Healthy Start works: A statewide profile of Healthy Start sites.* Sacramento, CA: Author.

134. Institute for At-risk Infants, Children and Youth, and Their Families. (1994). *The effect of putting health services on site, Example 1: A full services school assembly.* Tallahassee, FL: Department of Education, Office of Interagency Affairs.

135. Stroul, B. A. (1993). *From systems of care for children and adolescents with severe emotional disturbances: What are the results?* Washington, DC: CASSP Technical Assistance Center, Georgetown University Child Development Center.

136. Warren, C. (1999). *Lessons from the evaluation of New Jersey's school-based youth services program.* Prepared for the National Invitational Conference on Improving Results for Children and Families by Connecting Collaborative Services With School Reform Efforts, Washington, DC.

137. Alexander, J., Barton, C., Gordon, D., Grotpeter, J., Hansson, K., Harrison, R., et al. (1998). *Blueprints for violence prevention, Book 3: Functional family therapy.* Boulder, CO: Center for the Study and Prevention of Violence.

138. Ellickson, P. L. (1998). Preventing adolescent substance abuse: Lessons from the Project ALERT program. In J. Crane (Ed.), *Social programs that really work* (pp. 201–224). New York: Russell Sage.

139. Gillham, J. E., Reivich, K. J, Jaycox, L. H., & Seligman, M. E. P. (1995). Prevention of depressive symptoms in schoolchildren: Two-year follow-up. *Psychological Science, 6*, 343–351.

140. Lochman, J. E., Coie, J., Underwood, M., & Terry, R. (1993). Effectiveness of a social relations intervention program for aggressive and nonaggressive, rejected children. *Journal of Consulting and Clinical Psychology, 61*, 1053–1058.

141. Johnson, D. (1995). *An evaluation of the early mental health initiative's primary intervention program and enhanced primary intervention program for the 1994–95 academic year.* Submitted to the State of California Department of Mental Health. Rochester, NY: University of Rochester, Primary Mental Health Project, Inc.

142. Prinz, R. J., Blechman, E. A., & Dumas, J. E. (1994). An evaluation of peer coping-skills training for childhood aggression. *Journal of Clinical Child Psychology, 23*, 193–203.

143. Gottfredson, D. C., & Wilson, D. B. (2003). Characteristics of effective school-based substance abuse prevention. *Prevention Science, 4*, 27–38.

Our Published Works and Center-produced Resources on Addressing Barriers to Learning

14

PUBLICATIONS SINCE 1990

Motivational readiness and minors' participation in psychoeducational decision making. H. S. Adelman, V. M. MacDonald, P. Nelson, D. C. Smith, & L. Taylor (1990). *Journal of Learning Disabilities, 23,* 171–176.

School avoidance behavior: Motivational bases and implications for intervention. L. Taylor & H. S. Adelman (1990). *Child Psychiatry and Human Development, 20,* 219–233.

Intrinsic motivation and school misbehavior: Some intervention implications. H. S. Adelman & L. Taylor (1990). *Journal of Learning Disabilities. 23,* 541–550.

Issues and problems related to the assessment of learning disabilities. H. S. Adelman & L. Taylor (1991). In H. L. Swanson (Ed.), *Handbook on the assessment of learning disabilities: Theory, research, and practice.* Austin, TX: PRO-ED.

Perceived control, causality, expectations, and help seeking behavior. J. M. Simoni, H. S. Adelman, & P. Nelson (1991). *Counselling Psychology Quarterly, 4,* 37–44.

Mental health facets of the School-based Health Center movement: Need and opportunity for research and development. H. S. Adelman & L. Taylor (1991). *Journal of Mental Health Administration, 18,* 272–283.

Early school adjustment problems: Some perspectives and a project report. H. S. Adelman & L. Taylor (1991). *American Journal of Orthopsychiatry, 61,* 468–474.

The classification problem. H. S. Adelman (1992). In W. Stainback & S. Stainback (Eds.), *Controversial issues confronting special education: Divergent Perspectives.* Boston: Allyn & Bacon.

LD: The next 25 years. H. S. Adelman (1992). *Journal of Learning Disabilities, 25,* 17–22.

Two studies of low income parents' involvement in schooling. B. Klimes-Dougan, J. Lopez, H. S. Adelman, & P. Nelson (1992). *Urban Review, 24,* 185–202.

Learning problems and learning disabilities: Moving forward. H. S. Adelman & L. Taylor (1993). Pacific Grove, CA: Brooks/Cole.

School-based mental health: Toward a comprehensive approach. H. S. Adelman & L. Taylor (1993). *Journal of Mental Health Administration, 20,* 32–45.

A study of a school-based clinic: Who uses it and who doesn't? H. S. Adelman, L. A. Barker, & P. Nelson (1993). *Journal of Clinical Child Psychology, 22,* 52–59.

Utilization of a school-based clinic for identification & treatment of adolescent sexual abuse. S. R. McGurk, J. Cárdenas, & H. S. Adelman (1993). *Journal of Adolescent Health, 14,* 196–201.

School-based mutual support groups for low-income parents. J. Simoni & H. S. Adelman (1993). *Urban Review, 25,* 335–350.

Learning disabilities: On interpreting research translations. H. S. Adelman (1994). In N. C. Jordan & J. Goldsmith-Phillips (Eds.), *Learning disabilities: New directions for assessment and intervention.* Boston: Allyn & Bacon.

Transition support for immigrant students. J. Cárdenas, L. Taylor, & H. S. Adelman (1993). *Journal of Multicultural Counseling & Development, 21,* 203–210.

School-linked mental health interventions: Toward mechanisms for service coordination and integration. H. S. Adelman (1993). *Journal of Community Psychology, 21,* 309–319.

Mental health status and help-seeking among ethnic minority adolescents. L. A. Barker & H. S. Adelman (1994). *Journal of Adolescence, 17,* 251–263.

On intervening to enhance home involvement in schooling. H. S. Adelman (1994). *Intervention in School and Clinic, 29,* 276–287.

On understanding intervention in psychology and education. H. S. Adelman & L. Taylor (1994). Westport CT: Praeger.

Clinical psychology: Beyond psychopathology and clinical interventions. H. S. Adelman (1995). *Clinical Psychology: Science and Practice, 2,* 28–44.

Welcoming: Facilitating a new start at a new school. M. B. DiCecco, L. Rosenblum, L. Taylor, & H. S. Adelman (1995). *Social Work in Education, 17,* 18–29.

Upgrading school support programs through collaboration: Resource Coordinating Teams. L. Rosenblum, M. B. DiCecco, L. Taylor, & H. S. Adelman (1995). *Social Work in Education, 17,* 117–124.

Education reform: Broadening the focus. H. S. Adelman (1995). *Psychological Science, 6,* 61–62.

Appreciating the classification dilemma. H. S. Adelman (1996). In W. Stainback & S. Stainback (Eds.), *Controversial issues confronting special education: Divergent Perspectives.* Boston: Allyn & Bacon.

Mobility and school functioning in the early grades. P. S. Nelson, J. M. Simoni, & H. S. Adelman (1996). *Journal of Educational Research, 89,* 365–369.

Mental health in the schools: Promising directions for practice. L. Taylor & H. S. Adelman (1996). *Adolescent Medicine: State of the Art Reviews, 7,* 303–317.

Restructuring education support services: Toward the concept of an enabling component. H. S. Adelman (1996). Kent, OH: American School Health Association.

Restructuring education support services and integrating community resources: Beyond the full service school model. H. S. Adelman (1996). *School Psychology Review, 25,* 431–445.

Toward a scale-up model for replicating new approaches to schooling. H. S. Adelman & L. Taylor (1997). *Journal of Educational and Psychological Consultation, 8,* 197–230.

Addressing barriers to learning: Beyond school-linked services and full service schools. H. S. Adelman & L. Taylor (1997). *American Journal of Orthopsychiatry, 67,* 408–421.

Establishing school-based collaborative teams to coordinate resources: A case study. C. Lim & H. S. Adelman (1997). *Social Work in Education, 19,* 266–278.

Involving teachers in collaborative efforts to better address barriers to student learning. H. S. Adelman & L. Taylor (1998). *Preventing School Failure, 42,* 55–60.

School counseling, psychological, and social services. H. S. Adelman (1998). In E. Marx & S. F. Wooley, with D. Northrop (Eds.), *Health is academic: A guide to coordinated school health programs.* New York: Teachers College Press.

Psychosocial screening. H. S. Adelman & L. Taylor (1998). Scarborough, ME: National Association of School Nurses.

A policy and practice framework to guide school-community connections. L. Taylor & H. S. Adelman (1998). *Rural Special Education Quarterly, 17,* 62–70.

Mental health in schools: Moving forward. H. S. Adelman & L. Taylor (1998). *School Psychology Review, 27,* 175–190.

Confidentiality: Competing principles, inevitable dilemmas. L. Taylor & H. S. Adelman (1998). *Journal of Educational and Psychological Consultation, 9,* 267–275.

Reframing mental health in schools and expanding school reform. H. S. Adelman & L. Taylor (1998). *Educational Psychologist, 33,* 135–152.

Mental health in schools: A federal initiative. H. S. Adelman, L. Taylor, M. Weist, S. Adelsheim et al. (1999). *Children Services: Social Policy, Research, and Practice, 2,* 99–119.

Mental health in schools and system restructuring. H. S. Adelman & L. Taylor (1999). *Clinical Psychology Review, 19,* 137–163.

Addressing barriers to student learning: Systemic changes at all levels. H. S. Adelman & L. Taylor (1999). Introduction to thematic section for *Reading and Writing Quarterly, 15,* 251–254.

Personalizing classroom instruction to account for motivational and developmental differences. L. Taylor & H. S. Adelman (1999). *Reading and Writing Quarterly, 15,* 255–276.

A school-wide component to address barriers to learning. H. S. Adelman, L. Taylor, & M. Schnieder (1999). *Reading and Writing Quarterly, 15,* 277–302.

Scaling-up reforms across a school district. L. Taylor, P. Nelson, & H. S. Adelman (1999). *Reading and Writing Quarterly, 15,* 303–326.

Fundamental concerns about policy for addressing barriers to student learning. H. S. Adelman, C. Reyna, R. Collins, J. Onghai, & L. Taylor (1999). *Reading and Writing Quarterly, 15,* 327–350.

Keeping reading and writing problems in broad perspective. H. S. Adelman & L. Taylor (1999). Coda to thematic section for *Reading and Writing Quarterly, 15,* 351–354.

Moving prevention from the fringes into the fabric of school improvement. H. S. Adelman & L. Taylor (2000). *Journal of Educational and Psychological Consultation, 11,* 7–36.

Shaping the future of mental health in schools. H. S. Adelman & L. Taylor (2000). *Psychology in the Schools, 37,* 49–60.

Looking at school health and school reform policy through the lens of addressing barriers to learning. H. S. Adelman & L. Taylor (2000). *Children Services: Social Policy, Research, and Practice, 3,* 117–132.

Promoting mental health in schools in the midst of school reform. H. S. Adelman & L. Taylor (2000). *Journal of School Health, 70,* 171–178.

Toward ending the marginalization of mental health in schools. L. Taylor & H. S. Adelman (2000). *Journal of School Health, 70,* 210–215.

Connecting schools, families, and communities. L. Taylor & H. S. Adelman (2000). *Professional School Counseling, 3,* 298–307.

School learning. H. S. Adelman (2000). In W. E. Craighead & C. B. Nemeroff (Eds.), *The Corsini encyclopedia of psychology and behavioral science* (3rd ed.). New York: John Wiley & Sons.

Enlisting appropriate parental cooperation & involvement in children's mental health treatment. L. Taylor & H. S. Adelman (2001). In E. R. Welfel & R. E. Ingersoll (Eds.), *The mental health desk reference.* New York: John Wiley & Sons.

Impediments to enhancing availability of mental health services in schools: Fragmentation, overspecialization, counterproductive competition, and marginalization. H. S. Adelman & L. Taylor (2002). Paper commissioned by the National Association of School Psychologists and the ERIC Clearinghouse on Counseling and Student Services (ERIC/CASS). Published by the ERIC/CASS Clearinghouse. Retrieved from http:// smhp.psych.ucla.edu.

Building comprehensive, multifaceted, and integrated approaches to address barriers to student learning. H. S. Adelman & L. Taylor (2002). *Childhood Education, 78,* 261–268.

Lessons learned from working with a district's mental health unit. L. Taylor & H. S. Adelman (2002). *Childhood Education, 78,* 295–300.

Lenses used determine lessons learned. H. S. Adelman & L. Taylor (2002). *Journal of Educational and Psychological Consultation, 13,* 227–236.

School-community relations: Policy and practice. L. Taylor & H. S. Adelman (2003). In M. S. E. Fishbaugh et al. (Eds.), *Ensuring safe school environments: Exploring issues–seeking solutions.* Mahwah, NJ: Lawrence Erlbaum.

Creating school and community partnerships for substance abuse prevention programs. (Commissioned by SAMHSA's Center for Substance Abuse Prevention.) H. S. Adelman & L. Taylor (2003). *Journal of Primary Prevention, 23,* 329–369.

Toward a comprehensive policy vision for mental health in schools. H. S. Adelman & L. Taylor (2002). In M. Weist, S. Evans, & N. Lever (Eds.), *School mental health handbook.* Norwell, MA: Kluwer.

Aligning school accountability, outcomes, and evidence-base practices. H. S. Adelman & L. Taylor (2002). *Data Matters, 5,* 16–18.

So you want higher achievement test scores? It's time to rethink learning supports. H. S. Adelman & L. Taylor (2002). *The State Education Standard, Autumn,* 52–56.

School counselors and school reform: New directions. H. S. Adelman & L. Taylor (2002). *Professional School Counseling, 5,* 235–248.

Fostering school, family, and community involvement: Guide 7, Guidebook in series Safe and Secure: Guides to Creating Safer Schools. H. S. Adelman & L. Taylor (2002). Portland, OR: Northwest Regional Educational Laboratory.

Toward a comprehensive policy vision for mental health in schools. H. S. Adelman & L. Taylor (2003). In M. Weist, S. Evans, & N. Lever (Eds.), *Handbook of school mental health: Advancing practices and research.* Norwell, MA: Kluwer.

School community relations: Policy and practice. L. Taylor & H. S. Adelman (2003). In M. S. E. Fishbaugh, T. R. Berkeley, & G. Schroth (Eds.), *Ensuring safe school environments: Exploring issues-seeking solutions.* Mahwah, NJ: Lawrence Erlbaum.

Rethinking school psychology (Commentary on Public Health Framework Series). H. S. Adelman & L. Taylor (2003). *Journal of School Psychology, 41,* 83–90.

On sustainability of project innovations as systemic change. H. S. Adelman & L. Taylor (2003). *Journal of Educational and Psychological Consultation, 14*, 1–25.

Advancing mental health science and practice through authentic collaboration. H. S. Adelman & L. Taylor (2003). *School Psychology Review, 32*, 227–236.

Advancing mental health in schools: Guiding frameworks and strategic approaches. L. Taylor & H. S. Adelman (2004). In K. Robinson (Ed.), *Advances in school-based mental health.* Kingston, NJ: Civic Research Institute.

Mental health in schools: A shared agenda. H. S. Adelman & L. Taylor (2004). *Report on Emotional & Behavioral Disorder in Youth, 4*(3).

Classroom climate. H. S. Adelman & L. Taylor (2005). In S. W. Lee (Ed.), *Encyclopedia of school psychology.* Thousand Oaks, CA: Sage.

The school leader's guide to student learning supports: New directions for addressing barriers to learning. H. S. Adelman & L. Taylor (2006). Thousand Oaks, CA: Corwin Press.

The implementation guide to student learning supports in the classroom and schoolwide: New directions for addressing barriers to learning. H. S. Adelman & L. Taylor (2006). Thousand Oaks, CA: Corwin Press.

Reorganizing student supports to enhance equity. H. S. Adelman & L. Taylor (in press). In E. Lopez, G. Esquivel, & S. Nahari (Eds.), *Handbook of multicultural school psychology.*

Mapping a school's resources to improve their use in preventing and ameliorating problems. H. S. Adelman & L. Taylor (in press). In C. Franklin, M. B. Harris, & P. Allen-Mears (Eds.), *School social work and mental health workers training and resource manual.* New York: Oxford University Press.

Want to work with schools? What's involved in successful linkages? L. Taylor & H. S. Adelman (in press). In C. Franklin, M. B. Harris, & P. Allen-Mears (Eds.), *School social work and mental health workers training and resource manual.* New York: Oxford University Press.

MATERIALS PRODUCED BY THE CENTER FOR MENTAL HEALTH IN SCHOOLS AT UCLA

All the following resources can be downloaded at no cost from the Web site of the School Mental Health Project and its Center for Mental Health in Schools (see http://smhp.psych.ucla.edu).

The following documents represent a variety of resources, including

1. *Introductory Packets.* These provide overview discussions, descriptions or model programs, references to publications, access information to other relevant centers, agencies, organizations, advocacy groups, and Internet links, and a list of consultation cadre members ready to share expertise.

2. *Resource Aid Packets* (designed to complement the Introductory Packets). These are a form of tool kit for fairly circumscribed areas of practice. They contain overviews, outlines, checklists, instruments, and other resources that can be reproduced and used as information handouts and aids for training and practice.

3. *Technical Aid Packets.* These are designed to provide a basic understanding of specific practices and tools.

4. *Technical Assistance Samplers.* These provide basic information for accessing a variety of resources on a specific topic such as agencies, organizations, Web sites, individuals with expertise, relevant programs, and library resources.

5. *Guides to Practice.* They translate ideas into practice.

6. *Continuing Education Modules, Training Tutorials, & Quick Training Aids.* These provide learning opportunities and resources for use in inservice training.

7. *Special Reports & Center Briefs*

SOME RESOURCES FOCUSED ON PSYCHOSOCIAL PROBLEMS

- *Affect and Mood Problems Related to School-aged Youth* (Introductory Packet)
- *Anxiety, Fears, Phobias, and Related Problems: Intervention and Resources for School-aged Youth* (Introductory Packet)
- *Attention Problems: Intervention and Resources* (Introductory Packet)
- *Behavioral Problems at School* (Quick Training Aid)
- *Bullying Prevention* (Quick Training Aid)
- *Common Psychosocial Problems of School-aged Youth: Developmental Variations, Problems, Disorders, and Perspectives for Prevention and Treatment* (Guide to Practice)
- *Conduct and Behavior Problems in School-aged Youth* (Introductory Packet)
- *Dropout Prevention* (Introductory Packet)
- *Learning Problems and Learning Disabilities* (Introductory Packet)
- *School Interventions to Prevent Youth Suicide* (Technical Aid Packet)
- *Sexual Minority Students* (Technical Aid Packet)
- *Social and Interpersonal Problems Related to School-aged Youth* (Introductory Packet)
- *Substance Abuse* (Resource Aid Packet)
- *Suicide Prevention* (Quick Training Aid)
- *Teen Pregnancy Prevention and Support* (Introductory Packet)
- *Violence Prevention* (Quick Training Aid)

SOME RESOURCES FOCUSED
ON PROGRAM/PROCESS CONCERNS

- *Addressing Barriers to Learning: Overview of the Curriculum for an Enabling (or Learning Supports) Component* (Quick Training Aid)
- *Addressing Barriers to Learning: New Directions for Mental Health in Schools* (Continuing Education Module)
- *After-School Programs and Addressing Barriers to Learning* (Technical Aid Packet)
- *Assessing & Screening* (Quick Training Aid)
- *Assessing to Address Barriers to Learning* (Introductory Packet)
- *Behavioral Initiatives in Broad Perspective* (Technical Assistance Sampler)
- *Case Management in the School Context* (Quick Training Aid)
- *Classroom Changes to Enhance and Re-engage Students in Learning* (Training Tutorial)
- *Community Outreach: School-Community Resources to Address Barriers to Learning* (Training Tutorial)
- *Confidentiality* (Quick Training Aid)
- *Confidentiality and Informed Consent* (Introductory Packet)
- *Creating the Infrastructure for an Enabling (Learning Support) Component to Address Barriers to Student Learning* (Training Tutorial)
- *Crisis Assistance and Prevention: Reducing Barriers to Learning* (Training Tutorial)
- *Cultural Concerns in Addressing Barriers to Learning* (Introductory Packet)
- *Early Development and Learning from the Perspective of Addressing Barriers* (Introductory Packet)
- *Early Development and School Readiness From the Perspective of Addressing Barriers to Learning* (Center Brief)
- *Enhancing Classroom Approaches for Addressing Barriers to Learning: Classroom Focused Enabling* (Continuing Education Modules with accompanying readings and tool kit)
- *Financing Strategies to Address Barriers to Learning* (Quick Training Aid)
- *Financial Strategies to Aid in Addressing Barriers to Learning* (Introductory Packet)
- *Financing Mental Health for Children & Adolescents* (Center Brief and Fact Sheet)
- *Guiding Parents in Helping Children Learn* (Technical Aid)
- *Home Involvement in Schooling* (Training Tutorial)
- *Least Intervention Needed: Toward Appropriate Inclusion of Students With Special Needs* (Introductory Packet)
- *Mental Health and School-based Health Centers* (Guide to Practice)
- *Mental Health in Schools: New Roles for School Nurses* (Continuing Education Modules)

- *Parent and Home Involvement in Schools* (Introductory Packet)
- *Protective Factors (Resiliency)* (Technical Assistance Sampler)
- *Re-engaging Students in Learning* (Quick Training Aid)
- *Responding to Crisis at a School* (Resource Aid Packet)
- *School-based Client Consultation, Referral, and Management of Care* (Technical Aid Packet)
- *School-based Crisis Intervention* (Quick Training Aid)
- *School-based Health Centers* (Technical Assistance Sampler)
- *School-based Mutual Support Groups (For Parents, Staff, and Older Students)* (Technical Aid Packet)
- *Screening/Assessing Students: Indicators and Tools* (Resource Aid)
- *Students & Family Assistance Programs and Services to Address Barriers to Learning* (Training Tutorial)
- *Students and Psychotropic Medication: The School's Role* (Resource Aid Packet)
- *Support for Transitions to Address Barriers to Learning* (Training Tutorial)
- *Sustaining School-Community Partnerships to Enhance Outcomes for Children and Youth* (a Guidebook and Tool Kit)
- *Understanding and Minimizing Staff Burnout* (Introductory Packet)
- *Using Technology to Address Barriers to Learning* (Technical Assistance Sampler)
- *Violence Prevention and Safe Schools* (Introductory Packet)
- *Volunteers to Help Teachers and Schools Address Barriers to Learning* (Technical Aid Packet)
- *Welcoming and Involving New Students and Families* (Technical Aid Packet)
- *What Schools Can Do to Welcome and Meet the Needs of All Students and Families* (Guide to Practice)
- *Where to Access Statistical Information Relevant to Addressing Barriers to Learning: An Annotated Reference List* (Resource Aid Packet)
- *Where to Get Resource Materials to Address Barriers to Learning* (Resource Aid Packet)

SOME RESOURCES FOCUSED ON SYSTEMIC CONCERNS

- *About Mental Health in Schools* (Introductory Packet)
- *Addressing Barriers to Learning: A Set of Surveys to Map What a School Has and What It Needs* (Resource Aid Packet)
- *Addressing Barriers to Student Learning: Closing Gaps in School/ Community Policy and Practice* (Center Report)
- *Addressing Barriers to Student Learning & Promoting Healthy Development: A Usable Research Base* (Center Brief)
- *Evaluation and Accountability: Getting Credit for All You Do!* (Introductory Packet)

- *Evaluation and Accountability Related to Mental Health in Schools* (Technical Aid Sampler)
- *Expanding Educational Reform to Address Barriers to Learning: Restructuring Student Support Services and Enhancing School-Community Partnerships* (Center Report)
- *Framing New Directions for School Counselors, Psychologists, & Social Workers* (Center Report)
- *Guides for the Enabling Component—Addressing Barriers to Learning and Enhancing Healthy Development* (Guides to Practice)
- *Integrating Mental Health in Schools: Schools, School-based Centers, and Community Programs Working Together* (Center Brief)
- *Introduction to a Component for Addressing Barriers to Student Learning* (Center Brief)
- *Mental Health in Schools: Guidelines, Models, Resources, & Policy Considerations* (Center Report)
- *New Directions in Enhancing Educational Results: Policymakers' Guide to Restructuring Student Support Resources to Address Barriers to Learning* (Guide to Practice)
- *New Directions for School & Community Initiatives to Address Barriers to Learning: Two Examples of Concept Papers to Inform and Guide Policy Makers* (Center Report)
- *New Initiatives: Considerations Related to Planning, Implementing, Sustaining, and Going-to-Scale* (Center Brief)
- *Organization Facilitators: A Change Agent for Systemic School and Community Changes* (Center Report)
- *Pioneer Initiatives to Reform Education Support Programs* (Center Report)
- *Policies and Practices for Addressing Barriers to Learning: Current Status and New Directions* (Center Report)
- *Resource Mapping and Management to Address Barriers to Learning: An Intervention for Systemic Change* (Technical Assistance Packet)
- *Resource-oriented Teams: Key Infrastructure Mechanisms for Enhancing Education Supports* (Center Report)
- *Restructuring Boards of Education to Enhance Schools' Effectiveness in Addressing Barriers to Student Learning* (Center Report)
- *Sampling of Outcome Findings From Interventions Relevant to Addressing Barriers to Learning* (Technical Assistance Sampler)
- *School-Community Partnerships: A Guide*
- *Thinking About and Accessing Policy Related to Addressing Barriers to Learning* (Technical Aid Sampler)
- *Working Together: From School-based Collaborative Teams to School-Community-Higher Education Connections* (Introductory Packet)

Internet Sites for a Sampling of Major Agencies and Organizations to Support Learning

15

There are many agencies and organizations that help and advocate for those with learning, behavior, and emotional problems. The following is a list of major links on the World Wide Web that offer information and resources related to such matters. This list is not an exhaustive listing; it is meant to highlight some premier resources and serve as a beginning for your search. Many of the Web sites will have links to others that cover similar topics. In general, the Internet is an invaluable tool when trying to find information on learning, behavior, and emotional problems.

American Academy of Child & Adolescent Psychiatry

www.aacap.org

Site serves both AACAP members, and parents and families. Provides information to aid understanding and treatment of the developmental, behavioral, and mental disorders, including fact sheets for parents and caregivers, current research, practice guidelines, managed care information, and more. Provides fact sheets and other information.

American Academy of Pediatrics

www.aap.org

Has a variety of reports, publications, aids, and links about the academy's various programs and initiatives. Also provides information about their policies and practice guidelines.

American Psychiatric Association

www.psych.org

Site has a variety of reports, publications, fact sheets.

American Psychological Association

www.apa.org

Site provides news, reports, publication information, a consumer help center, information on continuing education, and more.

American School Counselor Association

www.schoolcounselor.org

Cosponsor of the New Directions for Student Support Initiative. Partners with Learning Network to provide school-counseling-related content for parents, including age- and grade-specific information to help enhance learning and overall development—both inside and outside school. FamilyEducation.com offers 20 free e-mail newsletters, expert advice on education and child rearing, and home learning ideas. Includes materials for kids with special needs, gifted children, and homeschooling families.

American School Health Association

www.ashaweb.org

Cosponsor of the New Directions for Student Support Initiative.

Multidisciplinary organization of administrators, counselors, dentists, health educators, physical educators, school nurses and school physicians; advocates high-quality school health instruction, health services, and a healthful school environment.

Association for Supervision and Curriculum Development

www.ascd.org

Cosponsor of the New Directions for Student Support Initiative. Addresses all aspects of effective teaching and learning, such as professional development, educational leadership, and capacity building; offers broad, multiple perspectives—across all education professions—in reporting key policies and practices. Focus is solely on professional practice within the context of "Is it good for the children?" rather than what is reflective of a specific educator role.

California Association of School Psychologists

www.caspsurveys.org

Cosponsor of the New Directions for Student Support Initiative. Provides liaison with state boards and commissions, represents school psychology to governmental officials and other policymakers; provides continuing professional development; publishes a quarterly magazine and annual research journal.

California Department of Education

www.cde.ca.gov

Cosponsor of the New Directions for Student Support Initiative. This state agency has established a division for learning supports and has resources relevant to a school's focus on addressing barriers to learning.

Center for Community School Partnerships

education.ucdavis.edu/cress/ccsp

Cosponsor of the New Directions for Student Support Initiative. Originally the Healthy Start Field Office; serves community-school partnership across California and provides national and international consultation in education reform and collaborative partnership policy.

Center for Cooperative Research and Extension Services for Schools

education.ucdavis.edu/cress

Cosponsor of the New Directions for Student Support Initiative. Brings together K–12 educators with university faculty, education extension specialists, and graduate students. Focuses on educational research, curriculum design, and new modes of professional development.

Center for Effective Collaboration and Practice

www.air.org/cecp

Identifies promising programs and practices, promotes information exchanges, and facilitates collaboration among stakeholders and across service system disciplines with a focus on the development and adjustment of children with or at risk of developing serious emotional disturbances.

Center for Mental Health in Schools

smhp.psych.ucla.edu

Approaches mental health and psychosocial concerns from the broad perspective of addressing barriers to learning and promoting healthy development. Its mission is to improve outcomes for young people by enhancing policies, programs, and practices relevant to mental health in schools. Web site has extensive online resources accessible at no cost.

Center for Prevention of Youth Violence, Johns Hopkins University

www.jhsph.edu

Cosponsor of the New Directions for Student Support Initiative. Brings together academic institutions, city and state agencies and organizations, community groups, schools, youth groups, and faith organizations to collaborate on both positive youth development and prevention of violence. By integrating research with education, professional development, and practice efforts, it provides an infrastructure facilitating academic-community collaborations, thus translating research into improved professional practice.

Center for School Mental Health Assistance

csmha.umaryland.edu

Cosponsor of the New Directions for Student Support Initiative. Focuses on the concept of "expanded school mental health"; offers technical assistance and training; holds annual conferences to advance mental health in schools.

Center for Social and Emotional Education

www.csee.net

Cosponsor of the New Directions for Student Support Initiative. A multidisciplinary educational and professional development organization; works with educators, parents, schools, and communities to develop proactive ways to promote academic achievement as well as prevent youth violence and other at-risk behaviors by fostering effective social and emotional education and character education for children and adolescents.

Center for the Study & Prevention of Violence

www.colorado.edu/cspv

At the Institute of Behavioral Sciences, University of Colorado at Boulder; provides informed assistance to groups committed to understanding and preventing violence.

Coalition for Community Schools

www.communityschools.org

Cosponsor of the New Directions for Student Support Initiative. Alliance of national, state, and local organizations in education K–16, youth development, community planning and development, family support, health and human services, government and philanthropy as well as community school networks. Advocates for community schools as the vehicle for strengthening schools, families, and communities so that together they can improve student learning.

Collaborative for Academic, Social, and Emotional Learning (CASEL)

www.casel.org

Cosponsor of the New Directions for Student Support Initiative. An international collaborative of educators, scientists, policymakers, foundations, and concerned citizens promoting social and emotional educational and development in schools. Online resources include publications, reports, news, and links.

Connect for Kids

www.connectforkids.org

Information for those who want to make their communities better places for kids. Through radio, print, and TV ads, a weekly e-mail newsletter and a discussion forum, provides tools to help people become more active citizens— from volunteering to voting—on behalf of kids.

Council for Exceptional Children

www.cec.sped.org

Largest international professional organization dedicated to improving educational outcomes for individuals with exceptionalities, students with disabilities, and/or the gifted. Has divisions focused on LD and behavioral disorders.

Education Development Center

main.edc.org

Cosponsor of the New Directions for Student Support Initiative. An international, nonprofit organization with more than 335 projects dedicated to enhancing learning, promoting health, and fostering a deeper understanding of the world.

Education World

www.educationworld.com

Education-based resource and Internet search site designed especially for teachers, students, administrators, and parents.

ERIC: Educational Resources Info Center

www.eric.ed.gov

Provides extensive information on all topics relevant to education.

Family Resource Coalition of America

www.familysupportamerica.org

For community-based providers, school personnel, those who work in human services, trainers, scholars, and policymakers. Provides resources, publications, technical assistance, and consulting, as well as public education and advocacy.

Federal Consumer Information Center

www.pueblo.gsa.gov

Publishes a catalog listing booklets from several federal agencies, including works related to learning, behavior, and emotional problems.

Federal Resource Center for Special Education

www.dssc.org/frc

Supports a national technical assistance network that responds quickly to the needs of students with disabilities, especially students from underrepresented populations.

Higher Education and the Handicapped

www.heath.gwu.edu

National clearinghouse offering statistics and information on post-high school for individuals with disabilities.

Indiana Department of Education

main.edc.org

Cosponsor of the New Directions for Student Support Initiative. Provides leadership, vision, and advocacy to secure optimum educational opportunity and benefit to the citizens of Indiana.

Johns Hopkins University Graduate Division of Education

www.spsbe.jhu.edu/ programs/grad_edu.cfm

Cosponsor of the New Directions for Student Support Initiative. Committed to the preparation and support of a new generation of educators prepared to meet the challenges of high academic standards, expanding technology, and increasingly diverse student populations. Graduate programs provide innovative, research-based alternatives for the initial preparation and continuing development of teachers, administrators, specialists, and school and community counselors.

LD Online

www.ldonline.org

Focuses on the education and welfare of individuals with learning disabilities. It is geared toward parents, teachers, and other professionals.

Learning Disabilities Association of America

www.ldanatl.org

National nonprofit advocacy organization. Site includes information on the association, upcoming conferences, legislative updates, and links to other related resources.

Mental Health Net (MHN)

mentalhelp.net

Guide to mental health topics, with more than 3,000 individual resources listed. Topics covered range from disorders such as depression, anxiety, and substance abuse to professional journals and self-help magazines that are available online.

Minnesota Department of Education

education.state.mn.us

Cosponsor of the New Directions for Student Support Initiative. Focused on improving educational achievement by establishing clear standards, measuring performance, assisting educators, and increasing opportunities for lifelong learning.

National Alliance of Pupil Service Organizations

www.napso.org

Cosponsor of the New Directions for Student Support Initiative. A coalition of national professional organizations whose members provide a variety of school-based prevention and intervention services to assist students in becoming effective learners and productive citizens.

National Association of Pupil Service Administrators

www.napsa.com

Cosponsor of the New Directions for Student Support Initiative. Provides a network of professionals who can assist in the development of programs designed to meet locally identified needs. Information on current trends and changes in legal and regulatory standards.

National Association of School Nurses

www.nasn.org

Cosponsor of the New Directions for Student Support Initiative. Core purpose is to advance delivery of professional school health services to promote optimal health and learning in students. Site has a variety of publications, training aids, and links.

National Association of School Psychologists

www.nasponline.org

Cosponsor of the New Directions for Student Support Initiative. Promotes the rights, welfare, education, and mental health of children and youth and advancing

the profession of school psychology.

National Association of Secondary School Principals

nasspcms.principals.org

Cosponsor of the New Directions for Student Support Initiative. National voice for middle school and high school principals, assistant principals, and aspiring school leaders from across the United States and more than 45 other countries. Site offers news, publications, research, professional development, and job opportunities.

National Association of Social Workers

www.naswdc.org

Cosponsor of the New Directions for Student Support Initiative. Works to enhance the professional growth and development of its members, to create and maintain professional standards, and to advance sound social policies. Site describes publications, resources, research, and so forth.

National Association of State Boards of Education

www.nasbe.org

Cosponsor of the New Directions for Student Support Initiative. Works to strengthen state leadership in educational policy making, promote excellence, advocate equality of access to educational opportunity, and ensure continued citizen support for public education. Site offers information, news, technical assistance, and links.

National Association of State Directors of Special Education

www.nasdse.org

Promotes and supports education programs for students with disabilities.

National Center for Community Education

www.nccenet.org

Cosponsor of the New Directions for Student Support Initiative. Promotes community and educational change emphasizing community schools by providing state-of-the-art leadership development, training, and technical assistance.

National Clearinghouse for Alcohol and Drug Information

www.health.org

Information service of the Substance Abuse and Mental Health Services Administration's (SAMHSA) Center for Substance Abuse Prevention (CSAP). World's largest resource for current information and materials concerning substance abuse. Has both English- and Spanish-speaking information specialists.

National Clearinghouse on Child Abuse and Neglect

www.calib.com

U.S. Department of Health and Human Services' resource for professionals, with information on the prevention, identification, and treatment of child abuse.

National Dropout Prevention Center

www.dropoutprevention.org

Offers clearinghouse and professional development on issues related to dropout prevention and strategies designed to increase the graduation rates.

National Information Center for Children and Youth With Disabilities

www.nichcy.org

National information and referral center for families, educators, and other professionals. Has a Spanish version accessible from the main Web page.

National Institute of Mental Health (NIMH)

www.nimh.nih.gov

Conducts and supports research nationwide on mental illness and mental health, including studies of the brain, behavior, and mental health services.

National Mental Health Information Center: Substance Abuse and Mental Health Services Administration (SAMHSA)

www.mentalhealth.samhsa.gov

The federal Center for Mental Health Services provides a national, one-stop source of information and resources on prevention, treatment, and rehabilitation services for mental illness via toll-free telephone services and publications. It was developed for users of mental health services and their families, the general public, policymakers, providers, and the media. P.O. Box 42557, Washington, DC 20015. Ph: 800-789-CMHS (2647) M-F (8:30–5:00 ET). TDD: 866-889-2647.

National Middle School Association

www.nmsa.org

Cosponsor of the New Directions for Student Support Initiative. Offers news and views, bookstore, position papers, professional development, research.

National Technical Assistance Center for Children's Mental Health

www.georgetown.edu/research/gucdc/cassp

Provides technical assistance to improve service delivery and outcomes for children and adolescents with, or at risk of, serious emotional disturbance and their families. Assists states and

communities in building systems of care that are child- and family-centered, culturally competent, coordinated, and community based.

National Youth Gang Center

www.iir.com/nygc

Purpose is to expand and maintain the body of critical knowledge about youth gangs and effective responses to them. Assists state and local jurisdictions in the collection, analysis, and exchange of information on gang-related demographics, legislation, literature, research, and promising program strategies.

Office of Special Education and Rehabilitative Services

www.ed.gov/offices/OSERS

Supports programs that assist in educating children with special needs, provides for the rehabilitation of youth and adults with disabilities, and supports research to improve the lives of individuals with disabilities.

Partnerships Against Violence Network

www.pavent.org

"Virtual library" of information about violence and youth at risk, representing data from seven different federal agencies. It is a one-stop, searchable information resource to help reduce redundancy in information management and provide clear and comprehensive access to information for states and local communities.

Public Citizen

www.citizen.org

Consumer organization (founded by Ralph Nader) fights for the consumer in Washington. Looking up the group's Health Research Group may be useful when researching learning, behavior, and emotional problems.

Region VII Comprehensive Center

region7.ou.edu

Cosponsor of the New Directions for Student Support Initiative. Promotes the learning of all students in its region (Indiana, Kansas, Illinois, Missouri, Nebraska, Oklahoma); provides technical assistance to local education agencies, schools, tribes, state education agencies, and community-based organizations.

School Social Work Association of America

www.sswaa.org

Cosponsor of the New Directions for Student Support Initiative. Dedicated to promoting the profession of school social work and the professional development of school social workers in order to enhance the educational experience of students and their families.

Teaching Learning Disabilities

www.teachingld.org

Provides up-to-date resources about teaching students with learning disabilities (a service of the Division for Learning Disabilities of the Council for Exceptional Children).

Urban Special Education Leadership Collaboration

www.urbancollaborative.org

Network of special and general education leaders working together to improve outcomes for students with disabilities in the nation's urban schools. Emphasis is on mutual support, sharing of information and resources, and planning/problem-solving partnerships to strengthen each member district.

What Works Clearinghouse

www.whatworks.ed.gov

Gathers studies of the effectiveness of educational interventions (programs, products, practices, and policies), reviews the studies that have the strongest design, and reports on the strengths and weaknesses of those studies against the WWC Evidence Standards.

Wisconsin Department of Public Instruction

www.dpi.state.wi.us

Cosponsor of the New Directions for Student Support Initiative. Web site has information on various programs and initiatives supported by the department as well as updates and recent news for parents and educators alike.

Regional Education Laboratories

http://www.ed.gov/prog_info/Labs

With support from the U.S. Department of Education, Office of Educational Research and Improvement (OERI), this network of 10 Regional Educational Laboratories serves geographic regions that span the nation. They work to ensure that those involved in educational improvement at the local, state, and regional levels have access to the best available information from research and practice. This site is one of many ways that the network reaches out to make that information accessible. While each laboratory has distinctive features tailored to meet the special needs of the geographic region it serves, they also have common characteristics—one of which is promoting widespread access to information regarding research and best practice.

Northeast and Islands Regional Educational Laboratory at Brown University (LAB at Brown U.)

- www.lab.brown.edu
- Serves CT, MA, ME, NH, NY, RI, VT, Puerto Rico, Virgin Islands

Laboratory for Student Success (LSS)

- www.temple.edu/lss
- Serves DC, DE, MD, NJ, PA

Appalachia Educational Laboratory (AEL)

- www.ael.org
- Serves KY, TN, VA, WV

SERVE

- www.serve.org
- Serves AL, FL, GA, MS, NC, SC

North Central Regional Educational Laboratory (NCREL)

- www.ncrel.org
- Serves IA, IL, IN, MI, MN, OH, WI

Southwest Educational Development Laboratory (SEDL)

- www.sedl.org
- Serves AR, LA, NM, OK, TX

Mid-continent Research for Education and Learning (McREL)

- www.mcrel.org
- Serves CO, KS, MO, NB, ND, SD, WY

WEST ED

- www.wested.org
- Serves AZ, CA, NE, UT

Northwest Regional Educational Laboratory (NWREL)
- www.nwrel.org
- Serves AK, ID, MT, OR, WA

Pacific Resources for Education and Learning (PREL)

- www.prel.org
- Serves American Samoa, Commonwealth of the Northern Mariana Islands, Federated States of Micronesia, Guam, HI, Republic of the Marshall Islands, Republic of Palau

Special Education Regional Resource Centers

The following six regional centers offer tools and strategies for achieving effective education and human services delivery systems: coordinating information, providing technical assistance, linking research with practice, facilitating interagency collaboration.

Northeast Regional
Resource Center

- www.wested.org/nerrc
- Serves CT, MA, ME, NH, NJ, NY, RI, VT

Mid-South Regional
Resource Center

- www.ihdi.uky.edu/msrrc
- Serves DC, DE, KY, MD, NC, SC, TN, VA, WV

Southeast Regional
Resource Center

- edla.aum.edu/serrc/serrc.html
- Serves AL, AR, FL, GA, LA, MS, NM, OK, TX, Puerto Rico

North Central Regional
Resource Center

- www.dssc.org/frc/ncrrc.htm
- Serves IA, IL, IN, MI, MN, MO, OH, PA, WI

Mountain Plains Regional
Resource Center

- www.usu.edu/~mprrc
- Serves AZ, Bureau of Indian Affairs, CO, KS, MT, NB, ND, NM, SD, UT, WY

Western Regional Resource Center

- interact.uoregon.edu/wrrc/wrrc.html
- Serves AK, AZ, CA, HI, ID, NE, OR, WA, and the Pacific Islands

Comprehensive Regional Assistance Centers

The U.S. Department of Education established the 15 Comprehensive Centers (CCs) to provide technical assistance services focused on the implementation of reform programs. The CCs work primarily with states, local education agencies, tribes, schools, and other recipients of funds under the Improving America's Schools, Act of 1994 (IASA). Priority for services is given to high-poverty schools and districts, Bureau of Indian Affairs schools, and IASA recipients implementing schoolwide programs.

Region I

- www.edc.org/NECAC
- Serves CT, MA, ME, NH, RI, VT

Region II

- www.nyu.edu/education/metrocenter/NYTAC.html
- Serves NY

Region III

- http://ceee.gwu.edu
- Serves DC, DE, MD, NJ, OH, PA

Region IV

- www.ael.org/page .htm?&pd=abo6721 &pc=2
- Serves KY, NC, SC, TN, VA, WV

Region V

- www.sedl.org/secac
- Serves AL, AR, GA, LA, MS

Region VI

- www.wcer.wisc .edu/ccvi
- Serves IA, MI, MN, NC, SC, WI

Region VII

- region7.ou.edu
- Serves IL, IN, KS, MO, NE, OK

Region VIII

- http://www.starcenter .org
- Serves TX

Region IX

- www.cesdp.nmhu.edu
- Serves AZ, CO, NM, NV, UT

Region X

- http://www.nwrac.org
- Serves ID, MT, OR, WA, WY

Region XI

- www.wested.org
- Serves Northern CA

Region XII

- sccac.lacoe.edu
- Serves Southern CA

Region XIII

- www.serrc.org/akrac
- Serves AK

Region XIV

- www.ets.org/ccxiv
- Serves FL, Puerto Rico, Virgin Islands

Region XV

- www.prel.org
- Serves American Samoa, Guam, HI, Federated States of Micronesia, Commonwealth of the Northern Mariana Islands, Republic of the Marshall Islands, Republic of Palau

Index

**CORWIN
PRESS**

The Corwin Press logo—a raven striding across an open book—represents the union of courage and learning. Corwin Press is committed to improving education for all learners by publishing books and other professional development resources for those serving the field of PreK–12 education. By providing practical, hands-on materials, Corwin Press continues to carry out the promise of its motto: **"Helping Educators Do Their Work Better."**